ENVY

A Liberty Press Edition

Helmut Schoeck was born in Austria in 1922. He was a student of medicine and psychology at the University of Munich from 1941 to 1945. He received his doctorate in philosophy from the University of Tübingen in 1948. In 1950, he came to the United States and taught at Fairmont State College in West Virginia. From 1953 to 1954, he was a postdoctoral fellow at Yale. From 1954 to 1965, he was a professor of sociology at Emory University. Since 1965, he has been a professor and the director of the Institute of Sociology at the University of Mainz in the Federal Republic of Germany. He became a naturalized United States citizen in 1956.

Envy: A Theory of Social Behaviour (1969) was first published in German as *Der Neid: Eine Theorie der Gesellschaft* (1966). The book has also been translated into Spanish (1970) and Italian (1974). Other work includes *Was Heisst Politisch Unmöglich? (What Means Politically Impossible?)* (1959) and *Geschichte der Soziologie* (1974). The latter has been translated into Spanish (1977) and Italian (1980). His most recent books are *Das Recht auf Ungleichheit (The Right To Be Unequal)* (1979) and *Die 12 Irrtümer unseres Jahrhunderts (The 12 Errors of Our Century)* (1985).

ENVY

A Theory of Social Behaviour

by Helmut Schoeck

Liberty Fund

Indianapolis

LibertyPress is a publishing imprint of Liberty Fund, Inc., a foundation established to encourage study of the ideal of a society of free and responsible individuals.

The cuneiform inscription that serves as our logo and as the design motif for our endpapers is the earliest-known written appearance of the word "freedom" (*amagi*), or "liberty." It is taken from a clay document written about 2300 B.C. in the Sumerian city-state of Lagash.

ACKNOWLEDGMENTS
The author and publisher would like to thank the following for permission to quote from copyright material:

George Allen & Unwin Ltd., and Humanities Press, Inc.: *Ethics,* Volume I, by Nicolai Hartmann.

W. W. Norton & Company, Inc.: Reprinted from *The Interpersonal Theory of Psychiatry* by Harry Stack Sullivan, M.D., by permission of W. W. Norton & Company, Inc. Copyright © 1953 by The William Alanson White Psychiatric Foundation. Copyright renewed 1981 by The William Alanson White Psychiatric Foundation.

The Viking Press, Inc.: From *The Portable Melville*, edited by Jay Leyda. Copyright © 1952 by The Viking Press, Inc. Copyright renewed 1980 by Jay Leyda. Reprinted by permission of Viking Penquin, Inc.

The Hogarth Press Ltd. and Basic Books, Inc.: From *Collected Papers of Sigmund Freud*. Authorized translation by Joan Riviere and Alix and James Strachey. Published by Basic Books, Inc., by arrangement with The Hogarth Press Ltd. and The Institute of Psycho-Analysis, London. Reprinted by permission of Basic Books, Inc., Publishers.

Library of Congress Cataloging-in-Publication Data

Schoeck, Helmut.
    Envy: a theory of social behaviour.

    Translation of: Der Neid.
    Reprint. Originally published: New York : Harcourt,
• Brace & World, 1969.
    Bibliography: p.
    Includes indexes.
    1. Envy. 2. Envy—Social aspects. I. Title.
BF575.E65S3213 1987   152.4'34   87-3080
ISBN 0–86597–063–7
ISBN 0–86597–064–5 (pbk.)

10 9 8 7 6 5 4 3

Contents

ENVY

1

Man the Envier

THROUGHOUT HISTORY, in all stages of cultural development, in most languages and as members of widely differing societies, men have recognized a fundamental problem of their existence and have given it specific names: the feeling of envy and of being envied.

Envy is a drive which lies at the core of man's life as a social being, and which occurs as soon as two individuals become capable of mutual comparison. This urge to compare oneself invidiously with others can be found in some animals but in man it has acquired a special significance. Man is an envious being who, were it not for the social inhibitions aroused within the object of his envy, would have been incapable of developing the social systems to which we all belong today. If we were not constantly obliged to take account of other men's envy of the extra pleasure that accrues to us as we begin to deviate from a social norm, 'social control' could not function.

Man the envier can, however, overshoot the mark and arouse or release inhibitions which have a retarding effect on the ability of a group to adapt to new environmental problems. Envy can also turn man to destruction. Almost all the fragmentary literature which has hitherto dealt with envy (essays, belles-lettres, philosophy, theology, psychology) has constantly seen its destructive, inhibitory, futile and painful element. In all the cultures of mankind, in all proverbs and fairytales, the emotion of envy is condemned. The envious person is universally exhorted to be ashamed of himself. And yet his existence, or the belief in his ubiquity, has at the same time always provided enough latent apprehension of other people's views to allow a system of social controls and balances to evolve.

3

Although some schools of modern psychology have practically deleted the word 'envy' from their vocabulary, as if it simply did not exist as a primary source of motivation, the available evidence leaves no doubt whatever of its universality. In almost all languages, from those of the simplest primitive peoples to those of the Indo-European group, in Arabic, Japanese and Chinese, there is invariably a term to indicate envy or the envious person. Proverbs of the most varied cultures deal with it in hundreds of different forms. Aphorists and philosophers have touched on it. For instance envy had a particular significance for Kierkegaard, who even attributed envy to those who aroused envy in others. In fiction envy often plays a role and sometimes a major one; and every one of us has encountered envy in his own life. It is the great regulator in all personal relationships: fear of arousing it curbs and modifies countless actions.

Considering the key role played by envy in human existence, and that nothing new in the way of conceptual apparatus was needed in order to recognize it, it is truly remarkable how few works have dealt exclusively with it. They include an essay by Francis Bacon; a short book by the Frenchman, Eugène Raiga, written in the late 1920s, and a Russian novella, *Envy,* of the same date; besides these, there is a novel by the almost forgotten nineteenth-century French author, Eugène Sue, several aphorisms in Nietzsche and a study by Max Scheler which in fact deals more with the special case of resentment than envy proper.

This book may disturb many readers, including those with widely differing opinions on social and political issues. I believe, though, that I can demonstrate two things: first, that envy is much more universal than has so far been admitted or even realized, indeed that envy alone makes any kind of social co-existence possible; secondly, however, I believe envy as the implicit or explicit fulcrum of social policy to be much more destructive than those who have fabricated their social and economic philosophy out of envy would care to admit.

That our fellow man is always potentially envious—and the probability as well as the degree of his envy increases in ratio to his propinquity—is one of the most disturbing, often one of the most carefully concealed yet most basic facts of human existence at all levels of cultural development. The inadequacies, the historical limitations of so many respected social philosophies and economic theories, become obvious when it is realized how much they depend on the assumption that human envy is the outcome of arbitrary, haphazard and purely temporary circumstances—in particular that it is the result of gross inequalities and may disappear once these are removed: in other words, that it can be permanently cured.

Most of the achievements which distinguish members of modern, highly developed and diversified societies from members of primitive societies—the development of civilization, in short—are the result of innumerable defeats inflicted on envy, i.e., on man as an envious being. And what Marxists have called the opiate of religion, the ability to provide hope and happiness for believers in widely differing material circumstances, is nothing more than the provision of ideas which liberate the envious person from envy, the person envied from his sense of guilt and his fear of the envious. Correctly though Marxists have identified this function, their doctrines have remained blind and naïve when faced with the solution of the problem of envy in any future society. It is hard to see how the totally secularized and ultimately egalitarian society promised us by socialism can ever solve the problem of the residual envy latent in society.

However, it is not only the determining philosophical and ideological content of a culture but also social structures and processes, themselves in part supported by or derived from ideological factors, which exert an influence on the part played by envy.

The world from the viewpoint of the envier

We must begin by looking at the world as seen by the envious man. A certain predisposition to envy is part of man's physical and social equipment, the lack of which would, in many situations, simply result in his being trampled down by others. We use our latent sense of envy when, for instance, we examine social systems for their efficiency: before joining an association or firm we try to discern whether it has any intrinsic structure which might arouse strong envy in ourselves or in others. If so, it is probably an organization which is not very well adapted to particular functions. In the recent past a few American colleges and universities have tried to attract able academic celebrities as professors by offering salaries perhaps twice as high as those earned by the standard full professor. I know of several cases of a man being unable to bring himself to accept the offer because, as he told me, he could not bear the thought of being the object of so much envy in the faculty.

Further, potential envy is an essential part of man's equipment if he is to be able to test the justice and fairness of the solutions to the many problems which occur in his life. Very few of us, when dealing with employees, colleagues, etc., are able to take a position which consciously ignores the existence of envy, such as that adopted by the master in the Biblical parable of the toilers in the vineyard. No matter how mature, how immune from envy a personnel manager or plant manager may himself be, when he has to deal with the taboo subject of wages or staff regulations he must be able to sense exactly what sort of measures are tolerable, given the general tendency to mutual envy.

The phenomenon described by the word 'envy' is a fundamental psychological process which of necessity presupposes a social context: the co-existence of two or more individuals. Few concepts are so intrinsic a part of social reality yet at the same time so markedly neglected in the categories of behavioural science. If I emphasize envy as a pure concept representing a basic problem, I am not claiming that this concept, or the theory of the role of envy, explains everything in human life, in society, or in cultural history. There are various related concepts and processes, as there are various other aspects of man's social existence, which cannot be explained by reference to his capacity for envy. Man is not only *Homo invidiosus,* he is also *Homo ludens* and *Homo faber*; but the fact that he is capable of associating in lasting groups and societies is primarily due to his being subject to a constant, frequently subliminal urge to be envious of all those deviating from a norm.

If we are to recognize the role of envy this phenomenon must be unmasked, as sex has been unmasked by psychoanalysis. I do not wish to give the impression, however, that I consider the tendency to envy as a universal ultimate cause: envy does not explain everything, but it throws light on more things than people have hitherto been prepared to admit or even to see.

Envy has the advantage of other modern terms such as ambivalence, relative deprivation, frustration or class war, in that as a concept it has a pre-scientific origin. For centuries, indeed for millennia, countless people who have never regarded themselves as social scientists have consistently and unanimously observed a form of behaviour—envy—which they described in words that were often the etymological equivalents of the same words in other languages.[1]

An exhaustive study of envy in its active and passive roles in social history is important not only because this emotion and motivational syndrome are crucial in individual human life; it is also relevant to politics, since the right or wrong assessment of the phenomenon of envy, the under- or over-estimation of its effects, and above all the unfounded hope that we can so order our social existence as to create people or societies devoid of envy, are all considerations of immediate political significance, particularly where economic and social policies are concerned.

If envy were no more than one of many psychological states such as homesickness, desire, worry, disgust, avarice and so on, one might be prepared to admit that on the whole most people know what envy is and what it involves. It would still be a rewarding task, and one of great importance to many fields of study such as child psychology, educational science or psychotherapy to classify systematically all that we know about envy and to develop it methodically into a theory. This book is also an attempt to do that. But a proper appraisal of man's potential for envy, a realization of its universality and persistence, could in years to come determine how much common sense is exercised in the domestic social and economic policies of parliamentary democracies, as well as in their dealings with the so-called developing nations. As we shall show, we are least capable of acting sensibly in economic and social matters when we face, or believe we face, an envious beneficiary of our decision. This is true especially when we mistakenly tell ourselves that his envy is a direct

---

[1] Bronislaw Malinowski once criticized the tendency to hide concrete phenomena, for which we have perfectly good terms, under pretentious neologisms: 'I must admit that from the point of view of field-work I have never been quite clear how we are going to test, measure or assess these somewhat formidable yet vague entities: euphoria and dysphoria. . . . When we try to translate the state of being satisfied . . . into concrete cases, we are faced not with the communal state of consciousness but rather with such individual factors as personal resentment, thwarted ambition, jealousy, economic grievance. . . . In any case, why not study the concrete and detailed manifestations of resentment and of satisfactions instead of hiding them behind euphoria and dysphoria writ large.' (In his introduction to: H. Ian Hogbin, *Law and Order in Polynesia*, London, 1934, pp. xxiv ff.; Hamden [Conn.], 1961.)

consequence of our being better off, and will necessarily wane when we pander even to unrealistic demands. The allocation of scarce resources, in any society, is rarely optimal when our decision rests on fear of other men's envy.

The loneliness of the envious man

The extent to which envy is a social form of behaviour, i.e., necessarily directed at someone else, is also apparent from the fact that without the other person the envier could never envy. Yet as a rule he specifically rejects any social relationship with the envied person. Love, friend-liness, admiration—these approaches to another person are made in the expectation of reciprocity, recognition, and seek some kind of link. The envier wants none of this: he does not—exceptional cases apart—wish to be recognized as envious by the object of his envy, with whom, given the choice, he would prefer not to associate. The pure act of envy can be described thus: the more closely and intensively the envier concerns himself with the other person, the more he is thrown back on himself in self-pity. No one can envy without knowing the object of envy, or at least imagining him; but unlike other kinds of human emotional relation-ships the envier can expect no reciprocal feelings. He wants no envy in return.

As people have always realized, however, the envier has little interest in the transfer of anything of value from the other's possession to his own. He would like to see the other person robbed, dispossessed, stripped, humiliated or hurt, but he practically never conjures up a detailed mental picture of how a transfer of the other's possessions to himself might occur. The pure type of envier is no thief or swindler in his own cause. In any case, where that which is envied is another man's personal qualities, skill or prestige, there can be no question of theft; he may quite well, however, harbour a wish for the other man to lose his voice, his virtuosity, his good looks or his integrity.

The motives for envy, the stimuli of envious feelings, are ubiquitous, and the intensity of envy depends less on the magnitude of the stimulus than on the social disparity between the envier and the envied. The kind of maturity achieved by an individual which enables him to conquer his own envy does not seem to be a universally attainable attribute. The reasons for the varying role or effectiveness of envy in different societies must be sought, therefore, in the ethos of the respective cultures. Both the envier, who must somehow come to terms with observed inequalities in his life, and the envied person in trying to ignore the other's envy (and both these emotional processes can sometimes occur simultaneously in one and the same person) will make use of creeds, ideologies, proverbs, etc., which will tend to reduce the power of envy and thus allow daily life to proceed with a minimum of friction and conflict.

Good luck and bad luck

It is not true, as many social critics would have us believe, that only the more fortunate people in this world, those with inherited possessions or chance wealth, have a vested interest in an ideology that inhibits envy. Such an ideology is in fact much more important to the envy-prone person, who can begin to make something of his life only when he has hammered out some sort of personal theory which diverts his attention from the enviable good fortune of others, and guides his energies towards realistic objectives within his scope.

One of the beliefs capable of repressing envy is the concept of the 'blind goddess' Fortune. A person is either lucky or unlucky, and whatever number he draws in life's lottery is unconnected with the good or bad fortune of his neighbour. The world has, as it were, an inexhaustible supply of good and bad luck. The most envy-ridden tribal cultures—such as the Dobuan and the Navaho—do not in fact possess the concept of luck at all, nor indeed the concept of chance. In such cultures no one is ever struck by lightning, for instance, without a malignant neighbour having willed it out of envy.

It is not easy to conclude from the general nature of a culture its degree of development or its economic institutions, e.g., which of its elements are generally regarded as immune from envy and which most vulnerable. Almost everywhere it is felt that universal values, such as personal health, youthfulness, children, have to be protected from the evil eye, the active expression of envy, and this is evident in the proverbs and the behaviour patterns that are employed by so many peoples to ward it off. It can, perhaps, be safely assumed that between individuals within a culture there is relatively little potential for envy in respect of those values and inequalities which serve to integrate their society, e.g., the formal pomp and luxury exhibited by a head of a state, such as that still displayed by some of the remaining monarchies in Europe.[2]

The capacity for envy is a psycho-social datum, not infrequently accompanied by marked somatic epiphenomena. Envy, as an emotion, can be treated as a problem of individual psychology; but there is far more to it than that, for it is also a sociological problem of the first order. How is it that so basic, universal and intensely emotional a constituent of the human psyche as envy—and the fear of envy, or at least the constant awareness of it—can lead to such different social consequences in various cultures? There are cultures which are obsessed by envy; virtually everything that happens is attributed to it. Yet there are others which seem to have largely succeeded in taming or repressing it. What causes such differences? Is it perhaps the varying frequency of certain types of personality and character? A considerable amount of research points in this direction. It may well be that certain cultural patterns encourage the envious or the less envious to set the tone; but this still does not explain what originally produced that tendency in a particular culture.

Although 'envy' exists in our language as an abstract noun and is used as such in literature, there is, strictly speaking, no such thing as envy. There are people who envy, even some people habitually prone to envy, and we can observe emotional stirrings in ourselves and others which would be defined as feelings of envy; yet it is impossible to experience envy as an emotion or as a mood in the same way that we can feel anxiety or sadness. Envy is more comparable with 'being afraid'; we envy something or someone in the same way that we are afraid of something or someone. Envy is a directed emotion: without a target, without a victim, it cannot occur.

A susceptibility to envy exists to a much greater degree in man than in any other creature. A prime cause of this is the duration of childhood, which exposes the human individual far longer than any animal to the

[2] A group which in 1966 might have been specifically classified as resentful of the monarchy and the display of royal pomp were the Amsterdam Provos. A dispute as to whether the crown may still fulfil an envy-free function in a society developed between Edward Shils and N. Birnbaum (see E. Shils and M. Young, 'The Meaning of the Coronation,' in *The Sociological Review*, Vol. I, December 1953, pp. 63–81; and N. Birnbaum, 'Monarchs and Sociologists,' idem, Vol. III, July 1955, pp. 5–23).

experience of sibling jealousy within the family. On rare occasions, as in certain poems, envy is invoked as a stimulant, as something sublime or constructive. In such cases the poet has made a poor choice of words; he is really referring to emulation. The really envious person almost never considers entering into fair competition.

Envy as such no more exists in a concrete sense than do grief, desire, joy, anxiety and fear. It consists, rather, of a set of psychological and physiological processes occurring in the individual which indicate certain qualities and which, if interpreted as the constituents of a whole, correspond to the meaning of one of these abstract words. In the most diverse languages the term 'envy' is sharply differentiated from other similar phenomena, yet it is remarkable how seldom 'envy' has been personified in art. Grief, joy and fear obviously lend themselves much more easily to representation. Nor can envy or an envious person be shown without some other point of reference. We can depict a person who is woebegone or joyful, but it is practically impossible to represent a man by himself in such a way that anybody who looks at the picture will instantly grasp that this man is envious. To do so requires a social situation, or symbols whose connection with envy is common knowledge to everyone within the particular culture.[3]

The case is different in regard to the institutionalization of envy in a social structure. Envy can become more easily institutionalized than, say, desire or joy. We hold days of national mourning or rejoicing, but it is hardly possible to give to any emotion other than envy the status of an institution. As examples of envy manifested in social forms one might perhaps cite instances such as steeply progressive income tax, confiscatory death duties and corresponding customs among primitive peoples, such as the 'muru raid' of the Maoris.

Envy represents an almost entirely psychological and social phenomenon. Conceptually it can be differentiated much more sharply from other or similar psychological processes than can the processes deriving from it, which the behavioural sciences today employ as conceptual

---

[3] In earlier centuries envy (or the envious man) was sometimes depicted as a man riding on a dog with a bone in its mouth, e.g., the illustration 'Envy' on p. 14 of Heinz-Günter Deiters' *Die Kunst der Intrige* (The Art of Intrigue), Hamburg, 1966. The picture is taken from a series of woodcuts entitled 'The Seven Deadly Sins' by an anonymous master from the Constance region, *ca.* 1480–90, in the Albertina, Vienna.

substitutes for envy. Aggression, ambivalence, hostility, conflict, frustration, relative deprivation, tension, friction—all these terms are justified, but should not be employed to mask or conceal the basic phenomenon of envy. Until the end of the nineteenth century, indeed in occasional instances up to about a generation ago, most authors who had cause to deal with this side of human nature were quite familiar with envy as a clearly defined phenomenon. Not all cultures possess such concepts as hope, love, justice and progress, but virtually all people, including the most primitive, have found it necessary to define the state of mind of a person who cannot bear someone else's being something, having a skill, possessing something or enjoying a reputation which he himself lacks, and who will therefore rejoice should the other lose his asset, although that loss will not mean his own gain. All cultures, too, have erected conceptual and ritual mechanisms designed as protection against those of their fellow men who are prone to this condition.

Most of the concepts and conceptual sequences by which we modern members of large, complex societies regulate our public affairs are inexplicable to a member of a primitive tribe, but our anxiety not to arouse envy and the situations which give rise to envy are immediately comprehensible to him and he can sympathize with our concern. This is quite clear from an abundance of ethnographical data.

Repression of the concept of envy?

It is most curious to note that at about the beginning of this century authors began to show an increasing tendency, above all in the social sciences and moral philosophy, to repress the concept of envy. This I regard as a genuine instance of repression. The political theorist and the social critic found envy an increasingly embarrassing concept to use as an explanatory category or in reference to a social fact. In isolated cases, and then only as a rider to other remarks, some modern authors have referred to envy as to something obvious, but even then they have almost invariably played down its significance. It may be invoked to explain a localized problem—why, for instance, some over-specialized critics refuse to find anything good to say about a book intended for a general readership; but the concept of envy is avoided if its recognition as an element of social reality would lead to the fundamentals of social policy being questioned.[4]

The indexes of relevant periodicals in the English language during recent years have been remarkably unproductive for the study of the concept of envy. There is not a single instance of 'envy,' 'jealousy' or 'resentment' in the subject indexes of the following periodicals: *American Sociological Review,* Vols. 1–25 (1936–1960); *American Journal of Sociology,* 1895–1947; *Rural Sociology,* Vols. 1–20 (1936–1955); *The British Journal of Sociology,* 1949–1959; *American Anthropologist and the Memoirs of the American Anthropological Association, 1949– 1958; Southwestern Journal of Anthropology,* Vols. 1–20 (1945–1964). It is true that individual articles may be found here and there in these periodicals over the course of the years in which short and very penetrating observations are made concerning envy, clearly attributing significance to the term. But to the people who made the indexes, terms such as 'envy,' 'resentment' and 'jealousy' were so remote that they disregarded them. Under terms as vague as 'aggression' a few contributions may be found in which 'envy' sometimes makes an appearance. In the anthropological journals it was not difficult to find phenomena which, conceptually speaking, should properly be termed envy by looking under 'witchcraft' or 'sorcery' in the index. But oddly enough, the term 'evil eye,' which is the concomitant of envy, is, without exception, again omitted from the aforementioned indexes.

Now and again we find envy and its problems mentioned under veiled or misleading titles, or as part of a treatise on something else, yet it is quite remarkable how often scientists have evaded this emotional syndrome. Why is it that for well over a generation writers have avoided tackling this subject, affecting as it does every human being? In such

---

[4] Oliver Brachfeld, for instance, wonders why 'Envy, curiously enough, has been rather neglected by the psychologists; one hardly comes across it except in some disguise, e.g. that of jealousy, etc.' (*Inferiority Feelings in the Individual and the Group,* New York, 1951, p. 109). Is it mere coincidence that so articulate an author as the young German sociologist Ralf Dahrendorf, for instance, managed to write his *Theory of Social Conflict* without once using the word 'envy'? I do not think so, because elsewhere he has had no hesitation in ascribing, twice on one page, feelings of mutual envy to American and European intellectuals. (*Gesellschaft und Demokratie in Deutschland* [Society and Democracy in Germany], 1965, p. 320.)

cases depth psychology has long since taught us to suspect that repression is at work. The subject has been felt by many writers well equipped to handle it to be distasteful, unpleasant, painful and politically explosive. Many remarks that will be cited in this book support this interpretation.

Much as I should like to agree with all those authors who for millennia have consistently described and condemned the negative and destructive aspect of envy once it has become an end in itself, data will be presented to show that man cannot exist in society without envy. The utopia of a society free from envy, and in which there will no longer be any grounds for envy, is unlikely to be replaced by the totally utopian plan of eradicating envy from human nature by means of education; although so far in the history of social experiment people have been rather more successful when attempting to create the second sort of society than when striving towards one composed of unenvious equals.

Every man must be prone to a small degree of envy; without it the interplay of social forces within society is unthinkable. Only pathological envy in the individual, which tinges every other emotion, and the society entirely designed to appease imagined multitudes of enviers, are socially inoperative. The capacity for envy establishes a necessary social warning system. Here it is remarkable how seldom the vernacular forms of different languages permit one to say directly to another person: 'Don't do that. It will make me envious!' Instead, we tend to talk in abstract terms of justice, saying that something or other is intolerable or unfair, or we relapse into sour and bitter silence. No child warns his parents against taking an ill-considered step by saying something like 'If you do/give/allow that, I shall be envious of Jack/Jill.' The taboo against an open declaration of envy is effective even at this level, although it is true that in both English and German one may say: 'I envy you your success/your property'—i.e., one may only speak of one's own envy when the actual situation between the participants, at least the 'official' version of it, excludes the possibility of genuine, destructive, malicious envy.

Oddly enough, in German one cannot even say: 'I resent you.' There is no such verb, and the alternative construction (literally, 'I have a resentment against you') sounds so clumsy and pompous that no one is likely to use it. In English one frequently hears and reads the expression: 'I resent that,' or 'I resent your action, your remark,' etc. This does not indicate resentment so much as a feeling of indignation or annoyance at a piece of thoughtlessness or carelessness on someone else's part, an unreasonable suggestion or an impugnment of our motives.

Acting as though there were no envy

To anticipate one of the main theses of this work: the more both private individuals and the custodians of political power in a given society are able to act as though there were no such thing as envy, the greater will be the rate of economic growth and the number of innovations in general. The social climate best suited to the fullest, most unhampered deployment of man's creative faculties (economic, scientific, artistic, etc.) is one where accepted normative behaviour, custom, religion, common sense and public opinion are more or less agreed upon an attitude which functions *as if* the envious person could be ignored. This represents a conviction shared by most members of such a society, enabling them to cope realistically, and relatively unconsumed by envy, with the evident differences that exist between people; the attitude, in effect, which enables legislators and governments to offer equal protection to the unequal achievements of the members of the community, while on occasion even offering them unequal advantages so that the community may benefit in the long run from achievements which initially, perhaps, only few are capable of attaining.

In reality these optimal conditions for growth and innovation are never more than partially reached. On the other hand many well-meant proposals for the 'good society' or the completely 'just society' are doomed because they are based on the false premise that this must be a society in which there is nothing left for anyone to envy. This situation can never occur because, as is demonstrable, man inevitably discovers something new to envy. In the utopian society in which we all would have not only the same clothes but the same facial expressions, one person would still envy the other for those imagined, innermost feelings which would enable him, beneath the egalitarian mask, to harbour his own private thoughts and emotions.[5]

[5] David Riesman has pointed out that in a materially egalitarian and consumption-oriented society such as the American, people are still prone to imagine that another

person enjoys greater sexual gratification and to envy him for it: 'If someone else has a new Cadillac, the other-directed person knows what that is, and that he can duplicate the experience, more or less. But if someone else has a new lover, he cannot know what that means. Cadillacs have been democratized. So has the sexual glamour, to a degree. . . . But there is a difference between Cadillacs and sexual partners in the degree of mystery. And with the loss or submergence of moral shame and inhibitions . . . the other-directed person has no defenses against his own envy . . . he does not want to miss . . . the qualities of experience he tells himself the others are having.' (*The Lonely Crowd*, New Haven, 1950, p. 155.) Man's fear of being envied for having a unique sexual experience may have led, at least in part, to the various rituals, designed to ward off envious spirits, performed prior to the consummation of marriage in many tribal societies.

2

Envy in Language

BOTH IN LITERATURE and in discussions with a number of people as to what they understand by envy I have been struck by the tendency to use the word 'jealousy' instead of 'envy,' the former no doubt being more tolerable to those who confess to it than the latter, which is an ignominious sentiment. The jealous man has been defeated in a struggle for power or in competition; he is not inferior in relation to the asset under contention as, by definition, the envious man is. Yet even the behavioural sciences often shirk the phenomenon of envy and of envious behaviour as though it were taboo, disguising the motive of envy with concepts such as ambivalence, aggression, tension, rivalry, jealousy and similar indirect descriptions.

The primary role of envy in human society and the comparatively unproblematical nature of common jealousy—or what is usually meant by the term—are apparent both from language and from proverbs.

Envy and jealousy in English

The Oxford English Dictionary[1] treats 'envy' and 'envious' as 'jealousy' and 'jealous.' About four columns are devoted to both terms.

'Envy' and 'envious' in modern English are derived from the Latin *invidia* and *invidiosus,* which have the same meanings. The verb 'to envy' corresponds to the Latin *invidere.* In Spanish, Portuguese and Italian there are similar derivatives from the Latin to denote the same states of mind.

---

[1] *Oxford English Dictionary,* Vol. 3, Oxford, 1933.

Early English examples are: 'There be others that be envious to see other in gretter degree thanne they.' 'No lawful meanes can carrie me Out of enuies reach.' 'It is much more shame to have envy at other for mony, clothing, or possessions.'

Definitions emphasize the feeling of hostility, spite and ill-will. According to these, envy is present when there is 'mortification and ill-will occasioned by the contemplation of superior advantages.' On the other hand, envy may simply mean that one wishes one might do the same as someone else. The first definition of envy as a verb is most specific: 'To feel displeasure and ill-will at the superiority of (another person) in happiness, success, reputation, or the possession of anything desirable.'

It is also called envy when a person withholds a thing from someone else out of spite; further on we shall have to consider the phenomenon of avarice and its relationship to envy. Thus in England at the beginning of the seventeenth century it was said of the peacock that he so envied men their health that he would eat his own droppings (then used for medicinal purposes).

Incidentally, the modern English words of Latin origin for 'envy' and 'envious' have practically the same meaning as those in modern German deriving from ancient Germanic words, which express the same states of feeling and of mind.

'Jealous' and 'jealousy' are given detailed treatment by the Oxford English Dictionary. Obviously 'jealous' at first denoted simply an intense or highly excited emotional state, and then came to include a craving for the affection of someone else. Later it came to designate the fear of losing another person's affections, just like 'jealous' in the modern sense. Sometimes 'jealous' has the sense of 'envious,' as in: 'It is certain that they looked upon it with a jealous eye.' Earlier there was also an English term 'jealous glass,' meaning the frosted glass used for ground-floor windows, analogous to the French *jalousie*. But the principal meaning of 'jealousy' remains the passionate endeavour to keep something that is one's own by right. In complete contrast to the envious man, therefore, one may postulate a man of jealous disposition whose mind is at rest once he knows that he is free of rivals. In 1856 Emerson wrote: 'The jealousy of every class to guard itself, is a testimony to the reality they have found in life.' Where jealousy acquires undertones of mistrust or hatred, what is meant is generally the suspicion that somebody is seeking to take something from us which we have hitherto enjoyed in tranquillity. In some cases jealousy may even represent the pugnacity of the rightful defender holding his own against the envious miscreant.

More precisely, the jealous man can never normally become a spontaneous, primary aggressor. His hostile behaviour begins only when a rival appears on the scene to give him specific reason for anxiety. This rival may be genuinely striving for an asset, or he may be driven by envy. Everyone is familiar with the type, often described in fiction, who wants to seduce his friend's fiancée, not because he wants to marry her, but only because he begrudges the other his happiness.

In contrast to the envious man, who usually knows exactly what provokes him, the jealous man is often in doubt as to the nature of his antagonist: whether he is a genuine, honourable rival on his own level or an envious man, ostensibly a rival but in fact intent merely on destruction. The envious man, on the other hand, may have hostile feelings towards a person who may actually be ignorant of his existence. Sociologically, therefore, envy and jealousy represent basically distinct social situations, for in jealousy two or more persons must confront each other in a relationship that is avowedly reciprocal.

The fully revised edition of the most comprehensive dictionary of American English, Webster's Third New International Dictionary of the English Language Unabridged, which appeared in 1961, devotes very little space to the terms 'envy' and 'envious.' Two examples of contemporary usage are cited: 'the sterile and envious principle of artificial equality' from *Time* magazine; and, 'examining the tire with envious appreciation.' 'Envious' is defined as a disgruntled emotional state arising from the possessions or achievements of another, a spiteful wish that the other should lose them. By contrast, the word 'jealous' is used when we observe or imagine with mistrust or dissatisfaction that someone is acquiring something which is really our due or which belongs to us.

Thus the decisive difference is evident: jealousy is only directed against a definite transfer of coveted assets or their removal elsewhere, never against the asset as such. Envy very often denies the asset itself. Further, 'jealous' may be used with no critical implications at all, as when John Galsworthy writes: '. . . conscious of their duty, and jealous of their honour.'

Webster's examples of envy eliminate this fine distinction and give samples of contemporary English, or more especially and significantly of American English, according to which one says 'I envy you' when it should in fact be 'I am jealous of your . . .' Thus Hollis Alpert writes: 'I have a wild envy of the man in the taxi with her,' while V. S. Pritchett writes: 'I often envy the writer who works in a university.'

The emphasis, in the definitions of 'envy' and 'envying' in Webster's third edition, is laid on the desire to possess what belongs to the other, not to see it destroyed. Indeed, this shift in emphasis corresponds almost exactly to the present American view of envy. Thus an American advertisement is able to declare that one should buy this or that in order to be envied—that is to say, so that the other man should at once do his utmost to get the same thing, not, as in earlier cultures, that he should try to damage it out of spite.

Jealousy as compared with envy is defined by Webster principally as fear of unfaithfulness or rivalry, but the dictionary also mentions that 'jealous' can be used in the sense of 'envious,' as in: 'Jealous because her coat isn't as nice as yours.' 'Jealousy' has rather the meaning of hostile rivalry, and we believe that, as opposed to genuine envy, it does not anticipate the downfall of the rival. Webster's example of this is: 'Intense local jealousies among existing villages.'

Envy and emulation

A masterly definition and description of envy is found in the *Encyclopedia of Religion and Ethics,* published in 1912. Therein, William L. Davidson, Professor of Logic at the University of Aberdeen, has this to say:

> Envy is an emotion that is essentially both selfish and malevolent. It is aimed at persons, and implies dislike of one who possesses what the envious man himself covets or desires, and a wish to harm him. Grasping-ness for self and ill-will lie at the basis of it. There is in it also a consciousness of inferiority to the person envied, and a chafing under this consciousness. He who has got what I envy is felt by me to have the advantage of me, and I resent it. Consequently, I rejoice if he finds that his envied possession does not give him entire satisfaction—much more, if it actually entails on him

dissatisfaction and pain: that simply reduces his superiority in my eyes, and ministers to my feelings of self-importance. As signifying in the envious man a want that is ungratified, and as pointing to a sense of impotence inasmuch as he lacks the sense of power which possession of the desired object would give him, envy is in itself a painful emotion, although it is associated with pleasure when misfortune is seen to befall the object of it.

The writer of the article also quotes Dryden:

> *Envy, that does with misery reside,*
> *The joy and the revenge of ruin'd pride.*

The article compares envy with jealousy. They have much in common yet represent completely different emotions. Jealousy differs from envy in being infinitely more spiteful, as well as more impassioned and less restrained. Jealousy arises out of an opinion as to what is one's due; it is not purely a sense of inferiority, as is envy. For the jealous man, furthermore, there is a twofold source of irritation and uneasiness, since three people are involved: he is not engaged with one rival only, but with two (individuals or groups). If I am jealous of somebody this is because he has won someone else's affections to which I think I have a right. Thus I hate not only the usurper but the person he has seduced.

Next, envy is compared with emulation, a term that has been equated with it. Americans, for example, prefer 'envy' to the obsolete use of 'emulation,' but are quite unaware of the shift in meaning. They have forgotten envy's spiteful, destructive aspect.

The article rightly considers emulation to be very different from envy. He who emulates, who seeks to do what another has done, is neither self-seeking, spiteful, nor filled with hatred. Emulation requires a rival, a competitor, but the latter does not have to be seen as an enemy. He may even be a friend whose example stimulates our own powers and talents. Behaviour that reveals emulation is observable in many animals and is also apparent in the simple games of young children.

Again, the article draws a distinction between ambition and emulation. While ambition may be laudable, it may also degenerate into a ruthlessness leading ultimately to methods of harming a rival very similar to those of the envious man. Emulation may turn into envy as when, for instance, shortly before the end of the race a runner realizes that he will not be able to outpace the winner and so tries to trip him up. The article cites the following distinction drawn by Joseph Butler in one of his sermons (Sermon 1, note 20):

'Emulation is merely the desire and hope of equality with, or superiority over others, with whom we compare ourselves. . . . To desire the attainment of this equality or superiority by the particular means of others being brought down to our own level, or below it, is, I think, the distinct notion of envy.'[2]

John Gay (1669–1745), philosopher and Fellow of Sidney Sussex College, Cambridge, gives a brilliant analysis of the phenomenon of envy in his study of the fundamental principles of virtue or morality.[3] He regards envy as a diabolical passion and concurs with Locke in believing it possible for some people to be completely devoid of it. Moreover, Gay rightly observes that most people, were they to give the matter some consideration, would remember the first time they ever felt themselves to be under the influence of envious emotions. This he sees as being especially important, since the ability to remember the first active experience of envy indicates the series of fundamental motives that leave their stamp on the personality. Because the most important experiences of envy cannot easily be forgotten, Gay believes, those people who think they have never been affected by it are probably right. He could not, of course, have been aware of such a factor as repression.

To begin with, Gay keeps to the common definition of envy as the anguish that besets us when we observe the prosperity of others; but this he at once qualifies with the statement that it is not the prosperity of all and sundry but of specific persons. What persons? As soon as we look around us to discover who it is we might envy we will, Gay maintains, find the source of this passion: the objects of envy invariably prove to be persons who had formerly been the envious man's rivals. Gay rightly comments on the importance of social proximity in envy. It is usually directed only towards persons with whom it has been possible to com-

---

[2] W. L. Davidson, 'Envy and Emulation,' in the *Encyclopedia of Religion and Ethics,* ed. James Hastings, Vol. 5, New York and Edinburgh, 1912.

[3] John Gay, *Concerning the Fundamental Principle of Virtue or Morality,* quoted from *The English Philosophers from Bacon to Hill,* ed. Edwin A. Burtt, The Modern Library, New York, n.d., p. 784.

pete. But to restrict envy to genuine and factual rivalry is to go too far, for it blurs its distinction from jealousy. There is no doubt that envy may occur where competition has been only imagined, or even where it is inconceivable. What is decisive, however, as we shall see repeatedly, is the envious man's conviction that the envied man's prosperity, his success and his income are somehow to blame for the subject's deprivation, for the lack that he feels. Now if the capacity for envy derives from the experience of sibling jealousy, this aspect of envy becomes explicable; for within a family the favouring of one child (even if this be purely imaginary) will necessarily involve discrimination against the other (or will arouse a sense of injury).

According to Adam Smith, envy, malice and resentment are the only passions which could bring someone to injure another's person or reputation, yet few people succumb frequently to these passions and the worst scoundrels only on occasion. And even if one does give way to such feelings, little is gained. Therefore, Smith opines, in most human beings envy is restrained by rational reflection.[4]

The evidence for Smith's confident assumption is, of course, the fact that it would not be possible to imagine any kind of orderly co-existence if the prevailing society had not succeeded in largely suppressing mutual envy.

Causal delusion in envy

Scheler is responsible for a very important conceptual clarification. He sees envy, in the ordinary sense of the word, as the product of the feeling of impotence

> which inhibits the striving after a possession that belongs to another. The tension between such striving and such impotence only leads to envy, however, when it is discharged into an act of hatred or vindictive behaviour towards the owner of the possession; when, that is, owing to a delusion, the other with his possession is experienced as the *cause* of our painful failure to have the possession. This delusion, whereby what is in fact our impotence to obtain the possession appears to us as a positive force 'opposing' our striving, has the effect of somewhat reducing the initial tension. Genuine

---

[4] Adam Smith, *Wealth of Nations,* Modern Library edition, p. 670.

envy is no more possible without the particular experience of such impotence than it is without the causal delusion.

Now it is significant that, as we shall show, many primitive peoples
(e.g., the Dobuans and the Navaho Indians), as well as some village
communities in more developed societies (e.g., in Central America),
bring about the kind of causal delusion described by Scheler, not
unconsciously or subconsciously like our contemporaries in modern
societies, but with intent: my neighbour's harvest *can* only have turned
out better than mine *because* he has somehow succeeded in reducing
mine by black magic. It is this view of the world, the magic thinking of
the primitive man within us—also discernibly at work in many other
forms of superstitious compulsive behaviour—which provides the dynamic of envy in modern, enlightened society.

Scheler declares explicitly:

> Mere displeasure at the fact that another possesses the thing which I
> covet does not constitute envy; it is, indeed, a motive for acquiring in some
> way the desired object or a similar one, e.g., by working for it, by buying it,
> by force or by theft. Only when the attempt to obtain it by these means has
> failed, giving rise to the consciousness of impotence, does *envy* arise.[5]

A definition in German

As early as the nineteenth century, Grimm's German Dictionary had a
definition of envy comprising all the essential elements we need for our
inquiry: 'Today, as in earlier language, envy [*Neid*] expresses that
vindictive and inwardly tormenting frame of mind, the displeasure with
which one perceives the prosperity and the advantages of others, begrudges them these things and in addition wishes one were able to
destroy or to possess them oneself: synonymous with malevolence,
ill-will, the evil eye.'

We shall now examine the elements of the definition:

1. Vindictive, inwardly tormenting, displeasure. These represent a
feeling of aggression already conscious of impotence, so that from the

[5] Max Scheler, 'Das Ressentiment im Aufbau der Moralen,' *Gesammelte Werke*, Vol.
3, Bern, 1955, p. 45.

start some of the aggression and a good measure of anguish and torment are somewhat masochistically turned back upon the subject. Later we shall examine the possibility that the intensely and chronically envious man may indeed be a person possessed by the desire—from whatever cause—to destroy himself, yet unable to tolerate that others who enjoy life, or at least courageously endure it, should survive him.

2. It is anguish to perceive the prosperity and advantages of others. Envy is emphatically an act of perception. As we shall see, there are no objective criteria for what it is that stimulates envy. And herein lies the error of political egalitarians who believe that it is only necessary to eliminate once and for all certain inequalities from this world to produce a harmonious society of equals devoid of envy. Anyone who has a propensity for envy, who is driven by that emotion, will always manage to find enviable qualities or possessions in others to arouse his envy. Experimental proof of this is not lacking, as shown *inter alia* by child psychology.

3. One begrudges others their personal or material assets, being as a rule almost more intent on their destruction than on their acquisition. The professional thief is less tormented, less motivated by envy, than is the arsonist. Beneath the envious man's primarily destructive desire is the realization that in the long run it would be a very demanding responsibility were he to have the envied man's qualities or possessions, and that the best kind of world would be one in which neither he, the subject, nor the object of his envy would have them. For instance, an envy-oriented politician regards a lower national income *per capita* as more tolerable than one that is higher for all and includes a number of wealthy men.

In the Bible (Genesis 26:14–15) we read: 'For he had possession of flocks, and possession of herds . . . and the Philistines envied him. For all the wells which his father's servants had digged . . . the Philistines had stopped them, and filled them with earth.' (In this respect, human nature has changed little since Old Testament times. Envy of a neighbour's herd of cattle and an assault on his water supply are the order of the day in many a village community in present-day South America, for example.)

Would many of our contemporaries, on hearing the word 'malice,' be likely to think at once of envy? The word 'malice' still plays a part in

English law today. In certain lawsuits, for instance, there has to be evidence that the slanderer or wrongdoer acted out of malice afore-thought. That malice underlies envy is understood.

At Oxford in 1952 a prize was awarded for an essay on the subject of malice. The writer, F. George Steiner, by the use of quotations from a large number of sources, shows how closely envy is linked with malice and to what extent both are the result of social proximity.

> A Flemish proverb has it that Malice is born of familiarity, and when Grotius proposed that there are no men malicious in a state of nature, he had in mind the lonesome creatures of a golden age. Malice is created by low garden fences, or in narrow streets, where men unceasingly rub shoulders, and this man's orchard casts a blighting shade over that man's vineyard. It is an elixir brewed by close contact. . . . Indifference yields no malice. . . .[6]

Steiner quotes passages from the Anglican liturgy and from the Latin poet Persius to demonstrate that envy is a universal human ailment. He regards as one of La Rochefoucauld's most terrifying maxims that in which the moralist remarks that there is something in us that warms the heart at the spectacle of a friend's misfortune. This is the hidden malice which generates envy.

Envy in proverbs

A nineteenth-century dictionary of proverbs contains 136 proverbs on the subject of envy, and a further 76 comprising words such as 'to envy' and 'envious.'[7] In these two hundred or more German proverbs, many of which have Latin, Danish, Russian, Hungarian, Polish and other equivalents, most of the general observations that can be made about envy are stated with surprising accuracy.

Let us advance some theses on the phenomenon of envy, in each case citing a popular saying.

1. Envy is above all a phenomenon of social proximity: American sociologists use the term 'invidious proximity,' or in other words, proximity that arouses envy.

---

[6] F. G. Steiner, *Malice*, Oxford, 1952, p. 16.

[7] *Das Deutsche Sprichwörter-Lexikon*, K. F. Wander (1863–1880), Bonn, 1874, p. 177.

Envy is always between neighbours.—The envious man thinks that if his neighbour breaks a leg, he will be able to walk better himself.

2. It is not the absolute differences between men which feed envy, but subjective perception, the optics of envy. In other words, the envious man sees what confirms his envy.

Envy turns a blade of grass into a palm tree.—A bush of broom, in envy's eye, grows into a palm grove.—The Russians say: Envy looks at a juniper bush and sees a pine forest.—In the eye of the envious man, a toadstool becomes a palm tree.—Envy sees faults sooner than virtues.—A number of Russian proverbs express the thought that the envious man sees only what is enviable in the other, and not his countervailing handicaps: Envy can see the ship well enough, but not the leak.—Envy sees the sea, but not the reefs.—Envy sees only the bridge, not the swamp it crosses.—Envy may see the bearskin but not the moths.—Envy looks at a swamp and sees a sea.—To envy, bad duck eggs will hatch out swans.—To envy, the pike in the fishpond is a golden trout.—The envious eye makes elephants of midges.—And the Russians say: The envious man sees with his ears as well.

These proverbs explain, too, why in all cultures it is not just good taste but virtually a compulsion never to mention one's own advantage, new possession or good luck to others unless in conjunction with a lack, a disadvantage or a mischance. Thus the owner of a new car will at once mention his long, wearisome journey to work; the sweepstake winner or recipient of an unexpected windfall immediately discovers a hundred commitments; the man who has been promoted at once reminds us that this now makes him more liable to a heart attack. In many societies, and notably among primitive peoples, this compulsion is so extreme that on principle no one can ever announce favourable news about himself or any member of his family.

3. Envy is a very early, inescapable and unappeasable drive in man, which induces the envious man constantly to react to his environment in such a way that his envy cannot be assuaged. Hence it is utterly hopeless to strive for a society which could be freed of envy by social reform.

Envy looks out even from the eyes of little children.—Envy is a beast that will gnaw its own leg if it can't get anything else.—Envy is inborn.—Envy is at home everywhere.—Envy never dies.—Envy and jealousy are immortal, but friendship and love brittle.—None lives in this world without envy.

Were envy a fever, the world would have been dead long since. (There are German, Danish, Italian, Latin and Swedish versions of this proverb.)—If envy were an illness, the world would be a hospital.— He who would be without envy must not tell of his joy.—The envious die, envy is inherited.—The more kindness is shown to an envious man, the worse he becomes.

This latter observation is particularly important because psychopathology has repeatedly confirmed it. The more one seeks to deprive the envious man of his ostensible reason for envy by giving him presents and doing him good turns, the more one demonstrates one's superiority and stresses how little the gift will be missed. Were one to strip oneself of every possession, such a demonstration of goodness would still humiliate him so that his envy would be transferred from one's possessions to one's character. And if one were to raise him to one's own level, this artificially established equality would not make him in the least happy. He would again envy, firstly the benefactor's character, and secondly the recollection retained by the benefactor during this period of equality of his erstwhile material superiority.

4. The envious man is perfectly prepared to injure himself if by so doing he can injure or hurt the object of his envy. Many criminal acts, in some cases perhaps even suicide, become more comprehensible if this possibility is recognized.

Envy stews in its own juice.—The envious man will often suffer injury himself so as to bring it on his fellow man.

5. Proverbs in many languages agree that the greatest damage done by the envious man is to himself. Envy is described as an utterly destructive, uncreative and even diseased state of mind for which there is no remedy.

Envy has never made anyone rich.—Envy cuts its own throat.—Envy will eat nothing but its own heart.—Envy envies itself.—Envy brings suffering to the envious man.—Envy devours its own master.—Envy is its own scourge.—Envy flogs itself.—Envy makes life bitter.—The envious man injures no one so much as himself.

6. Like primitive peoples, whose fear of their fellow tribesmen's black magic invariably ascribes to them the motive of envy, proverbs repeatedly indicate how easily the passively envious man can become an aggressive criminal. For the envious man it is not enough to wait until

fate overtakes his neighbour so that he can rejoice (his *Schadenfreude* is attested by countless proverbs): he lends fate a helping hand.

No sooner is envy born than he consorts with the hangman and the gallows.—Envy never laughs till a ship founders with its crew.—Envy makes corpses.

In Islamic literature, most proverbs are ascribed to the Prophet himself, to one of his companions or, with the Shi'ites, to one of their imams. Islam's ethics and wisdom in proverbs regard envy (*Hasad*) as one of the greatest ills. Al-Kulaini writes:

> 'Envy devours faith as fire devours wood,' the Prophet is held to have said. 'Fear Allah, and be not envious among yourselves' is a saying ascribed to Jesus. . . . The plagues of religion are envy, vanity and pride. . . . Moses is held to have said: 'Men should not envy one another what I give them out of my fulness.' And another Imam declared: 'The true believer is he who wishes others well and who does not molest them, while the hypocrite is a man who is envious and who does not suffer any other to be happy.'[8]

Imputation of envious motives

Nowadays we are generally reticent and inhibited when it comes to the imputation of envious motives. Sociological and political publications of the period from about 1800 to 1920 investigated the effects and the nature of envy far more freely and thoroughly than is done today. Nevertheless, a few contemporary quotations will indicate the kind of context in which envious motives are discussed today. The *Time* essay (February 21, 1969), discussing 'May-December Marriages,' declared: 'Envy as well as enmity is aimed at Supreme Court Justice William O. Douglas, 70, veteran of two other alliances with pretty young things, and now married to 26-year-old Cathleen Heffernan.'

In 1964 a woman journalist explained the partial failure of the Ford Foundation's 'Artists-in-Residence Project' in Berlin, namely, the isolation of the visitors and the remarkable reactions—amounting to pure envy—of local artists, and quoted the revealing comments of a Berlin artist: 'No one rolls out the red carpet for me when I arrive in London or

[8] On envy in Islam, cf. Dwight M. Donaldson, *Studies in Muslim Ethics*, London, 1953, pp. 91 ff.

Paris' and, 'My studio is much smaller than the Ford artists' studios.' Much envied, too, were the monthly stipends (up to $1,250) of these people.[9] No one but Americans, who so often cultivate a blind spot so far as envy is concerned, could conceivably have attempted such a project.

Thus, from time to time advertising copy in the United States presents envy as an emotion not at all to be feared, and one that the man who responds to the advertisement will arouse in his neighbours and colleagues: 'If you've never been a Waldorf guest, you could, unthinkingly, believe it to be expensive.' It then continues: 'The admiration (if not envy) of the folks at home is included in the room rate. . . .'[10] German advertising copy, too, has now begun to adopt this allusion to the fact of being envied, which is used as a selling point for a product. Thus, at the end of 1965 huge posters on the sides of streetcars in Mainz promised the lucky owners of a washing machine that they would be envied by others. And a truck manufacturer's advertisement in the German daily papers, in 1966, showed a picture of an upholstered seat in one of their trucks with the caption: 'You will be envied for sitting in this seat.' In 1968 the same slogan was used by IBM in ads to recruit workers for its plants in Germany.

In American business life, however, the inhibiting and destructive aspects of envy are sometimes recognized and mentioned. In the monthly publication of the U.S. Chamber of Commerce there appeared in 1958 an article on the seven deadly sins of management, dealing explicitly with the role of envy in business. Envy was said to be found sometimes in superiors towards their more talented and efficient subordinates or among colleagues who, from envy, band together in cliques against an efficient man.[11]

And in 1966 a German daily paper, on the subject of the training period of college graduates destined to become executives in big concerns, recommended that 'the intended future position of the man should not be made public so early' lest the trainee be deliberately misled 'as a result of the envy' this would arouse. Its motive: 'Many of the firm's

[9] C. Jacobsen, 'Halbzeit bei der Ford-Stiftung,' *Die Zeit,* October 9, 1964, p. 9.

[10] *New York Times,* December 7, 1961, p. 29.

[11] *Nation's Business,* Washington, D.C., April, 1958, p. 48.

employees would themselves have liked to have a period of training that was equally comprehensive and well paid.'[12]

A study made in 1961 of social conflict in modern business revealed widespread envious feelings, with particular reference to possible envious feelings resulting in loss of production. The study even revealed minor acts of mutual sabotage to the detriment of the firm, the motive being given unequivocally as envy. The manager of the production planning department said: 'There are envious foremen. When the foreman sees that someone is earning a great deal, he tries to curry favour by telling us: "We can cut down the piece-rate, then." '[13]

Confessing one's envy

There can be no doubt that we have the rarest and also the most unequivocal evidence for the role of envy when the envious man ultimately admits publicly to his own envy and confesses that he has harmed another person from that motive. So far I have read only one such admission. The author of a biting review wrote in 1964:

'I was, looking back on it now, jealous because he, with his background of mathematics in which I was always weak, had found rational thinking easy. Must I now say in so many words that I take back everything I wrote. . . ?'[14] But significantly this man still hides behind the less painful, and here conceptually false, term 'jealousy.'

The only public discussion of envy that I know of in which both participants spoke of their own envy took place during an unscripted talk on the B.B.C. between Arnold Toynbee and his son Philip. Philip, the ex-Communist (as it transpired during the broadcast), in the course of a discussion on the progress of morality, declared: 'What about envy? Envy and covetousness have always seemed to me to be very much the same thing. . . .'

A.T.: '. . . I notice how much American businessmen talk about the wickedness of envy.'

[12] 'Nachwuchskräfte sollen sich am Anfang überall unterrichten,' *Die Welt*, No. 128, June 4, 1966.

[13] Wolfgang Kellner, *Die moderne soziale Konflikt. Seine Ursache und seine Überwindung im Betrieb*, Stuttgart, 1961, pp. 142–51.

[14] G. H. Theunissen, 'Der Fall Max Bense,' *Die Zeit*, April 24, 1964, p. 9.

P.T.: 'Meaning how wicked of the poor to want to have more money?'
A.T.: 'Yes . . . I think that to feel envy is unfortunate for the person who
feels it, even if the person he feels it against justifies the feeling by
deserving it.' The father overlooked his son's naïve insinuation of class
warfare and considered envy rather in the traditional sense in which it is
depicted here.

Both Toynbees next told of their own experience of envy. The son
envied authors praised by critics, especially when he himself was ad-
versely criticized. The father thought he had not often been envious.
Both saw envy as an obstacle that prevented people from engaging in
worthwhile activity. The father suggested that neither of them had
suffered unduly from envy, not through any merit of their own but
through good luck, both having jobs, for instance, which they had
chosen for themselves. Finally, Arnold Toynbee recalled his envy of the
French for being able to go on with their writing even under German
occupation.[15]

[15] A. and P. Toynbee, *Comparing Notes*, London, 1963.

3

The Envious Man and
His Culture

NO SYSTEM OF ETHICS, no religion, no popular wisdom recorded in proverbs, no moral fables and no rules of behaviour among primitive peoples have ever made a virtue of envy. Quite the opposite, in fact; by means of the most diverse arguments, human societies—or the men who have to live in a society—have persistently sought as far as possible to suppress envy. Why? Because in any group the envious man is inevitably a disturber of the peace, a potential saboteur, an instigator of mutiny and, fundamentally, he cannot be placated by others. Since there can be no absolutely egalitarian society, since people cannot be made truly equal if a community is to be at all viable, the envious man is, by definition, the negation of the basis of any society. Incurably envious people may, for a certain time, inspire and lead chiliastic, revolutionary movements, but they can never establish a stable society except by compromising their 'ideals' of equality.

The history of early human thought on the subject of social relations has never, so far as is known, shown evidence of any illusions about the nature of envy.

Most communities have developed or adapted customs and views that enable individual members of a tribe to be unequal in one way or another without being harmed by the envy of the others.

Ethnological material shows how inescapable is the problem of envying and being envied in every aspect of human social existence. The member of a certain social class at a certain stage of his country's economic or political development, the individual in a certain group situation, every person in a private capacity will, when confronted by the imagined envy of others towards himself, be inclined to see it as a special case. He may console himself: it is the nature of things in the society in which he lives. Given certain conditions, feelings of envy will manifest themselves.

But if one is to realize how little envy depends on specific classifications of difference in status, or on cultural or political stages of development, a thorough and detailed examination of ethnographical material is required. Envy is one of the inevitable accompaniments of human social life, and no anthropology that evades this problem can be regarded as complete.

Thirty years ago Richard Thurnwald wrote:

> Among primitive peoples we find the same kinds and the same proportion of dispositional types of temperament as there are among ourselves. They influence each other, fit in together or repel one another. In the play of personalities individuals gain ascendancy and respect as successful hunters, skilled dancers, imaginative singers, effective magicians, cunning killers or impressive orators. Among tribally related families who meet each other on equal terms, individual excellence may be greeted with displeasure and envy. Aversion is shown towards the emergence of a strong leadership. It was not rare for men such as dread magicians to be killed or compelled to flee by their communities—a primitive form of ostracism. This attitude is, indeed, responsible for the slow rate of cultural growth because it resists innovation.[1]

Are any societies devoid of envy?

Wherever in a certain culture we do find institutions which appear to take no account of envy or jealousy, they are exceptions which do not invalidate what has been said above. Many African tribes, for example, which practice polygamy, have a norm prescribing that the husband must show strict impartiality, sharing his favours equally between all his wives. The Kriges clearly demonstrated this in the case of the Lovedu, among whom the wives, who have their own individual huts arranged in a semicircle around their husband's, always keep a careful watch to see if he spends just a little too much time in one of them, or singles out one particular wife. If a wife enjoys only two to four hours in the day of a

[1] R. Thurnwald in: *Lehrbuch der Völkerkunde*, ed. K. Th. Preuss, Stuttgart, 1937, pp. 236 ff.

husband whom she shares with others, she guards these as jealously as a monogamous wife who can lay claim to her husband against other females for the whole twenty-four hours.[2] Polygamy does not exclude susceptibility to sexual jealousy, which is universal among human beings.

It is equally false to speak of a relatively unenvious society because, for instance, it has no 'salary taboo' as a device to obviate envy. The Swedes regard themselves as an envious people, and there is an expression 'royal Swedish envy.'[3] Yet in Sweden anyone is allowed to examine any other citizen's tax return. There is, in fact, a private firm which yearly produces a much-consulted list giving the incomes of all families where these are more than about $3600 a year. Institutions of this kind may represent a deliberate exploitation of democratic envy for the purpose of enforcing honesty in taxation matters. Thus if data which are kept secret in some societies in order to obviate envy are made public in another society, this does not mean that its attitude is less envious. In the United States, secrecy is generally assured in the matter of tax returns. Yet between 1923 and 1953, in the state of Wisconsin there was a law permitting anyone to inspect any of his fellow citizens' tax returns, with all details and particulars. Not until 1953 was the right of the inquisitive or envious man curtailed by a new law which required of him a fee of one dollar, entitling him only to be told the total tax paid by another person.[4] And in some states democratic vigilance demanded that every civil servant's emoluments and expenses, together with his name and place of

---

[2] ' . . . polygyny . . . must create special interrelations within its structure, between husband and wives, between children of different wives, and between fellow wives . . . . The polygynist must be most circumspect in his relations with his wives. He must treat them all with strict impartiality. Should he wish to give one a present, all must receive similar gifts. If he spends more time with one than another, this may be the cause of serious domestic discord. He must always be weighing and balancing lest preference shown to one should lead to trouble and unpleasantness.' The Lovedu are quite aware of the situation. The term for fellow wives is to be translated as 'people who roast one another.' And the existing tension occasionally affects different wives of the same man living in different villages. (E. J. Krige and J. D. Krige, *The Realm of a Rain-Queen*, London, 1943, pp. 70 ff.)

[3] F. Rose, *Umgang mit Schweden* (Vol. 12 of the series 'Umgang mit Völkern'), Nuremberg, 1954, p. 13.

[4] *Time*, June 29, 1953.

residence, should be recorded annually in a book available in every public library. Anyone hearing of this institution might conclude that Americans were little plagued by envy, for if they were, they could not afford thus to publicize salaries. But as may be observed, the frankness shown by the Department of Finance not infrequently leads to personal conflicts such as the salary taboo elsewhere seeks to avoid.

The more data comparative cultural anthropology provides, the more evident it becomes that we cannot infer, from the lack of certain institutions and typical practices, a corresponding absence of any one basic human drive. This applies especially to envy. Individual cultures have evolved various, sometimes of course rather weak, mechanisms to enable their members to get along with each other despite envy.

It is not easy to test a theory about envy. The existence of the motive of envy can, of course, be proved, where there is express mention of envy or of concern about it, and most languages have a word for it. Again, if a person wants other people to have less than he has or nothing at all, instead of granting others the right to have more, or if he inflicts damage on another without himself benefiting thereby, envy can at least be assumed. It is more difficult to find evidence for the absence or minimal role of envy in a culture or in a given social situation. At best it could be said that someone had been able to suppress his envy and hence to accept the other's privilege or advantage with good grace. But it is virtually impossible categorically to declare that in a given social situation or custom none of those involved feels envy. Yet we are fully justified in believing a man who, at an interview, spontaneously admits to being envious. He would be generally much more likely to conceal the fact. But we cannot implicitly believe anyone who maintains that this thing or that would not arouse his envy.

Nor are we any the wiser if we conclude from the existence of certain social institutions such as primogeniture or polygamy that there is no envy or jealousy. Not infrequently these very customs give rise to black magic or other modes of behaviour which show that anyone who is injured by the institutionally tolerated behaviour of, say, father or spouse, is in a favourable position to react enviously. Again and again in ethnographical literature we come upon accounts of sons who killed the brother favoured by primogeniture, or of a first wife who killed a second or third wife, despite the general custom of polygamy in her tribe.

Social life would be impossible if cultures did not succeed within reason in forcing those who have real cause for envy or jealousy to co-operate. For after all, a society in which there was never cause for envy, a society of total and constant equality, would not be workable even as a theoretical experiment. Thus in some tribes a father, especially if he is a medicine man, will bequeath his magic tricks to the eldest son only, much to the jealous anger of the others. And yet as long as such a tribe finds it essential to believe in magic in order to endure the threat of adversity, it is clearly good sense for that power not to be diffused throughout the group. Magic which is common knowledge is not magic at all. Thus all we can ask is how well or how badly a society has eliminated, deflected or restricted envy in certain spheres of life. We can never say that in such and such a culture and such and such a social situation none of the participants is envious or jealous. Rather, some cultures may successfully attempt to achieve a condition in which much social activity can proceed *as if there were no envy.*

Every society and every culture may lend such esteem to a certain position, achievement or spiritual state (e.g., ecstasy) that there will inevitably be some individuals who believe they have been hard done by. Distinctions and differences which arouse envy are the concomitant of all social existence. In some societies, prestige accrues from the possession and manipulation of property or wealth, in others from formalized scholarship (in Imperial China) and in Hindu and Buddhist cultures from spiritual perfection. But it is not only differences in prestige that are a source of envy and resentment; most cultures, as the anthropologist H. G. Barnett emphasized, provide opportunities for one man to excel, thus becoming a cause for envy even when his achievement as such has little or nothing to do with the society's general system of prestige: ' . . . the potential causes of resentment are countless.'[5]

The Navaho are the largest Indian tribe still to survive in the United States. The existence they lead on their reservation is wretched. The Navaho has nothing to correspond to our concept of 'personal success' or 'personal achievement.' Nor can he have good or bad luck. Anyone who prospers or, according to their notions, grows rich, can only have done so at someone else's expense. Hence the Navajo who is better off feels himself to be under constant social pressure to be lavish in hospitality

---

[5] H. G. Barnett, *Innovations. The Basis of Cultural Change,* New York, 1953, pp. 401 f.

and generous with gifts. He knows that if he fails in this, 'the voice of envy will speak out in whispers of witchcraft' which would make his life in society 'strained and unpleasant. . . .'[6]

Again, the primitive fisherman, even when he has had only one lucky catch, has to reckon with his comrades' envy. Raymond Firth, an expert on the island peoples of Polynesia, describes relations among a group of fishermen:

> If a man catches only one or two fish while no one else has any success then he will give them to other members of the crew and not keep any. If he did retain his fish, allowing the others to go away empty-handed, then he runs the risk of slanderous talk. 'One man may go and not say anything; another man may go and criticize, "that fish which he brought in, he did not give it to me but kept it for himself." ' There is no ritual reason why a man should not eat of his own catch—a reason which sometimes obtains in other communities. The custom is explained on a rational, social basis. If a man catches fish with his net in the lake, for instance, it is quite legitimate for him to keep them for himself 'because he is alone.' It is when he is a member of a crew that the former custom operates. It is described directly as 'the blocking of jealousy' (te pi o te kaimeo).[7]

A practice that serves to obviate envy may be openly prescribed by tribal custom for that very purpose. In other cases an unexplained taboo attempts the same thing. Thus it was observed that a Siriono Indian hunter in Bolivia might not eat any part of the animal he had killed. Were he to break the taboo, the same kind of animal could never again fall to his arrow. Originally this taboo meant that the quarry was spared. About twenty years ago, however, Holmberg remarked that the rule was already being frequently broken.[8]

The Siriono, a tribe leading an excessively meagre existence in

---

[6] C. Kluckhohn, *The Navaho*, Cambridge (Mass.), 1946; *Navaho Witchcraft* (Papers of the Peabody Museum of American Archaeology and Ethnology, Vol. 22, No. 2, Cambridge (Mass.), 1944); see especially p. 68.

[7] R. Firth, *Primitive Polynesian Economy*, London, 1939, p. 282.

[8] A. R. Holmberg, *Nomads of the Long Bow. The Siriono of Eastern Bolivia* (Smithsonian Institution: Institute of Social Anthropology Publication, No. 10). Washington, 1950. The field work was done during 1941–42.

sub-units of fifteen to twenty-five people, show a few remarkable behavioural traits explicable as an attempt to avoid the envy of their tribal associates. The individual generally eats alone and at night, because he does not wish to share his quarry with others. If he eats by day, a small crowd of people outside his immediate family gathers round him. They stare at him enviously. Although he hardly ever gives them anything, he is nevertheless disturbed. Even Allan Holmberg, an American anthropologist, while living with them, eventually adopted this practice of eating alone.[9]

For the most part the Siriono give proof of extreme individualism, though they will conform, often reluctantly, to some norms of the group. A man who has given food to a relative can expect some in return, but he nearly always has to demand it.[10] Food (meat being especially scarce) is hardly ever shared with anyone in the sub-unit who does not belong to the nuclear family (wife, or perhaps the favourite wife and children). The Siriono accuse each other of hoarding food, but cannot do anything to stop this.[11] They are constantly denouncing each other for stealing food. Typically, every man hides anything edible. Females may even hide morsels of meat in their vagina rather than share them. A returning hunter will hide his quarry outside the camp and join the group with every sign of dejection. Not until nightfall will he return, perhaps with his wife, to the hiding place and eat the animal he has killed.[12] There is nothing to be seen here of the close community which allegedly exists among primitive peoples in pre-affluent times—the poorer, it is held, the greater the sense of community. Sociological theory would have avoided many errors if those phenomena had been properly observed and evaluated a century ago. The myth of a golden age, when social harmony prevailed because each man had about as little as the next one, the warm and generous community spirit of simple societies, was indeed for the most part just a myth, and social scientists should have known better than to fashion out of it a set of utopian standards with which to criticize their own societies.

[9] Op. cit., p. 36.
[10] Op. cit., p. 60.
[11] Op. cit., pp. 60, 61.
[12] Op. cit., p. 62.

4

Envy and Black Magic

FOR MOST PEOPLE, the first association of the word 'witch' is with fairystories, with *Macbeth* or with witch burning. Before we examine primitive thinking on the subject of witches, the expression of the general fear inspired by the envious fellow tribesman, a few concepts will need clarification. In Europe as elsewhere, 'witch' originally meant something like 'vagrant,' a threatening, ill-intentioned person. The connection with the evil eye, the eye of the envious man, appears early. From time immemorial suspicion of witchcraft or black magic has fallen upon those who have had cause to be envious—of someone less ugly than themselves, of lucky parents, or the peasant with a good harvest and healthy cattle, etc. After all, bad luck can befall only those who have something to lose: good health, beauty, possessions, family. In the attempt to come to terms emotionally with the problem of misfortune, it seemed reasonable to look around for people who might be envious.

During the witch trials in Europe the accused were precisely those persons who had somehow aroused the suspicion that they were envious and hence desirous of harming others. Gradually, however, the envious man himself became the accuser, the accused being people who were good-looking, virtuous, proud and rich, or the wives of wealthy citizens. This double role played by envy in witchcraft is again apparent among primitive peoples. The outsider, the cripple, anyone at all handicapped, is suspected and regarded as responsible for damage. Yet the same primitive man is capable of asserting that another member of his tribe is only rich, powerful, a good dancer or hunter because he has gained by black magic something that should have belonged to his fellow tribesmen.

Accounts of primitive peoples in all parts of the world offer a wealth of evidence as to belief in witches and the practice of witchcraft. It is a constant aspect of primitive existence. Some tribes, such as the Navaho of North America, the African Azande and the West Pacific islanders, the Dobuans, seem to have a particularly strong belief in witchcraft, but basically the picture is the same wherever the investigation is made.

In his analysis of resentment, Max Scheler has already compared the incurably envious person with the witch figure. He maintains that resentment can 'never develop without the mediation of a specific feeling of impotence.' There are types of social situation, he says, in which, quite aside from their individual character, the people concerned are particularly liable to resentment. Scheler sees a connection between the female sex and the figure of the witch:

> The *woman,* because she is weaker and hence more vindictive, and by very reason of her personal, unalterable qualities is forced to compete with other members of her sex for man's favour, generally finds herself in such a 'situation.' Small wonder then that vengeful deities, such as that sinister serpent's brood, the Eumenides or Furies, first grew up within a female-dominated matriarchy. . . . This may also account for the fact that there is no male counterpart to the figure of the 'witch.'[1]

Rightly though Scheler has observed and explained the peculiar affinity between the 'second sex,' as Simone de Beauvoir resentfully called it, and the envious figure of the witch, the deviations found in other cultures are equally remarkable.

Although English has masculine nouns such as 'sorcerer' and 'wizard,' English-speaking ethnographers nearly always select the female noun 'witch' when they wish to designate such persons. Yet among primitive peoples the witch is by no means confined to the female sex: for instance the Navaho Indians believe that both men and women can become witches, but that there are far more male witches. Out of 222 cases of accusation of witchcraft, Kluckhohn discovered that 184 involved adult males, 131 of these being of great age. All the females accused were also very old. The Navaho are usually so afraid of the sorcery of old people that they do their best to propitiate them with lavish

[1] M. Scheler, 'Das Ressentiment im Aufbau der Moralen,' *Gesammelte Werke,* Vol. 3, Bern, 1955, p. 52.

hospitality and the like, even though the person concerned may be extremely unpleasant. Kluckhohn explains this by, among other things, the high value set by the Navaho on a long life. Those who achieve it seek to keep it, often at the cost of younger people. These Indians are generally suspicious of all persons in extreme positions—the very rich, the very poor, the influential singer, the extremely old. They believe that only dead relatives can become hostile spirits. A person must belong to the dead man's clan to be able to see his spirit.[2]

The extent to which Navaho life is overshadowed by the ubiquity of witches is matched only by their unwillingness to discuss it. White men have often spent years among them without obtaining any exact idea of the seriousness and extent of this cultural feature. Even those Navaho who have completely emancipated themselves from all the other aspects of their tribal religion are still subject to the fear of witches.[3]

Some anthropologists see in witchcraft beliefs a useful safety valve, an understandable and desirable institution whereby intersocial tensions are regulated. Kluckhohn, however, maintains that the destructive and inhibiting effect of these ideas has been grossly underrated, and that they are much more likely to give rise to timidity and to restrict social relations than to bring about a healthy abreaction of aggressive feelings.[4]

Envy and suspected witchcraft

Kluckhohn leaves no room for doubt as to the immediate connection between envy and suspected witchcraft. Among the Navaho a person becomes a witch (having inherited the craft from one of his parents) 'in order to wreak vengeance, in order to gain wealth, or simply to injure wantonly—most often motivated by envy.'[5] A special kind of witchcraft, frenzy witchcraft, is black magic directed principally against those who are prosperous. A Navaho described this to Kluckhohn as follows: 'That's when they see you got the best of goods all the time, good children, good wife. That man from over there, that bad man might think, "We'll break up that home." '[6]

[2] C. Kluckhohn, *Navaho Witchcraft*, pp. 15, 59.

[3] C. Kluckhohn, *The Navaho*, pp. 128 f.

[4] C. Kluckhohn, *Navaho Witchcraft*, p. 68.

[5] Ibid., p. 15.

[6] Op. cit., p. 111.

Another Indian tribe, the Hopi, are reputed to be very peaceable. In their culture, social harmony is prized as the highest good. But when a Hopi seeks to explain illness, death and similar misfortunes, he believes, like the Navaho, that there are witches in his immediate neighbourhood.

The Hopi Indians know the danger of envy. Their principal rule is never to brag or boast. 'People may steal the boaster's things and begin sorcerous operations.'[7] The ideal Hopi, as revealed by several inform- ants, condemns envy as a useless emotional state. He is supposed to banish envious thoughts.[8] The same things are regarded by the Hopi as enviable as is the case elsewhere: 'A man being envious of someone else because he has more money and a better house.'[9] Or: 'Your heart aches for a person who has more than you have. You say, "I ought to have that."' The Hopi language has the word *unangtutuiqa,* meaning in fact 'he is sick at heart,' and translated by American ethnologists as 'en- vious, jealous.'[10] The Zuñi Indians share with the Hopi a distaste for competitive behaviour and open aggression, and sacrifice individuality to the collective. But this does not eliminate envy. Both very poor and particularly rich Zūni can be suspected of witchcraft. The constant threat of an accusation of witchcraft serves to maintain social conformity. The similarity between European stories of witchcraft and Zuñi stories has been remarked upon.

A deceived husband or a jilted lover is described in Zuñi legend, not as feeling vengeful and filled with hatred of his rival, but as a man to whom it is intolerable that he alone should be unhappy: the whole tribe, all its members, whether guilty or not, must likewise be destroyed. Zuñi folktales state expressly that the husband deprived of happiness desires no one else ever to be happy. And when a Zuñi who thinks he has been deceived or unfairly treated indulges in daydreams, what he generally longs for is that others should suffer as he does. The deserted wife may wish that the tribe's arch-enemy, the Apaches, will come and destroy the village.[11]

[7] R. B. Brandt, *Hopi Ethics,* Chicago, 1954, p. 328.

[8] Op. cit., pp. 143, 148.

[9] Op. cit., p. 156.

[10] Op. cit., p. 129.

[11] Ruth Benedict, in 'An Anthropologist at Work, Writings of Ruth Benedict,' ed. by Margaret Mead, Boston, 1959, p. 234 (from *Zuñi Mythology,* Vol. 1, New York, 1935.).

In North America there were some Indian tribes among whom ethnologists discovered remarkably little general fear of witchcraft, but who
nevertheless regarded the central values of their existence as under
threat. The Comanche of the open prairie, for example, were courageous
people, and the role of aggressive warrior was reserved for men between
twenty and forty-five. If an old man failed to adapt himself with good
grace to the role of peaceable old age, he was suspected of envious
magic. He might even be killed by the relatives of someone who suspected him of being a witch. Understandably, the Comanche generally
revered as chiefs those men who had *not* especially distinguished themselves as young warriors, and who were therefore unlikely to regret their
lost youth.

It is also generally true of the Central American Indian cultures that
envy and covetousness are regarded as anomaly or crime. The Indians
know a kind of illness which is produced by magic, called by them
envidia, and which is invoked by an envious person. The victim has the
undeniable right, recognized by the community, to kill his enemy if he
can be discovered. For this reason it is inconceivable that anyone should
admit his envy.[12]

Edward Evans-Pritchard's work on witchcraft and black magic among
the Azande in Africa is regarded as being among the most accurate
studies of such phenomena. His observations and conclusions are in
complete agreement with the general theory of envy we have outlined in
this book. Repeatedly he describes the constant preoccupation of the
Azande with the envy of others, and their resultant behaviour. The
Azande system of values, their culture, their popular beliefs, all condemn the envious man. Like us, they have the concept of a gentleman, a
man who is respected, upright and trustworthy. He stands up for himself,
and may take ruthless action against all those who in any way harm him,
his family and his friends; nor does he have to evince false modesty. But
an important feature is that he does not envy those around him.[13]

The proverbs of this tribe are very similar to those of Europe: 'Envy
and jealousy kill the strongest man.' 'Malice leads the way, black magic

[12] J. Gillin, *The Culture of Security in San Carlos. A Study of a Guatemalan Community of Indians and Ladinos,* New Orleans, 1951, pp. 122, 124.

[13] E. E. Evans-Pritchard, *Witchcraft (Mangu) among the Azande (Sudan Notes and
Records,* Vol. 12), Khartoum, 1929, pp. 163–249, 215.

follows.' 'First there is covetousness, next there is witchcraft.' These and other moral failings are always cited as the prelude to *mangu,* envious black magic.[14] Azande parents warn their children over and over against being malicious, envious or jealous, or delighting in the sorrows of others. Probably few primitive peoples are so conscious of the danger of envy as the Azande. Whoever speaks ill of his neighbour without apparent reason is at once held to be envious. Not every envious person, indeed, becomes a witch. A lesser form of *mangu* is feared in forms of envy too mild to lead to punishable misdeeds. But anyone who is held to be envious is shunned, and is no longer invited to join the others in communal events.

The Azande draw a very clear distinction: *mangu* as such is not the cause of crime, but only the power to satisfy an envious disposition by doing harm to others.[15] They believe that anyone may become a witch. No one can ever be quite sure of anyone else. And since no one can know whether or not he is suspect, envy must always be restrained in public.[16] Evans-Pritchard considers this belief to be socially most beneficial. Since the Azande look upon every neighbour as a potential witch, the envious man can avert suspicion only by controlling his envy. But on the other hand, those of whom he is envious may also be witches who wish him ill. For this reason, too, he has to be careful.[17] Not only are physically deformed people regarded as witches but also those who are habitually unfriendly, bad-tempered, dirty, quarrelsome and secretive.[18]

The spells of the Azande, designed to protect him against magic, always refer to the envy of some other person, and it is in general quite plain to him that no matter in what way he excels or how he prospers, there will always be those who will envy him his possessions, his descent, his appearance, his skills as hunter, singer or orator, and will therefore seek to destroy him.[19]

---

[14] Op. cit., p. 212.

[15] Op. cit., p. 215.

[16] Op. cit., p. 220.

[17] E. E. Evans-Pritchard, *Witchcraft, Oracles and Magic among the Azande,* Oxford, 1947, p. 117.

[18] Op. cit., p. 112.

[19] Op. cit., pp. 206 f.

Evans-Pritchard compares the Azande idea of envy-magic with our concept of good and bad luck. If there is nothing we can do about a misfortune, we console ourselves with the impersonal 'It was just bad luck.' The Azande ascribes it to *mangu* which originates from a certain person.[20]

The enemy in our midst

In his study 'The Enemy Within,' dealing with sorcery among the Amba in East Africa, E. H. Winter draws this distinction: that whereas witches exist only in the imagination of the Amba, the European observer can be in no doubt that there are individuals among them who do in fact practise black magic, who engage in magic practices, that is, in order to harm their fellow tribesmen. For the Amba the basic distinction between witch and sorcerer lies in the motivation underlying their activity. Sorcery is practised as a result of ordinary motives: envy, jealousy and hatred. It is provoked by the occurrences of daily life, by social situations in which feelings of hatred arise. For this reason the Amba find it understandable if someone takes to magic, although they do, of course, condemn it.

Witches, on the other hand, bring down upon men every conceivable kind of misfortune, driven by their lust for human flesh—a desire incomprehensible to the normal Amba. Winter then suggests the following analogy: the sorcerer who kills a relative for his inheritance corresponds to the murderer in our society, while the witch corresponds to the pathological murderer whose motives we cannot discover. We find this analogy unacceptable because the whole of the literature on the subject of African sorcery shows that the envious man (sorcerer) would like to harm the victim he envies, but only seldom with any expectation of thereby obtaining for himself the asset that he envies—whether this be a possession or a physical quality belonging to the other. As we can show again and again, every culture sees the envious man's reward either as the pleasure of having deprived the man he envies of something, or else of 'punishing' him for owning the coveted asset, supposing this to be indestructible—fame won by heroic deeds, for instance. Yet the Amba and their interpreter, Winter, may very well be right in believing that

[20] Op, cit., p. 148.

someone becomes a sorcerer only if his envy is specifically aroused. In certain circumstances a man may resort to magic only once in his life. He is not, like the witch whose cannibalism is a threat to everyone, a constant and universal danger. No one can protect himself against him. 'In theory at least a person can protect himself against the sorcerer (envious man) by avoiding any occasion to provoke the annoyance or the jealousy of others'—or, as we would put it, by the avoidance of envy.[21]

In his study of sorcerers in North Sukumaland (Tanganyika, East Africa) R. E. S. Tanner has occasion to refer to the specific dynamic of envy in witchcraft.[22] The Sukuma regard black magic as a planned, deliberate crime. The sorcerer is in no way seen as an evil-doer who arbitrarily strikes out at mankind in general; rather, he is preoccupied with his greed, his envy. He hopes for material gain from his magic. Again, the degree to which the sorcerer is suspected of being a man whose envy is unappeasable is evident from the fact that, by completely ostracizing him, the community sometimes forces him to leave the district. At times, anxiety over what such a man may perpetrate out of envy may even lead to his being lynched. Similar instances have been reported in other cultures, in Central America, for example, where persons suspected or convicted of envy-magic are driven out.

The Sukuma word for magic, *bulogi,* derives from the verb 'to fear.' Tanner stresses that the Sukuma community is not sorcerer-ridden. But if someone suffers misfortune he always wonders what cause a relative or neighbour may have to practise sorcery on him. Among the Sukuma as elsewhere sorcery is practised only in situations of proximity and close association. They have a noteworthy tendency to accuse successful or prosperous men of sorcery. In one such case, Tanner explains, the magician and chief co-operated in making and substantiating the accusation—'Something that was, in fact, a political act based on jealousy.'

Thus in every society there are at least two possible tendencies and manifestations of envy to be reckoned with: the man who is not well off, or only moderately so, may be seized with envy against relatives or neighbours and practise destructive magic and arson. The victim and

[21] E. H. Winter, 'The Enemy Within,' from *Witchcraft and Sorcery in East Africa,* ed. John Middleton and E. H. Winter, London, 1963, pp. 280 f.

[22] R. E. S. Tanner, 'The Sorcerer in Northern Sukumaland, Tanganyika,' *The South-western Journal of Anthropology,* Vol. 12, pp. 437 ff.

other more or less interested persons may attribute to him the motive of envy. As suspicion grows, everyone in the community, whether rich or only fairly prosperous, is driven to fear the incurably envious man. Eventually he may be expelled. The danger to the group lies in the destructive envy of an individual—the sorcerer.

This situation can also be reversed, in which case social tension arises from the envy felt by several persons against one who may be richer, more popular or more successful than they. The majority then spread the rumour that the happy man owes his success to illicit sorcery. Tanner mentions a notorious case in Sukumaland: A chief was suspected of employing the spirits of dead fellow tribesmen for the cultivation of his fields as the number of people to be seen working there was not enough to explain their excellence and yield. Tanner rightly describes this as a manifestation of envy of success or superior work rather than the expression of occult ideas.

In common with most other individual field studies, Tanner's work fails to offer us a theory based on the phenomena he describes. The universality of such sorcery cannot be founded merely on sporadic hatred. The writer expresses his agreement with the currently popular theory of pent-up emotions without legitimate (e.g., orgiastic) outlet. Hence it is suggested that before contact with Europeans and European jurisdiction, there were far fewer evil sorcerers than there are today. Escape into destructive magic is therefore explained almost apologetically as a reaction to the pressure of white administration and colonization. Yet the increase in envy-based magic—which is vouched for solely by the memory of old members of the tribe—might, I believe, only be connected with the arrival of Europeans in so far as it was in fact their colonization that, for the first time, brought to the tribes a rule of rational law and thereby created a socio-economic situation in which individual success—and thus reason for envy—became possible in any degree.

The Lovedu

In his description of the Lovedu in Africa, more especially in a chapter on witchcraft and black magic, Krige presents many observations in which the element of envy is clearly distinguishable. If a man in that tribe falls sick his thoughts turn at once to the possibility of witchcraft, especially if he has been in conflict with someone or knows he has an enemy. A person who is known to be resentful or someone who is generally unpopular will be the first to be considered responsible for any ill that may befall a man.

> A person with an unpleasant face very often earns the reputation of being a witch. . . . A very old person, too, is apt to be thought a witch; his long life is attributed to his bartering the lives of younger relatives for his own. Just as people with grievances are suspected of witchcraft, so successful ones are thought to be especially liable to being bewitched—those who reap better crops than others, successful hunters, those favoured by their European masters.[23]

Krige regards it simply as projection if their success is also liable to be attributed to witchcraft on their part.

Here, perhaps, one may introduce a generalization: Evidently primitive man—and the Lovedu can be regarded as representative of hundreds of similar simple peoples—considers as the norm a society in which, at any one moment of time, everyone's situation is precisely equal. He is possessed by the same yearning for equality as has for many years been apparent in political trends in our modern societies. But reality is always different. Since he has failed to grasp the empirical causes of factual inequalities, he explains any deviation upwards, or downwards, from the supposedly normal—i.e., emotionally acceptable—society of equals as having been caused by the deliberate and malicious activity of fellow tribesmen. The suspicion increases with the closeness of the relationship.

Krige analyses fifty of the witchcraft cases he observed. The motives that predominate are envy and jealousy. Only fifteen of those cases took place between unrelated persons; of these, only five involved sexual jealousy (e.g., the abandoned girl seeking revenge); the other ten had to do with jealousy and resentment arising out of economic and social differences. Any conspicuous gadget, such as a sewing machine acquired in town by a neighbour, is especially calculated to cause envy and hence black magic. The witches' envy was also aroused by another's

[23] E. J. Krige and J. D. Krige, *The Realm of a Rain-Queen,* London, 1943, pp. 269.

ability to drive a car, to find work in a town or to dance particularly well. Very often complex jealousies were at work, involving sexual and economic motives. Causes of envy mentioned by Krige are position, prestige, personal attractiveness, bride prices, the distribution of possessions, and the yield from herds of cattle.[24]

The whole of pre-scientific literature, as for example proverbs, concerning the phenomenon of envy, invariably lays stress on social proximity between the envious man and the object of his envy. This factor is also apparent from Krige's material. Not only are relatives and neighbours those most often involved, but it is regarded as exceptionally difficult to bewitch a stranger with any success. The Lovedu believe that only a mother can never harm her children with witchcraft, just as they can never harm her. And this is precisely the very relationship in which envy would appear least probable.

Exaggerated modesty, the understatement so typical of the Englishman, which occurs in Chinese culture too, is also a convention of the Lovedu. When a man comes back from a visit to another district, the neighbours greet him with the question: 'What do they eat over there?' or, betraying envy: 'What are they keeping from us, the people you've been with?' To which the invariable answer is: 'They're just about starving'—even when they have everything in plenty and have shown regal hospitality. It is even feared that to be over-zealous will arouse suspicions that a man is striving for success: if one passes a field where a Lovedu man or woman is working and remarks: 'Working hard, eh?' they will always answer: 'We're hardly working at all.'[25]

A bright child who matures early is regarded by the Lovedu as a future witch. Life is spent in perpetual fear of envy. Possessions bring no prestige.[26] And there is no socio-economic stratification in Lovedu society. The culture—that is, the total system of norms—of this Bantu tribe shows deeply rooted inhibitions of all kinds which can be traced back directly to intensive mutual envy, and which plainly show, too, how they specifically restrict development.[27]

[24] Op. cit. pp. 264 ff.
[25] Op. cit. p. 18.
[26] Op. cit. p. 290.
[27] Op. cit. p. 286.

Competition is impossible

Krige was especially impressed by the impossibility of exploiting competition between craftsmen. Often one potter will commend to a customer another potter's wares. It is pointless to attempt to make a craftsman work faster by threatening to give the job to someone else. Even if a Lovedu urgently needs money to pay his taxes, he shies away from lucrative occupations. He is also extremely reluctant openly to compare himself with others. Indeed, his language does not provide expressions—comparative forms, for example—with which to make distinctions. It is difficult to extract from him any expression of opinion as to the relative merit of manufactured articles, individual achievements or other cultural attributes. In regard to the articles of everyday life, the aim is equality with others, as Krige stresses. A common expression is 'What are you keeping from me?' Krige interprets this as meaning: 'Aren't I entitled to the same share of your generosity as the others?' Even when they implore their ancestors for help or for some favour, they must say: 'But only in the same measure as the rest.'[28] Where the inhabitants of one village recover from smallpox while those of another village die, a Lovedu's only explanation is witchcraft on the part of the survivors.[29]

In a culture incapable of any form of competition, time means nothing. The word for slowness, for the absence of any bustle or hurry, is the same as that for what is good, or virtue.

It is, however, imperative that primitive man's superstition should not be equated with his chronic state of envy of his fellow tribesmen, or one be used to explain the other. A self-pitying inclination to contemplate another's superiority or advantages, combined with a vague belief in his being the cause of one's own deprivation, is also to be found among educated members of our modern societies who really ought to know better. The primitive people's belief in black magic differs little from modern ideas. Whereas the socialist believes himself robbed by the employer, just as the politician in a developing country believes himself robbed by the industrial countries, so primitive man believes himself robbed by his neighbour, the latter having succeeded by black magic in spiriting away to his own fields part of the former's harvest.

[28] Op. cit. p. 287.
[29] Op. cit. p. 270.

However, man's envy-motive may already permeate the individual act of cognition at every historical stage of his understanding of the world and emphasize those manifestations which lend support to the envious man's suspicions. But unless every person had a basic tendency to make envious comparisons, envious black magic would not necessarily arise, even in the case of primitive man, out of magic ideas. The envious man creates the means to revenge himself on the object of his envy. He will always seek to order his world so as to nourish his envious feelings.

It cannot be proved, from the nature of the means chosen to impair another's prosperity, that these were employed out of envy. Primitive man, when he makes use of black magic because someone has injured a member of his family, is acting from a legitimate feeling of outrage. The government adviser who successfully suggests to the legislature a special tax on certain luxury goods or on envy-provoking forms of income may himself sincerely believe in the economic reasonableness of his policy. It would therefore be false to imagine that wherever black magic is used, whether by primitive man or by a peasant in a tolerably advanced country, in order to harm his neighbour and quite manifestly out of envy, what is involved is merely the unfortunate consequence of superstition that enlightenment could exorcize. The false premise that one man's gain necessarily involves the others' loss is still indulged in by some modern economic theorists; while these do not make use of black magic, they often have recourse to methods no less absurd, such as, for instance, a special kind of tax which ends up by damaging the very people it was supposed to help.

On the one hand there is an inadequate grasp of environmental factors which consists in immediately seeing every inequality of the other as diminishing one's own prosperity, with resultant envy, resting at least in part on a false understanding of the causes of inequality. On the other hand the primitive man, too, may be envious of his neighbour without misinterpreting the circumstances in terms of magic. Sorcery is simply his most immediate means of putting someone down out of envy. Both the primitive man who seeks to harm the object of his envy by means of irrational ritual (helped along, perhaps, with poison), and the senior official in a bureaucracy who quietly sabotages the promotion of a subordinate because he secretly envies the man to be promoted, are acting from the same motives. They differ only in their methods.

Black magic versus persons unknown: envy of the other's easier future

The primitive man—and sometimes also the less primitive man—who uses black magic to make things equally unpleasant for others; the wealthy father or trustee who is tight-fisted so that the next generation shall, as students, have as hard a time as he did; the factory manager, the departmental head, the board of directors who oppose the acquisition of air-conditioning plant or labour-saving machinery because that wasn't the way things were when they joined the firm—all these irrational embodiments of a Spartan complex have fundamentally the same object. Someone they know, and often enough someone they don't, has to suffer on equal terms the lot that was theirs in the past. True, the proverb says that sorrow shared is sorrow halved. But the true companion in sorrow is the one who, through no action on our part, either voluntarily or as a result of external circumstances, endured the painful situation at the same time as ourselves. If, merely to appease his own recollection of having suffered a disagreeable experience, a difficult examination, say, or a repellent task, someone takes it upon himself out of a sense of *Schadenfreude* to burden another person's future with the same difficulties, he is elevating his envy to the status of a Goddess of Fate. But a case like that of an older person, for objectively convincing educational reasons—reasons not serving merely to disguise envy—imposing something difficult upon a younger person either to test him or to temper him physically or mentally does not come under this heading. Again, one may still sympathize with genuine mountaineers who try to sabotage a scheme for a funicular to the finest peaks, because in their opinion only the man who has braved the dangers and difficulties of the climb deserves the view at the end of it. There might be a suggestion of jealousy about the mountain itself, but hardly of envy. Yet the person, often designated typical by the natives themselves, who practises sorcery against the stranger only because the latter might otherwise have an easier life than himself, is found in the most diverse parts of the world and within the framework of widely differing cultures; his persistent recurrence gives rise to the fundamental question as to what human drive or motive is involved, especially as traces of it are on occasion perceptible in some of our affluent contemporaries.

In our opinion this is typical of the fundamental attitude from which the more complex processes of envy are built up. The evidence of such a basic impulse in man, independent of his absolute material situation and directed towards someone who may be a stranger, or may indeed be a purely hypothetical person, leaves room for doubt whether it is ever justifiable to state the principle that the object of envy is responsible for the envy (A. Rüstow, among others). The vandal, in our own society, who, for instance, strews nails over the road because he cannot stand people who drive cars, may still be impelled by a specific experience of envy. It is 'meaningful' to imagine oneself owning a nice car and saying: 'Well, if *I* can't have it, at least I can spoil the pleasure of people who can.' But the primitive man who has just experienced a deprivation or escaped a danger and wishes to inflict it magically on others has in no way been provoked by his victims. He wishes to drag down others (who may, of course, be personally known to him) to that level of existence to which he has been temporarily reduced. While there are some forms of envy having at least a certain 'progressive' element, this particular action bears the mark of retaliation. 'Since I cannot revenge myself on fate and often there is no such concept in a culture for my painful lot, I shall look for some other person upon whom to wish the same suffering.'

A truly classic description of envious black magic is that of Karsten, drawn from his observations among the Jivaro Indians:

> When the Indians try to produce rain by magical means they nearly always do so merely out of wickedness, that is, to cause their fellow tribesmen harm or annoyance, especially when they are travelling on the river. When in 1917 I came from my long river expedition down to the Achuares on the middle Pastaza, I was surprised by heavy rains which lasted for weeks, caused the Bobonaza to swell, and made the ascension of the river extremely trying for my Indian crew. When at last we approached Canelos, one of my Indians said that he would make the rains continue so that other travellers would have the same difficulties as we had had.[30]

There is, perhaps, no case of envy so pure as that directed against others who, we believe, are about to experience less privation, fear, etc.,

[30] R. Karsten, *The Head-Hunters of Western Amazonas. The Life and Culture of the Jivaro Indians of Eastern Ecuador and Peru (Societas Scientiarum Fennica. Commentationes Humanarum Litterarum,* Vol. VII, No. 1), Helsinki, 1935, p. 452. Between 1917 and 1928 Karsten spent a total of three years among these tribes.

than we ourselves have just endured and finally left behind. In this instance the envious man's own future course of life can in no way be compromised by the others' gain, by the alleviation of their circumstances. It is only the memory of his own disagreeable past that makes him begrudge others anything better. This kind of envy, which greatly impedes all progress in a society, also occurs between generations in a family: fathers are annoyed because nowadays things are much easier for their sons. Angry outbursts of this kind may be observed in families in Western industrial nations and in the most primitive tribes where the younger generation has enjoyed certain advantages through contact with Europeans.

Envy between generations

Tradition asserts, with a fatal effect upon deliberate innovations, that what was good enough for the father is good enough for the son. Here we have the conflict between generations. Older members of a group will generally adopt a negative attitude towards innovations which younger people try out or initiate; their feeling arises from comparison, accompanied by envy or jealousy. Where the son follows the same profession as his father, or is a partner in the same firm, the term 'jealousy' might apply. Where the innovation is concerned with increased comfort or prestige and is attempted by the son or a member of the younger generation in a field in which the fathers can in no way assert themselves, the term 'envy' would be more appropriate.[31] That in some cases a father's envy of his children's educational opportunities has to be reckoned with has come to light in recent studies of unused educational opportunities.

There have, of course, been older people, including fathers, who have smiled benevolently on a younger man's innovation, and have encouraged or even promoted it. Had there been no such exceptions to social control by tradition, there would have been fewer innovations. But sometimes, even in cases of an older man objectively helping his junior to put through an innovation, undertones of resentment are discernible.

Everyone will understand the impediments which the older generation

[31] See, for example, among others, Franz Hess, *Die Ungleichheit der Bildungschancen*, Olten and Freiburg i. Br., 1966, pp. 155 f. Also Willy Strzelewicz and others, *Bildung und gesellschaftliches Bewusstsein*, Stuttgart, 1966, p. 606.

puts in the way of the younger through envy of its renown. Similar motives come into play when the innovation proposed by the younger man (its discovery or merely its adoption) conceals an imagined reproach to the older man for not having thought of it himself. We are, however, penetrating into deeper layers of emotional life when we seek to understand why the older generation, in keeping a Spartan hold on the younger, tries to forbid or disparage those objects or institutions which represent increased comfort.

Incidentally, the cruel initiation rites that are customary in a wide number of primitive tribal societies, and which close the stage of adolescence, might conceivably be understood as the expression of general existential envy which members conscious of their age feel towards those whose life still lies before them.[32]

[32] For instance, in the African tribe of the Masai several authors (Fox, Merker) have noted that the members of one generation are extremely jealous of generations older or younger than themselves. Specifically, as Ralph Linton once pointed out, the age group just before the status of 'old men' is pushed over that threshold by the new crop of adolescents. They are therefore extremely cruel to the youngsters during the initiation rites.

5

The Envy-barrier of the
Developing Countries

THE FUTURE, the only field where the fruits of any development are to be reaped, lends itself to a co-operative approach, to exploitation by men able to exchange and co-ordinate their ideas, knowledge and desires. But this is conceivable only when fear of the other's envy, of his possible sabotage or malicious sorcery, has to some extent been overcome. No one can even begin to have rational aspirations for the future unless he has a realistic view of what that future may be; but no such prognosis can be made so long as each member of the group carefully keeps hidden *his* view of the future. Nor can a view that is conducive to social and economic development be formed within a group until its individual members are able, in frank discussion, to compare, weigh and synchronize all their different pictures of the future. It is precisely this, however, which more than anything else is impeded by the ever-present fear that basically everyone, more especially our near neighbour, is potentially envious and that the best defence against him is to pretend complete indifference about the future.

A ruthless, charismatic leader may, in certain circumstances, force *his own* view of the future on others, over a short space of time and when threatened by danger from without (although there have been cases where even the most obvious danger was not enough to overcome the inhibition of communal action by envy). Since the leader cannot do everything himself, however, the undertaking suffers in its execution precisely from mutual suspicions among his followers.

Institutionalized envy

An expert on South American peasant cultures and village communities, Eric Wolf, singled out the phenomenon mentioned above. He speaks of 'institutionalized envy' which manifests itself in phenomena such as backbiting, the evil eye and the practice or fear of black magic. Wolf cites other experts on these societies—Oscar Lewis, John Gillin and Clyde Kluckhohn—in his refutation of the romanticism according to which the close communal spirit of village communities and the great measure of 'equality' between their inhabitants lead to a pervasive feeling of goodwill.

Institutionalized envy (so far as I know, Wolf is the only one to have used this concept), or the ubiquitous fear of it, means that there is little possibility of individual economic advancement and no contact with the outside world through which the community might hope to progress. No one dares to show anything that might lead people to think he was better off. Innovations are unlikely. Agricultural methods remain traditional and primitive, to the detriment of the whole village, because every deviation from previous practice comes up against the limitations set by envy.[1]

Identical observations—using the terms 'envy,' 'resentment' and *'Schadenfreude'*—are found in some articles by American cultural anthropologists who in 1960 addressed themselves to the subject of personal relations in peasant societies.

Sol Tax attributes the unprogressiveness, the slowness of change towards economically productive and rational behaviour patterns that he observed among the Indians of Guatemala, to the facts of life in 'a small community where all neighbors watch and where all are neighbors.' Specifically, Tax thought: 'It is impossible to rule out envy and the fear of envy; or accusations of greed, and the fear of such accusations.'[2]

In Haiti, G. E. Simpson found that a peasant will seek to disguise his true economic position by purchasing several smaller fields rather than one larger piece of land. For the same reason he will not wear good clothes. He does this intentionally to protect himself against the envious black magic of his neighbours.

[1] E. R. Wolf, 'Types of Latin American Peasantry. A Preliminary Discussion,' *American Anthropologist,* Vol. 57 (1955), pp. 460 f.

[2] G. M. Foster, 'Interpersonal Relations in Peasant Society,' *Human Organization,* Vol. 19 (Winter 1960/61), pp. 175 ff.; cf. in the same issue the articles by O. Lewis, p. 179, and J. Pitt-Rivers, pp. 180 f. Exactly corresponding observations on the intense fear of envy by fellow villagers inhibiting all progress are found in the work mentioned

The social sciences have put forward numerous theories on the assumption that the normal man seeks a maximum in production and in property. All men today, including those of the so-called developing countries, ostensibly desire the greatest possible progress. These theories, however, overlook the fact that in a great many situations the object of human activity is a diminution; that regularly recurring modes of human behaviour have as their object the lessening of assets, not just their replacement by other assets. Everyone who has attempted to describe envy has pointed out the purely negative character of the phenomenon. No one is to have anything and no one is to enjoy himself. A tribe of North American Pueblo Indians showed the beginnings of division of labour. The various magic and cult tasks such as rain-making, fertility magic, exorcism of witches, etc., were delegated to certain 'societies' in the pueblo. At times, however, the other villagers imagined that the magic powers of these 'specialists' were chiefly used for such people's personal gain. Steps were taken, therefore, to liquidate them, and those individuals who in any way seemed better off were 'brought into line' by the destruction of their property or, in slighter cases, by official warnings.

How little mutual envy, in a relatively simple society, depends upon objectively ascertainable differences in the standard of living of its members is apparent from a study of personal relations in a Jamaican village, carried out between 1950 and 1951. This mountain village is inhabited by 277 English-speaking Negroes. The descendants of former slaves, they are now independent, competitively minded peasants who take their various products to market. The accumulation of money and land is among their principal motives. About 80 per cent of the inhabitants earn a tolerable livelihood, and only 3 per cent of the adults are in need of assistance. Yet we read in the study: 'No matter how "indepen-

---

earlier by J. Gillin, pp. 116, 114, 124, 122. In that Guatemalan society there is a diseased condition called *envidia*, literally envy, which these people believe is caused in the victim by the magic of an envious man.—C. J. Erasmus (*Man Takes Control, Cultural Development and American Aid*, Minneapolis, 1961, p. 80) speaks of an 'envy pattern' which sometimes prevents more successful peasants in Haiti from introducing up-to-date agricultural methods.—S. Tax ('Changing Consumption in Indian Guatemala,' *Economic Development and Culture Change*, Vol. 5, Chicago, 1957, pp. 151, 155).

dent" (wealthy) a person might be, he generally believes that everyone else, no matter how obviously poor, is better off and has accumulated more money.' One of the worst things a man can do is to inquire into someone else's financial circumstances. There can be no doubt that this attitude is a protection against envy. But everyone is filled with insatiable curiosity regarding such information. Imaginary personal poverty is generally blamed upon another, presumed or believed to be richer. The frequent damage to crops caused by hurricane or drought is still usually attributed to some evil sorcerer at work on behalf of an envious neighbour. Nearly every villager is convinced that his neighbour dislikes him and is excessively envious of him. These feelings are, of course, mutual. It is impossible for several families to pool resources or tools of any kind in a common undertaking. It is almost equally impossible for any one man to adopt a leading role in the interests of the village.[3]

The problem of envy is again brought out clearly in William Watson's study of social cohesion in an African tribe in Northern Rhodesia, whose members, through working in the copper mines and in the towns, are gradually adopting a money economy. These are the Mambwe, whose cohesion as a tribe in village communities has been far less impaired than might be expected by the industrial wage labour of many of its members. Watson made his observations in 1952 and 1953.

There was an ever-present cause for ill-feeling in the fact that competent men, not belonging to the 'nobility' of a chief's family but having been educated in a mission school, were able to attain 'wealth' by personal work in the market economy of their district. The outward sign of wealth is usually a brick house. A decisive factor in the success of such people seems often to have been the resolve to leave the area of the chief where they were born in order to seek their fortunes in some other

[3] Y. A. Cohen, 'Four Categories of Interpersonal Relationships in the Family and Community in a Jamaican Village,' *Anthropological Quarterly,* Vol. 28 (New Series, Vol. 3), 1955, pp. 121–47. C. S. Rosenthal reports similar actions designed to avert envy in the Jewish community of a small Polish town before 1938 ('Social Stratification of the Jewish Community in a Small Polish Town,' *American Journal of Sociology,* Vol. 59, 1953, p. 6): 'People were very much afraid of other people's jealousy. It was pointed out endlessly that you are not allowed to take out other people's eyes, that is, that one should avoid making others jealous.' What is remarkable about this expression is its connection with belief in the 'evil eye.'

district, since the social controls inhibiting an individual's financial success and the community's redistributive claims are then not so great.[4]

Watson records one case of a self-made man of this kind, a 'commoner,' who, by marrying into the 'royal family' of another chief, was able to obtain permission to take an eminent political position within the tribe in keeping with his wealth. This can sometimes succeed. But Watson describes another man whose success story clearly shows not only how one who is economically superior in a primitive society is suspected of supernatural machinations, but how the effectiveness of his powers is believed to be in direct proportion to his ability to damage his neighbour.

Adam was forty-one years old and had been educated as a carpenter at a mission school. He now owned, after various excursions as a wage-earner, the only brick house in the village. He also did a great deal for his relatives. But, 'Like all successful men, Adam is supposed to "know something" (i.e., to possess magical knowledge). He is said to know how to tame crows through magic, so that they take maize from other people's gardens and grain-bins and bring it to his own.'[5]

Watson also describes some successful farmer-traders who live under considerable social pressure, not only because they have to reckon with competition in a limited market, but also because they are constantly suspected of black magic. 'The Mambwe accuse all successful men of practising sorcery.' Exactly like the Dobuans in the Pacific, the Mambwe are convinced that if the field a man has sown regularly produces a crop better than his neighbour's, this is not the result of better methods of cultivation but of sorcery, which has inflicted a corresponding degree of damage on other fields. Successful men are regarded as sinister, supernatural and dangerous. A contributing factor is that they do not live like the rest of their tribe. Their brick houses isolate them from the others, and if the village community migrates they stay behind.[6]

---

[4] W. Watson, *Tribal Cohesion in a Money Economy. A Study of the Mambwe People of Northern Rhodesia* (The Rhodes-Livingstone Institute), New York, 1958, pp. 82 f.

[5] Op. cit., pp. 122 f.

[6] Op. cit., p. 209. In connection with this, Watson points out the similarity with the Bemba, a neighbouring tribe, of which A. I. Richards reported: '. . . to be permanently much more prosperous than the rest of the village will almost certainly lead to accusations of sorcery.' (*Land, Labour and Diet in Northern Rhodesia,* London,

Fear of the evil eye

One of today's best experts on the village culture and mentality of the lower classes in Mexico, Oscar Lewis, gives an interesting account of the way in which, in one village, fear of other people's envy determines every detail of life, every proposed action. A safety zone is secured by extreme secretiveness, by the anxious concealment of everything private. Men withdraw into themselves and avoid all intimacy:

> The man who speaks little, keeps his affairs to himself, and maintains some distance between himself and others has less chance of creating enemies or of being criticized or envied. A man does not generally discuss his plans to buy or sell or take a trip. A woman does not customarily tell a neighbor or even a relative that she is going to have a baby or make a new dress or prepare something special for dinner.[7]

Here, clearly apparent, is the fear of envy, the 'evil eye' of the other, which threatens all our prospects, all the assets to which we aspire. To some extent this fear still persists in many enlightened people. We are reticent about many prospects for which we hope or strive until they are realized or fully secured. But it is difficult to envisage what it means for the economic and technical development of a community when, almost automatically and as a matter of principle, the future dimension is banned from human intercourse and conversation, when it cannot even be discussed. Ubiquitous envy, fear of it and those who harbour it, cuts off such people from any kind of communal action directed towards the future. Every man is for himself, every man is thrown back upon his own resources. All striving, all preparation and planning for the future can be undertaken only by socially fragmented, secretive beings.

1939, p. 215.) Watson compares his findings with the work of the Kriges which I have quoted, and also with the two following studies; all of them emphasize that the invariable price the successful African has to pay for his above-average position is his fellow tribesmen's sense of their property and welfare being harmed by his sorcery: M. Hunter, *Reaction to Conquest. Effects of Contact with Europeans on the Pondo of South Africa,* London and New York, 1936, p. 317; M. Gluckman, 'Lozi Land Tenure,' *Essays on Lozi Land and Royal Property* (Rhodes-Livingstone Papers No. 14), Cape Town, 1943, p. 37.

[7] O. Lewis, *Life in a Mexican Village: Tepoztlán Restudied,* Urbana, 1951, p. 297.

In contrast to the enthusiasm of the eighteenth and nineteenth centuries for the communal spirit of unspoilt, simple societies, reality has a very different aspect. If, in this Mexican village, an accident befalls or threatens a man's property

> few hasten to inform the owner, who may not discover it until it is a total loss. In one case, a widow's pig was killed by a bus. Although it was known that she was the owner, no one told her about the accident. By the time she learned of it, most of the meat had been cut away by near-by residents, and she was left with only the head and tail.

This, too, is significant. Very often the envious man, while not indeed acting so as to harm another, will not voluntarily do anything out of what is called humanity, a feeling of decency (concepts still incomprehensible to the vast majority in this world) to avert another's harm. There are innumerable situations in which envy can vent itself by the mere fact of remaining passive. And that envy is responsible for the remarkable behaviour of the people in this Mexican village becomes quite evident from the following passage:

> There is a greater readiness to commiserate in another's misfortune than to take joy in his success, resulting in a more widespread sharing of bad news than good. There is an almost secretive attitude toward good fortune, and boasting is at a minimum. People . . . do not ordinarily advise each other where a good purchase or sale is to be made, how an animal can be cured, or in what ways a crop may be improved.

'Whoever helps me is my enemy'

It can well be imagined what effects a basic attitude of this sort can have upon the well-meaning, optimistic programmes of development advisers who work on the assumption that a few tricks, a few technical or agricultural skills, having been demonstrated once or twice, will automatically spread like wildfire from family to family and village to village. Lewis further observes:

'Articles and market baskets carried through the streets are kept carefully covered from prying eyes. . . .' In general, there is an absence of altruism, generosity, charity, and the spirit of sharing. . . .' These qualities, which show a positive attitude towards one's fellow men typical of Americans, are effective enough in their country of origin. Since 1949, however, they have contributed largely to encouraging American optimism in regard to the so-called developing countries, where the existing cultures make it difficult for the natives to comprehend them. The development-aid politicians could have learned a great deal by reading studies such as those referred to here:

> Doing favors for others is rare and creates suspicion. Favors are generally associated with people *de cultura* who, it is said, do favors to get favors.
> When young people or children show kindness or pity to outsiders they are frequently 'corrected' by their mothers. Children are scolded for giving things to their friends or for being trusting and generous in lending articles to persons outside the family.[8]

In the early fifties the husband-and-wife team, Gerardo and Alicia Reichel-Dolmatoff, spent more than a year doing field work in the mestizo village of Aritama in North Colombia. In this culture, too, they found the envy-motive, fear of mutual envy being a determining factor.

> The individual performance of magical practices intended to be harmful to other people is one of the most dominant aspects of supernatural beliefs in Aritama. Every individual lives in constant fear of the magical aggression of others, and the general social atmosphere in the village is one of mutual suspicion, of latent danger, and hidden hostility, which pervade every aspect of life. The most immediate reason for magical aggression is envy. Anything that might be interpreted as a personal advantage over others is envied: good health, economic assets, and so on. All these and other aspects imply prestige, and with it power and physical appearance, popularity, a harmonious family life, a new dress, authority over others. Aggressive magic is, therefore, intended to prevent or to destroy this power and to act as a leveling force. As a system of social control, Black Magic is of tremendous importance, because it governs all interpersonal relationships.[9]

[8] Op. cit., p. 297.

[9] G. and A. Reichel-Dolmatoff, *The People of Aritama. The Cultural Personality of a Colombian Mestizo Village,* Chicago, 1961, p. 396.

The buyer is a thief

There is only one explanation for all unforeseen events: the envious black magic of another villager. Although some persons are particularly suspect, every adult is a potential enemy armed with black magic. The inhabitants of Aritama do not believe in the possibility of natural death. Every illness is caused by a personal enemy. Economic loss, a poor harvest, cattle disease, and even the sudden emergence of undesirable characteristics—drunkenness, violence, impotence, laziness, unfaithfulness—all these are regarded as the product of someone else's hostile, envious intentions. If somebody suddenly decides to leave the village, either temporarily or permanently, the decision is always assumed to have been brought about by the magic of an enemy who wants to be rid of the other man. When a family has to sell some property—house, cattle or land—the new owner regards it as self-evident that he will be hated and envied because he has taken over the property. And it is especially believed of the vendor of a house that for the remainder of his life he will vindictively pursue the buyer with black magic.[10]

The fact, in itself remarkable, that the vendor of property hates the buyer, whom he seeks to damage, is probably explicable by his persisting claim on the property. Even where the sale was genuine and paid for in good money, the vendor envies the buyer his superiority which lies in his ability to pay, that is, in an active quality. What we have here is, I believe, a very widespread human reaction. The buyer is never quite safe from the envy of the seller, who himself retains a faint suspicion that he has been cheated of something (in return for something so transient as money). We are familiar, too, with the craftsman and artist who is by no means prepared to sell his products or works of art to just anyone. But here the benign effect of modern anonymous mass production of all imaginable goods becomes apparent, for it enables us to purchase virtually anything without having to reckon with the envy of the producer. The romantically inclined, who still continue to regret the days when nearly every commodity had to be purchased from an individual maker, have no idea how subtly the relations between producer and customer strangled the free circulation of goods. In modern society there is evidence of similar

[10] Op. cit., p. 398.

limitations on the free market in many fields. They are based on snob-bery rather than on envy, though both may be involved. A conceited architect or painter will not sell his work to anyone just because he has enough money. Some car manufacturers, indeed, even seek to ensure that their products do not go to those whose position is not in keeping with their wealth. And when the Princeton University Press published a difficult mathematical work on the theory of games, the many profes-sional gamblers who ordered a copy had their cheques returned with the remark: 'You wouldn't really understand it.' Evidently it was thought undesirable that the small edition of this specialized work should be cast before swine, that is to say the gamblers of the American underworld.

The salesman-employee may also envy the customer when he has not himself produced the article but is not able to buy it, as has been observed of American salesgirls. This is not a case of simple envy connected with a particular object, such as that of the maker of an article who pursues its buyer with feelings similar to those of a mother-in-law towards her son's wife.[11]

The Reichel-Dolmatoffs show emphatically the extent to which liter-ally nothing in Aritama is safe from the villagers' envy and from their black magic. If one member of a group works faster and better than the rest, his place of work is marked with a cross before he arrives the following morning. The envious man then says three Paternosters and three Ave Marias. This is supposed to make the good worker slow, tired and thirsty. Agricultural implements, such as machetes, are very vulner-able to damage by sorcery. The same applies to all hunting and fishing gear, to traps, guns, hooks and nets. According to the Reichel-Dolmatoffs, even a hunting dog's keen scent can be destroyed for ever by the machinations of an enemy who is envious of the dog's owner.[12]

In Aritama, as almost everywhere else, the evil eye (*mal ojo*) is an important and special form of malevolent magic. It can cause sickness, drought and decay. Significantly, 'economic assets such as houses, crops, domestic animals, or fruit trees are said to be much more exposed to the Evil Eye than people themselves. The reason: envy.'[13]

[11] C. Wright Mills, *White Collar. The American Middle Classes.* Paperback ed., New York, 1956, p. 174.

[12] Reichel-Dolmatoff, op. cit., p. 402.

[13] Op. cit., p. 403.

From this the merciful effect of private property is evident, though it is seldom recognized. It is not the cause of destructive envy, as the apostles of equality are always seeking to persuade us, but a necessary protective screen between people. Wherever there have ceased to be any enviable material goods or where these have for some reason been withdrawn from envy's field of vision, we get the evil eye and envious, destructive hatred directed against the physical person. It might almost be said that private property first arose as a protective measure against other people's envy of our physical qualities.

In the village of Aritama, where everyone trembles before everyone else's envy, Reichel-Dolmatoff discovered only the following degrees of relationship where black magic could not be practised—hence those in which a large measure of envy can evidently be suppressed: between father and son and between mother and daughter, although even here there may be considerable tensions. Between husband and wife, among siblings and in any other form of kinship, on the other hand, there are very frequent cases of malicious witchcraft. Outside the family, anyone and everyone is suspect.

In some tribes—for instance, the African Lovedu—envy-motivated sorcery takes place almost entirely among relatives, while there is little to fear from strangers. This again testifies to the importance of social proximity in envy. In Aritama, on the other hand, suspicion is so general that no one will say of a clearly innocuous person that he does not practise black magic, but rather, that he is not known to do so (*'Todavía no se le ha sabido'*).[14]

'Loss of face' in China and avoidance of envy

Again, the Asiatic's proverbial fear, especially evident in Imperial China, of 'losing face' is basically nothing more than a ritualized attitude designed to avoid envy, and more especially a form of self-training to avoid the *Schadenfreude* of others. This was clearly demonstrated by Hu Hsien-chin, an anthropologist, in a study of the Chinese concept of 'face' published in the United States in 1944.[15]

[14] Op. cit., p. 404.

[15] Hu Hsien-chin, 'The Chinese Concepts of "Face",' *American Anthropologist,* Vol. 46, 1944, pp. 45–64.

The degree of loss of face (*lien*) depends upon the situation of the subject. Public opinion takes account of extenuating circumstances in the lives of the poor and underprivileged and allows such persons to retain face after actions which would cost better-situated people theirs. The holder of a strong economic position may use it only in such a way as not to infringe moral tenets. The description of the process of social control in China reminds one of the 'other-directed person,' as portrayed by David Ziesman: Hu Hsien-chin wrote:

> The consciousness that an amorphous public opinion is so-to-say supervising the conduct of the ego, relentlessly condemning every breach of morals and punishing with ridicule, has bred extreme sensitivity in some people. This is particularly obvious where the taking of the initiative may incur failure. . . . A young person who fails to pass an examination will sometimes feel the shame so keenly as to commit suicide.

From this it is already apparent how fear of losing face inhibits individual actions and modes of behaviour such as are necessary for economic progress. The explanation that follows brings to light the motive of envy:

The Chinese anthropologist believes that Western observers are wrong in attributing the excessive modesty with which the Chinese seek to disparage their achievements or their positions to hypocrisy, humbug or lack of self-confidence. Rather, he says, it is a case of a carefully institutionalized attitude designed to avert envy. Anyone setting too high a value on his abilities or his stamina perpetrates the social sin of regarding himself as better than his fellow men. 'As physical violence is discountenanced, so is every action that might call forth unpleasant feelings, such as envy and dislike, in other people. A person given to boasting will not have the sympathy of his group when he fails; rather will he incur ridicule.'

For the Chinese, however, it was not necessary to see himself confronted by public opinion or by an actual group in order to restrain his behaviour; the maxim 'Behave so that the result of your actions will arouse the minimum of envy in your fellow men,' imprinted upon him as a commonplace from childhood onwards, equipped him with the knowledge of how to act so as to retain *lien*. And to make absolutely sure that no one would be envious, self-deprecation (as in mutual forms of address) was taken to what Westerners regarded as absurd extremes.

Habitual avoidance of envy and the inhibition of development

Reichel-Dolmatoff described a common method of avoiding envy in the village of Aritama:

> In this suspicion-ridden atmosphere any calamity is immediately attributed to the magic of an enemy who, through ill will and envy, caused the trouble. The best prophylactic measure an individual can take, in all cases, therefore, consists in not appearing enviable in the first place and in pretending to be poor, ill, and already in trouble.[16]

In his study of the Dobuans, one of the most envy-ridden of cultures, Fortune raises the question, difficult but justified, as to whether such a community is poor because inhibited by mutual envy, or whether envy is a consequence of the general frugality of their existence. Fortune generally uses 'jealousy' but quite evidently means 'envy.'

> In this society it is not possible to say that the attitudes of the social organization are created by the attitudes of the magical outlook, or that the attitudes of the magical outlook are created by the attitudes of the social organization. It is, however, possible to show a unity of feeling throughout. Jealousy of possession is the keynote to the culture.
> In social organization this jealousy is found in a conflict between the kin and the marital groupings. In gardening this jealousy obtains between gardeners. All illness and disease and death are attributed to jealousy, and provoke recrimination. It is also possible to show that poverty and a great pressure of population upon land accords well with the prevalent tone of jealousy of possession. But here again it is not possible to say whether poverty has created the jealousy or vice versa. Either point of view could be put forward. Accordance is all that can be demonstrated, and in truth it is probable that the more accordance there is in the elements of a culture the stronger an intensification of the mutually agreeable elements will result. They will react upon one another.[17]

[16] Reichel-Dolmatoff, op. cit., p. 403.

[17] R. F. Fortune, *Sorcerers of Dobu. The Social Anthropology of the Dobu Islanders of the Western Pacific*, New York, 1932, p. 135.

Sometimes even primitive peoples realize that because some of their fellows are courageous enough to defy the envious eye, they prosper. The Tiv are a pagan people numbering some 800,000. They inhabit the Benue valley in northern Nigeria and eke out a meagre agricultural existence. Ten years ago an anthropologist gave an account of their economic system:

> Tiv are very scornful of a man who is merely rich in subsistence goods (or, today, in money), they say . . . that jealous kinsmen of a rich man will bewitch him and his people by means of certain fetishes in order to make him expend his wealth in sacrifices. . . . A man who persists in a policy of converting his wealth into higher categories instead of letting it be dispersed by his dependants and kinsmen is said to have a 'strong heart'. . . . He is both feared and respected. . . .[18]

The word *tsav* indicates the magic substance of the heart which fends off envy. Not everyone has it. 'Is a person in any way outstanding, if only as a singer, dancer, hunter? He has some *tsav*, though perhaps only a little. Is a man healthy, possessed of a large family and prosperous farms? He is a "man of *tsav*, " or he could not have warded off the envy of others either in its physical or mystical expression.'[19] The Tiv, like many other primitive people, do not recognize natural death. If someone dies it is always attributed to the envious magic of another. As long as the anthropologists remained in the area, one of their informants felt safe, but afterwards he hoped 'to survive by doing as little as possible to attract envy.'[20]

The envy-barrier to vertical mobility in ethnically stratified societies

About twenty years ago a group of American anthropologists studied a small mountain township in the south of Colorado, founded about 1870

[18] P. Bohannan, 'Some Principles of Exchange and Investment among the Tiv,' *American Anthropologist*, Vol. 57, 1955, pp. 66 ff.

[19] Laura Bohannan in the book, edited by Joseph B. Casagrande, *In the Company of Man*, New York, 1960, p. 386.

[20] Op. cit., p. 393.

and having some 2,500 inhabitants, partly of Spanish and partly of Anglo-Saxon descent. They were especially interested in the Anglo-Saxon upper stratum and the Spanish-speaking group below it. Special attention was paid to the ways in which a capable person could climb from the Spanish group (58 per cent of the population) into the dominant, English-speaking stratum. The majority of the Spanish-speaking inhabitants did not arrive until 1920, principally from Spanish villages in northern New Mexico. They comprise the lower occupation groups. A very few own land or other commercial property; most depend on wage-labour in local agriculture.

Why is it so difficult for individuals to rise out of this group? The study gives four main reasons: 1. Traditional behaviour patterns which do not sufficiently prepare a Spanish person for contact with Anglo-Saxon culture. 2. The goals for social advancement are determined by the model of the Anglo-Saxon group, which therefore involves the unlearning of the goals prescribed by Hispanic culture. 3. The English-speaking group, in spite of a certain caste spirit, is sufficiently open to absorb really able members of the Spanish community, thus depriving their original group of leaders. 4. The most revealing factor for our thesis, however, is that concerned with the envy, inhibiting advancement and success, shown by the Spanish towards all those of their own kind who appear to be on the way up. Success is equated with betrayal of the group. Whoever works his way up socially and economically is regarded as the 'man who has sold himself to the Anglo-Saxons (Anglos),' 'who climbs on the backs of his own people.' Those Spanish-Americans who have attained a modest economic position just above the Spanish stratum are called *orgullosos,* 'the arrogant'; a feeling of contempt for others less successful is falsely attributed to them. This is expressed even more plainly by the word coined for them, *agringados,* meaning 'Americanized.' Many of those using these words at once admitted that their people were envious (*envidiosos*) and for that reason neither could nor would follow (*seguir*) those already assimilated. The discovery of these motives led the authors to believe in a circular system of inhibitions: the more gifted among the Spanish-speaking people are reluctant to take a leading role because they know how much they will be envied and suspected. The majority, however, keep their distance from potential leaders, because they believe the latter have no use for them. Thus, while some remain in the Spanish 'ghetto,' the few economically ambitious ones migrate as soon as possible into non-Spanish society. The writers even believe that discrimination by the Anglos is insufficiently clear-cut for the good of the Spanish group: aspiring members of the Spanish group can only climb upwards separately and individually, and are not cast back into their group as embittered leaders who might be able to do something for their own people in the collective.[21]

The crime of being a leader in the community

Even those societies which have not been successful in neutralizing the envy of the majority towards the unequal few, of course, need chiefs and men in authority, that is, persons exercising the functions of a leader. But in many cases the effect of envy and the leader's fear of provoking it, which determine his actions, are clearly discernible in the description of the leader's role. Thus Cyril S. Belshaw describes how, among the Southern Massim, an island people in Melanesia, the pressure of envy so restricts the leader that, whether in the interests of equality or from the fear of too evidently profiting himself from an innovation, he sometimes refrains from the very undertakings that would further the progress of the whole community.

The Massim value administrative ability and organizing talent in their leaders, like most Melanesian peoples. Formerly these men were chiefly concerned with the production and exchange of ceremonial goods. Such a man's technical success may be ascribed to his good magic or supernatural gifts, whereas all the European observer sees is his altogether worldly talent for organization. In any case the high esteem accorded to managerial talent has served to prepare this society for modern commercial behaviour.[22] Any yet many undertakings come to a halt; somehow the leaders prematurely drop a project on the very eve of success. Why? Firstly, the leader in this culture must show great discretion. Were he to display impatience, his men might desert him. He must not shout, nor may he show annoyance, and he must court public opinion at every

---

[21] J. B. Watson and J. Samora, 'Subordinate Leadership in a Bicultural Community. An Analysis,' *American Sociological Review,* Vol. 19, 1954, pp. 413–31.

[22] C. S. Belshaw, 'In Search of Wealth,' *American Anthropologist Memoir,* February, 1955, p. 80.

decisive step; and just because he has been chosen leader, he must constantly ask himself: 'What does my life look like, seen through the envious eyes of my followers?' 'A leader does not openly set himself above other people. There is a reinforcement here to the prestige which accrues from sharing wealth, bringing the leader face to face with the necessity of increasing the level of living of those about him, through sharing, almost *pari passu* with his own.'[23]

Belshaw demonstrates here what harm envy, or its institutionalized consideration, can do to the process of economic and technical growth. It is virtually impossible to undertake innovations in a society, to improve or even to develop an economic process, without becoming unequal. But when can a leader or innovator ever be sure that he will not incur the ill-will of those who do not immediately benefit from his activity? The leader hemmed in by envy may choose a course such as Belshaw describes in detail, whereby he directs his ambition towards a high level of consumption of goods which he cannot easily share. The demand for sharing may also defeat a well-intentioned scheme for expansion by which the whole village would ultimately profit. Among the Massim there was a half-caste who gave up various independent undertakings because he could not stand the envy of the others, finally preferring to work as an employee in a European firm.

Sometimes an ambitious man is able to further his own cause by moving with a few selected relatives to another community where they may participate fully in his economic advancement. Should he not wish to move away, yet still be unable to stand the envious hostility of his own village, the following procedure applies: he attempts to live as close as he possibly can to the customary level. He may permit himself and his family minor, inconspicuous luxury articles, or food with a higher protein content, but his wealth is silently hoarded or is shared out in lavish ceremonies. However much respect such behaviour may earn him, it contributes little to the economic progress of the population as a whole.

A leading expert on undeveloped countries, S. Herbert Frankel, demonstrated in 1958 how great is the influence of envious and tyrannical relatives upon the individual who wishes to get ahead in Africa.

[23] Op. cit., pp. 60 f.

A characteristic of wide areas of that continent is the small community with a meagre subsistence and embedded in a rigid culture. The community looks askance at any man who is in process of advancement. Frankel compared this mentality with the extreme egalitarianism in some developed countries where the exceptionally able, hard-working and successful man is often regarded as the kind of fellow one would rather not have around and who should be taxed with especial severity.

Frankel describes the difficulties of an important Ghanaian tribal chief. This man had worked for thirty years as a clerk in the offices of a number of European export firms. He knew that the only way to political influence lay in the accumulation of savings with which to finance a political organization. For him, this was enormously difficult. Whenever his relatives supposed him to have saved anything, they applied the thumbscrew of family obligations. Frankel noticed how people in West Africa hung about at the entrances of banks and fell upon their relatives when the latter emerged after drawing out a sum of money. The chief in question had to transfer his account from bank to bank because his relatives succeeded in eliciting information from the bank clerks about his savings. He began to build a house which he purposely left unfinished so that he could tell his relatives, 'You see, I have no more money, I am a poor man.' At last they believed him and he was able to prosper without interference.[24]

Fear of success

Whether from zeal, from the joy of discovery or out of curiosity, innovators, like explorers or inventors, may ignore the inhibiting social controls of their environment. Generally speaking, however, every innovation must be adopted by a large number of individuals to make itself felt in any culture. Yet anyone who wants to play the role of innovator is typically subject to a twofold social control.

The agent for a private or public agricultural development programme in an Indian village advises one of the peasants to use specially prepared seed or a new kind of fertilizer for the next harvest—advice which is

[24] Lecture given in September 1958 at the Congress of the Mont Pelerin Society in Princeton, New Jersey.

seldom followed. When we asked why this was so, an elderly Indian with long experience as a missionary in Indian villages, and knowing nothing of our theory replied: 'Should the innovation, as promised, produce an especially good harvest, the man would go in fear of *nazar lagna.* ' This is an Urdu word of Arabic origin meaning 'to look' or eye, not normally used in that sense, but only in relation to the malevolent, destructive, envious look of another person or of a demon. He fears both the envy of his fellow villagers and that of some kinds of spirit.

Nazar lagna is, of course, also to be feared if anyone in an Indian village regards himself as healthier, better-looking, blessed with more children, more prosperous, etc., than his neighbours. Understandably, this fear is much increased where a man anticipates his being conspicuous among the villagers as a result of some innovation which he has voluntarily adopted.

So far as I can ascertain, there seems today to be no Hindi word for the 'evil eye.' Rather, the Hindu uses the Urdu term *nazar lagna.* Urdu is the language of the Mohammedans who lived among the Hindus as a minority from about A.D. 1100 up to the partition of India. Among Arabs and other Islamic peoples, fear of the evil eye is particularly marked, manifesting itself, among other things, in the use of the veil and the method of building houses facing inwards. It is easy to see how the dynamic of a minority problem led to the borrowing by the Hindus of the corresponding word for someone else's malevolent, envious magic from a minority of a different faith. In Urdu *nazar* means look and is also used in this neutral sense. *Nazar lagna* means evil eye, and is used by Hindus only in this form.

In confrontation with a proposed innovation, there is, on the one hand, fear of its success. At the same time—as my informant explained—the peasant thinks of the possible consequences of failure. Far more than its discoverer, the man who applies an innovation proposed by another unfailingly lays himself open to the most heartless *Schadenfreude* and ridicule if he fails to produce results. This dilemma, which for the individual arises in its most extreme form in a tradition-bound culture, is also to be found in advanced cultures and represents one of the worst inhibitions to processes of development. But the motive, the emotional and social dynamic, for the twofold social control undeniably arises, as can be shown again and again, out of an immediate awareness of potential envy in the social environment. The unsuccessful innovator is assailed by mockery and ridicule because he dared to risk something for which the majority had neither the courage nor the drive. But again, he is threatened by the silent danger of *nazar lagna* if he succeeds. It is pertinent to reflect at this point that nearly all primitive religions, but also some of the more developed peoples, have the idea of an envious supernatural being—sometimes even a being who can ridicule man. It must have been one of Christianity's most important, if unintentional, achievements in preparing men for, and rendering them capable of, innovative actions when it provided man for the first time with supernatural beings who, he knew, could neither envy nor ridicule him. By definition the God and saints of Christianity can never be suspected by a believer of countering his good luck or success with envy, or of heaping mockery and derision upon the failure of his sincere efforts.

6

The Psychology of Envy

O BSERVATIONS DRAWN FROM a wide variety of simple tribal cultures show conclusively, then, that envy, and especially fear of being envied and hence 'bewitched,' is independent of the size of the object and of its qualities. Frequently, mere trifles are involved. However, it may be objected, and justifiably so, that these are trifles only in our own view and that, to the man in the primitive society, they represent real values which one person has and the other has not. This is true up to a point. But again, there are other clear instances of acute envy being focused on assets other than those of the material values of a particular village or tribe. To this can be added our observations of the stimuli that induce envy in modern, developed, industrial communities. And these, too, support the hypothesis that envy is not directly proportional to the absolute value of what is coveted, but very often concentrates upon absurd trifles to such a degree that, in some situations, the best means of protection against the envy of neighbour, colleague or voter is to drive, say, a Rolls-Royce instead of a car only slightly better than his, or, if Brighton is his resort, to choose a world cruise rather than a holiday in Sicily. In other words, overwhelming and astounding inequality, especially when it has an element of the unattainable, arouses far less envy than minimal inequality, which inevitably causes the envious man to think: 'I might almost be in his place.'

Child psychology, drawing on the experience of sibling jealousy, may help to explain why envy concerns itself with small differences rather than with really big ones. In so far as the propensity for envy is chiefly acquired through experiencing and suffering sibling jealousy, what is involved is almost a conditioned reflex naturally oriented towards stimuli of low threshold values. Within a family or sibling group the coveted possession is generally similar to that already possessed (often it is, indeed, exactly the same and it is only in the resentful child's imagination that it appears finer, newer, more expensive, bigger and better). Unconsciously the envious one almost expects, so to speak, that his emotion will be aroused by minimal differences between himself and another, just as it was during his childhood and adolescence.

The Viennese psychiatrist Victor E. Frankl, with the intention of establishing a basis for existential psychotherapy, and drawing upon his experience in a concentration camp, has in his writings shown repeatedly how relative is the degree and extent of human suffering. The more uniformly oppressive and destructive an environment appears to the outside observer, the more its victim, in the course of his daily suffering, is able to discover and fasten upon what is positive among those qualitative differences which are perceptible to him alone. Now the fact that there is no stage of environmentally caused human suffering at which those involved are unable to sense, at any given moment, perceptible inequalities in their respective lot, permits, Frankl says, the existence of reciprocal envy even in this situation. He recalls the feeling of envy aroused in him by the sight of a squad of ordinary prisoners, presumably able to have baths and to use toothbrushes. But there was something else to envy among the inmates of the concentration camp: the frequency with which prisoners were beaten up varied according to the particular guard supervising their work. Again, those prisoners were found enviable whose work did not necessitate their wading through deep, soft clay, etc.

Yet Frankl also shows that even the most appallingly maltreated and handicapped person is able, in the interests of his psychological well-being, to extract new strength for the future from this very experience of impotence.[1]

Comparative ethnology leaves no room for doubt as to the universality of sibling jealousy. While in a particular culture it may be subdued to some extent, most primitive peoples are acutely aware of this problem, often resorting to remarkable taboos so as to avoid its worst consequences.

[1] V. E. Frankl, *Man's Search for Meaning,* Boston, 1962, pp. 33, 43, 45, 63. This is a new edition of *From Death-Camp to Existentialism,* Boston, 1959. First German edition: *Ein Psychologe erlebt das Konzentrationslager,* 1946.

Among the Sioux Indians of the North American prairies, an adult Sioux was heard to vaunt the number of years his mother had allowed to elapse between his birth and that of her next child, thus showing how greatly she had preferred him as a child to the delights of sexual intercourse.[2]

A tribe of Dakota Indians in Canada went to great pains to counteract jealousy between twins. These were considered to be one person. They had to be treated with absolute equality, for otherwise sibling jealousy would assume such immoderate proportions that one twin might do away with the other.[3]

A ritual performed by some Indians of Guatemala, when a new child is born into the family, consists in beating a fowl to death against the body of the previously born child. This is held to absorb, as it were, the hostility which would otherwise be directed against the new-born child.[4]

A field worker reports the belief held in an Arab village that an elder child's jealousy might be so intense as to cause the death of the younger.[5] Among the Dobuans, in the Pacific, whom we have already encountered as an envy-ridden society, the avoidance of sibling jealousy plays a special role. From puberty onwards, brothers are not allowed to sleep side by side. It is believed that poisonous blood would pass from one to the other and thus lead to fratricide. In point of fact, as Fortune supposes, the brothers' incompatibility springs from jealousy over primogeniture. The Dobuan father never passes on his magic powers and methods to more than one of his sons; if he has six sons, five receive nothing. But the right of primogeniture may be over-ridden on the grounds of preference. Hence brothers are violently jealous of each other because of the unpredictability of inheritance and are therefore kept apart by the norms of their culture.[6]

[2] G. Devereux, *Reality and Dream, Psychotherapy of a Plains Indian,* New York, 1951, p. 66.

[3] Ruth Sawtell Wallis, 'The Changed Status of Twins among the Eastern Dakota,' *Anthropological Quarterly,* Vol. 28 (New Series, Vol. 3), 1955, p. 117.

[4] B. D. Paul, 'Symbolic Sibling Rivalry in a Guatemalan Indian Village,' *American Anthropologist,* Vol. 52, 1950, pp. 205–18.

[5] H. Granqvist, *Child Problems among the Arabs. Studies in a Muhammedan Village in Palestine,* Copenhagen, 1950, p. 81.

[6] R. F. Fortune, *Sorcerers of Dobu,* New York, 1932, pp. 16 f.

It would, however, be false to see the constellation within the nuclear family—that is, sibling jealousy and a certain rivalry with the parent of the same sex—as the only cause or source of the capacity of envy. It is, indeed, the immediate family of each individual, as depth psychology and innumerable examples from all types of culture show beyond doubt, that is the primary field where people learn to play each other off and where nearly everyone undergoes his first painful experience of envy. Yet we ought rather to envisage the history of envy in terms of phyloge- netic aggressive drives, found also in animals without siblings, which are already inherent in the organism and which, in man, as a result of his exceptionally prolonged childhood within the social field of his family and the circle of his siblings, are sharpened and modified in an acute way to produce the typical phenomenon of the capacity for envy.

It would be quite in keeping with present-day ethology to assume that there are physiological differences in the strength of individual ag- gression which are virtually if not completely independent of social factors and therefore of early social experiences. These differences cause one man to become violently envious as a result of sibling jealousy, and another to manage very much better, that is, with less envy, similar experiences within the family.

Sigmund Freud's view of envy

So far as I have been able to ascertain, Freud's most detailed treatment of envy appeared in some considerations entitled *Group Psychology and the Analysis of the Ego.*[7] Freud attempts to reach a conclusion on the ontogenesis of the herd instinct.

> Nor is the child's fear when it is alone pacified by the sight of any haphazard 'member of the herd,' but on the contrary it is brought into existence by the approach of a 'stranger' of this sort. Then for a long time nothing in the nature of herd instinct or group feeling is to be observed in children. Something like it first grows up, in a nursery containing many children, out of the children's relation to their parents, and it does so as a reaction to the initial envy with which the elder child receives the younger one. The elder child would certainly like to put his successor jealously

[7] S. Freud, *Collected Works,* Vol. XVIII, London, 1955, pp. 120–1.

aside, to keep it away from the parents, and to rob it of all its privileges; but in the face of the fact that this younger child (like all that come later) is loved by the parents as much as he himself is, and in consequence of the impossibility of his maintaining his hostile attitude without damaging himself, he is forced into identifying himself with the other children. So there grows up in the troop of children a communal or group feeling, which is then developed at school.

This reaction formation, as Freud calls it, leads in the first instance to a clamour for 'justice,' for equal treatment for all: 'If one can't be the favourite oneself, at all events nobody else shall be the favourite.'

Freud admits that such a transformation of jealousy and its replacement by mass emotion or group solidarity might seem improbable were it not repeatably discernible even in adults. He cites as an example the fan club (though at the time that particular expression was not known to him), an instance being the banding together of a popular singer's female admirers, all of whom, though they would far rather scratch each other's eyes out, yet delight in their idol through communal action in the ecstatic group since none can have him for herself.

Freud then gives a penetrating analysis of the idea of 'social justice':

> What appears in society in the shape of *Gemeingeist, esprit de corps,* 'group spirit,' etc., does not belie its derivation from what was originally envy. No one must want to put himself forward, every one must be the same and have the same. Social justice means that we deny ourselves many things so that others may have to do without them as well, or, what is the same thing, may not be able to ask for them. This demand for equality is the root of social conscience and the sense of duty.

In this connection, Freud recalls the story of Solomon's judgement: 'If one woman's child is dead, the other shall not have a live one either. The bereaved woman is recognized by this wish.'

Next, Freud endeavours to combine his theory of the sense of solidarity and of egalitarianism with the 'leader-principle.' Incidentally, his observations and their interpretation together form an astonishingly illuminating sociology of National Socialism in Germany under Hitler, when the 'leader-principle' was carried to absurd lengths while at the same time being combined with an almost equally fanatical attachment to the principle of equality. Freud writes:

> Thus social feeling is based upon the reversal of what was first a hostile feeling into a positively-toned tie in the nature of an identification. So far as we have hitherto been able to follow the course of events, this reversal seems to occur under the influence of a common affectionate tie with a person outside the group. We do not ourselves regard our analysis of identification as exhaustive, but it is enough for our present purpose that we should revert to this one feature—its demand that equalization shall be consistently carried through. . . . Do not let us forget, however, that the demand for equality in a group applies only to its members and not to the leader. All the members must be equal to one another, and a single person superior to them all, but they all want to be ruled by one person.

The sporadic outbursts of hostility encountered by anyone who questions the principle of the idea of equality might, on the basis of Freud's finding, be partly explained by the fact that people harbour this idea all the more unconditionally and fanatically for having repressed and transformed into a feeling of solidarity their original sibling jealousy or other form of envy.

As it happened, many of Freud's followers, and especially those in the Anglo-Saxon countries, were politically committed people, to whom the literal implementation of the concept of equality meant a great deal. This may explain why no one really seemed to have wanted to pursue the implications of Freud's initial grasp of envy for questions of social policy.

In 1950 the psychoanalyst Franz Alexander, however, directly questioned Karl Marx's theory in the light of Freud's view of envy, pointing out that 'if class struggle is the essence of social life, it must be based upon human psychology. . . . Why should the dictatorship of one of the groups lead to a millennium of social justice? Obviously it can be achieved only by a miraculous change of human nature. . . .' Alexander then explored the origin of the sense of social justice, along the lines of Freud, and left little hope that this change of human nature, to fit a social theory, is likely to be forthcoming since 'envy and competition are deeply rooted in early family life and are latently present in the adult and influence his relationship to other members of society.'[8]

[8] Franz Alexander, 'Frontiers in Psychiatry,' in *Frontiers in Medicine,* New York, 1951, pp. 9–12.

Abram Kardiner gave a very plausible explanation of the fact that Freud did not fully recognize sociological problems, and more especially that he barely considered the large number of phenomena connected with social envy in the adult world.[9]

It was Freud's basic thought that in many groups the corporate identity of their members is imposed upon the individual who is forced at the same time to suppress his jealousy of the others and to replace it with the demand for justice and equality. This desire for equality is, as it were, the ransom paid by the group for the renunciation of the jealousy that endangers it. The urge for equality in its turn gives rise to a social conscience and the sense of duty. Solidarity is thus obtained by a specially enforced mutation of the original hostility or jealousy. With this theory we can agree. However, Freud's error originates, as Kardiner has pointed out, in the fact that he sees aggression as an instinct: '. . . he cannot regard inequalities in distribution of wealth and goods as a source of aggression, a tendency which already shows itself in the nursery.'

Kardiner believes that he and Linton, relying upon the Marquesan and Tanalan societies, have shown that Freud's instinct theory is inappropriate as an explanation of the origin of intra-group hostility and of vandalism and the increasing severity of the super-ego. Thus it was possible to show clearly that, in the Tanala-Betsileo culture, both aggressive and masochistic forms of vandalism (possession by spirits and the use of black magic) always increased whenever a food shortage began.

To Kardiner and Linton, therefore, the only aspects of Freud's sociology which empirical methods of comparative cultural analysis prove to be false are those 'based on the instinct theory and those derived from parallelism between phylogeny and ontogeny. He comes close to discarding the latter at several points in his sociology, but ends by including, with the old, a new orientation, which he does not develop and which is inconsistent with the old. All these factors conspired to prevent Freud from examining current social realities, and from reconstructing the reactions of man to his effective social environment.'

Some psychoanalytical studies that have the term 'envy' either in their titles or in their indexes have somewhat remarkably confined their accounts to mutual envy between the sexes relating to each other's

[9] A. Kardiner, *The Individual and His Society. The Psychodynamics of Primitive Social Organization*, New York, 1939, pp. 375 f., 379, 403.

sexual organs. It is a decisive assumption in much psychoanalytical thinking. To me it seems astonishing, however, that writers trained, or interested, in psychology should have allowed themselves to be so taken up with mutual envy between the sexes over a small anatomical feature as to pay not the slightest attention to the immeasurably greater role of envy in the totality of man's existence.[10]

The psychoanalyst Phyllis Greenacre speaks of a Medea complex which she claims to have found in women who suffered in childhood a traumatic experience consisting principally in pre-pubertal feelings of envy, comparisons and anxiety relating to primary and secondary sexual characteristics in both sexes. A basic situation especially conducive to this experience was one in which another child was born into the family of a patient, herself then not sixteen months old and therefore not yet able to talk. The sight of the new-born child at the mother's breast filled the little girl with unverbalized oral feelings of extreme intensity. Similar jealousy can sometimes be observed in domestic animals on the arrival of a new baby.[11]

The duration and intensity of sibling jealousy in many cases are recorded in a book by the psychiatrist Emil A. Gutheil on the language of dreams. However, he tends to use the term 'envy' where 'jealousy' would in fact be applicable. Thus he writes of a patient:

> Contrary to his conscious state of mind, this patient offers dreams full of
> activity, dreams carrying strong emotions, which however are of a distinctly

---

[10] Cf. D. Wyss, *Die tiefenpsychologischen Schulen von den Anfängen bis zur Gegenwart,* 2nd ed., Göttingen, 1966, p. 81. B. Bettelheim believes that ' . . . certain psychological phenomena have not received the attention they deserve. Particularly, penis envy in girls and castration anxiety in boys have been overemphasized, and a possibly much deeper psychological layer in boys has been relatively neglected. This is a complex of desires and emotions which, for want of a better term, might be called the "vagina envy" of boys. The phenomenon is much more complex than the term indicates, including, in addition, envy of and fascination with female breasts and lactation, with pregnancy and childbearing.

'Though this male envy has been recognized, it has received relatively little notice in the psychoanalytic literature.' *Symbolic Wounds. Puberty Rites and the Envious Male,* 1954, p. 99. Melanie Klein, *Envy and Gratitude. A Study of Unconscious Sources,* London, 1957.

[11] P. Greenacre, *Trauma, Growth, and Personality,* London, 1953, p. 233.

anti-social character. It is his criminal envy, his intolerance toward single
members of his family along with his emotional fixation to his family which
cause the symptom of an apparent 'emotionlessness.'

A nineteen-year-old girl envies her younger brother, who had received
a greater share of her parents' attention. She wished she might be as
young as he and told of a dream in which she imagined herself back
inside her mother: 'I am in a bed with my brother. We have rolled
ourselves up like embryos.' Gutheil gives accounts of several other of his
patients' dreams from which it is usually apparent that in waking life
inhibitions against work, or similar difficulties, are caused by envy of a
more successful friend, brother-in-law or sibling.[12]

The material obtained from dream analysis does at least provide
evidence for my thesis that the feeling of envy and jealousy is experienced and learnt primarily in the sibling group and that these feelings, on
reaching a certain intensity, have an exceptionally inhibiting and destructive effect upon the personality.

Ian D. Suttie, a psychiatrist, in his book on the origins of love and
hate, speaks of 'Cain jealousy.' The need to control this he sees as
providing the ethical 'Leitmotiv' of mother-cults. This sibling jealousy is
the earliest and most powerful in the development of the individual.
Suttie also mentions primitive peoples, for example the Bantu, who 'take
elaborate measures to counteract Cain jealousy.' He tells us that among
the aborigines of Central Australia, the mother eats every second baby,
sharing it with the older child. Suttie explains this as follows: 'Not only
can the child go on "eating the mother," but she even lets it *eat the
younger baby.*'[13] This use of cannibalism to attenuate sibling jealousy
recalls the custom recorded above in which, on the birth of another child
in the family, a fowl is beaten to death against the body of the older child.

Suttie emphasizes that sexual jealousy must be regarded as the main
source of all controls, whether these be social controls (taboos) or
endopsychic ones such as inhibition and repression. He sees Cain jealousy as providing the most important motive for socialization: sibling

[12] E. A. Gutheil, *The Language of the Dream,* New York, 1939, pp. 39, 68, 87, 195,
212, 228.

[13] J. D. Suttie, *The Origins of Love and Hate,* London, 1935, pp. 107, 110.

jealousy is biologically unavoidable (with the exception, perhaps, of the youngest child) and is a very early experience.

The social function of sexual jealousy

Next to sibling jealousy comes sexual jealousy, which is connected with it and may exceed it in intensity. But in contrast to the problem of sibling jealousy, most societies have succeeded, thanks to the universal institution of incest taboos, in eliminating at least enough sexual stimulus situations within close groups to ensure the basic unit of human society, the family. Murdock examined the nature and scope of the incest taboo in two hundred fifty tribal societies. He came to the conclusion that presumably only those societies (tribes) have survived, and thus become the object of research, which had succeeded in producing, through their rational and irrational beliefs on the subject of incest, effective inhibitions that reduced to a minimum conflicts within the family.

No society has ever succeeded in getting along without the social unit of the nuclear family (parents and children). Every attrition of that unit weakens and endangers the whole society. As Murdock emphasizes, however, there is no more destructive form of conflict than sexual rivalry and jealousy. The incest taboo alone makes possible the co-operative and stable family group. Without totally neglecting other causes, Murdock places the functional theory in the foreground: both the interest of the individual and the whole function of society demand internalized social controls or inhibitions, supported by the strict norms of the culture concerned which, from the start, prevent the feeling of jealousy at the most critical points of interpersonal contact in a society. Murdock cites Freud in support of his theory. From him he gets the fruitful theoretical proposition that every social phenomenon as widespread and as deeply imprinted as, for instance, the horror of incest, must have its origin in the nuclear family. But Murdock's theory then goes beyond Freud's far too simple Oedipus theory. For, after all, most of the Freudian mechanisms and their products—projection, sadism, regression and so forth—are rarely tolerated or encouraged by society. In the case of the incest taboo, however, we have an inhibition which, without exception, is embedded in valid forms of culture.

Murdock supplements Freud's theory with that of the sociological function of the incest taboo, of which he points out the economic and technical advantages. Every family has its own individual culture wherein many discoveries, improvements and linguistic innovations initially evolve and, through adoption by other members of the family, become patterned and are stabilized. Now in so far as incest taboos enforce marriage outside the family, they contribute to the spread of these new cultural elements. Murdock suggests that a society with incest marriage might succumb in conflict with other societies having incest taboos, because of the inadequate diffusion of important cultural elements, or at least because of excessive differences in family custom. We too make use of a similar argument to demonstrate the positive function of those social and psychological processes and institutions which reduce envy within a society.

Finally, Murdock seeks to answer the question of why the universal incest taboos are extended so regularly to distant relatives and to quite different kinship categories in individual societies. Since theories of psychoanalysis and sociology supply no answer, Murdock turns to the principle of stimulus generalization in behavioural psychology, particularly as developed by C. L. Hull. According to this principle every habitual reaction learned in connection with a stimulus or constellation of stimuli can also be aroused by similar stimuli or stimulus situations. Avoidance behaviour in conformity with the incest taboo is said to follow this principle. The mother's sister will generally resemble her. Yet this alone would not explain the scope of the incest taboo. Hence Murdock adds to this the sociological theory of conflict avoidance. Within the kinship, the clan and the community, generalized incest taboos contribute to social peace. Recently, however, D. F. Aberle and others have objected to Murdock's purely sociological theory of incest taboo on the grounds that it is also observable in animals.[14]

Further psychoanalytical aspects

A few years ago a group of American psychiatrists tried to create a scale by which to measure the degree of hostility in clinical situations. Thirty

[14] G. P. Murdock, *Social Structure*, New York, 1949. David F. Aberle (and five others), 'The Incest Taboo and the Mating Patterns of Animals,' *American Anthropologist,* Vol. 65, April 1963, pp. 253–65.

male and thirty female patients were questioned exhaustively, and any
signs of hostility were assessed by three observers in accordance with
the following 'aspects of hostility': resentment, verbal hostility, indirect
hostility, physical attack, mistrust, general hostility and strength of
hostile impulses. It is revealing, in the light of our investigation, that this
particular study totally disregards envy, mentioning only resentment.
This is said to be a feeling of annoyance over actual or imagined
ill-treatment. The writers begin by discussing the various meanings of
the term 'hostility' in the literature of psychiatry. Basing themselves
upon an investigation by Grayson, they find that hostility signifies
among other things: (a) a negative emotional state, (b) destructive
impulses, (c) aggressive behaviour and (d) a reaction to frustration
(thwarting of a desire). While they realize that hostility is made up of a
number of sub-concepts, they do not once advance the phenomenon of
envy.[15]

A very penetrating and useful distinction between envy and jealousy
was drawn by the American psychoanalyst Harry Stack Sullivan, based
upon the two- or three-group model.

> Before going further, let me discriminate my meaning of the terms
> jealousy and envy, which are often tossed around as synonyms. There is a
> fundamental difference in the felt components of envy and jealousy; and
> there is also a fundamental difference in the interpersonal situation in
> which these processes occur, for envy occurs in a two-group, with perhaps a
> subsidiary two-group made up of the person suffering envy and his auditor,
> while jealousy always appears in a relationship involving a group of three or
> more. I define envy, which is more widespread in our social organization
> than jealousy, as pertaining to personal attachments or attributes. It is a
> substitutive activity in which one contemplates the unfortunate results of
> someone else's having something that one does not have. And envy does not
> cease to be envy when it passes from objects to attributes of another human
> being, for envy may be an active realization that one is not good enough,
> compared with someone else. Although it involves primarily a two-group
> situation, one of the two may be a more-or-less mythological person.
>
> Jealousy, on the other hand, never concerns a two-group situation. It is
> invariably a very complex, painful process involving a group of three or

[15] A. H. Buss and others, 'The Measurement of Hostility in Clinical Situations,'
Journal of Abnormal and Social Psychology, Vol. 52, January 1956, pp. 84 ff.

more persons, one or more of whom may be absolutely fantasized. Jealousy is much more poignant and devastating than envy; in contrast with envy, it does not concern itself with an attribute or an attachment, but, rather, involves a great complex field of interpersonal relations. While data are hard to get, apparently jealousy occurs frequently in adolescence. . . .[16]

Again, Sullivan rightly recognizes the relationship between self-pity and envy. Though he in no way sees envy itself as self-pity, the latter may sometimes take its place. Self-pity may arise in the most diverse situations in which a person already having a low opinion of himself may get into difficulties. Self-pity eliminates envious comparison with others which might endanger our self-esteem.[17]

In his account of the phenomenon of resentment, Sullivan indicates its psychosomatic components:

Thus resentment is the name of the felt aspect of rather complex processes which, if expressed more directly, would have led to the repressive use of authority; in this way resentment tends to have very important covert aspects. In the most awkward type of home situation, these covert processes are complicated by efforts to conceal even the resentment, lest one be further punished, and concealing resentment is, for reasons I can't touch on now, one of our first very remarkable processes of the group underlying the rather barbarously named 'psychosomatic' field. In other words, in the concealing of resentment, and in the gradual development of self-system, processes which preclude one's knowing one's resentment, one actually has to make use of distribution of tension in a fashion quite different from anything that we have touched on thus far. . . .[18]

Guilt and shame

Starting from psychoanalysis, Gerhart Piers distinguishes between feelings of shame and feelings of guilt, both as regards their origin and their dynamics, thus creating a pair of terms which enable him to distinguish two kinds of envy. Of all the more concrete forms or states of emotional

[16] H. Stack Sullivan, *The Interpersonal Theory of Psychiatry,* New York, 1953, pp. 347 f.

[17] Op. cit., 355.

[18] Op. cit., 213.

tension, guilt and shame are two of the most important, not only in the pathology of emotion but also in character formation and the socialization of the individual.

The painful inner tension termed a feeling of guilt always occurs when the barrier set up by the super-ego is reached or exceeded. By contrast, the feeling of shame arises out of the conflict between the ego and the ego-ideal. In more simple terms, we feel guilt when we have undertaken or attained something which, though desired by the elemental driving forces within us, we know to be incompatible with the official norms of our group—incompatible, that is, if we seek its realization. Guilt is therefore the consequence of trespass. Shame arises, on the other hand, if we have not been able to do or to attain something which, according to the ideal we have set ourselves, we should have been able to achieve. Hence shame is indicative of failure.

Piers prefers the wider term 'shame' to that of 'inferiority feeling' because the latter presupposes comparison with some outside, other person. In the case of being ashamed, the comparison is between the actual self and the perfect, or at least adequate, self to which we aspire. For the man who is tormented by feelings of inferiority has no potential which he has failed to exploit. The man who is ashamed knows or believes that what he has done is below the level he should have attained.[19]

Piers next observes that envy is often suppressed or restrained by a feeling of guilt at being envious. This type of envy is usually rooted in the oral aspect of sibling jealousy. The unconscious train of reasoning is more or less as follows: 'The other gets more than I. I must take it away from him or kill him.' This type of envy, as Piers remarks, is generally accompanied by resentment which may be so strong that it will colour the whole personality. This resentment, resulting from impotence in the face of authority, is directed against the parents, who, consciously or unconsciously, are accused of favouritism towards the sibling. Resentment can also be turned against a mere image of parental authority, ultimately against God or fate.

Piers then draws attention to another type of envy. This he believes to

---

[19] G. Piers and M. Singer, *Shame and Guilt. A Psychoanalytical and Cultural Study*, Springfield (Ill.), 1953, pp. 6, 11.

be the consequence of the maturation process and the non-oral aspects of competition with parents and siblings. In this case, the unconscious syllogism runs: 'The other is so much bigger and better than myself. I am so small. I can never be his equal.' This form of envy (invidious comparison)—in contrast to the other—is held in check by shame and not by a feeling of guilt.

Piers also mentions that these two types of envy correspond to the two forms of sibling jealousy for which Franz Alexander suggested the terms 'regressive' and 'progressive,' the first being ascribed to the oral, the latter to the phallic, stage of child development.[20]

Do animals seek to avoid envy?

About thirty years ago at his laboratory in Florida Yerkes observed among his chimpanzees signs of some kind of social conscience. This he sometimes calls altruism.[21] Consideration of another, and a bad conscience about him (not just fear) leading to inhibition of action, are among the most important results of evolution, and Yerkes believed he had found indications of the history of this feeling among these same anthropid apes, for in man a large part of its formation remains buried deep in the unconscious or subconscious, or is concealed out of modesty and shame. Yerkes may have been thinking of motives such as envy when he wrote: 'For in these matters we are not honest, frank, and straightforward even with ourselves, much less with the prying scientist.' Next, Yerkes describes an experiment with isolated chimpanzee couples, each consisting of male and female, from which it was hoped to observe whether a chimpanzee could be inhibited in spontaneous action (of taking as much food as he could seize) by a feeling for the other animal's disappointment.

A tasty item (a banana, apple or orange) was offered to the chimpanzee couple at a fixed point in the cage wall. One of the two could take it. The small size of the titbit meant that it could not be shared. In the

[20] Op. cit., pp. 23 f.

[21] R. M. Yerkes, 'Conjugal Contrasts among the Chimpanzees,' *Journal of Abnormal and Social Psychology,* Vol. 36, 1941, pp. 175–99. See also 'The Life History and Personality of the Chimpanzee,' *American Naturalist,* Vol. 73, 1939, pp. 97–112. Ibid., 'Chimpanzees,' 1943.

first series of experiments, the box method, the food was placed in a wooden container with a lid. This box was made available at short intervals throughout the day. It was rare for both chimpanzees to try to get hold of the titbit.

In the second and more prolonged series of experiments, the researchers used a wooden chute which was fixed to the side of the cage at a certain time every day. During the daily period of experiment, the experimenter let the titbit roll down the chute into the cage at ten- or thirty-second intervals. A signal drew both the chimpanzees' attention to the fact that they were about to be fed. During the first series of tests, the male, Pan, first came and took the titbit. The female, Josie, sat contentedly by, obviously assenting to Pan's right to take everything he wanted. Pan, on the other hand, according to Yerkes, was quite obviously not at ease over this one-sided taking of the food. 'He talked low and questioningly to himself in a manner never before noticed.'

Pan went on asserting his precedence until the seventh experiment. But then Josie snatched the titbit out of the chute before Pan's outstretched hand reached it. 'Without show of resentment he left the chute and she took possession. He neither returned nor gave sign of restlessness or dissatisfaction.' Upon which Yerkes asks: 'The aforementioned conversation-like vocalization may have been an intimation of conscience or of deference toward a consort. Was it?'

The following day the female was able to take the food out of the chute without interference from Pan although he evidently wanted it. On the third day the picture was different: both chimpanzees approached the chute expectantly. Josie took control and Pan quietly walked away. After taking one bite, however, Josie left the chute, hurried across to the male and brought him back to the feeding-place where she presented herself to him sexually, but without success. But with the female beside him, visibly eager to have the food, Pan stood in front of the chute and took the next bits of banana that came down.

At the third experiment, however, she again forestalled him. Pan immediately went away and did not return to the feeding-place. That day Josie got nine of the ten portions presented during the experiment. The next day the male tried once more to take a titbit. Josie screamed at him, and during the following days she took the food almost always alone and without interference from Pan.

When the female's period of heat was over, the pair's social behaviour changed. At the signal both animals at once approached the chute, their hands ready to snatch the food. Now Pan asserted his precedence, taking the food as it arrived without regard for Josie, who looked annoyed. Pan took no notice of this, seizing the food but remaining friendly towards Josie. The following day Josie accepted happily and with good grace the priority claimed by Pan to the titbit. On one of the subsequent days, however, Yerkes and his colleagues noticed a new form of behaviour in Pan which they held to be very significant: during the feeding period Pan suddenly ran into the corner of the cage and tried to attract the attention of two females in another cage about forty feet away. Neither was in heat. Yerkes interpreted this behaviour as an attempt on Pan's part to find a pretext for abandoning the chute with its periodic descent of food to Josie, his companion, who in fact made use of the opportunity.

The next day Pan left the feeding-place without the pretext of interest in other females, but this time he ran to the other side of the cage and stared into the distance without there being anything the observers could see that might be attracting his attention. A minute later Pan returned to the chute where Josie was engaged in taking out the food. But before reaching her, he changed course, sat down to one side and quietly watched her. When Josie had finished, Pan's appetite was tested with an extra feeding; he was quite evidently eager to eat.

Yerkes believed that these observations gave evidence of a kind of conscience or social consideration towards the female to whom Pan wanted to give another chance. It should be emphasized that these experiments were made in connection with additional titbits at a special time of day and did not involve the animals' regular feeding.

Special significance accrues to these experiments from the fact that human psychiatry and psychology make use of the concept of food-envy (*Futterneid*). It is easy to see how food, the most important commodity in the living being's environment, was decisive, from the point of view of developmental psychology, in the formation of envy and envy-avoiding conduct. The decisive nature of food-envy in human conflict and in resentment is apparent from the fact that conflicts within small groups that have long been dependent on their own resources can be lessened by giving every one of its members uninterrupted access to large amounts of food: during the Second World War, for example, the crews of

submarines were kept relatively free of conflict by every member of the
crew being allowed constant access to food.

Further ethological studies in aggression

John Paul Scott, a zoologist, in his short monograph *Aggression* (1958),
which is concerned mainly with neurological, genetic and animal psychology data, does at least discuss jealousy, particularly between siblings. He bases himself upon unspecified clinical studies according to
which the motives for aggressive behaviour often originate in the situation of close family life.[22] Scott believes that these causes do not arise
with animals because they do not have the prolonged relations, typical of
man, between members of a family or of kinship. Scott mentions that not
only the deposed elder or eldest child may have reason for hostile
feelings, but also the younger child who believes the elder to be privileged. Scott does not think it possible for parental behaviour ever to have
any effect upon sibling jealousy, of which a certain measure is actually
beneficial for the development of the personality. Incidentally, he also
discusses other forms of jealousy, such as that of the neglected husband
who believes that because of their young child his wife has no time for
him.

Scott does not, however, go on to the subject of envy. He goes no
further than the concept of aggression, which he defines as 'the act of
starting a fight.' He attempts a theory of multiple causation for this form
of behaviour.

Some of the observations reported by Scott from the animal world
have a certain significance for our knowledge of the early stages of envy.
Hungry mice fight over food when they are able to carry it away, but not
if it is fastened down or is offered in powdered form. While male mice
never fight over females, there are sexually motivated fights among
many apes (baboons), dogs, stags, buffalo and mountain sheep.

The occurrence among animals of fights over territory is perhaps of
greater note for a theory of envy. Mammals and birds show this behaviour. Scott cites a study of prairie dogs according to which groups of the
wild animals in the Western prairies of the United States each possess a

---

[22] J. P. Scott, *Aggression*, Chicago, 1958, pp. 39–41.

certain territory and leave other prairie dogs alone so long as they do not cross the frontier. Konrad Lorenz has also given detailed accounts of territorial fighting among animals.[23]

According to Scott, all these situations which stimulate aggressive behaviour also apply to man. On the basis of a few experiments he then concludes that aggression is learned behaviour, and that children therefore could be brought up to be *non*-aggressive people by being denied the chance to fight. A happy and peaceful environment would 'automatically allow a child to grow up completely accustomed to consort peacefully with friends and relations.' Here again we have the limitless optimism of the American experimental psychologist. However, Scott does remind us that aggression is caused by other things than learning.[24]

It is noteworthy that Scott mentions various experiments and observations which considerably restrict the time-honoured frustration theory of aggression. *Frustrated* animals can be driven into forms of behaviour other than attack; other animals again (e.g., mice) become even more aggressive the more successful they are in battle—when, in fact, they are *not* thwarted.[25]

The pecking order

In 1951 Eduard Baumgarten had already stressed the fact that certain forms of behaviour in animals can be seen as envy-like types of response.

> As an example of the *fight for rank* among animals, the farmyard pecking order has recently been much discussed. The rankling impulse in envy would appear to be an analogy on the one hand with the merciless and irrevocable classification of an individual in the precise rank ascribed to it within such an animal society, on the other hand with the possibility every animal has of moving up to a higher rank by engaging in a fight for it. This possibility nags at the envious man's heart, along with the feeling of humiliation that weakness, either of constitution or position (actual inferiority of rank), should prevent him from attempting the fight.[26]

[23] Op. cit., pp. 7 f.

[24] Op. cit., p. 22.

[25] Op. cit., pp. 32 f.

[26] E. Baumgarten, 'Versuch über mögliche Fortschritte im theoretischen und praktischen Umgang mit Macht,' *Studium Generale,* 4th year, 1951, pp. 540–58.

It is not, however, altogether clear what Baumgarten means by this: we cannot know whether the lowest-ranking animal in a pecking order experiences anything corresponding to human envy; the only indication that this was so would be behaviour aimed unequivocally at harming the group, and/or his superior in the pecking order, which would not procure for the creature any sort of material gain (e.g., food). An experiment would be needed in which the supposedly resentful animal could in fact destroy or remove from reach the food of others, without however—as it is aware from the start of its destructive action—itself getting the food (or even more significantly, doing this at the cost of its own meal). Konrad Lorenz, in a letter to the author, agreed that this would indeed be the crucial experiment to show the presence of envy in an animal. But to date, as far as I have been able to ascertain, this experiment has not been carried out by any ethologist.

However, Baumgarten may perhaps have had in view something in the nature of 'royal envy.' The man of higher rank does not wish his subordinates to enjoy the same privileges. He is niggardly with supplies, which he rations so that none of his subordinates may be too comfortable. This, too, is envy, but exercised from a position of effective power. Behaviour has sometimes been observed which would be interpreted as revealing this kind of envy: the higher-ranking animal, although itself unable to eat any more, or satisfied sexually, denies both food and partner to lower-ranking animals. It is as if it were saying: 'If I've got to stop, there's no reason for you to go on enjoying yourselves.' This behaviour, seen from the point of view of developmental psychology, certainly contains an element of envy.

Baumgarten also mentions vindictive acts among animals provoked by envy:

An especially rankling form of envy respecting 'undeserved' differences in rank also has its prototype in animals. A relatively low-ranking female may, in favourable circumstances, advance by several degrees to the status and power which the relatively high rank of her mate happens to confer. The same applies to the offspring. The rank she has thus secured without a fight may be respected while her lordly consort is about; in his absence, female and young experience every refinement of persecution. The finest nuances of human squabbles over rank are foreshadowed here. Everyone is familiar with the refined sarcasms of, say, a superior assistant, servant, or subordinate on the subject of his master's privileged ineptitudes, or perhaps the analogous sarcasm of the man whose work is dull, slow, and commonplace about the men of rank and power who may be favoured by a trend, a fashion or a technical or theoretical system, which they either brought to flashy effect themselves, or adopted skilfully amid a blaze of publicity.[27]

For instance, we regard it as the expression of a sense of social justice when a strong man spontaneously goes to the assistance of another who is being attacked by somebody stronger than the victim but weaker than the rescuer. Such 'noble' behaviour can be observed notably in school playgrounds, in groups of children and among siblings, but also in certain groups of adults and among strangers. Now where the case is one of defending the weakest in the group so that he may not go short of food, it is even more applicable to the matter under investigation: Why does the stronger one, who is in any case well provided for, bother about securing enough for the weaker or weakest one, who is not even a member of his own inner group? Before considering pretentious terms such as 'sympathy,' 'egalitarian justice,' 'compassion' or 'nobility,' it might be worth taking a look at animals.

Many years ago Konrad Lorenz mentioned behaviour on the part of animals that was analogous to moral conduct. For instance, he describes the strict order of precedence that obtains in all jackdaw colonies: if any two jackdaws quarrel, a third, their superior in rank, intervenes with reflex-like authority on behalf of the lowest-ranking combatant.

> In the jackdaw colony those of the higher orders, particularly the despot himself, are not aggressive towards the birds that stand far beneath them: it is only in their relations towards their immediate inferiors that they are constantly irritable; this applies especially to the despot and the pretender to the throne—Number One and Number Two.

Hence, what appears to us to be chivalry is in reality an innate reaction which does, of course, function in the preservation of the species. It also, however, secures the position of the animal which happens to be stronger against those which, for the time being, cannot assert themselves against him and so direct their aggression towards those beneath them.[28]

[27] Op. cit., p. 548.

[28] K. Lorenz, 'Moral-analoges Verhalten geselliger Tiere,' *Universitas,* 11th year, 1951, p. 548.

Experiments in social psychology and the reality of envy

Experimental social psychology shows a number of proved results arrived at from experiments with subjects in various cultures demonstrating the degree to which the average man is inclined to mistrust his own
senses as soon as he is associated with an actual or fictitious group
which, unknown to him, has been instructed to pass on false information.[29] The experiment succeeds not only when the intentionally false
observations are reported by conniving participants whom the man being
tested holds to be better qualified than himself, or whose feigned rank is
such as to impress him. In this case it might be a question of a subordi-
nation drive, which may well also be involved. During a military exercise, in industry, in an anatomical laboratory or in a clinic where X-ray
photographs are being examined, for instance, there will always be
subordinates who will suppress their own observations or give an interpretation either consciously or semi-consciously corresponding to that of
their superior, for fear of a clash with him.

These experiments, however, are highly pertinent to our theory of
envy avoidance, if they are planned in such a way that the group which
deliberately falsifies its observations is either unknown to the experimental subject, indifferent to him, or else completely simulated, but in
no case represents a superior. 'Simulated' is now a current social science
term for such experiments. For in these experiments it can be seen that
the participant, suddenly unable to trust his senses, cannot bear to swim
against the (social) current since he does not wish to seem too clever, a
know-all and so forth. He is afraid of the others' resentment, their
envious annoyance, giving him to understand that only a snob or an
incurable egghead could reach conclusions that differed from their own.

About ten years ago Stanley Milgram experimented with subjects,
first at Harvard and then in Norway and France, to see if their respective
national cultures and characters played any part in conformity. The
subject, sitting in one of six cells, was given the false impression that the
other five were also occupied. In reality they were empty, and an
impression of the presence and co-operation of other people was given
by phase-ins on tape. The subject listened through earphones to two

---

[29] S. E. Asch, 'Effects of Group Pressure upon the Modification and Distortion of
Judgments,' *Groups, Leadership and Men,* ed. Harold Guetzkow, Pittsburgh, 1951.

notes, and had to say which of the two was the longer. Before giving an opinion, however, he was able to listen to what was said by the fictitious five other people. The experimenter, by use of the tape, could give these fake opinions every kind of distortion. The degree of social control could be increased by angry remarks, indignant murmurs, etc.

These experiments generally showed an astonishing conformity, as did the earlier ones by S. E. Asch (who got the subject to estimate the length of lines): the individual inclines rather to mistrust his own ears or eyes than to persist in going against the finding of a group. But Milgram was able to increase the degree and frequency of independence by a second experiment in which the subjects believed that their findings would be used as a basis for the design of air traffic control systems.

It is not so conclusive for our present considerations that in all his experiments Milgram found a higher conformity drive in Norway than in France, although this finding agrees with other observations indicating more complete social control in the former than in the latter. When the subjects did not have to speak into the microphone, thereby communicating their observations to the supposed group, but simply wrote them down, both French and Norwegian subjects showed greater independence, but the latter again less than the French. Milgram continues:

> It is very puzzling that the Norwegian so often voted with the group, thus with the incorrect observation, even when given a secret ballot. One possible interpretation is that the average Norwegian, for whatever reason, believes that his private action will ultimately become known to others . . . one subject said he feared that because he had disagreed too often the experimenter would assemble the group and discuss the disagreements with them.

The urge to conform was even more evident in the statement of another Norwegian who, along with the group, had heard incorrectly in twelve out of fifteen observations. ' "In the world now, you have to be not too much in opposition. In high school I was more independent than now at the university. It's the modern way of life that you have to agree a little more. If you go around opposing, you might be looked upon as bad." '[30]

[30] S. Milgram, 'Nationality and Conformity,' *Scientific American,* Vol. 205, 1961. Quoted from the reprint in *Readings in General Sociology,* ed. R. W. O'Brien and others, Boston, 1964, pp. 54 ff.

Reminded that he was permitted to disagree on a secret ballot, he declared: ' "Yes, I tried to put myself in a public situation, even though I was sitting in the booth in private." '

It would be difficult to think of more striking experimental proof of David Riesman's theory and concept of the other-directed person than the behaviour of those Norwegians.

Conformism and the fear of envy

The way in which envy is linked with all these experiments becomes apparent as soon as we ask ourselves why a man is not prepared to trust his senses and to defy a group. What is he afraid of? What could the other students, whose identity he does not even know, do to him if he trusted himself and contradicted them? Why is he afraid of being himself?

The nature of the sanctions, or alternatively of the unexpressed thoughts about him most feared by the subject, can be recognized from the experiment in Norway and France, where the phased-in remarks increased to the maximum the urge to conform. A faint snicker was one of the milder sanctions. But the phasing-in of the sentence: 'Skal du stikke deg ut?'—'Are you trying to show off?'—had a decisive effect upon the Norwegian subjects: conformity with the group rose to 75 per cent. Furthermore, they accepted the criticism impassively.

In France the sentence used was 'Voulez-vous vous faire remarquer?' ('Trying to show off?') Its effect on the subject was somewhat slighter. But in contrast to the Norwegians, about half the Frenchmen answered the critics angrily. (Incidentally, in a control experiment with forty Norwegian workmen, Milgram found their behaviour very similar to that of the students.)

What, then, is basically feared by the man who, against his better judgement, conforms to the group, is verbal reprisal, a reproach for wanting to be better, more knowledgeable, cunning and observant than the group. In other words, an expression of envy of his particular abilities, his individuality and his self-assurance.

But at this point another question arises. Is the misled subject trying to conform to the judgement of the group because to make a wrong observation would embarrass him or put him to shame, or is he, while convinced that his observation is correct, afraid only of seeming a know-all? The effect of the verbal reprisals used by Milgram in his experiment indicates the latter. Where the subject was brought to recant his own observations by taunts such as 'Can't you see or hear, man?, or 'Wake up!' the shame factor could be assumed. Hence a definitive distinction between the two motives is hardly possible because the group—or another person—more often than not seeks to force the individualist, whose superiority is secretly feared, to conform by denigrating his judgement, although they know he is right.

What is perhaps of significance to our general considerations is the comparison made by Milgram between the considerable conformity shown by the Norwegian in the experiment in perception and his calm acceptance of extremely restrictive social measures 'in the interests of the welfare of the community.' Milgram writes:

> I found Norwegian society highly cohesive. Norwegians have a deep feeling of group identification, and they are strongly attuned to the needs and interests of those around them. Their sense of social responsibility finds expression in formidable institutions for the care and protection of Norwegian citizens. The heavy taxation required to support broad programs of social welfare is borne willingly. It would not be surprising to find that social cohesiveness of this sort goes hand in hand with a high degree of conformity.

The braggart experiment

Once more we look in vain for any awareness of the fact of envy in an experimental study in social psychology by Albert Pepitone on *Attraction and Hostility,* [31] which appeared in 1964. It concerns experiments with small groups in which an interviewer was supposed to anger the subjects by a display of various types of vanity or arrogance; from one experiment to the next subjects were given fictitious biographical data concerning the supposedly arrogant interviewer, so that in one case his behaviour was to some extent justified by his achievements, in another

---

[31] A. Pepitone, *Attraction and Hostility. An Experimental Analysis of Interpersonal and Self-Evaluation,* New York, 1964.

extreme case less so. The series of experiments was commissioned by the U.S. Office of Naval Research and used exact quantitative methods.

The author is clearly so completely taken up in the American cultural ethos, which 'officially' does not recognize envy of the successful man, that he does not even take the concept of envy into consideration where its stimuli are manifestly built into the experiment. Thus in one case the interviewer is identified as a well-known professor earning an exceptionally high fee as an adviser to government departments. The question as seen by Pepitone, and tried out on students, who seldom have enough money, was as follows: Will the man who, in a taped discussion played back before students, appears especially overweening and self-absorbed be more, or less, unfavourably criticized by the audience if they regard him as a highly paid specialist or as a routine researcher? According to Pepitone's hypothesis, the more highly situated the arrogant man, the more favourable the judgement. But the author completely overlooks the fact that in some subjects, unconscious envy of the successful man would, in fact, counteract such a reaction which might otherwise 'logically' be expected. It is easy to see how a man inclined to envy can more readily tolerate, and dismiss as mere awkward behaviour, vain mannerisms in a person he believes to belong to his own level, than he can in another person who, just because his prestige and fortune have set him at the top, should behave modestly. So long as the experimenter disregards this consideration, the whole of his research must, as in the above case, be quite inaccurate.

Pepitone discusses a hypothesis according to which the hostility shown by the subjects (the term 'envy' would often be far more specific) towards the braggart is the result of a feared loss of status; that is, the subject's self-esteem is impaired by the ostensible behaviour of the person acting as stimulus. From the final result of this series of experiments, the hypothesis would seem implausible. For as a consequence of the author's blind spot in regard to envy, the hypothesis fails to take into account the fact that the man whose envy has been aroused by another may very easily show symptoms of hostility (as by making derogatory, sarcastic remarks) although in no way feeling his own status—hence his social position—to be threatened or shaken.

Pepitone, laudably enough, is concerned with going beyond the frustration-aggression theory of hostility, and it might have been hoped that in a chapter on reactions to the braggart there would be a few findings on the subject of envy. That hope is disappointed, however. Pepitone does, of course, succeed in making the subjects annoyed with the braggart; there are exclamations such as 'No man could be as good as that!' But it never occurs to Pepitone to introduce the idea of envy, not even when the braggart in the crassest possible way impresses upon the subject, a student, how much better off financially he himself had been at university. In one sentence only does Pepitone so much as approach the problem of envy: 'The boaster's self-evaluation also must be believed or considered plausible, for without the *invidious comparison* [i.e., envious comparison, *invidia*] there would be no threat [to the self-evaluation of the subject].'[32]

Yet instead of examining the problem of envy more closely, Pepitone coins an elaborate concept of 'anger which then motivates status-defensive behavior.'

It is true that a number of earlier writers—Schopenhauer, for example—have clearly realized that the average envious man will expose the object of his envy to spiteful, destructive criticism so as to be able to live with himself. Pepitone's experiments served merely to confirm what has long been an everyday experience. Yet it is difficult to imagine why, having so anxiously avoided the concept of envy, he believes, like many another social psychologist, that he has discovered something new in science. The concluding remark in his chapter on the boaster is correspondingly superficial: 'When all is said and done, at least part of the negative attitudes toward the boastful interviewer [the stimulus in the experiment] could have been due to his egregious [experimentally foreseen] breach of good taste.[33]

However, the question as to why etiquette in most cultures regards boasting as a breach of good taste remains unasked; the connection between modesty and the avoidance of envy, so evident to earlier writers, is no longer discerned by Pepitone.

In general Pepitone adheres to those theories of hostility according to which rejection and dislike of another person increase in proportion to the threat to one's own status.[34] The theory is correct in so far as it agrees with the observation repeatedly recorded in this book that envy is chiefly

[32] Op. cit., pp. 78 f.

[33] Op. cit., p. 88.

[34] Op. cit., pp. 222 f.

directed against people within the same social group and at the same level, and very rarely at those considerably above us. Schopenhauer said the same thing when he pointed out that composers or philosophers were far more envious among themselves than, for instance, a less famous composer or a very famous philosopher.

Basically, however, Pepitone and social psychologists of the same persuasion would have to assume that a lower-placed subject whose self-evaluation is correct, that is, realistic, ought not to react with hostility to a more highly-placed stimulus person, as long as the former is convinced that this person is justified in behaving so haughtily because this accords with his level of achievement. Such a theory, however, completely overlooks the fact that in common experience the envious man always manages so to alter his perspective as to make the man he envies appear to have no merit. Pepitone, in accordance with American popular ethics, assumes with considerable naïveté that most people feel a strong need to establish the true value of others and to order their feelings accordingly. In the experiment Pepitone sought to induce situations in which the boastful person would in no way be able to constitute a threat to the subject's status, but the reactions he obtained were still negative; this too he explains merely as 'college-boy culture' where boasting is again a breach of good taste.[35]

In my opinion, the basic error in this experiment is the actual concept of the boaster, the swaggerer, the vain man. For in themselves these words mean a man who, from the point of view of society, has a self-evaluation that is objectively false. But what can be made of a person—for instance, a Nobel Prize winner or some other internationally prominent figure—whose behaviour corresponds to his position? According to the social psychology which Pepitone represents and which ignores the concept of envy, the subject would feel no hostility towards such people because he would see no discrepancy between behaviour and position. In reality, however, men do not behave according to formula. This current American social psychology is, in a sense, itself suffering from the weakness, recently discovered by one or two European critics, of failing to pursue the real and inevitable conflicts in society. Pepitone and others maintain that, in a society where privilege,

[35] Op. cit., p. 224.

proficiency and reward were properly ordered, there simply would not be any hostility. They fail to realize how very little envy is concerned with reward and proficiency. Of course, this is small wonder. As recently as 1964 the psychoanalyst Marvin Daniels, in a brief paper on the dynamics of morbid envy in cases of chronic learning disability, remarked upon the curious disregard for this phenomenon in psychological and psychoanalytical literature.

> Envy . . . lends itself to phenomenal disguises which often confound the teachers, parents and psychotherapists whom it spitefully confronts. Its basic importance has long been underestimated in psychoanalytic and psychological circles. And, finally, we might well be living in a culture which favours the propagation of envy.[36]

And in 1961, Leslie Farber, in a very brief article on the faces of envy, also wondered why psychoanalysts have paid so little attention to envy. The classical Freudian considered envy as just a by-product of other processes and had little interest in its ramification. To Farber, however, envy is a primary emotional substratum from which emanate specific manifestations that enter into many interpersonal relations as well as in other areas of personal experience.[37]

[36] Marvin Daniels, 'The Dynamics of Morbid Envy in the Etiology and Treatment of Chronic Learning Disability,' *Psychoanalytic Review*, Vol. 51, 1964, pp. 45–56.

[37] Leslie Farber, 'Faces of Envy,' *Review of Existential Psychology and Psychiatry*, Vol. 1, 1961, pp. 131–9.

7

Envy as Seen by the Social Sciences

THE MUTUAL AND SPONTANEOUS supervision exercised by human beings over each other—in other words, social control—owes its effectiveness to the envy latent in all of us. If we were quite incapable of envy and, more important, if we were also convinced that our behaviour would not be envied by anyone, that mutual, tentative exploration of the threshold of social tolerance—a constant social process upon which the predictability of social life depends—would never occur.

Without envy there could be no social group of any size. The other-directed process comprised in this concept consists of emotional, probably also endocrine processes which influence our perceptions as well as our rationalized cognitive acts. Envying is as much a constituent of social existence as it is generally concealed, repressed and proscribed. Similar denials and repressions in respect of an even far more basic kind of motivational system, the sexual, have been investigated and described in detail since the beginning of the twentieth century. It is not uncommon for a behavioural factor essential to our existence to be passed over in silence for a long time.

The threat of envy, arising between human beings at almost any time through any deviation from the standard or norm, not only has this in itself necessary function; it also constantly sets the limit of variability in the patterns of social behaviour and social organizations.

The awareness, conscious or subconscious, of the often only latent or potential envy of others, has the same kind of effect as a gravitational field: our socially relevant, or at least socially visible, behaviour is kept within certain limits and is unable to deviate too far from the centre of consensus. In so far as virtually all members of a group or society are endowed with this inhibition, each keeps the other in check and is prevented from displaying arbitrary innovations in his own behaviour.

This view of the problem would seem to me more enlightening than the usual one, according to which we are at all times so intent on gaining the approval and acceptance of others that we conform. It would be more realistic not to regard this as the primary motive. Often enough we conform whether or not the sympathy of the rest is, or should be, of especial importance to us: we fear what they might do—or not do—if we were to arouse their envy of our courage to deviate from the norm.

Individual and group

The fact that modern social psychology always substitutes the motive of 'acceptance' or 'wanting to be popular' for the obviously more apt motive of the avoidance of envy, is in itself a symptom of a process of repression.

Sociologists, especially American sociologists, have investigated in many variations the repeatedly observable fact of conformity. The members of a group, whether as sub-group or as individuals, exact from every other member, and especially from the newcomer, certain kinds of conformity. 'They' want 'adaptation' and 'adjustment.' They punish non-conformity. These studies, however, never ask whence this tendency comes, and why conformity of behaviour is demanded of the individual even in fields having little or nothing to do with the real functions of the group. What is particularly striking and unexplained here are those cases in which a hold is gained over some members by others—usually those who make themselves out to be spokesmen or in some way specially qualified representatives of the group—where no one personally feels that the recommended norm is either pleasant, practical or rewarding. Indeed, the more unpleasant in practice, the more irrational and awkward the norm to which members have to adhere, for whatever reason (perhaps because the controlling body simply wants it that way), the more fiercely do they watch each other for any laxity or failure.

Could it be that in culture and society, man sees himself, often perhaps unconsciously, as so much of an individual that any kind of group membership is inherently repugnant to him? He feels himself robbed of an asset—his very individuality. He has to be a member of a group so as to earn his living, to acquire a certain education etc., but he feels himself somehow diminished by belonging to a group, even if he prefers that particular group to other possible ones. He can then most easily compensate for his partial loss of individuality occasioned by membership of the group, or mitigate the pain of that loss, by taking an active part in depriving other members of their individuality.

It is malicious glee in the torment of the newcomer who has yet to adapt himself to the group, *Schadenfreude* in the sanctions applied to a non-conforming member, that automatically makes of every one of its members a watch-dog and a whipper-in. The kind of group is immaterial: it could be a parliamentary political party, a school class, a boarding school, a platoon of recruits, a group of office workers, a group of industrial workers, an age group in a primitive society, prisoners, or simply a sibling group within a family.

Despite some influential social theories, it may be that man experiences his membership of a group not as fulfilment but as diminution. Thus membership of the group would be for man a compromise with his true being, not the culmination of his existence but its curtailment. This is a necessary experience for nearly everyone if he is to acquire certain values such as economic security, the acceptance of his children into society, etc. But even in the most 'socially minded' man there is a residue of stubborn, proud individualism, the core of his existence as a human being which fills him with *Schadenfreude* when he is able to help impose upon others the same loss of individuality that he himself has painfully experienced.

Power and conformity

From this we derive a hypothesis of a process of social control that can be decisive in the establishment of a new power structure. This book is not primarily concerned with forms of domination, power and force; yet the sociology of power and domination should not overlook the factor of envy, since it is always the wish of those who subject themselves to power that others, still able to evade that power, should also subordinate themselves and conform to it. Phenomena such as the totalitarian state and modern dictatorship cannot be fully understood if the social relations between those who have, and those who have not yet conformed, are overlooked. Let us take a typical case:

A new centre of power has come into being. It may be merely a routine change, it may be usurpation or a party acceding to power by legitimate or illegitimate means, or again it may be a new departmental manager in a plant or officer in a military unit. A previously existing vacuum or balance of power has been altered; a new centre of power, whether vested in a group or an individual, exists, and it seeks to expand and to establish itself by bringing under its domination those groups and persons who have not yet submitted to it. At this stage some individuals or groups will already have lined up behind this new power, whether out of greed, cowardice, stupidity or genuine enthusiasm. But these men who have already submitted to the new power are not satisfied with conforming, themselves and almost invariably develop intense feelings of hostility towards those who continue to stand aside sceptically appraising the new power and considering whether to remain aloof.

This behaviour, if judged according to an independent system of values, may be altogether laudable. But to the system in question it may very well seem dilatory and subversive, as in Herman Wouk's novel *The Caine Mutiny* some of the officers and crew of a small warship dislike the new captain from the start, and sabotage his command. Tension, usually originating with the conformists, then arises between those who conform and those who do not. Why is this?

Anyone who has already adapted himself against his will, whether out of cowardice or for the sake of comfort, begrudges others their courage, the freedom they still enjoy. Anyone who has already committed himself to the new leaders, from calculation or from real enthusiasm, sees both himself and his chosen power group endangered by those who obviously prefer, and see it as politically feasible, to keep their distance. Those at the periphery of the power centre, though in no way entitled to wield authority, now begin to exert pressure on other people in the course of daily social life, within the framework of local groups and among business or neighbourhood connections, with the object of getting them to conform as well.

There is a variety of familiar social situations in which a similar ambivalence is apparent. A small professional group, such as a university department, a business or a small military unit, naturally desires, as a group, to gain the respect, recognition and support of other groups and institutions. Therefore every mark of distinction and every special achievement of every member of the group is of intrinsic interest to every other member. And if the group is lucky enough to be given, or is able to choose, as its head someone who is sufficiently sure of his own value, or at least willing to combine it for the sake of his leading role with the achievement of his whole group, he is likely, as *primus inter pares,* to be able to do everything possible to provide every member of the group with ample opportunity for development. Observation shows, however, that even under such ideal conditions individual members are generally careful, if not anxious, to remain within certain limits: nobody wants to stand out too much, at least not if his potential achievement is unlikely to be compensated for within a short time by additional prestige or something similar accruing to the majority. At the same time everyone who sees and has a chance of rapid advancement knows that a success, at present open only to him, would also contribute to the prestige of the group as a whole, and that no one would dare to criticize him officially and in public. But secretly he fears the many small acts of sabotage which might be practised, sometimes almost unconsciously, by his fellow workers or colleagues who constantly compare themselves with him—because of their envy at his having achieved, or succeeded in, something ahead of them.

Envy in the sociology of conflict

The German sociologist Dahrendorf chooses the word 'envy' when explaining why the American sociologist C. Wright Mills, so prominent as a writer, was mercilessly branded a heretic even by those who shared his political opinions: 'But much more can be read between the lines. They betray the intense mixture of anger, hatred and envy characteristic of the attitude of the profession towards its successful outsiders.'[1]

But when dealing with a fundamental theory of social conflict, Dahrendorf stops one step short of the concept of envy. Georg Simmel's sociology of conflict contains a detailed and fascinatingly perceptive phenomenology of envy; shortly after him, Max Scheler also made a thorough study of the problem. But Dahrendorf writes almost forty pages about this problem in his essay on social conflict without once mentioning the word 'envy.'[2]

[1] R. Dahrendorf, *Die angewandte Aufklärung. Gesellschaft und Soziologie in Amerika,* Munich, 1963, p. 188.

[2] R. Dahrendorf, *Gesellschaft und Freiheit,* Munich, 1963, pp. 197–235.

In the first place the very word or concept 'conflict' partly conceals the phenomenon of envy. If I seek to define all hostility between men as conflict, I presuppose a concrete relationship, a mutual awareness, a preying on one another, etc. But the envious man can, in fact, sabotage the object of his envy when the latter has no idea of his existence, and when true conflict exists only in the envious man's imagination and perhaps not even there. Conflict may, of course, sound more decorous, more democratic or more acceptable to our socially sensitive ears than does the old, starkly unequivocal word 'envy.' If I see two men (or groups) engaged in conflict, I have no need to ascertain which is the inferior. But if I speak of envy I must assume that one of the two opponents realizes the fact of his inferiority in situation, education, possessions or reputation.

In Dahrendorf and others envy vanishes from sight, because 'conflict situations' in which the one party's motivation arises unmistakably from his inferior resources are simply subsumed under much more abstract concepts, in which the concept of envy is barely discernible to most people. For example:

> All other inequalities of rank which may appear as the immediate structural point of departure or as the object of conflict—grades of prestige and income, unequal distribution of property, education etc.—are only emanations and special forms of the very generalized inequality in the distribution of legitimate power.

I would also question whether the term 'conflict' is at all suitable in sentences such as the following:

> The inequality of rank of one party in general social conflict can mean a great many things. In this case what is meant may be inequality of income or of prestige: conflict between those on a higher or significantly lower wage scale; conflict between the highly regarded technicians in the printing trade and the lowlier ones in mining. . . .[3]

Between income groups and professional groups of this kind there cannot be any real conflict; at the most it may arise when envy is generated between unequally paid workers within the same industry, as

[3] Op. cit., p. 213.

happened with the British engine-drivers who went on strike because the lower-ranking railway workers' wage was too close to their own. For the 'frictions' referred to above, for the mutual jostling between groups that can in fact take place only in the minds of individual members, the only correct word is 'envy.'

It may partly be the sociologists' predilection for observable processes which has led them to substitute the phenomenon and concept of conflict for that of envy. Envy is a silent, secretive process and not always verifiable. Conflict is overt behaviour and social action. Between the two, and partaking both of envy and of conflict, one might conceivably place tension. The preoccupation with conflict and conflict situations has led, however, to the neglect of numerous aspects of human and social relations which are explicable in terms of envy but not in terms of conflict. For envying can take place between the envier and the person reacting to envy without the least sign of conflict.

Of course envy in individuals and in groups may lead to behaviour and to actions which could rightly be subsumed under the sociology of conflict. But conflict or aggression should not, as unfortunately happens so often, be confused with envy, which makes researchers eventually pay more attention to conflict than to the primary phenomenon.

The sociology of conflict overlooks the fact that between the envious and the envied man no real possibility for conflict need exist. In contrast to jealousy, what is often particularly irritating to the envious man, and conducive to greater envy, is his inability to provoke open conflict with the object of his envy.

Conflict without envy

It is possible, though rarely so, for true conflict to arise between individuals and between groups which has nothing or very little to do with envy. (Where priorities are concerned, envy is always likely to be present.) If, for example, two opponents confront each other in a conflict situation, each holding the other in high esteem but each believing he must adhere to a different rule, envy would not enter into it.

Both fiction and history contain instances of close friends, or at any rate characters neither of whom could find anything to envy in the other, becoming firm opponents in an impending conflict because one obeys a universal moral law, the other a more limited, specific law. The conviction that I, from direct and observed experience, am following what I adjudge to be the right law, the proper standard, need not cause me to envy my opponent and need not arouse his envy against me. This could only happen after the conclusion or settlement of the conflict, when the loser was compelled to realize that for some reason he had obeyed the wrong law (wrong not only in pragmatic terms but revealed as false in the light of reappraisal). The consequence may then be intense anger, resentment, envy, against the victor: Why wasn't I clever or experienced enough to see at once that my choice of values was objectively the wrong one?

But so long as both opponents in the conflict situation believe un-hesitatingly and firmly in the absolute, or at any rate overwhelming, rightness of the accepted law upon which they take their stand, the entire conflict can be played out in circumstances that are completely *devoid of envy.*

And even when both opponents voluntarily recognize the same rules in a contest, or in business competition, they can remain untouched by any feeling of envy while the conflict is still in progress, as long as neither side knows who is going to win.

Sociological ambivalence

In 1965 an American sociologist, Robert K. Merton, published an essay in which he grappled laboriously with new concepts, on the subject of 'sociological ambivalence,' in which problems of envy were patently involved but were left untouched. Merton speaks of the ambivalence produced by the social structure between teacher and pupil when the pupil who has finished his education is unable to find a position comparable to that of the master. Later Merton investigates the 'hostile feelings' which society appears to harbour towards self-employed professionals, despite their manifest contributions to the general welfare. Here again he introduces the concept of ambivalence, coined by Eugen Bleuler in 1910, and shies away from the much simpler primary notion of envy.[4]

[4] R. K. Merton and E. Barber, 'Sociological Ambivalence,' in *Sociological Theory, Values, and Sociocultural Change. Essays in Honor of P. A. Sorokin,* ed. E. A. Tiryakian, New York and London, 1963, pp. 92 f., 95, 106 f.

What is even more striking is the fact that when, in present-day European investigations as to why working-class parents are reluctant to send their children to grammar school, envy and the *Schadenfreude* of neighbours, mentioned in so many words in the answers to the questions, are disguised by the sociologists with elegant flourishes like 'affective distance' or 'traditionalism buttressed by social sanction': 'Our neighbours think we're too big for our boots and are just waiting for things to go wrong.' 'My buddy said, "Don't go and get ideas into your head."' 'They think we're stuck up, and are just waiting for him to drop out.' 'They say, "Look at the show-off."'[5]

Perhaps contemporary sociology is so ready to overlook the phenomenon of envy, a sensation which arises primarily in the aggressor, because it looks predominantly for interaction, for social interrelation. Anyone who concerns himself principally with social contacts and interaction is all too likely to neglect the behaviour of those who keep aloof and regard with envy and resentment the very people with whom they are *not* in social contact. But again, in applauding healthy and regular social interaction, we must not forget that this may occur between persons one of whom is intensely envious of the other.

As various criminal cases show, envy may be a very well-concealed and well-disguised form of behaviour whose victim discovers it in friend, servant, colleague, nurse or relative only when it is already too late. Shakespeare depicted a character of this kind in Iago. As a rule, envy is partly the result of social proximity, although this may be replaced by memory or imagination. The man who is marooned on an island, in the depths of the country or in prison imagines what he is missing, and what others—whether he knows them or not—are at that moment enjoying; he envies them without any social contact. One has only to recall the Count of Monte Cristo.

Today the social scientist is constantly being asked for a formula for the ideal society. But if envy is taken to be one of the chief causes of social friction, conflict, sabotage (minor and major) and various forms of crime, it is very difficult to determine whether it will best be

[5] R. Dahrendorf, *Bildung ist Bürgerrecht*, Hamburg, 1965, pp. 70 f. Here Dahrendorf refers to J. Hitpass, *Einstellungen der Industriearbeiterschaft zu höherer Bildung. Eine Motivuntersuchung*, 1965, from which the quoted remarks of the workers who were questioned derive.

diminished or relatively contained in a society having a maximum or a minimum of points of social contact.

Georg Simmel on envy

In Chapter 4 of his *Sociology,* which is concerned with conflict, Georg Simmel investigates the phenomenon of envy, which he sees as contained within the concepts of hatred, jealousy and ill-will. Like so many authors, Simmel is immediately confronted by terminological ambiguity:

> Finally, there is a fact, apparently of merely individual importance, yet in reality very significant sociologically, which may link extreme violence of antagonistic excitement, to close proximity: jealousy. Popular usage is not unequivocal in regard to this term, often failing to distinguish it from envy.

As we have already seen, Simmel here underrates the precision of the German language (as also of English and French). The big dictionaries, already available in his day, could have given him a clue. Simmel continues:

> Both affects are undoubtedly of the greatest importance in the formation of human relations. In both, an asset is involved whose attainment or preservation is impeded by a third party, either truly or symbolically. Where attainment is concerned, we should speak of envy, and where preservation, rather of jealousy; in this the semantic differentiation of the words is in itself, of course, quite meaningless and of importance only for the distinction of the psycho-sociological processes.

Here I would not agree with Simmel unconditionally: the use of the words is not incidental, as we have already shown in Chapter 2. Proverbial lore, as well as the literature of different cultures, has, over the course of centuries, ranged so much precise knowledge under the distinct concepts 'jealousy' and 'envy' that we should retain the existing terminology. On the whole Simmel, too, adheres to tradition:

> It is peculiar to the man described as jealous that the subject believes he has a rightful claim to possession, whereas envy is concerned not with the

right to, but simply with the desirability of, what is denied; it is also a matter of indifference whether the asset is denied him *because* a third party owns it, or whether even its loss or renunciation by the latter would fail to procure it for him.[6]

Jealousy or envy?

Simmel's definition needs greater precision: the expression 'jealousy' should be restricted to an asset upon which there is a legitimate claim, even if the jealous man is subjectively mistaken about his possible loss of that asset. A child in a family undoubtedly has a true a priori claim to its parents' kindness, help and love, yet it may be tormented by jealousy of its siblings if it only *believes* it isn't getting enough. Conversely, the husband whose wife is estranged from him has a right to claim her affections even though, seen objectively, her alienation is genuine. Simmel's final observation is wholly correct, namely, that the envious man, in certain circumstances, does not even want to have the coveted asset, nor could he enjoy it, but would find it unbearable that another should do so. He becomes ill with annoyance over someone else's private yacht although he has never wished to board a ship in his life.

Simmel clarifies this further:

> Jealousy . . . is determined in its inner direction and tone by the fact that a possession is withheld from us *because* it is held by another, and that were this to cease, it would at once become ours: the feelings of the envious man turn rather upon the possession, those of the jealous man upon the possessor. It is possible to envy a man's fame without oneself having any pretensions to fame; but one is jealous of him if one believes that one is equally or more deserving of it. What embitters and corrodes the jealous man is a kind of emotional fiction—however unjustified and senseless—that the other has, so to speak, taken the fame away from him.[7]

To continue with the example of fame, there is a further distinction to be made: if there is only one foremost literary prize and one poet has

---

[6] G. Simmel, *Soziologie. Untersuchungen über die Formen der Vergesellschaftung*, Munich and Leipzig, 2nd ed., 1922, p. 210.

[7] Op. cit., pp. 210–11.

missed getting it, he may be jealous of the prize-winner; but the chemist who, contrary to his expectations, has not received the Nobel Prize for his discovery can only envy his colleague the physicist who does get it. In other words, in the case of jealousy there must be real competition, but as soon as parallel attainment of the coveted asset is or could have been factually possible, envy alone is involved.

Finally, Simmel says of jealousy that it is 'a feeling so specific in degree and kind that, having arisen as the result of some exceptional emotional combination, it aggravates the situation which gave rise to it.' This observation is very important. But it is also true of envy. For the envious man, too, by use of his imagination will often aggravate a real situation to such an extent that he never lacks cause for envy.

Begrudging others their assets

Simmel arrives at an interesting clarification of terms, distinguishing him from nearly all other writers on the subject, in his description of ill-will, of begrudging, which have always been central aspects of envy.

> Approximately halfway between the clearly defined phenomena of envy and jealousy there is a third, belonging to the same scale, which might be termed begrudging: the envious desire for an object, not because it is of itself especially desirable to the subject, but only because others possess it. This emotional reaction develops two extreme forms which mutate into the negation of the subject's own possessions. On the one hand there is the passionate form of begrudging which prefers to renounce the object itself, would indeed rather see it destroyed than allow another to have it; on the other, there is complete personal indifference or aversion to the object, and yet utter horror at the thought that someone else possesses it. Such forms of begrudging permeate human relations in every degree and variation. That great problematical area where human relations to things turn into cause and effect of their personal interrelations is largely covered by this type of affect.[8]

These few sentences of Simmel's contain an observation of great importance. He does not give specific examples, yet what he has indi-

[8] Op. cit., p. 211.

cated here is the psycho-social dynamic, the source of numerous socially or culturally derived regulations usually known as 'sumptuary laws.'

Sociology of sexual jealousy

The American sociologist Kingsley Davis analyses jealousy and sexual possession as examples for his functional theory of society. He thinks it may seem surprising that an individual emotion, something purely psychological, might contribute to an understanding of culture and social organization, yet he attributes to jealousy a function not only in the individual's emotional state, but also in his immediate linkage to social organization:

> . . . the manifestations of jealousy are determined by the normative and institutional structure of the given society. This structure defines the situations in which jealousy shows itself and regulates the form of its expression. It follows that unless jealous behaviour is observed in different cultures, unless a comparative point of view is adopted, it cannot be intelligently comprehended as a human phenomenon.[9]

The same applies to envy. Curiously enough, Davis concerns himself with it only incidentally, seeing it, in contrast to jealousy, not as the attitude of a possessor but as that of an observer or potential rival who would like to have what another has without envisaging any possibility of getting it away from him. Envy, he says, cannot assert itself simultaneously with jealousy in the same person, since the latter emotion presupposes a certain right. Other authors, as we have seen, believe in the possibility of a blend of jealousy and envy, each intensifying the other. Davis sees in envy an inevitable phenomenon of all social life. Anyone who has not got everything that he has been led to regard as desirable will be envious of others. 'But since envy usually goes contrary to the established distribution of this world's valuables, it is frowned upon by the group as a whole.'[10]

Davis shows in detail how wrong those writers were who have seen in sexual jealousy the expression of a completely physical state of affairs.

[9] K. Davis, *Human Society*, New York, 1949, p. 175.
[10] Op. cit., p. 182.

Because there are instances among a number of primitive peoples in which it is permissible for a man, apparently without any feeling of jealousy, to put his wife at another's disposal, it should not be concluded that these are cultures or types of personality devoid of jealousy. Closer investigation almost invariably reveals that the favours of the wife are shared only with certain others whose right to share them is prescribed by the culture, while within the same society unauthorized 'adultery' may immediately evoke jealous reactions.

Even non-sexual jealousy follows the patterns of intimacy prescribed by the relevant culture. In our own culture, for instance, an uncle would not normally be jealous were his nephew to have a very tender and close relationship with his own father. In societies with matrilineal descent, in which it is customary for the relationship between uncle and nephew to be unusually close, a very jealous uncle is sometimes known to object to the nephew loving his natural father more than his uncle.

Davis saw the social function of jealousy as being mainly to stimulate defensive behaviour whenever an interpersonal relationship, sanctioned by the culture and regarded as a property relationship, is threatened or disrupted by a trespasser not admitted by the culture as a legitimate rival. When several men are seeking the hand or the favours of a girl who belongs to none, this is denoted as true rivalry which, pathological excesses apart, turns into indifference or friendship, in accordance with the norms of most cultures, as soon as the girl has chosen one of them.

In other forms of possession, besides that relating to the object of value in a personal bond, human societies generally distinguish between, on the one hand, the socially desirable and sanctioned activity of rivalry and competition, in which all participants must play the game with a good grace, and 'trespass' on the other. Trespass arouses jealousy and thus evokes protective measures in the form of laws.

The blind spot in regard to envy in the present-day behavioural sciences

How well modern experimental social science and psychology, in fact most behavioural sciences, have succeeded in skirting the phenomenon of envy—so precisely described in pre-scientific literary and philosophical experience—is apparent from the latest encyclopaedic work representing those disciplines. *Human Behavior: An Inventory of Scientific Findings,* by Bernard Berelson and Gary A. Steiner, was published in 1964. In seven hundred pages we are presented with all that is verifiably known of human behaviour to date, arranged according to categories such as child psychology, perception, learning and thinking, motivation and small-group behaviour. The book is intended as an inventory. The authors write: 'Our ambition in this book is to present, as fully and as accurately as possible, what the behavioral sciences now know about the behavior of human beings: what we really know, what we nearly know, what we think we know, what we claim to know.'

The subject index fails to mention either envy or resentment. Jealousy in mentioned once; turning, then, to page 54, we find a diagram giving the approximate ages at which different emotions are felt for the first time. According to this, jealousy, as a derivative of 'distress,' is felt for the first time between the eighteenth and twenty-fourth months of life. This, the only mention of the phenomenon in the entire book, refers to an article published in 1932(!).

At this point we would recall the vast literature of cultural anthropology dealing with the phenomenon of superstition in innumerable human groups, which never fails to deal, in full and exact detail, with the function of envy. But Berelson and Steiner mention superstition once only, in the entry on learning and thinking—an experiment with pigeons, reported by Skinner in 1953, on the reinforcement of conditioned reflexes, which is said to explain why the most glaring evidence fails to convince people that their superstitious rites are ineffective. This, if we are to go by the pigeon experiment, is because the more often our superstitious action fails to produce the desired result, the less we are discouraged by its failure, and because it is in the nature of things that, say, a rain dance will rarely be followed by rain, the principle is valid that superstition persists with such obstinacy because it so seldom works, not in spite of the fact that it so seldom brings success.[11]

We look in vain in the index for irrationality or irrational behaviour. Nor is anything to be found about competition, rivalry and imitation. Nothing, in fact, that could in any way lead to the periphery of the

---

[11] B. Berelson and G. A. Steiner, *Human Behavior: An Inventory of Scientific Findings,* New York, 1964, p. 156.

phenomenon of envy. A single reference to *sibling* jealousy cites a psychiatric essay of 1951, six lines of which are quoted, informing us that *sibling* jealousy observed by a mother in her own children may reactivate her own childhood experiences.[12]

The most productive of the entries in the index are those under aggression and social conflict. Here, perhaps, we shall find something about envy, the more so since the stock answer of American researchers, when asked about envy, is nearly always that this represents a minor variant of the phenomenon of aggression.

According to this compendium, the modern behavioural sciences tell us about aggression: severely punished children tend to become aggressive men. Next comes the hypothesis, against which the authors have placed a large question mark, that societies like Germany, in which children have a disciplined upbringing, tend in consequence to have authoritarian political systems.[13]

On page 258 we are informed, in a paltry couple of lines, that there is apparently something called 'need aggression,' the need for aggressive behaviour, which may assume such forms as murder or sadism. Envy is not mentioned once. On pages 267–70 the frustration theory, according to which the cause of aggression is not the attacker but the man who thwarts his drives, is described in some detail. Experimental proof is offered: In a summer camp for boys half of them were deliberately deprived, or given too little of something. The disappointed boys vented their displeasure on an ethnic minority—meaning that after the deprivation experiment they answered a questionnaire on Japanese and Mexicans more unfavourably than before the experiment.

The classic aggression-frustration hypothesis put forward by John Dollard (and others) in 1939 states that the occurrence of aggression always presupposes the existence of frustration, that is, the thwarting of aspiration. Berelson and Steiner comment on this with a question mark. But whatever may be thought of this hypothesis it does seem a little strange that not even at this point is envy so much as considered.

The few remaining allusions to aggression refer chiefly to behaviour discriminating against ethnic minorities. In various works it is claimed

[12] Op. cit., p. 72.
[13] Op. cit., pp. 72, 81, 82.

that economically underprivileged people have a tendency towards discrimination. This observation could, of course, be extended to include envy, but it is not.[14]

Even the inventory's relatively numerous passages on conflict, social conflict and social class, however, entirely fail to mention the envy-motive. Other expressions such as 'revolution,' 'justice,' and 'equality,' where a discussion of our problem might conceivably have been expected, are simply not listed.

Although Berelson and Steiner found themselves greatly restricted by the meagre fare provided by a social science, dependent as it is on evidence drawn chiefly from rats, cats and pigeons, these authors nevertheless do not hesitate now and then to draw upon animal experiments for analogies and comparisons which might illuminate everyday situations in human existence. One such example shows once more how people stop just short of discussing the motive of envy-avoidance.

First there is an account of animal experiments concerned with 'approach-avoidance conflict,' where the issue is as follows: Where a goal possesses both pleasurable and frightening aspects, thus being at once attractive and potentially painful, there is a point on the way to the goal at which the organism becomes irresolute, and begins to waver; if it then proceeds further towards the goal, it reaches a point just short of it where avoidance behaviour becomes more marked. This is called 'approach-avoidance.'

In human existence, according to Berelson and Steiner, this can mean, for example, that a man will approach an attractive but dangerous sport in which, at the last moment, he will not engage. Or else someone would like to buy a luxury article, approaches it repeatedly, visits the shop window more and more frequently, takes hold of the door handle, even goes into the shop, but at the last moment avoids making the purchase. Why? 'Perhaps because the pain or guilt associated with the expenditure rises more sharply as the point of commitment is approached than does the attractiveness of the item.'[15]

If it were realized precisely what part envy and envy-avoidance play in purchases of this kind, one might assume, from this example of Ber-

[14] Op. cit., pp. 281, 514–16.
[15] Op. cit., pp. 273 f.

elson's and Steiner's interpretive method, that it would have been entirely appropriate within the framework of their book to describe obvious forms of behaviour related to envy, hypothetical and incapable of proof though they might be. But nowhere does this occur in all the seven hundred pages of an inventory dated 1964 that purports to convey our present state of knowledge about man, especially man in his social context. Were an imaginary inhabitant of another planet to seek information from this book about *Homo sapiens,* the idea would never occur to him that anything like envy existed on this planet.

Theories of hostility

Though exponents of modern social sciences (sociology, social psychology, cultural anthropology) have concerned themselves exhaustively with the phenomenon of hostility, they have managed to write whole chapters about this subject, even in recent works, without ever asking what it is that underlies hostility.

Neil J. Smelser, a sociologist, in 1962 put forward a comprehensive theory of collective behaviour, by which he means group behaviour such as panic, mob action, riot, fanatical sects, etc. There is a detailed discussion of hostility, with references to literature on the subject, but not a single mention of such phenomena as envy, resentment and malevolence; 'hostility' is the only term. Even when he is investigating 'hostile belief' and 'hostile outbursts,' the envy which can only too easily be shown to underlie it never comes into view. It is vain to look in Smelser's index for envy, resentment, jealousy, egalitarianism or the sense of justice. Perhaps unconsciously, he carefully evades every phenomenon and every concept that could lead him even indirectly towards anything to do with these aspects of human nature. We find little here even about aggression, which, as we have seen elsewhere, is a favourite form of evasion for those refusing to face the fact of envy.

In Smelser's analysis of 'hostility' we do in fact discover why modern social science is so apt to overlook envy. There is repeated discussion of theories of hostile behaviour according to which such behaviour is the consequence of a perceived threat to a person's real economic, sexual, professional or social position. The authors admit, of course, that the possessor of these hostile feelings incorrectly assesses, exaggerates or actually invents the ostensible threat (American literature is concerned chiefly with hostility towards minorities such as Negroes and Jews, the subject feeling threatened in his own sphere by minority claims, power, etc.). But the point of departure is invariably that hostility is aroused when the subject imagines a real threat to his own real position.[16]

The guilt of the attacked

According to this view of the hostile man, ill-feeling can never really arise if the subject does not see himself in any way effectively threatened by the object of hostility. It is a view that obliterates the age-old familiar and precisely formulated phenomenon of envy and envious hatred, which can, indeed, exist when the object of envy does not or cannot in any way constitute a threat to the envious man. It is far more true that men in all cultures feel threatened primarily by the envious man. Modern social science thus entirely reverses the situation: the primary threat issues from the person who is potentially enviable. But the social scientist ignores that envy. Hostility thus becomes a secondary phenomenon that will disappear as soon as all groups in a society are placed in a situation where everyone is equally secure and free from threat.

It is, of course, right to suppose that a white lower class which fears unemployment is specially prejudiced against its Negro equivalent in the same country, or that a middle class with diminishing wealth and prestige can easily be stirred up against a prominent well-to-do Jewish minority in its midst. But the hope, implicit or explicit, that all substantial hostilities will disappear as soon as a group or individual in a society ceases to worry about livelihood or position, is just as unrealistic and unfounded as the rather more extreme theory that there would be no more envy or resentment in a truly egalitarian society.

It is immediately apparent that these two assumptions about a peaceable society have different models in view. One can imagine a very stable society in which everyone had an absolutely assured and adequate place but in which at the same time there were a distinct hierarchy, marked social stratification and considerable inequalities. Those sociologists who believe that only the threatened man is hostile would see such a society of total social security as free of hostile feelings. But to sociolo-

[16] N. J. Smelser, *Theory of Collective Behavior,* New York, 1962, p. 106.

gists who recognize the existence of phenomena such as envy and resentment that society would still be prone to disturbance as a result of provocative inequality. Only a permanently equal society would offer freedom from envy and hence from aggression—a state of mutual friendship between its members.

As we have been able to show repeatedly in this book from many different angles and cultural viewpoints, neither of these utopian societies, even if they were to approach their ideal, would be able to turn human beings into contented and peaceable sheep, as 'progressive' social science promises.

Once the process of envying has begun, the envious man so distorts the reality he experiences, in his imagination if not actually in the act of perception, that he never lacks reason for envy. The same applies to the man who feels insecure.

Everyone in his lifetime must have had an experience such as the following: Against the advice of some onlooker, one sets to work on something difficult, carpentry, say, which one insists on doing in one's own way. Suddenly the malice of inanimate objects asserts itself. Things begin to go wrong. How often do we then exclaim: 'You wanted that to happen!' Yet we know perfectly well that the annoyance of our companion whose advice has been spurned cannot possibly affect the natural course of things. For primitive man there is never any question of the other man's guilt in such a case: he is always convinced of it.

But this archaic magical way of interpreting our environment, in seeing our neighbour's evil eye on it, as it were, has not been so completely discarded by modern man that in most of us it cannot recur. It still persists in rural areas, and subliminally. In practical terms this means that if there ever were a society in which the individual or every group was guaranteed absolute economic security, and hence where no one could really threaten or objectively harm another, there would still remain plenty of unpleasant personal and group experiences which would still unerringly be attributed to other people's malevolence.

Why a society of unenvious equals?

The blind spot in regard to the problem of envy in the social science of this century, and particularly in 'human behavioural science' in the United States, cannot be fortuitous. It can be plainly shown how authors shy away from the concept or phenomenon of envy, how they veil it in euphemism, how, if they are very brave, they mention it briefly as a peculiar hypothesis, to discard it at once with an expression of pitying scorn.

Many different observers, including some of the most progressive sociologists, have noted, often with approval, the resentment and sense of defiance to be found in the personality of many modern social scientists (Ruth Benedict, M. Tumin, C. Wright Mills, George Simpson). In American sociology and anthropology it is almost proverbial that the majority of professionals are men who are discontented with their place in society and culture, former members of some kind of underprivileged group or class—men, in short, rebelling against their own society. The proof is easy to find and the sources are so numerous that they can hardly be questioned. See, for instance, Edward Shils:

> Professor [C. Wright] Mills implies that sociology has more to gain from a hostile attitude toward the existing order than from uncritical incorporation into it. It is true that, in taking this position, he stands in a distinguished tradition. Nonetheless, neither his viewpoint nor its opposite is correct. Neither the unqualified hatred of the outsider nor the uncritical affirmation of the patriot opens the path to truth about society.[17]

[17] Resentment towards one's own society as the sociologist's necessary point of departure is supported by, for example, the New York sociologist George Simpson (*A Sociologist Abroad*, The Hague, 1959, p. 168). C. Wright Mills maintains the same thing. For this he was criticized by Edward Shils ('Professor Mills on the Calling of Sociology,' *World Politics*, Vol. 13, July 1961, p. 608). The cultural anthropologist Julian H. Steward, commenting on Ruth Benedict as revealed in her writings, published posthumously by Margaret Mead, in his review (*Science*, Vol. 129, February 6, 1959, pp. 322 f.), said: 'As a scholarly profession, anthropology has drawn more than its share of non-conformists who are comforted by its findings that each culture has its own values and standards of behaviour and that the demands of our own society are no more right in an absolute sense than those of any other. Ruth Benedict, however, seemed to be an exception. Her outward calm, mild demeanour, and Mona Lisa smile seemed to indicate a good adjustment to her world. The error of this inference is startlingly disclosed by the materials published for the first time in Dr. Mead's book. These materials reveal a tortured, non-conformist individual who finally found a creative outlet, and we hope relief, in anthropology. . . .

'Ruth Benedict's diaries and an unfinished autobiographical sketch, "The Story of My Life . . . ," expose with surprising candour the black depressions and self-doubts that made her early life almost insupportable. These feelings, however, were so

The common denominator for this discontent, this unrest, is the egalitarian impulse; most of the problems experienced or imagined by such minds would theoretically be solved in a society of absolute equals. Hence the constant and strangely tenacious preoccupation of Anglo-Saxon social science with models and programmes for a society of absolute equals. The utopian desire for an egalitarian society cannot, however, have sprung from any other motive than that of an inability to come to terms with one's own envy, and/or with the supposed envy of one's less well-off fellow men. It must be obvious how such a man, even if only prompted by his unconscious, would carefully evade the phenomenon of envy or at least try to belittle it.

It is true that certain American sociologists have repeatedly encountered the problem of envy and have actually named it—Kingsley Davis, for example, in his textbook of sociology, or Arnold W. Green. But what is significant is that the greater the currency of other hypotheses, such as the frustration theory, the more consistent is the neglect of every approach, even in contemporary specialist literature, to a recognition of envy. Practically never has envy as an hypothesis been raised in order to be refuted or subjected to criticism; instead, it has been ignored, as too embarrassing. Envy touched too painfully on something personal which it was preferable to keep buried. This silence within the wider professional fraternity of behavioural scientists and psychologists about a central problem of man's social existence has had the result, however, of making their younger colleagues, who themselves might have had no grounds for repressing the phenomenon, less than fully perceptive of its existence.[18]

---

carefully concealed that Ruth Benedict was in effect two persons, a private self and a social self. The double pattern began in her earliest childhood, when Ruth Benedict shut part of herself off from her friends and family and lived in a secret world of imagination. . . .

'The inner torments and introspective search for an answer to life continued well into adulthood. Ruth Benedict tried teaching and *embraced social causes* to no avail. In large measure, she saw her difficulty as a consequence of being a woman in our own culture.' (Italics mine.)

[18] Arnold W. Green, *Sociology,* 4th ed., New York and London, 1964, considers the problem of equality and envy in American society. He is fully aware of his position as an outsider.

A disinclination to concern oneself with envy may also be connected with the following: Almost without exception all research concerning man has, when faced by envy, seen it as a serious disease. The latent ubiquity of this ailment is known, but it is also known that no society could exist in which envy was raised to the status of a normative virtue. Invariably it is emphasized that envy, once having taken root, is incurable, although it is not part of our normal endowment. Even superstition, the primitive 'anthropology' of simple societies, sees envy as a disease, the envious man as dangerously sick—a cancer from which the individual and the group must be protected—but never as a normal case of human behaviour and endeavour. Nowhere, with very few exceptions, do we find the belief that society must adapt itself to the envious man, but always that it must seek to protect itself against him. [19]

[19] The extent of envy-avoidance in a population can also be ascertained from opinion polls. In the summer of 1966 the Institut für Demoskopie at my request repeated a question which had been put to the West German people some ten years before. The tendency to avoid envy had actually risen slightly. Of those asked, 53 per cent thought it sensible not to show how well one had got on. Among civil servants the figure rose to 63 per cent. The breakdown of the answers according to religion, refugee or native citizen, region, small or medium-sized town, shows only insignificant differences. West Berlin alone is noticeable for having less tendency to understatement.

8

Crimes of Envy

Murder from envy

As we have already observed, one function of private property is to protect people against the envy and aggression of the physically less well endowed. For a society in which everyone owned an equal amount of property, or where property was shared out by the state, would not be an idyll devoid of envy but a hell in which no one could feel physically secure. Even in present society there are frequent cases of crimes whose motive is obviously envy of some physical superiority.

In 1963, after a basketball game in New York City, a drab-looking day labourer drove his car at the good-looking hero who had won the game and who was standing on the pavement with his parents and friends. The murderer, who had no interest whatever in the losing team, declared that he just could not stand seeing the glamour of that handsome athlete.[1]

Arson prompted by envy of more gifted fellow students may end in murder, as a story which appeared in the *New York Times* on June 1, 1967, strongly suggests. It may even happen at an élite university, with a very high academic standard, should it dare to offer an exceptional opportunity to the favoured few. During 1967 buildings housing Cornell University students were the victims of three fires, all very similar. In the worst fire, on April 5, eight students and a professor died in the blaze. On May 23 a second fire broke out in a building housing students, and a third occurred on May 31 in a building occupied by some of the students evacuated from the house burned on April 5. All three fires involved

[1] 'Youth Is Accused of Killing City College Star with Car,' *New York Times*, December 16, 1963.

dormitories housing students who were enrolled in a special programme for exceptionally brilliant students. It is a programme that may lead to a Ph.D. in six years instead of the usual ten or more years of undergraduate and graduate work. Only 45 of Cornell's more than 13,000 students are enrolled in that special programme. Four of the eight students who died in the April 5 fire were members of the special Ph.D. group. Most of the students who were threatened by the fire on May 23 were also enrolled in the special programme, as were seven of the nine students who were driven out by the fire of May 31. Neither the District Attorney nor the County Coroner believed that it was all due to coincidence. The fires could have been started only by human agency. The Coroner did not use the word 'envy' but spoke of 'human malice,' a term often enough used in place of 'envy,' as we have seen in Chapter 2. By November 24, 1967, the Department of Police, City of Ithaca, New York, informed me that no arrests had been made, and the Coroner's hypothesis had been neither eliminated nor substantiated.

In 1953 a middle-aged spinster in Munich took her friend's baby out for a walk in its pram. Suddenly she pushed baby and pram into the Isar River. The investigation, in which the psychiatrist Ernst Kretschmer took part as expert witness, disclosed that the culprit was suddenly overcome with envy of her friend's happiness which the child symbolized.[2]

In May 1959 American daily papers carried an account from Swannanoa, in North Carolina, under the headline: 'Co-ed Chopped in Envy may be Disfigured.' According to the account given on May 21 by United Press International, this is what happened: An attractive twenty-year-old student, Rose Watterson, was attacked and mortally wounded while asleep in her room in Warren Wilson College; the hatchet struck her four times between her left eye and her throat. The culprit was her former room-mate, Patricia Dennis. The newspapers carried pictures of the two girls. Before the attack, Rose was undoubtedly pretty, though not exceptionally so, Patricia distinctly less attractive, a bit on the chubby side and, even in the photograph taken before the deed, her expression almost hostile. At the first hearing she stated her motive to have been jealousy and envy of her prettier room-mate.

[2] Information in a letter from Dr. Heinz Häfner, July 17, 1953, according to which Professor Kretschmer was to bring his expert opinion to bear on the Munich child murder in a publication.

In August 1959 thirty-six-year-old Stephen Nash was executed in San Quentin in California. He spent the last two years of his life in solitary confinement because his fellow prisoners could not stand his constant boasting about having murdered eleven people, among them several boys. Nash, who refused spiritual consolation before his execution, even at the trial clearly revelled in giving detailed descriptions of how he stabbed the victims. When the judge announced the verdict with the remark: 'You are the most wicked person who has ever appeared in this court,' Nash smiled. According to his own statements, he committed the murders for the following reason: 'I never got more than the leavings of life, and when I couldn't even get those any more, I started taking something out of other people's lives.'[3] The court psychiatrist declared Nash to be not responsible for his own acts. As a result of his many previous convictions, Nash had already been examined by court psychiatrists in 1948 and 1955, but he had always been declared not dangerous to the public.

Although it is barely hinted at as a hypothesis in the Warren Committee's report, the letters and reported remarks of President John F. Kennedy's assassin leave little room for doubt that Lee Harvey Oswald's central motive was envy of those who were happy and successful, and whose symbolic representative he murdered in the person of the young President, a man truly favoured by fortune. If one endeavours, in the light of available biographical material, to understand Oswald's frame of mind, one is forced to conclude that he would not have raised his gun against an older, less handsome president, married to an inconspicuous wife, and one whose style of life, constantly reported in the press and on television, had not been that of modern royalty. Various press commentaries, without using the word 'envy,' came close to this interpretation. For instance: 'Kennedy was Oswald's victim, because the young prince at the White House was and had everything that Oswald, the perpetual failure, never could be or have.'[4]

[3] Associated Press report from San Quentin, California, August 21, 1959.

[4] 'The Marxist Marine,' *Newsweek,* December 2, 1963, p. 23. About Oswald: 'As the diabolical psychologist in Richard Condon's *The Manchurian Candidate* says . . . "The resenters, those men with cancer of the psyche, make the great assassins."' Further, in his foreword to the new edition of Svend Ranulf's study of moral indignation and middle-class psychology, Harold D. Lasswell suggests that the murderer of the President might be understood as an envious man. S. Ranulf, *Moral Indignation and Middle-Class Psychology,* New York, 1964, p. xiii.

On March 15, 1960, American papers published an Associated Press story from Victorville, California: 'Jealous of Woman's Wealth, Boy says in Iron-Rod Killing.' Seventeen-year-old David Marz, son of a worker in a dry cleaner's plant, killed the mother of a school friend. The motive he gave the authorities was explicitly envy of the family's prosperity. David was often invited to use the family's private swimming pool and became more and more envious because, as he explained to the judge, the Hodge family had a lot of things his own family couldn't afford. David had no previous police record.[5]

Mr. Floyd Jones, detective of the homicide division, in charge of the Marz case, supplied me with the following information:

> David's parents and the victim had been close friends since David's infancy. One thing David mentioned during our conversations was that one of the victim's sons, who is in his class at Victorville High School, was going away to a scout camp for the summer, and the funds were being donated by his estranged father and grandfather and other members of the Hodge family. The subject did sincerely want to go on the same summer camping trip, but his parents could not afford it, and there was no one close to his mother or father who could provide the necessary funds. While he refused to admit that the camp trip was one incident which aroused his envy, investigating officers felt it had a great deal to do with his feelings toward the Hodge family at this particular time. The plans for the camping trip were made by the Hodge boy only a few days prior to the murder of his mother.
>
> When first interrogated, David Marz steadfastly refused to admit any knowledge of the brutal beating. After approximately one hour's conversation with David, which was recorded on tape, David interrupted officers while the tape was being changed with the remark, 'There's no use wasting any more tape. I did it.' Then he gave a detailed account of how he had burgled the Hodges' home and another house on the same property during the evening before the murder, both houses being empty at the time he prowled through them. Following the burglaries he returned to his home, where he was sleeping on a camp bed near the swimming pool. Significantly, the pool's cement was cracked and the pool could not be used by his family. He lay there about two hours without falling asleep, and at approximately 1:30 decided to return to the Hodges' and hit Mrs. Hodge on the head.

[5] 'Jealous of Woman's Wealth, Boy says in Iron-Rod Killing,' the *Atlanta Journal,* March 15, 1960, p. 19.

When questioned about his motive for wanting to strike Mrs. Hodge, David was at a loss to explain. He said, 'I don't know,' several times. Then he finally said, as tears came to his eyes, that he didn't know, but he guessed it was because other women always had so much more than his mother. Although pressed for more specific information, David was unable to put into words any better explanation for his actions. The similarity of this motive to the one attributed by the French novelist Eugène Sue, as we shall see in Chapter 10, is astounding. Later, in an interview following the re-enactment of the crime, on March 15, 1960, David stated in a conversation with an officer that if his reason for committing the crime were to be expressed in one word, it would probably be jealousy, but, as before, he was unable to explain why the mother of his friend was the victim.

In 1963 a seventeen-year-old Negro in Georgia, U.S.A., shot a school friend. The alleged motive was jealousy of the victim's being elected head of their class. Before this, it was stated, the culprit had 'out of envy torn down several of his victim's election posters.'[6]

In the spring of 1957, in the neighbourhood of Detmold, West Germany, a Turkish music student was murdered by a Greek music student. Of this case a journalist wrote: 'What was the motive? Detectives groped their way blindly until they received the following information: both young men were studying singing at the Detmold Academy of Music. . . . The murdered man was the more gifted and successful. Socially, too, the Turk had shown himself to be superior.'[7]

The envious murderer, whose motive should not be confused with that of the armed robber, is widely encountered in ethnological literature dealing with primitive peoples. For example, intense envy might arise among members of a South Sea Island canoe crew if, during a long voyage undertaken for barter trade, one of their number did better than the others. Poison and black magic were often his lot.[8] It cannot be said too often that there is no sign that any primitive community, however simple or however tightly knit, has ever inspired its members with that

[6] The *Atlanta Journal,* October 28, 1963.

[7] G. Zöller, 'Scotland Yard in Wiesbaden,' *Rheinischer Merkur,* March 18, 1960, p. 24.

[8] R. F. Fortune, *Sorcerers of Dobu,* New York, 1932, p. 210.

spirit of collective ownership which eliminates envy by eliminating private property, as Western utopia-mongers would have us believe.

Again, envy has always been among the motives of those who accuse others of some crime and who, as witnesses, will actually distort their observation and information until they finally persuade themselves of the accused man's guilt. Modern criminology records what is called the 'persecution of a beautiful woman' suspected of murder, for whom things are said to be little better than at the time of the witch trials. Before the First World War, Karl Kraus, for example, wrote about this subject; his essays have recently been reissued by Heinrich Fischer under the title *Sittlichkeit und Kriminalität*[9] (Morality and Criminality).

The purest form of existential envy manifests itself during a catastrophe when people, through envy of others with possibly better opportunities for survival, select *one* among several different means of escape, and seek to destroy the alternative possibilities of flight or rescue. In his book *The Boat* Walter Gibson tells what happened during the Second World War after the torpedoing in the middle of the Indian Ocean of the Dutch ship *Rooseboom,* carrying 500 evacuees from Malaya. Gibson, one of the 135 survivors, states that in one lifeboat not only did five soldiers band together one night to murder and throw overboard twenty of the survivors, but even those who were driven by hunger and thirst to jump overboard seemed to envy the fact that others, who wished to remain in the boat, still had a chance of survival which they themselves had surrendered. Gibson recalls:

> That was a strange feature of every suicide. As people decided to jump overboard, they seemed to resent the fact that others were being left with a chance of safety.
> They would try to seize the rations and fling them overboard. They would try to make their last action in the boat the pulling of the bung which would let in the water. Their madness always seemed to take the form that they must not go alone, but must take everyone with them.[10]

---

[9] P. Kipphoff, 'Hetzjagd auf die schöne Frau. Vorurteil, schlechtes Gewissen und Eifersucht von den Hexenverfolgungen bis zum Mariottiprozess,' *Die Zeit,* April 10, 1964, pp. 10 f.

[10] W. Gibson, *The Boat,* London, 1952, p. 35.

Vandalism

Vandalism is a well-known concept in the criminal law of English-speaking countries, being the senseless and malicious damage to, or destruction of, private or public property without any material gain to the perpetrator, although it often necessitates considerable effort on his part in order to wreck something.[11] German law does not recognize this offence as a special concept. Thus, when one March morning in 1966 twenty private cars parked in a street in Wiesbaden were found to have had their tires painstakingly slashed, the police made the following statement to the press: 'We're puzzled as to the motive. It's not, of course, the problem that we've had before, when somebody has been annoyed or cheated, perhaps deported from country A, later in country B pulls his knife on all cars with A number plates, leaving them with slashed tires.' The detective can understand mere vengeful acts, however irrational they may be, but when there is no ostensible reason for revenge, vandalism appears to him as inexplicable. Yet it is simple enough to put oneself in the position of a young lout or someone less well off, or even in that of the man who has several times failed his driving test and is driven into an envious rage by the mere sight of a car waiting for its lucky owner. The repression of envy as a comprehensible and, anthropologically speaking, obvious motive, is so fundamental in most of us that even an experienced detective appears unwilling to go into the matter—either with the accused or privately, in his own mind.

The word 'vandalism,' designating wanton destruction, usually of an

[11] F. M. Thrasher, *The Gang. A Study of 1313 Gangs in Chicago,* 1st ed., 1927, reissued by J. F. Short, Jr., Chicago, 1963, pp. 77 f. See also T. R. Fyvel, *Troublemakers,* 1962. As a current concept of criminal sociology, vandalism also appears in D. C. Gibbons, *Changing the Lawbreaker,* Englewood Cliffs, 1965, p. 35, which refers to M. B. Clinard and A. L. Wade, and others, 'Toward the Delineation of Vandalism as a Sub-Type of Juvenile Delinquency,' *Journal of Criminal Law, Criminology and Police Science,* Vol. 48, 1958, pp. 493–9. A. K. Cohen, *Delinquent Boys. The Culture of the Gang,* Glencoe (Ill.), 1955, pp. 183 ff., sees vandalism as the chief behavioural characteristic of asocial juvenile gangs in America and almost attains the concept of 'envy' when he calls this hoodlum sub-culture malicious and full of gratuitous hostility. The journal *Federal Probation,* organ of the Federal Prison Industries in the United States, presented a symposium on vandalism in the issue of March 1954 (Vol. 18).

asset that is culturally—i.e., aesthetically—over the head of the culprit, has been used since 1794, when Bishop Henri Grégoire of Blois first coined the term in connection with the alleged destruction of works of art in Rome, during its occupation by the Vandals in 455. The few belated works on vandalism available from twentieth-century German sources are concerned exclusively with showing that the Vandals did not behave in Rome like 'vandals.' To us, the point under dispute is irrelevant.

Like arson—though its victim is usually someone known to the envious man—mere vandalism, which may of course be arson, is an act that can best be accounted for by resentment or envy. Vandalism is a recurrent, everyday phenomenon of American life, and is practised more especially in new schools for the children of the poorest classes, particularly those of minority groups. On November 20, 1959, a leading article in the *New York Times* expressed indignation at the fact that architects of new schools were compelled to take account of possible vandalism. New school buildings in New York City were to have fewer and smaller windows, and these were to be protected by wire netting, steel bars and fences, thus making schools look like prisons. This influence of vandals upon school architecture was a result, according to the *Times,* of the huge number of acts of vandalism in New York. After the opening of a new school in East Harlem in February 1959, 589 windows had been broken by November. In 1958 the New York Department of Education had to replace 160,000 windows and make good the damage done by 75 cases of arson. Various observers believe that one reason for the increase of vandalism in the United States is the authorities' reluctance to make a direct approach to the culprits' parents for compensation.

It would seem to us that the frequent acts of vandalism, particularly in *new,* modern and well-equipped American schools built for the underprivileged, are evidence of the envy-motive behind the criminal act. To the slum child, the daily contrast between his 'home' and the school's air-conditioned chrome-and-glass luxury is an irritant. If he is also burdened with learning difficulties, he sees school as a world to which he will never belong. He knows that when his schooldays are over there will be no comparable place of work waiting for him. What, then, is more probable than that he should give free rein in vandalism to his rage and resentment? Revealingly the chronic acts of vandalism by high-school students, typical of the mid-fifties, have now, ten years later, reached the colleges. The emotional roots, in many cases, appear to be the same.

It is true that in the United States cases of vandalism involving children of the middle and upper classes are also becoming more frequent. Even here, however, the culprits may be turning against too perfect an environment which they did not themselves help to create. They are trying to see how much grown-ups are prepared to stomach. The increasingly broadminded 'understand-all, forgive-all' attitude of judges in juvenile courts where near-adult youths may appear might well, I believe, have some bearing on the increase of acts of vandalism by children from good homes.

Typical vandalistic behaviour is manifested by the culprit who, in November 1952, in Bridgeport (Connecticut) set fire to eight cars and said to the police: 'I couldn't afford to own an automobile . . . and I didn't want anyone else to have one.'[12] This seemed to him more satisfactory than stealing a car.

An almost tragi-comic variation of the envy-motivated delinquent was the English trade-unionist who habitually started wildcat strikes in his factory. When called to account by his union he explained his action: 'I shut the works down on several occasions because it was a nice day and I wanted to go fishing.—I did not want the other fellows to have more money in their pay packets than I did.'[13]

Envious building

Early German legal terminology actually recognizes the case of the envious man, who, in certain circumstances, is prepared to incur expense in damaging another person. Grimm's Dictionary quotes the following definition from the Augsburg building regulations: 'It is held to be envious building [Neidbau] when a prospective building is planned clearly to the detriment of a neighbour and without pressing need, or where such a building has little or no purpose, while representing great damage, and loss of light and air, to the neighbour.'

The self-destructive element in envy is plainly apparent. Just as the

[12] *Time* Magazine, November 3, 1952.

[13] *Fortune* Magazine, July 1952, p. 60.

envious man often does not wish to possess but merely to see destroyed the property he covets, he may begin by hurting himself—or at least by incurring unnecessary expenditure—simply in order to torment the man he envies. The concept of 'envious building' must have been very widespread. Thus G. H. Zinck's *Ökonomisches Lexikon* (2nd edition, 1744) defines it as 'a building forbidden in many places by law being erected not so much in the interests of the builder as out of malice, to the disadvantage and annoyance of a neighbour.'

Vengeful violence

Erich Fromm has little new to offer beyond the overworked 'frustration theory' of envy. He sees hostility based upon jealousy and envy as analogous to the aggressive behaviour of animals, children and neurotic adults; envy and jealousy are special forms of frustration, i.e., a wish thwarted or denied. According to Fromm, envy results from the fact that A not only fails to get what he wants, but that B has got it. He cites the Bible stories of Cain and of Joseph as 'classic versions' of envy and jealousy.

Following a very brief discussion of these two emotional states, Fromm introduces the concept of 'vengeful violence.' This is found mainly among the impotent (naturally, *not* only in cases of sexual impotence) and among cripples. The destruction of self-confidence in such people is said to produce but one reaction, *lex talionis*, or 'an eye for an eye.'

Fromm correctly interprets vengeful violence, as encountered today, more especially in the United States and in certain population groups, as the consequence of an experience of weakness, and he is also right in stressing that men who lead a full, productive life seldom meditate or resort to revenge, even if offended or disappointed. More questionable is his belief that it would be possible to establish by means of a questionnaire a direct connection between economic need, depressed circumstances, and the degree of such vengeful feelings among, say, the lower classes of the industrial countries. Fromm recalls here the nationalism of the lower middle class. He refers in this connection to the intensive and often fully institutionalized revenge mechanisms among the primitive peoples, explicable on the one hand by the Freudian concept of narcissism (which Fromm expands) and on the other by 'psychic scarcity' in the primitive group.[14]

From this, Fromm proceeds to 'compensatory violence,' a substitute activity for what is productive, hence itself a result of impotence. The sadist, the wantonly destructive vandal, is explicable in these terms. Sadistic pleasure in destruction as a substitute for positive activity, either denied or of which the subject is incapable, is seen by Fromm as the necessary outcome of an 'unlived and crippled life.' Yet this does not explain why throughout history so many people have become famous who were undeniably handicapped or crippled in one sense or another, and did not take the way of compensatory violence but chose instead the available means to positive achievement, their original handicap more often than not acting as a spur.

The very low rate of crime, so often noted during the post-war years in West Germany, among refugees and their children—an indubitably underprivileged group whose members could not fail to notice plenty of differences to give them cause for envy—would seem to lend probability to the following hypothesis: Envious crime—a concept which embraces most juvenile crime and vandalism in the United States—will occur chiefly in those societies whose official credo, constantly recited in school, on the political platform and in the pulpit, is universal equality. The less the individual can explain realistically the visible difference between himself and his neighbour, the more likely certain types of people are to lose self-control and to have recourse to crime motivated by envy. In contrast to this, every refugee was aware of a reason for his present deprivation that was quite unconnected with his new environment since he, along with millions of others, had been driven out of his homeland. Such feelings of aggression as may have existed were mostly directed against forces and persons which had little connection with the relative well-being of the new environment.

Sheldon and Eleanor Glueck, two American criminologists specializing in juvenile crime, asserted in a study of the subject in 1952:

> Turning next to the *feeling of resentment* or frustration, envy or dissatisfaction, this emotional attitude is far more frequent among the delinquents

[14] E. Fromm, *The Heart of Man: Its Genius for Good and Evil*, New York, 1964, pp. 27 ff.

than among the boys within the control group (74 per cent: 51 per cent). Persons in whom this attitude is strong are not so much concerned with the positive attempt or hope of bettering their own situation as with the desire that others should be denied the satisfactions and enjoyments which they feel are being withheld from themselves. Resentment, in other words, is different from mere envy or the wish to have what somebody else has got.[15]

It should be recalled here that there is a tendency in English to speak of envy as if in a sense harmless, as though nothing was involved but 'wanting something too,' the fulfilment, without resentment, of further desires. When it is thus disguised, many Americans, as I discovered by questioning them, are able to conceal from themselves the true nature of the phenomenon of envy. Apart from that concession to usage, however, the Gluecks recognized exactly what envy involves: the consuming desire that no one should have anything, the destruction of pleasure in and for others, without deriving any sort of advantage from this. A great many observations would seem to indicate that this tendency plays a significant role in the criminal personality.

[15] S. and E. Glueck, *Delinquents in the Making,* New York, 1952, p. 149.

9

The Envy of the Gods
and the Concept of Fate

I N THE MOST DIVERSE CULTURES and at all stages of man's development
we encounter the idea that man is threatened by the envy of supernatural beings. The envy of the gods, to which the Greeks attached such
significance, finds an echo in other religions. Often the dead are thought
to be envious, the more so if they were closely related to us.[1] This belief
is supported by the observation made among many primitive peoples
that their fear of ghosts, often amounting to panic, relates only to the
spirits of dead relatives. 'Why was it I who escaped death?' is one of
those age-old human enigmas which may perhaps lie at the root of one of
mankind's most widespread feelings of guilt. Many of the seventy-five
hibakusha (survivors of Hiroshima), for instance, interviewed by Robert
J. Lifton and described in his recent book, *Death in Life, Survivors of
Hiroshima,* told of their intensely ambivalent feelings: pleasure at having
survived was overshadowed by the pain of being alive *because* someone
else was dead. It is indeed true that in some cases *hibakusha* managed to
survive only by ignoring someone else who needed help. This is one of
the most basic dilemmas of human existence in any situation that is a
matter of life and death, whether in war or in a burning theatre. Yoko Ota
calls it 'the shame of the living,' perhaps the most fundamental human
guilt. I can still hear the words of J. B. Priestley in a B.B.C. broadcast on
May 8, 1945, in which he reflected on the painful riddle that posed itself
to his fellow Englishmen, indeed to all Europeans: 'Why did I stay alive
while so many perished?' Lifton writes: 'The survivor can never, inwardly, simply conclude that it was logical or right for him, and not

[1] This is also plainly evident in fairy-tale. Cf. H. von Beit, *Symbolik des Märchens,*
Bern, 1952, p. 72.

others, to survive. If (others) had not died, he would have had to; if he had not survived, someone else would have.'

Anyone who is alive, who feels or knows himself to be healthier, to eat better, to have a more flourishing crop or herd of cattle, will inevitably feel a faint sense of guilt towards those who have died or who are less fortunate. To restrain himself and to forestall such behaviour as ostentatious enjoyment or irresponsible boasting—so that envy could not even raise its head—man evolved ideas of a god, deities or powers who pursue him with the eye of envy and who punish him when he exceeds the limits.

Clearly it is very difficult for man in whatever culture, our own included, to localize and to define envy and the envious man. As Nilsson stresses, the ancient Greeks hardly ever attributed envy to one particular god or supernatural being but rather to a divine principle, a general, vaguely conceived power. There may well have been good reasons for this. It has sometimes been observed, as by Francis Bacon, or in the witchcraft beliefs of some primitive peoples, that envious man becomes really envious and malicious only when he sees that he has been detected by the object of his envy; this fact is due to the shame he feels at the inferiority which the discovery of his envy discloses. Hence the Greeks were careful not to ascribe envy to any particular god, daring to do so only sometimes in the case of Zeus, probably because he was too majestic to be accused of petty envy; his motive was seen to be, rather, a sublime sense of justice; he punished the over-powerful in the interests of compensating justice and not because he was himself envious.

The case of dualistic religions is somewhat different; these have little difficulty in ascribing envy as a motive to the principle of evil, Satan, as can be seen in Manicheism, in which Satan is moved by envy to pit himself against the light. Among the Persians, demons were believed to be responsible for envy in man. It is surely not far-fetched to suppose that a civilization of unequal citizens was able to arise under the aegis, as it were, of the Christian religion because the latter early condemned envy, which was personified in the devil, whereas God and all the saints were represented as, by definition, utterly incapable of envy towards mankind.[2]

[2] F. Bertholet, article on the envy of the gods in *Die Religion in Geschichte und Gegenwart,* Tübingen, 1930, Vol. 4, p. 488.

Agamemnon's homecoming

Aeschylus impressively illustrates the Greek fear of divine envy in his description of Agamemnon's return. The motive for human envy, as the successful man encounters it, is discovered in his very first speech:

> Rare are those mortals who a friend arrayed
> In fortune's smiles with eyes unenvying view:
> The fateful poison rankling at the heart
> A double smart inflicts; the sufferer mourns
> His own peculiar woes—then at the sight
> Of others more successful, sighs again.
> I know mankind full well, nor need to learn
> That empty as the shadow of a shade
> Are many who with smiles my presence hail. [3]

Clytemnestra, his wife, plotting the murder of her husband, has laid out a purple carpet and seeks to persuade Agamemnon to walk over it into the palace. This is no casual gesture, but, as Ranulf points out, deliberate treachery. The more Agamemnon can be involved in actions which notoriously incite the envy of the gods, the more likely is the murder to succeed. The hypocritical or naïvely frivolous method of egging on an unsuspecting person (or one acting consciously against his better judgement) to do something provocative of envy so that those who are provoked shall do one's dirty work—obstruction, say, or revenge—may be observed in many cultures.

Clytemnestra greets her husband with a fulsome panegyric:

> Oh! blest immunity from threatened woe!
> Envy, begone—too well we grief have known.
> Most loved of mortals, from this car descend
> But sully not in dust, great king, thy feet
> Which scarce have rested from the glorious work
> Of trampling down proud Troy: ye thoughtless slaves,
> Why this delay? forget ye my commands,
> With trappings to spread o'er your monarch's way?
> Be his whole path empurpled. . . .

[3] *The Agamemnon of Aeschylus*, London, 1831, p. 210.

Agamemnon at once rejects her adulation. He does not wish to see his path laid 'with hateful robes':

> Reserve such honours for the gods; frail man
> Should tremble for himself when he delights
> With stately mien to tread o'er gorgeous robes.

In the ensuing exchange between him and his wife, she seeks to dispel his fear of the envy of the gods. Finally Agamemnon gives way, but he removes his shoes and enters the house over the purple carpet with considerable uneasiness:

> Let some slave unloose
> These sandals, for with envious glance some god
> May blast me should I walk with covered feet.
> I blush to sully, thus, such precious robes,
> Objects so costly. . . .[4]

This is not enough for Clytemnestra. Again she expresses what no Greek who feared the envy of the gods would ever choose to say: 'We shall never lack for purple carpets, we have never learnt what it is to be poor.'

The chorus then takes up the motive of envy with the parable of a ship on a fair voyage which can best succeed in avoiding hidden reefs if a good measure of her cargo is voluntarily jettisoned.

The Danish sociologist Svend Ranulf, whose two-volume work on the Greeks' remarkable concept of the envy of the gods is one of the rare studies to deal with envy in detail, noticed unmistakable distaste in classical scholars, who showed a general unwillingness to assume that the ancient Greeks could ever really have ascribed to their gods anything so monstrous and despicable as envy.

Thus the Danish philologist A. B. Drachmann, to whom Ranulf owes the inspiration for his work, cites the subsidiary concept of the Greek sense of cosmic harmony. It is, he maintains, an aesthetic element in Greek thought: the envy of the gods is nothing other than the sym-

[4] Op. cit., pp. 215, 216.

metrical balance of good and bad fortune among men.[5] At this point Ranulf asks whether something is not being read into the Greeks simply because we, today, do not find it deifying that our envy-mechanism should come from the gods. As an example of the horror this idea inspires in nineteenth-century scholars, Ranulf cites U. von Wilamowitz-Moellendorff, who in his introduction to *Agamemnon* discusses the envy of the gods:

> Every child knows 'Polycrates' Ring,' the story told by Herodotus. . . . It illustrates the idea that unalloyed happiness ineluctably turns into great misery. This is but an expression of a far-reaching emotion. Everything that is perfect, beautiful, rich or brilliant is especially threatened because it provokes the envy both of men and of the gods. More especially when one of these things is ostentatiously displayed or openly publicized by one's own praise or that of others, the danger of envious destruction is more likely than ever. For envy need not damage by physical contact: the evil eye can bewitch and compel from afar. Man and god can thus wish evil upon others. Hence the cautious man protects himself by secretiveness or by apparent self-abasement. . . . Now it is certainly a good and just feeling that men should be aware of their own weakness. . . . The admonition to modesty and moderation in all things is also truly Greek. But here it plays only the most minor role. Rather, it is the basest aspects of man's nature which freely manifest themselves—envy which fears harm from its fellows because itself wishing them harm, and unseemly fear that cravenly drags down the gods to its own despicable mentality. . . . Hence the avoidance of the use of a certain divinity's name for such as is deemed harmful. . . .[6]

Erwin Rohde was similarly repelled by the Greek idea of the envy of the gods.

In the second half of the nineteenth century, envy as a governing principle was, indeed, almost universally proscribed. True individual thinkers like W. Roscher, Jacob Burckhardt, Friedrich Nietzsche, and Oliver Wendell Holmes in America recognized certain emergent social philosophies which evidently appealed to the envy-motive. But generally

---

[5] S. Ranulf, *The Jealousy of the Gods and Criminal Law at Athens,* Copenhagen, 1933, Vol. 1, p. 117.

[6] U. von Wilamowitz-Moellendorff, *Griechische Tragödien übersetzt,* Vol. 2, 6th ed., 1910, pp. 21 f.

under the influence of Christianity, with its God incapable of envy towards man, to students of ancient Greece the concept of a divine envy was an absurdity.

The Greek concept of fate

Every culture must have an explanation to offer to its members for the varying lots that fall to them. Some cultures have been successful in this task, others relatively unsuccessful. The connection between the concept of fate and human envy may, I believe, be illustrated from Homer's view of that concept.

Nilsson describes the social situation which, to many people of the Mycenaean period, represented a problem: 'Many of those who took part in the great campaigns will have lost their lives, some will have returned laden with booty and riches, others with nothing but their scars.'[7] It is revealing that the conception of fate, Moira, should be expressed in phrases all of which mean a part, share or portion. Nilsson writes: 'A goddess designated by such words cannot be personal or concrete.' The sense of 'portion' should be adhered to. 'Each had his share of the booty, or portion of the meal, the size of the share of the spoils being regulated by a binding convention, size and quality of the portions of food by a form of etiquette which we encounter several times.'[8]

Yet life, Nilsson continues, is full of unexpected events, 'and these are spoken of simply as man's share in life, his portion of what happens, as he would speak of his share of the booty or his portion of the meal.' But even when things go wrong, he will still speak of his share of what happens. 'Death is the last and final lot of man. Thus the Moira of death is spoken of more often than any other.'[9]

The distribution of portions is governed by custom and convention. If a man takes more than his due he has to bear the consequences. 'Order, however, is part of the essence of the conception of the Moira.'[10] Nilsson

---

[7] M. P. Nilsson, *Geschichte der griechischen Religion*, Vol. 1: 'Bis zur griechischen Weltherrschaft' (*Handbuch der Altertumswissenschaft*, ed. W. Otto, Section 5, Part 2, Vol. 1), Munich, 1955, p. 344.

[8] Op. cit., p. 338.

[9] Op. cit., p. 339.

[10] Op. cit., p. 339.

considers in detail the contradiction and the difficulties arising from the confrontation of personal gods and ineluctable fate. He believes that in the final analysis the gods are subordinate to the Moira. Shares of the booty and portions were distributed by the great. This would suggest the conception that someone distributed the lots, the portions, in respect of individual lives. With the possible exception of Zeus, the distributors are not individual gods, however, but, according to Nilsson, a general regulating power.[11]

The above description of the early Greek concept of fate throws important light on our view of envy and the need for a culture to come to terms with it.

We know that there is no stronger or more primordial stimulus to envy than the distribution of unequal portions of food. Man is perhaps best able to come to terms with this experience when the distributor, who has the power to distribute 'unjustly' (in the sense of the householder in the parable of the labourers in the vineyard), is seen by the recipient as presiding over an order, and as one against whose word and wisdom no one can rebel. For this reason, social systems governed by a monarchy generally have less trouble with the problem of envy than do democratic ones where the sharing out of goods in short supply is equally necessary but is not seen as unassailably legitimized.

To the Greek of that time it may have seemed very probable that indeed all unequal portions in life were due to the agency of a regulating power that could not be personified. In effect, they felt it better not to visualize too clearly, or imagine in concrete form, the distributor of lots, lest 'he' or 'she,' through the very fact of our thoughts being directed towards the divinity or the conceptually imagined demon, might notice us and begin to wonder what our lot should be. Man feels safest when the distributor of his lot in life remains anonymous, when his fate is, so to speak, what he draws in the lottery. If the distributor of lots were to be seen in too human a guise, we would necessarily ascribe to him envy, or a closely related 'book-keeping' sense of justice. Thus anyone who has so far drawn really good lots in life is unlikely to believe in a personal distributor who, after a few years, might say: 'This man has done well for long enough, now I'll let him draw a few blanks.' Zeus alone, as the supreme arbiter of life and death, sometimes appears in the *Iliad*, for

---

[11] Op. cit., p. 342.

example, as directing the battle in company with Fate. Since no one can draw death as his lot more than once, in contrast to the many thousands of portions of good and bad he received during the course of his life, the conception of a particular god who holds the scales of fate, and decides when a man's time has come, is more readily tolerable, perhaps even comforting.[12]

Nilsson cites some stories from Porphyry that are characteristic of the endeavour to avert the envy of others found in the Apollonian piety of the Greeks. Invariably the comparison involves two sacrifices made to the god, one magnificent, such as a herd of cattle, the other meagre, perhaps a few handfuls of corn from a sack. Asked which sacrifice was more acceptable, the god invariably indicated the lesser. We are given a deep insight into the underlying psychology, however, when the poor man in the story proceeds to empty the whole of his sack of corn upon the altar, whereupon he is told by the Pythia that he is now twice as abhorrent to the god as he had previously been acceptable. Nilsson concludes: 'This is a case, not of good or bad conscience, of contrast between rich and poor or pure and impure, but of boasting and vainglory. . . . What is stressed is that man should not pride himself on his piety, nor should it be ostentatious.'[13] (The consequences of his doing so need only be recalled: In witch-hunts, such as those in New England, the victims were often exceptionally pious people, whose show of godliness had drawn down upon them the envy of others.)

The Christian religion has been able only partially to solve the social problem as to how the believer who is a perfectionist can protect himself against the envy and attack of those who, in their own eyes, are less perfect. For in a monastery, the very place where virtually every cause for mutual envy has been eliminated, envious suspicion is focused upon another's over-zealous concern for his religious duties or his religious advancement.

Nemesis

The classical conception of a divine power that represents the principle of envy is linked most often with the word 'nemesis.' In Homer, all it

---

[12] Op. cit., pp. 343, 344.
[13] Op. cit., p. 615.

means is dislike, a general distaste for what is unjust. The goddess Nemesis is of much later date; she is the guardian of just measure (no one having too much or too little), but she is also the express enemy of too much happiness.

Already in Herodotus, Nilsson discovers a tendency to call the divinity 'envious.' He uses the word *phthonos,* also found in Pindar, as an alternative for Nemesis. However, Nilsson is doubtful about the translation 'envy,' whose connotations, he feels, are too malevolent.[14] The confrontation of man's hubris and its consequence of divine nemesis appears early. In Homer, who used both terms, hubris means presumption, trespass. The underlying conception, in the sense of the Moira, is that of a man who has taken portions in excess of his due. Gradually there grew out of this the idea of justice. Later it was to mean not only equality before the law, but also 'a fair share of the goods of the state, both spiritual and material. This idea of equality was deep-seated; it was the driving force behind constitutional struggles, and upon it democracy was built.'[15]

Oddly enough, as Nilsson demonstrates, the conception of hubris and nemesis gradually came to be applied to distributive justice in the life of the individual: 'The higher a man climbs, the lower he must fall so that a balance is achieved. He is best off whose fortune is modest, since his misfortune will be modest in proportion.'[16] In this conception, avoidance of envy is already clearly apparent in the form in which it is found in nearly every culture.

Nilsson leaves no room for doubt as to the major part played by envy, and fear of it, among the Greeks. He cites Svend Ranulf's comprehensive account, with one aspect of which, however, he disagrees: 'Envy is indeed a prominent trait, especially of Athenian democracy; but as Ranulf's examples are mainly those of divine envy, he falls into the error of conceiving the gods individually, as Homer does, whereas in fact envy is ascribed only to the gods in general, and of isolating this conception from that of fate of which it is correlative.'[17]

[14] Op. cit., p. 699.
[15] Op. cit., pp. 699 f.
[16] Op. cit., p. 700.
[17] Op. cit., p. 696.

Nilsson gives numerous examples from Greek thought, according to which every man must pay for happiness with unhappiness. Sophocles, Pindar, Herodotus and others return to the idea again and again; its clearest expression is probably Herodotus' story of Polycrates and Amasis, familiar to us from Schiller's poem of Polycrates' ring. Nilsson selects this particular story to illustrate the point that disproportionate praise brings misfortune in its wake. It must be countered by some form of self-abasement, such as spitting in one's bosom or an obscene gesture. In this the Greeks behaved in the same way as primitive peoples. What we have here is the evil eye complex. Croesus, according to Herodotus, was struck by fate because he regarded himself as the happiest of men. Again and again one finds sayings and warnings such as: God's lightning strikes the largest animals, the biggest buildings, the tallest trees. Whatever excels, God disables.

Nilsson rightly supposes that this sort of outlook on life leads to quietism. 'Since the greatest are most vulnerable to the blows of fate, it is better to be among the lesser ones.'[18]

Acting in the face of divine envy

This view of Nilsson's corresponds with my basic thesis on the inhibiting effect of envy in all societies. But again, Nilsson asks the significant question as to why fear of hubris and nemesis did not cripple the Greeks' delight in action and achievement; he finds at least part of the answer in the fact that envy had been blunted because no individual god was ever identified with it, but only a very general divine force—in the final analysis a kind of fate. What will be, will be. If I am destined to achieve something that brings nemesis down upon my head, that is part of my lot. Simple fatalism restored to man so much courage and defiance that he was prepared to risk incurring the envy of the gods, not merely to tremble before it.[19]

The British Hellenist E. R. Dodds's penetrating work, *The Greeks and the Irrational* (1951), in discussing Ranulf and Nilsson, attempts a more far-reaching interpretation of divine envy. He makes use not only of ethnological data from other cultures, but also of more recent psycholog-

[18] Op. cit., pp. 696 ff.
[19] Op. cit., p. 701.

ical theories. His view of the phenomenon enables it to be included in my general theory of envy.

Aeschylus spoke of the envy of the gods as of a venerable and immemorial doctrine. Dodds points out that the idea that too much success, if boasted about, involves supernatural danger is found independently in the most diverse cultures. Hence it must be deeply rooted in human nature, as can be seen from our own custom of touching wood immediately after making an optimistic or boastful remark which a subsequent event might cause us to regret.[20]

Lévy-Bruhl and others have found among many primitive peoples a non-moralizing belief that awareness of one's own favourable position invites danger from some sort of power. This conception appears in a moralizing form in ancient China: 'If you are rich and of high degree, you become proud and so expose yourself to inevitable ruin. If all goes well with you, it is expedient to keep yourself in the background' (*Tao Tê Ching,* 4th century B.C.).

In this connection it is tempting to recall the song from the American musical *Oklahoma!* ('I got a wonderful feeling, everything's going my way'): It is no doubt an indication of the relatively carefree American national character and the American's relative freedom from fear of divine envy—a fact of decisive importance—that a song of this kind could become popular and even conceivable as a folk song. Most cultures would regard this self-satisfied couplet as a most dangerous challenge to fate.

Dodds also cites the Old Testament, in which God's envy is mentioned several times, as for instance in Isaiah (10:12ff.), and believes that the uninhibited boasting of Homeric characters shows that the envy of the gods was not really taken seriously at that time. It was not until late archaic and early classical times that the fear of *phthonos* assumed the proportions almost of a religious threat. The notion then gradually became a moralistic one: it is not just that the mere sin of too much success incurs the punishment of a divine power simply because the latter is envious; rather, it is believed that success leads to *koros,* self-satisfaction, which in turn gives rise to hubris, the arrogance of assured success. And this is punished.[21]

---

[20] E. R. Dodds, *The Greeks and the Irrational,* Berkeley and Los Angeles, 1951, p. 30.
[21] Op. cit., pp. 30 ff.

Like Nilsson, Dodds is inclined to seek a sociological explanation for the fear of divine envy: personal circumstances in Greece were frugal and dangerous; class conflict, changes in social stratification, and the general advance of hitherto oppressed elements of the population may have been responsible for the popularity of the idea that the misfortune of the rich, great and famous was willed by God. In contrast to Homer, for whom the rich were also as a rule especially virtuous, a poet like Hesiod, the bard of the helots, as a king once called him, gives voice to ideas of a divine distributive justice.[22]

The most determined attempt at an interpretation in terms of class warfare is that made by Svend Ranulf in the study already mentioned. Dodds allows that *phthonos* could be regarded simply as the projection of the unsuccessful man's resentment of the successful man, and rightly observes: 'Certainly human and divine envy have much in common; both, for instance, operate through the evil eye.' But Dodds then seeks to limit Ranulf's theory by recalling Piaget's remark that children sometimes think the opposite of what they really want, as though reality were scheming to thwart their wishes. Dodds agrees with A. R. Burn in seeing signs of such ideas in Hesiod. He attributes them to the emotional situation of the young man who, like the Greeks of this period or the children of our Western culture, suffered a very strict parental upbringing which he secretly called in question. Thus the resulting repressed guilt feelings have produced an attitude of such mistrust towards reality that even one's true wishes are, if possible, kept concealed.[23]

We would offer a much simpler explanation: The tendency observed in children, as it were teleologically, to keep as a potential what they really long for by thinking the exact opposite, is found in many taboos of primitive peoples who always circumscribe what they fear or desire in order to ward off the one and prevent the loss of the other. But beneath this lies nothing more than the quite general fear that the envy of companions, sublimated in the form of vaguely feared spirits or powers, might thwart the fulfilment of the wish were this to become known.

[22] Op. cit., p. 45.
[23] Op. cit., p. 62.

'Pleasure is forbidden!'

Paul Tournier, a Swiss psychotherapist, believes, like other psycho-analysts, it can be assumed that strict parents are largely responsible for instilling in their children the idea that everything that gives pleasure is sinful. Many parents told him that one thing they remembered from their upbringing was the principle, 'Pleasure is forbidden!' Thereafter the adult cannot enjoy anything without a bad conscience spoiling his pleasure.

'People who have been brought up with this idea burden themselves with heavy duties or unnecessary sacrifices, their only object being to allow themselves some subsequent pleasure without a bad conscience. They keep complicated mental accounts, behind which anxiety is always present in some degree. . . .'[24]

Tournier points out that this compulsive behaviour has little to do with Christianity, which in principle does not conceive God as a being who begrudges his children any kind of pleasure, even if it is undeserved. The feeling of guilt is, indeed, regarded as a definite sin, that of melancholy.

Here we would attempt a wider interpretation. Anyone who is familiar with the anxiety and fear of various primitive peoples—a feeling to which they always succumb whenever they have been lucky—and who also knows the extreme laxity with which these people are so often brought up, is unlikely to see over-strict parental control as the chief cause of a bad conscience about pleasure and happiness. What is involved is rather the primeval anxiety in man arising from the experi-ence of envy. It has little to do with any particular culture or form of society, or with the type of upbringing, though these may intensify or diminish it. Though strict, puritanical parents may, by their remarks and the values they represent, induce feelings of guilt in their children, they are themselves the victims of their own anxiety about envy. And if this were to be referred back to the parents' parents, we would be involved in an infinite regression.

The condition of anxiety, the feeling of guilt, the fear of a retributive catastrophe (Polycrates' ring)—all this is a combination of superstition and empirically verifiable (i.e., realistic) anxiety about another per-son's—usually a neighbour's—envy. More precisely, nearly all super-

[24] P. Tournier, *Echtes und falsches Schuldgefühl*, Zurich and Stuttgart, 1959, pp. 15 f.

stition can be found to derive its dynamic from this particular anxiety about envy, and may be interpreted as a system of ritual environment-control directed against envy. It is deeply rooted in every one of us, more or less independently of the actual culture and its level of civilizing technology. This can be demonstrated. A situation of happiness, of assured health, of imminent success is described to someone who is then asked to imagine himself in that situation. Having done this, he is asked: 'What is the first thing you'd do?' The answer is nearly always: 'I'd touch wood, or make this or that sign.' On being further pressed, and asked to think back as to why he would have done this, he is likely, for the first time in his life, to discover his fear of the envy of some anonymous other, which he has thus sought to assuage. But as long as the Christian (or at least the man still partially imbued with Christian culture) in his attitude to his fellow men still intuitively models his conduct on a supernatural exemplar, the potential innovator's neighbour, fellow villager or colleague will, in ideal circumstances (reality being often in default), represent less of an inhibition or threat than would have been the case in the pre- or non-Christian world.

Incidentally, agnostic and atheistic societies, as well as states and régimes, have profited by the opportunity for individual achievement made possible by Christianity, because they have often developed a system of incentives which rewards the individual extravagantly but is tolerable to him only because he feels in some measure secure against the envy of his companions—thanks to the persistence, albeit in diluted form, of Christian values.

The hour of fate in Scandinavian mythology

The heathen mythology of the north also contains ideas which are partly reminiscent of the Greek view of divine envy. These, too, will have helped members of a community to come to terms emotionally with the obvious inequalities of fortune.

As Karl Simrock shows, fate makes a personal appearance

in the Regin, the world-ordering, world-advising powers which are the gods themselves and hence not, of course, a power superior to the gods. . . . They 'impart' to man his 'modest share,' disclosing it in judgement, as we see in the *Gautreks,* Chapter 7, how Hrossharsgrani (horse-hair bearded) wakes his ward, Starkadr, at midnight, telling him to go with him. They go by boat to an island, disembark and find a crowd of people assembled in a forest clearing. They are attending a court of justice. Eleven men sit on chairs; the twelfth chair is vacant. Thereupon Hrossharsgrani takes the twelfth chair, being greeted by all as Odin. Now he demands that the judges determine Starkadr's fate. Upon which Thor begins to speak: 'Alfhild, Starkadr's mother, chose, instead of Asathor, a dog of a Jutex to father her son: therefore I shall cause Starkadr to have neither son nor daughter and to be the last of his race.' Thereupon Odin speaks: 'I shall cause him to live for three generations.' Thor speaks: 'In every generation he shall perform a deed of envy, a deed of shame.' Odin speaks: 'I shall cause him to have the best weapons and raiment.' Thor replies: 'I shall cause him to have neither lands nor estates.' Odin says: 'My gift to him is that he shall have much money and goods.' Thor replies: 'I lay upon him that he shall never think he has enough.' Odin speaks: 'I bestow on him victory and skill in battle.' Thor retorts: 'I bestow this upon him, that from every battle he returns wounded to the bone.' Odin speaks: 'I give him the art of the skald, so that poetry is to him as speech.' Thor retorts: 'He shall not be able to remember his poetry.' Odin speaks: 'I shall cause the noblest and best men to honour him.' Thor speaks: 'He shall be hated by the whole people.' Then the judges tell Starkadr everything that has been said, and thus the court ends. Thereupon Hrossharsgrani returns to the boat with Starkadr.

In the same way that Thor qualifies each of Odin's gifts with a codicil— just like the youngest fairy, Norn or wise woman in our fairy stories—so Odin is able to mitigate Thor's harmful impositions and to compensate for the land that he denies Starkadr by a profusion of movable property.[25]

It is clear that in this saga an attempt is being made to deal with the problem of fate, and the (envy-provoking) gifts fortune bestows on man, by explaining one man's actual fate on earth as a dispute between envious and generous powers. Here we have the projection of human envy on to the world of the gods, as with the Greeks. In this connection it is interesting to find the expressions 'deed of envy,' 'deed of shame,' factors which Odin seeks to eliminate from Starkadr's fate by apportioning to him that which would render him free of envy.

As we have seen again and again, it is enormously important for any

[25] K. Simrock, *Handbuch der deutschen Mythologie mit Einschluss der nordischen,* 4th ed., Bonn, 1874, p. 164.

human community to find some sort of explanation for the disparate fates, fortunate or unfortunate, of its members. This is necessary in order that the man who is favoured by fate may not suffer too much from a bad social conscience, that is, from the fear of being consumed by envy of the favoured man. Some cultures have not succeeded in achieving this either by psychological, mythological or religious means. Northern mythology seeks to tackle it by the concept of the hour of fate. Since every individual has his own personal and unique hour of birth, the painful problems that face every community as a result of disparate fates can be solved by coupling fate with the moment of birth. Simrock gives examples of these facts:

> Otherwise fate is impersonal, as the following account shows. . . . It is said of the Valkyrie that they set out to work Orlog, to mete out fate, to decide wars. Fates are laid and set, primeval decrees, primeval decisions, which man cannot escape, and to which even the gods are subject.
> Fortune is pre-determined and depends on the hour of birth: our fortune is sung in the cradle, an expression that alludes to those gift-bestowing Norns or fairies who come to the newly born child to 'create' its fortune. In Old High German the hour itself is called *hwila* and the fortune linked with it *hwilsalida* or *vilsaelda,* no doubt also imagined as personal, since it resembles the gift-bestowing Norns. The influence of the stars is a belief of later date, and refers to the 'star of the Wise Men'. . . . Those born at a lucky hour were called children of fortune. When it was said of them that they were born with a caul (lucky cap), also known as a helmet, the idea had some connection with nature, since some children are in fact born with a thin membrane round the head. This used to be carefully preserved and buried beneath the threshold. The child's guardian spirit, or a part of his soul, was supposed to dwell therein.[26]

Shame and guilt

The psychoanalyst Gerhart Piers has thrown some light on the personality change which helps to explain the modern creative era of relative freedom from the fear of being envied. Piers distinguishes between two personality types which may be seen as corresponding to two cultural types: the person burdened by a sense of guilt and the person filled with

[26] Op. cit., p. 165.

shame. A person who feels guilt is reticent and his character constrained. His early identifications, together with later ones based upon them relate to nonconstructive images. The guilt-laden person is disinclined to act, is passive and turns against the self. Piers writes: 'Guilt-engendered activity is at best *restitution* (sacrifice, propitiation, atonement) which rarely frees, but brings with it resentment and frustration rage, which in turn feed new guilt into the system.'[27]

By contrast, Piers sees the shame-driven individual as having better potentialities for maturation and progress. Shame arises when someone fails to attain the goals he has set himself; guilt frequently results from that very attainment of goals which, for the good of others, it is felt, would have been better unattained. The guilt-ridden person, therefore, is inclined in the first instance to placate the real or supposedly envious, the evil eye of others. Both mechanisms, however, that of shame and that of guilt, are necessary, if the child is to become a socialized adult, but these elements may be over-compensated either in an individual or in a culture.

Social conformity achieved through a sense of guilt will essentially be one of submission, that achieved through shame will be one of identification. According to Piers, Western culture seems to have undergone a gradual change:

> The highly patriarchal, feudal and hierarchical society before the Reformation put a high emphasis on guilt. Guilt before God was an accepted and practically unalterable fact; everyone was essentially equal in this so that there was no distinction or possibility of achieving any distinction except by degrees of submission; humiliation before God-Father was of the essence of human existence and no matter for shame.

This development he sees as having reached its climax in the Reformation. At the same time a new trend emerged. This was the emphasis put upon individual responsibility (Luther's *On the Liberty of a Christian Man*). According to Piers, the importance attached to an immanent conscience, over and above the allegiance to a transcendental God, reflects the internationalization of guilt, which is absorbed into the self.

Piers believes, however, that such a process contains the beginning of

[27] G. Piers and M. B. Singer, *Shame and Guilt. A Psychoanalytical and Cultural Study,* Springfield, 1953, pp. 28 f.

a turning away from the irrationality of this guilt concept. Although Protestantism retains the dogma of original sin, it provides the opportunity, particularly in Calvinism with its division into the 'elect' and the 'rejected,' for differentiation and for constructive self-comparison with others. The growing emphasis on rationality, work and success demands aggressiveness without guilt. This trend has been increased by capitalism and technology.

Whereas previously work was seen and experienced as a God-inflicted punishment, as drudgery which enables us to expiate the pressing sense of guilt, toil and work now become idealized. They are the road to accomplishment and distinction. Piers writes: 'The beggar in early Christianity could be God's child, a successful penitent, and even glorified as saint: in Protestant acquisitive status society, he "ought to be ashamed." '[28]

Religion without envy

Max Weber distinguishes between the two basically different attitudes that may be assumed by a supernatural power in a given religion towards the good fortune and well-being of the believer: (1) its joyful unenvying recognition, or (2) the envy of gods or demons.

> In spite of, not through, the gods, and frequently in opposition to them, the hero maintains a more than ordinary stature. In this the Homeric and part of the ancient Indian epic is characteristically opposed both to the bureaucratic-Chinese and the priestly-Judaic historiography, in that in the latter the 'legitimacy' of good luck as God's reward for approved virtue is far more strongly in evidence. On the other hand, the connection between misfortune and the anger and envy of demons or gods is extremely widespread.

In this connection Weber recalls that anyone inflicted with an infirmity, or sorely tried by fate, is regarded in nearly all popular religions, that of ancient Judaism, and in particular that of modern China, as one smitten by divine anger, who may not consort with the godly and fortunate before the face of God. Indeed, in 'almost every ethical form of

[28] Op. cit., pp. 35 f.

religion, the privileged classes and the priest who serves them see the individual's positively or negatively privileged social position as in some way religiously deserved, and only the forms of legitimizing the fortunate position change.'[29]

To draw the simplistic conclusion from these views—in the sense of Marxism, perhaps—that religion is exploited by the upper classes to provide opium for the lower, would be to ignore what we have repeatedly shown to be imperative in any society: to make discrepancies in status emotionally tolerable to the individual and capable of being rationalized. Systems of belief designed to control envy might be despised as social opium were it possible to demonstrate that the definitive elimination of certain economic conditions relating to property, class, etc. would eradicate mutual envy from this world. But this cannot be done.

It would seem more probable that the social need to achieve control over the worst problems of envy in human co-existence has brought about the reorientation of existing systems of religion so as to legitimize noticeable differences in individual circumstances in the interests of social peace. Thus, as has repeatedly been seen, the American cultural ethos, the popular mentality in the nineteenth century, created, quite independently of religious conceptions but in conjunction with them, a myth of the successful man which, much to the distress of the social critic, made inequalities emotionally tolerable. It would, however, be wrong to assume that individual authors or other interested parties had conjured up a myth and imposed it upon public opinion in order to legitimize and protect economic inequality. In many cases, rather, the existence of such an ideology alone permitted a mode of behaviour leading to inequality of achievement in business. At least it would seem probable that the human qualities and modes of behaviour requisite for the settlement and domination of the North American continent had helped to produce an ideology capable of legitimizing a state of progressive inequality.

New Testament ethics and the modern world

The ethic taught by the New Testament sought to secure differentiated human existence in a world full of envious people and unlikely to evolve

[29] Max Weber, *Wirtschaft und Gesellschaft,* Tübingen, 1925, Vol. 1, p. 281.

into a society of equals. A society from which all cause for envy had disappeared would not need the moral message of Christianity. Again and again we find parables the tenor of which is quite clearly the immorality, the sin of envy. One should love one's neighbour as one-self—for the very reason that this will protect him against our envy and hostility. Naturally, the avoidance of certain arrogant and ostentatious gestures, such as extravagance—but not of meaningful activity, the feast, excellence of achievement—is essential, if only to appease the envious. In such passages the New Testament nearly always mentions the envious man, exhorting him, in as much as he is mature and a Christian, to come to terms with the inequality of his fellow men.

In the West, the historical achievement of this Christian ethic is to have encouraged and protected, if not to have been actually responsible for the extent of, the exercise of human creative powers through the control of envy.

Yet the envious succeeded in perverting that ethic by adapting the message to their own ends: kill-joy, ascetic morality whispers persuasively to the joyful, lucky or successful person: 'Feel guilty, feel ashamed, for you're envied by those beneath you. Their envy is your fault. Your very existence causes them to sin. What we need is a society of equals, so that no one will be envious.' Thus it is no longer the envious who must discipline and control themselves and practise love of their neighbour, it is their victim who must change—and change for the worse, in conformity with envy's own yardstick.

Yet the mere conquest of envy, taught in categorical parables in which the envious man is shown to be displeasing to the Lord and no reasons are given why inequality of treatment, opportunity and happiness in this life should be accepted and not begrudged, is not the whole import of the New Testament. On the eschatological plane the oppressed, the un-fortunate and the victims of fate are further told, perhaps in order to help them overcome their envy of more fortunate companions and contemporaries:

'After death there is in store for you (maybe) a kingdom of heaven where all (in so far as they manage to get there) will be equal. All men are equal before God, whether kings or beggars when in this world; indeed, the poor have an even better chance of going to heaven.'

But here again the envious have succeeded in usurping the New Testament message. The doctrine, progressively secularized, came to mean a mission to establish an egalitarian society, to achieve a levelling-out, a state of uniformity here and now, in this world. The egalitarian utopia is respectably cloaked in the stuff of the New Testament. Since all will be equal before God (and have been created equal *ab initio* for the purpose of ultimate transcendental equality), all must be as equal as possible in society here on earth. This doctrine cannot, without chicanery, be read anywhere into the New Testament. Nor should the fact be overlooked that the realization of an egalitarian society would render the context of Christian ethics, for a greater part, superfluous.[30]

[30] See, e.g., Theodoros Nikolaou, *Der Neid bei Johannes Chrysostomus,* Bonn, 1969.

10

The Envious Man
in Fiction

THE ONLY LITERARY WORKS with the title *Envy* seem to be a French
and a Russian novel and a German short story. But Herman Melville's last work, *Billy Budd,* deserves that title. It is perhaps the most
profound attempt in fiction to discuss the problem of envy in human
existence.

Herman Melville

Billy Budd, a big, fair, good-looking sailor on board a merchantman, is
impressed into the Royal Navy. His captain complains to the naval officer
of the great loss this means to him. In Budd he is losing one of his best
sailors and one who, by sheer kindness and availability, has made a
peaceful crew of the wild rabble on board. When Budd first arrived, the
captain says, only one person took an immediate dislike to him, a bad
character whose motive he states precisely: envy of the newcomer
because everyone else liked him so much.[1] After picking a quarrel with
Billy Budd, however, the envious character was so promptly and thoroughly thrashed that from then on he, also, was one of his friends. The
captain fears unrest in his crew if Budd, the peacemaker, leaves it. But
characteristically Budd himself voluntarily submits to conscription
aboard the warship.

Melville depicts Budd not only as an exceptionally handsome and
skilled young seaman; we are also told that he is probably a foundling of
aristocratic birth. But Budd has a slight impediment—excitement de-

[1] H. Melville, 'Billy Budd,' in *The Portable Melville,* ed. J. Leyda, New York, 1952,
p. 643.

prives him of the power of speech. Billy Budd's downfall stems from the person of the master-at-arms, John Claggart. Melville intimates by hints about Claggart's origins and his civilian career that this is a man who, on several counts, is seething with resentment against society and life in general.

Billy Budd gets on well with his shipmates. He is popular and in addition does his utmost to carry out his duties with painstaking efficiency. Having, at the very beginning of his service, witnessed the flogging of a sailor for a minor mistake, Billy seeks to avoid attracting the attention of his superiors. But he soon notices that minor accidents keep befalling him. His gear, carefully stowed, is in disorder. The malice of inanimate objects constantly thwarts his endeavour to be a perfect seaman. He discusses this with an old sailor who explains that the master-at-arms is down on him. This Billy cannot believe, since his shipmates have told him that the master-at-arms always calls him 'the sweet and pleasant young fellow.' For Billy, Claggart always has a friendly word and a smile.

Melville several times describes the petty officer's envious look of hatred when he knows himself unobserved either by his victim or by the other sailors. Melville also muses on the fact that the envious man's chosen victim is seldom able to detect the intentions and feelings of his persecutor from his expression or behaviour. Resentment and envy are hostile feelings that are easily concealed, and which it is often essential to disguise if the plot is to succeed.

Billy Budd, Melville's embodiment of everything that is innocent, good and harmless, cannot comprehend why Claggart, whom he seeks to please by the exemplary performance of his duties, pursues him with the bitterest envy simply because Billy is the man he is. Thus, before relating the tragic events, Melville interpolates an analysis of envy.

After Melville has shown the reader what Billy and a number of his shipmates refuse to believe, namely, that 'Claggart is down on him,' and has confirmed this through the mouth of one of the crew, he looks for possible motives. Several are discussed and rejected before, very cautiously and gradually, Melville advances envy. At first, all he says is:

> . . . yet the cause [of Billy's persecution by the master-at-arms], necessarily to be assumed as the sole one assignable, is in its very realism as much

charged with that prime element of Radcliffian romance, *the mysterious,* as any that the ingenuity of the author of *The Mysteries of Udolpho* could devise. For what can more partake of the mysterious than an antipathy spontaneous and profound, such as is evoked in certain exceptional mortals by the mere aspect of some other mortal, however harmless he may be, if not called forth by this very harmlessness itself?[2]

The novelist thus perceives something that the modern social scientist is seldom able to perceive, because the latter seeks the primary cause of evil outside the perpetrator. Envy, hatred and hostility may be provoked in the aggressor while the man with whom the stimuli originated can in no way prevent this from happening. Only self-disfigurement or self-abasement might prevent envy in the other. With an understanding of the problems of human relations on board a warship—problems which modern small-group research, in costly and laborious experiments, claims to have solved anew—Melville describes the social climate in which the drama is played out:

> Now there can exist no irritating juxtaposition of dissimilar personalities comparable to that which is possible aboard a great warship fully manned and at sea. There, every day among all ranks almost every man comes into more or less of contact with almost every other man. Wholly there to avoid even the sight of an aggravating object one must needs give it Jonah's toss or jump overboard himself. Imagine how all this might eventually operate on some peculiar human creature the direct reverse of a saint.[3]

Many a novelist and most sociologists of our time would be content to cut short the analysis of Claggart at this point. Melville continues: 'But for the adequate comprehending of Claggart by a normal nature these hints are insufficient. To pass from a normal nature to him one must cross "the deadly space between." And this is best done by indirection.'[4]

So far, Melville has not introduced the concept of envy or resentment. He first recounts a conversation he had once had with a scholar on the

[2] Op. cit., pp. 672 f.

[3] Op. cit., p. 673.

[4] Op. cit., p. 673.

subject of worldly wisdom and the understanding of human nature. The scholar seeks to convince Melville that worldly experience does not of itself entail knowledge of the deeper labyrinths of human nature. He concludes with the remark: 'Coke and Blackstone [jurists whose writings are legal classics] hardly shed so much light into obscure spiritual places as the Hebrew prophets. And who were they? Mostly recluses.'

At first, Melville says, he did not see this. Now, faced with the task of explaining Claggart's antipathy to Billy Budd, he believes he understands his old friend's advice and says:

'And indeed, if that lexicon which is based on Holy Writ were any longer popular, one might with less difficulty define and denominate certain phenomenal men. As it is, one must turn to some authority not liable to the charge of being tinctured with the Biblical element.'[5]

Melville is no doubt inferring that the problem of envy is frequently discussed in the Old and New Testaments. Yet he himself goes on for nearly three more pages before he lets fall the decisive word. He is set to prove conclusively that the malice in Claggart is something which the environmental theory, later so popular, cannot explain. The evil in Claggart lies at his very core, quite independent of the world around him.

Melville quotes a definition of 'natural depravity' attributed to Plato: 'Natural Depravity: a depravity according to nature.' Melville hastens to warn us against the error of believing that what is meant here is the depravity of the whole of mankind, in Calvin's sense. It is found only in certain individuals. And 'Not many are the examples of this depravity which the gallows and jail supply.' Claggart's depravity, for which Melville is seeking the right word, is always dominated by the intellect. In a brief and masterly paragraph that might have come from the pen of a Scheler or a Nietzsche, the author of *Billy Budd* takes us into the phenomenological sphere of the envious personality—without having once mentioned the word 'envy':

> Civilization [by which Melville clearly means something like the educated, worldly-wise, urbane man], especially if of the austerer sort, is auspicious to it. It folds itself in the mantle of respectability. It has its certain negative virtues serving as silent auxiliaries. It never allows wine to

[5] Op. cit., p. 674.

get within its guard. It is not going too far to say that it is without vices or small sins. There is a phenomenal pride in it that excludes them from anything mercenary or avaricious. In short the depravity here meant partakes nothing of the sordid or sensual. It is serious, but free from acerbity. Though no flatterer of mankind it never speaks ill of it.[6]

A man so endowed by nature should, Melville thinks, be altogether subject to the law of reason. In reality, however, such natures are capable of the greatest irrationality, and such a man will, 'toward the accomplishment of an aim which in wantonness of malignity would seem to partake of the insane . . . direct a cool judgement, sagacious and sound.'[7] Melville sees such people as blinded by their madness, though to the ordinary observer their actions are indistinguishable from the normal. They never announce their true aim, yet their methods and mode of behaviour are always completely rational. Claggart was that kind of man, possessed of an inward malice not wholly explicable from his environment, but which, as Melville writes, was innate—in other words, 'a depravity according to nature.'[8]

The reluctance to attribute envy

Up to this point the author has not once used the word 'envy.' But in Claggart's characterization there is some evidence of those envious characteristics so often found in literature: he hides behind the mask of negative virtues such as spartan asceticism, his malignity is not to be bought off, he is unbribable, he never speaks ill of mankind, he appears to be extremely reasonable and yet is capable of the folly of self-injury if he can thus get at the object of his envy.

Here Melville interposes the digression on lawyers, experts and clerics. He asks whether the phenomenon (still not called envy) just described in Claggart which is always denied, or at least concealed, is not the motive behind the deed for which juries in many a criminal case vainly rack their brains. Surely, then, recourse should be had to men who know about the 'rabies of the heart,' rather than to ordinary doctors?[9]

[6] Op. cit., pp. 674 f.

[7] Op. cit., p. 675.

[8] Op. cit., p. 675.

[9] Op. cit., p. 676.

This shows remarkable insight in Melville. There has remained in criminological literature and practice up to the present a noticeable aversion towards express reference to the envy-motive, although there is convincing evidence in other sources of its significance in crime.

Not till now, forty pages after the beginning of the story, does Melville introduce the concept of envy, in a section headed 'Pale ire, envy, and despair,' the words Milton uses to characterize Satan. From this point, envy recurs again and again as the motive behind the master-at-arms' persecution of Billy Budd. Claggart is himself handsome, but his frequent ironic remarks about the sailor's beauty are explained by the author as envy:

> Now envy and antipathy, passions irreconcilable in reason, nevertheless in fact may spring conjoined like Chang and Eng in one birth. Is envy then such a monster? Well, though many an arraigned mortal has in hopes of mitigated penalty pleaded guilty to horrible actions, did ever anybody seriously confess to envy? Something there is in it universally felt to be more shameful than even felonious crime. And not only does everybody disown it but the better sort are inclined to incredulity when it is in earnest imputed to an intelligent man. But since its lodgement is in the heart not the brain, no degree of intellect supplies a guarantee against it.[10]

The passion of envy is kept secret by all men, regardless of their culture and language, more fearfully and shamefully than any form of erotic passion or perversion. To become a topic for literature and polite conversation, the latter needed a Sigmund Freud and his school. And it is no coincidence that Melville wrote this novel, in which envy is depicted in all its dangerous ugliness, at the end of his very long life fraught with privation and disappointment; for he must completely have resigned himself to his personal fate and to his lack of success in his own time.

In Claggart it was no vulgar envy that the author depicted, not just morbid jealousy which 'marred Saul's visage perturbedly brooding on the comely young David.' 'Claggart's envy struck deeper.' He sensed that Billy's outward beauty was related to a nature innocent of evil and envy. It was this strange moral phenomenon that drove Claggart to extremes of envy.

Melville even recognizes the paranoid aspect of such envy; because

---

[10] Op. cit., p. 677.

Claggart found it both inconceivable and intolerable that Billy should fail entirely to return his hatred, he read deliberate insults into chance happenings, like the spilling of the soup, so that his envy of Billy could find nourishment in self-righteous contempt and indignation.[11]

The blind spot in Melville scholars towards the envy-motive in Billy Budd

It is not just the social sciences of this century that exhibit a blind spot so far as envy is concerned, but also its literary criticism. When a writer of Herman Melville's standing devotes many pages of his last work to preparing the reader, in exemplary fashion, for the dominant motive of the drama's enigmatic central character, when he provides in addition what amounts to a phenomenology of envy from the standpoint of depth psychology, and when he chooses this concept, in a special series of words taken from Milton's *Paradise Lost,* as a chapter heading, it might be supposed that Melville scholars, at least when treating of this novel, would be bound to mention, if only once, Melville's attempt to solve the riddle of envy and of crime resulting from it. We look in vain for any such mention. A systematic survey of works on *Billy Budd* reveals that most of them totally disregard the problem of envy. This is the more surprising in that Melville repeatedly referred to the motive in other works, and was concerned with its metaphysics in discussing John Milton.[12]

---

[11] Op. cit., pp. 678 f.

[12] Cf., for example, 'Jackson, in *Redburn,* who seemed specially to hate a young sailor—Redburn himself—on account of his youth, fair cheeks, and good health . . . Radney of The Town-Ho's story in *Moby Dick* (ch. 54), who also envies a handsome and popular sailor.' (*Herman Melville: Billy Budd, sailor, reading Text and genetic Text, edited from the Manuscript with Introduction and Notes,* by H. Hayford and M. M. Sealts, 2nd ed., London and Chicago, 1963, p. 32.) Or in H. F. Pommer: 'Redburn believed that one cause of Jackson's hatred for him was *envy* of his physical well being: For I was young and handsome . . . whereas he was being consumed by an incurable malady that was eating up his vitals. A similar case was that of the Belfast sailor who was continually being abused and snubbed by Jackson, who seemed to hate him cordially, because of his great strength and fine person, and particularly because of his red cheeks' (*Redburn,* pp. 72, 356, 356–7, 374, 376.) Jealousy not very different from this was part of Satan's motivation too: Milton, *Paradise Lost,* IX, 119–30. (*Milton and Melville,* Pittsburgh, 1950, pp. 85 f.)

In some 280 pages of what is now apparently a manual much used by American college students, Merlin Bowen offers an analysis of Melville. It deals exhaustively with *Billy Budd,* from page 216 to 233, and in ten other passages in various parts of the book. While there is frequent mention of Claggart as the symbol of evil, there is not one word about the envy-motive, so unmistakably stressed and carefully developed by Melville.

Bowen avoids the term, stating only that Claggart is filled with malice and evil. His longest section concerns the conflict of motives in Captain Vere. And even when he returns on occasion to the supposed motives of the informer, Claggart, he does not get beyond generalizations (the puzzle of depravity), or mentions only that most superficial motive, shown clearly enough by Melville to derive from envy: '. . . Claggart whose covert hatred, feeding upon a supposed injury . . . '[13] Melville would not have had to construct half the novel upon the envy-motive had

---

The connection between Melville's *Billy Budd* and Milton's portrayal of envy in Satan is obvious: 'Finally there is the heading of the second chapter analyzing the master-at-arms' character: "Pale ire, envy, and despair." (*Billy Budd,* XIII, p. 48). These words Milton used of Satan's emotions upon first sight of Eden (*P.L.* IV, 115). Melville used them to introduce his analysis of Claggart's envy upon sight of Billy— and perhaps to hint at the cause of Claggart's pallor. "Claggart's was no vulgar form of (envy)" . . . ' (*Billy Budd,* XIII, p. 48). (Op. cit., p. 88.)

The same observation is found again in R. Mason's *The Spirit above the Dust. A Study of Herman Melville,* London, 1951: 'And Melville, by quoting as epigraph to the section introducing Claggart the half-line 'Pale ire, envy and despair' from the scene of Satan's approach to Eden, explicitly confirms the reference' (p. 252).

L. Thompson, *Melville's Quarrel with God,* 1952, discusses the parallel in greater detail: 'In this particular Billy was a striking instance that the arch-interferer, the envious marplot of Eden, still has more or less to do with every human consignment to this planet of earth' (p. 366); 'The many cross references between *Billy Budd* and *Paradise Lost* are sometimes obvious and sometimes subtle; but one of the most obvious is a direct quotation which Melville uses as the title or motto for chapter eleven: 'Pale ire, envy and despair' . . . Melville uses these words to describe Claggart's mixed feelings when he looks on Billy. Envying Billy his innocence, Claggart yet views that innocence with disdain . . . Melville's handling of it recalls the remarks of Milton's Satan as he enviously soliloquizes, while watching Adam and Eve' (pp. 370 f.).

[13] M. Bowen, *The Long Encounter, Self and Experience in the Writings of Herman Melville,* Chicago, 1960, p. 229. N. Arvin, *Herman Melville,* London, 1950, also fails to mention envy as Claggart's motive.

he merely intended to explain Claggart's hatred of Billy Budd in terms of what Claggart supposed to be insolence on Billy's part. No reader, indeed, could possibly deduce from Bowen's book that in *Billy Budd* Melville had given one of the most detailed analyses of envy and one, moreover, of crucial importance in the plot.

A. R. Humphrey's *Melville* comprises 114 pages, more than three of which are devoted to *Billy Budd*. The author leaves no doubt as to the importance attached by Melville to the analysis of Claggart's character: 'Among the finest things in Melville's work is the analysis of Claggart's mixed yearning and malice, real in its strangeness. . . . The analysis is probing, adumbrative, quietly troubled, and more interesting than any sensationalism could be. It presents, one might say, original sin according to agnosticism.'[14] There is no mention of envy in Humphrey's work.

In a study devoted to Melville's shorter works, Richard Harter Fogle has occasion to mention Claggart only once. All he says is: 'Claggart, the master-at-arms . . . who is pure evil according to nature.'[15] The nature of this evil, made so plain by Melville, is not mentioned.

Tyrus Hillway, in the 176 pages given to the novelist's work, unreservedly considers *Billy Budd* to be Melville's best and most mature achievement. It is not only his final work, the product of the decade between his seventieth and eightieth birthdays, but a statement of his philosophy, a novel written without any thought of financial gain, or contemporary readership, a work hastened only by the prospect of premature death. One would have thought that Hillway would, if only in one sentence or phrase, have intimated to the reader that Melville discusses the problem of envy. But the word 'envy' does not appear even once. Claggart is the embodiment of evil—nothing more.[16]

Geoffrey Stone's depiction of Melville, more than three hundred pages long, is aimed at the general reader. Billy Budd and Claggart are dealt with at length. The latter is one of the only two characters in the whole of Melville's opus to be dominated by evil.[17]

Yet here, too, we look in vain for an indication that in this novel and

---

[14] A. R. Humphrey, *Melville,* Edinburgh and London, 1962, p. 113.

[15] R. Harter Fogle, *Melville's Shorter Tales,* Norman, 1960, p. 138.

[16] T. Hillway, *Herman Melville,* New York, 1963.

[17] G. Stone, *Melville,* New York, 1949, p. 27.

Claggart's character Melville is investigating the problem of envy. Stone quotes long passages from the novel on the subject of the master-at-arms' motivation, but avoids all those in which Melville uses the term 'envy.' Stone even goes into what he declares to be the modern interpretation of Claggart, according to which he is a homosexual, no less, whose unrequited love for the beautiful sailor turns into ambivalent love-hate and eventually into mortal hatred. This interpretation Stone rejects: 'Melville constantly addresses himself to the metaphysical implications of Claggart's depravity, and if these are not his chief concern with the matter, we are left with the curious spectacle of a highly intelligent old man devoting the last three years of his life to pondering a simple case of thwarted pederasty.'[18] Here Stone is right, but there is not a single word to suggest that Melville devoted three years of his life to the anatomy of envy. The few authors, however, who have gone into the matter, demonstrate how obvious the chief subject of Melville's concern really is.

Milton R. Stern, for instance, devotes seven pages to a detailed interpretation of Claggart, mentioning the envious element several times.[19] F. O. Matthiessen puts it most clearly, perhaps, in his work on American literature: '. . . Claggart . . . whose malignity seems to be stirred most by the envious sight of virtue in others, as Iago's was.' And elsewhere:

> To characterize what Claggart feels, Melville has recourse to the quotation, 'Pale ire, envy and despair,' the forces that were working in Milton's Satan as he first approached the Garden of Eden. Melville has also jotted down, on the back of his manuscript, some remembered details about Spenser's 'Envy': and in his depiction of Claggart's inextricable mixture— longing and malice—he would seem to be reverting likewise to the properties he had noted in Shakespeare's conception of this deadly sin.[20]

---

[18] Op. cit., p. 313.

[19] M. R. Stern, *The Fine Hammered Steel of Herman Melville*, Urbana, 1957, pp. 227 ff. Claggart's envy is also mentioned twice by J. B. Noone, Jr., 'Billy Budd, Two Concepts of Nature,' *American Literature*, Vol. 29, 1957, p. 251. And by W. Berthoff, *The Example of Melville*, Princeton, 1962: 'Claggart . . . is envious and despairing' (p. 200).

[20] *American Renaissance: Art and Expression in the Age of Emerson and Whitman*, London, 1941, pp. 435, 505.

Eugène Sue's Frederick Bastien: Envy

Sue's novel about envy differs from other literary treatments of the problem in its psychotherapeutic approach. Long before psychoanalysis and depth psychology existed, Sue showed how a mature experienced man comes to the aid of a family doctor and, by tenacious, detailed work, seeks to find the reason for the patient's psychological distress by putting together his isolated remarks and fragmentary notes (which he had tried to destroy) of his supposed experiences during the critical period. In the novel, the patient's corrosive, personality-destroying envy is successfully overcome and is sublimated into an attitude of noble and honourable competition for objective values with the man he envies; they vie with each other in saving the lives of families threatened by flood. The youth, tormented by envy, gains an insight into his motives. Many readers may find that the way in which envy is eliminated is too simple. Allowing for the relative naïveté of the novel, the credibility or otherwise of the subplot and Sue's own standing as a writer, we believe that his account of a successful psychotherapy of envy is convincing, and might well stand as a model for a psychotherapist today.

It is remarkable, too, that Sue should believe in the possibility of liberating a man from envy. Most stories that have envy as their central theme show the downfall of the envious man, who becomes a criminal or, at the end of his unhappy, unsuccessful life, unburdens himself of some great offence committed from envy. In Sue, however, the success of the psychotherapy is assumed from the start in that his hero has grown up without sibling jealousy, in close communion with a kindly and infinitely experienced mother.

Sue gives one of the most accurate clinical accounts of the envy-syndrome to be found in fiction. Melville alone, perhaps, excels him in detail. In contrast to some other authors who use 'jealousy' and 'envy' indiscriminately or as alternatives, Sue discovers the fundamental difference. He begins with a young person brought up in pyschologically ideal circumstances, unaware of the feeling of envy, but yet made sensitive to the material and aesthetic values of life by his gifted mother. Without transition, Sue puts his hero in a situation where he is able to compare standards and styles of living and, step by step, we see envy germinating. The diagnosis is not withheld from the reader, but those around the envious boy have the utmost difficulty in recognizing the true motive for the hatred of another that is gradually becoming manifest. It takes them months.

This double camouflaging of the envy-motive is a consistent feature: the envious man will confess to almost any other sin or emotional impulse (in Sue's novel it is intention to murder) before he will confess to his own envy. And to those around a person impelled by envy, this is the very last motive they will think of, and that with great reluctance. Not only does Sue depict this circumstance convincingly and with great accuracy but he uses it to construct a dramatic plot.

The extent to which Sue concerned himself with envy is evident from the phenomenology of this emotion which the novel slowly develops before our eyes.

The sixteen-year-old boy whom mounting envy transforms in the course of a few months from being happy and studious into a savage hater, well on the way to becoming a murderer, had a rather lonely childhood, spent on a small farm with his pretty young mother. This woman, who had been married against her will and had rejected her husband, lived apart from him on a minimal income. The misfortunes start when the family doctor obtains permission for mother and son to visit a neighbouring château and its grounds while its owner, the young marquis, and his grandmother are away. The son is not only embittered by the château servants' high-handed treatment of his mother and the doctor during their short visit, but for the first time becomes painfully aware of the meanness and poverty of his own home.

Sue then describes his condition as follows: 'He felt a strange, growing sense of moral unease . . . a feeling which, although still ill-defined, made him so ashamed that for the first time in his life he failed to confide in his mother, afraid of her perceptivity. . . .'

A little later when he sees his pretty mother sitting at home in front of her wretched dressing-table, he suddenly recalls the rooms in the château. Envy grips him, and he says to himself: 'Wouldn't the elegant, sumptuous boudoir which I saw at the château have been put to better use by a charming person like my mother instead of that octogenarian marquise?'[21]

---

[21] E. Sue, *Frederick Bastien: Envy*, Boston, no date, Vol. 2, pp. 49 f.

Frederick's growing envy is concealed from those around him. It can only be guessed at through certain changes in him. A beggar, to whom he had formerly always given something, now gets a mere 'You would only laugh at my paltry alms. Ask M. le Marquis—he should play the benefactor in these parts—he's rich enough. . . .'

Even before he has seen the marquis, he envies him for being able to live in such luxury. The gradual exacerbation of this genuine envy is depicted most convincingly by Sue. But to bring the youth to the point of planning murder, he introduces some further motives. While mother and son are out for a walk, the marquis comes riding after them, having picked up the mother's cape which she had inadvertently dropped. Innocently, she remarks on the young nobleman's good manners, thereby adding jealousy to the envy already felt by her son. A little later, while the boy is watching his mother's old carriage-horse being unharnessed in front of the house in the village street, a hunt passes by; the old horse tries to join it, but is driven off by the marquis with his whip. The young man's hatred and envy know no bounds.

Sue explains the suddenness and intensity of this envy by Frederick's aesthetic sensibility, derived from his mother, who, with slender means, has succeeded in creating surroundings that are in good taste. The author implies that a young man who had grown up in uncouth or dull surroundings would not have been so painfully aware of the contrast with the château.

A psychotherapy of envy

The subsequent chapters depict the growing incomprehension between Frederick and his mother, the family doctor and the latter's friend. All have noticed a serious psychological change, the nature of which remains hidden because Frederick, ashamed of his envy, becomes increasingly stubborn and withdrawn.

> The first period of envy from which Frederick suffered had been, so to speak, passive. The second was active. His suffering then was impossible to express; hidden, concentrated in the depth of his soul, his agony could find no outlet and was constantly and fatally aroused by the sight of the château of Pont-Brillant, which he could not help seeing, no matter where he looked, for the ancient building dominated the horizon from afar. The more

conscious Frederick became of his bitter affliction, the more he felt the need to conceal it from his mother, persuading himself in his grim despair that such failings as his deserved nothing but scorn and loathing, and that even a mother could not show pity for them.[22]

Probably wishing to titillate the reader with yet another sensation (but one which fails to materialize), Sue now stages a scene in a grotto, where Frederick overhears a remark by the marquis' grandmother to the effect that his, Frederick's mother would make a good mistress for the marquis. Envy is teamed with jealousy, and the author describes the progressive deterioration of Frederick's physical condition—jaundiced complexion, hollow cheeks, a bitter smile, abrupt and clumsy movements, an impatient manner of speech.

The youth determines to murder the marquis: '. . . then if I kill him . . . he will no longer enjoy all the pleasures for which I envy him so . . . his luxuries will cease to be an insult to the poverty of myself and all those others who have even more cause for complaint than I have.'[23]

The murder does not come off, but the doctor's friend, David, who has taken on the job of tutor to Frederick in order to help the young man, knows what is afoot. Like a detective, he seeks the motive. He finds the decisive clue in some partly erased drafts of an essay. There David reads, 'For people who are fated to drag out their existence in humiliating obscurity, it is their inability . . . to raise themselves up and . . .'

And elsewhere: 'Why, by what right . . . ?'

And a sentence almost wholly erased: '. . . for . . . great and holy revolution . . . the weak . . . have become the strong; vengeance has come at long last . . . then . . . terrible . . . but beautiful in its . . .'[24] At this point, the tutor understands the motive of his protégé.

Next Sue gives what amounts to a psychotherapy of envy. David confronts Frederick with his affliction. 'The cause of your illness is your envy!' Overcome with shame, the boy tries to evade the issue but learns from David that destructive envy can be metamorphosed into what is constructive, into honourable competition.

The dialogue in which David persuades his pupil to transform his envy

[22] Op. cit., p. 56.

[23] Op. cit., p. 91.

[24] Op. cit., p. 157.

into an incentive, and to try to emulate the marquis in those fields open to
him, expounds a philosophy of life that must be anathema to any social
revolutionary. Basically this is the much-maligned Horatio Alger myth
of America, the conviction that all is well with the *status quo* since the
glamour of the privileged and successful has the positive function of
providing an example, and of stimulating special mobility in the young
person at the bottom of the ladder. Everyone, it informs us, could make
something of himself and of his life if he really wanted to. And the mere
destruction or expropriation of the upper classes would help no one.
Thus it is not surprising to find Georg Lukács recalling Karl Marx's
biting criticism of Eugène Sue, who, he alleges, 'cravenly adapted
himself to the surface of capitalist society . . . out of opportunism
distorting and falsifying reality.'[25]

A novel which shows, if somewhat naïvely and superficially, how
social envy could be cured must indeed have been a vexation to the
socialists of the mid-nineteenth century. Yet this fact is remarkable in
itself.

While a hundred years ago it was a meaningful and rewarding task for
one of the most popular French novelists to depict the torment caused by
envy of the privileged and its possible cure, in the second half of the
twentieth century very few people would be interested in reading a
modern novel about a young man consumed with envy of the luxuries of
a multi-millionaire, and eventually cured by a psychoanalyst. To the
modern detective searching for a motive, it would seem as improbable
that someone should murder a millionaire out of envy as Frederick's
motive seemed to those around him.

Yuri Olesha's Envy: *The problem of envy in Soviet society*

In the very short novel *Zavist* (Envy), by the Russian Yuri Karlovich
Olesha (1899–1960), we have one of the few literary works in which the
envy of the hero, who is depicted somewhat unsympathetically by the
author as a miserable failure, reveals to us the whole spectrum of envy.[26]

The object of envy is a successful, powerful, hustling technocrat, the

[25] G. Lukács, *Schriften zur Literatursoziologie*, 2nd ed., Neuwied, 1963, pp. 224 f.

[26] Yuri Olesha, 'Envy' in *Envy and Other Works*, Anchor Books, New York, 1967.

food specialist Commissar Andrei Petrovich Babichev. In view of the fact that the feeling of envy derives originally from food-envy, and that Olesha, like most others, must have suffered considerably from hunger after the October Revolution, it seems hardly a coincidence that through-out the whole novel the critical eye of envy fastens scornfully, again and again, upon food and the processes of eating and digestion. The story begins literally with the commissar's colon.

Kavalerov, the hero, is the narrator in the first part of the book. He is an 'angry young man,' already in thrall to alcoholism, and he personifies envy, as does the commissar's brother, Ivan, a romantic failure who hates his brother, as representing not only success but also the new machine age and mass organization, which Ivan tries to sabotage.

The novel closes with the utter defeat of the two envious men. But so unmercifully are the commissar and his world laid bare and caricatured through the eye of envy that Olesha, who became famous overnight as a result of this, his first novel, was allowed to enjoy his popularity for only a short time. Soon he became the object of personal attack, no doubt partly because he was seen in official Communist circles as a social critic dangerous to the régime.

Olesha has several times admitted that the figure of Kavalerov is autobiographical. He identified himself with that character, and the attacks on his hero's trivial and vulgar nature inflicted a deep and personal hurt.[27] The similarity between the author and the young man in the novel is patent. Olesha's youth was spent in the secure ambience of a middle-class family of officials in pre-Revolutionary Russia. He tells us that he valued the world of private property, and this is also apparent from some of the lovingly drawn pictures in his memoirs.[28] The first ten years of Communist Russia were the years of his early manhood, from nineteen to twenty-eight. During that time he made his living as a journalist. It is not difficult to imagine how the world of new-style Party bosses in the Russia of 1925 appeared to him. His hatred and envy are set down on paper, and he had the courage to choose the single word 'envy'

---

[27] R. Mathewson, 'The First Writers' Congress. A Second Look,' in *Literature and Revolution in Soviet Russia 1917–1962. A Symposium,* ed. M. Hayward and L. Labedz, London, 1963, p. 65.

[28] Y. Olesha, 'Jottings of a Writer,' in *Envy and Other Works,* pp. 201 ff.

for his title. The novel, perhaps to his own surprise, attracted immediate attention.

Envy and the commissar

The plot is simple. Kavalerov is picked up by the commissar after being thrown out of a bar and is put up in the latter's provocatively fine apartment. He observes all his benefactor's private and professional moves, which he so interprets as continually to exacerbate his hatred and envy. Gradually he becomes aware that he is merely filling a temporary vacancy in the commissar's favour as in his apartment, occasioned by a visit to the country of another young man, Makarov, whom the commissar has taken in or adopted as a sort of son. During his short stay with the commissar, Kavalerov also gets to know the latter's brother, Ivan, as well as Ivan's daughter, Valya, who is engaged to Makarov.

In *Billy Budd*, Herman Melville, fully conscious of the problems involved and of people's general aversion to acknowledging this feeling, hesitantly guides the reader towards the metaphysic and the depth psychology of envy. This common aversion may be linked with the Anglo-Saxon cultural ethos. By contrast, Olesha postulates envy as an accepted phenomenon. Apart from the title, the term is not used by the envious man himself until quite late in the story, when he realizes that his spiteful farewell letter to his benefactor will be interpreted by the latter an envious.[29] But nowhere does Olesha give any intimation of envy's abysmal, uncanny role in human existence, which Melville found so fascinating.

That no exception was taken by Soviet literary critics to the naked portrayal of envy scarcely ten years after the October Revolution is not to be wondered at. Olesha introduces the feeling of envy at the point of demarcation between generations. It is the old, decadent, outdated representatives of pre-revolutionary Russia who envy the new Soviet man, the dynamic, efficient commissar. Why, then, the excitement? With the extinction of that generation, the problem of envy would also vanish from Communist reality. Although Olesha may have known that envy, whose points of view and emotional states he so effectively por-

---

[29] Olesha, 'Envy,' p. 47.

trays, is part of man's basic equipment and will exercise a disruptive influence in the very societies that depend upon an eventual utopian state of egalitarianism, this is nowhere hinted at in his novel.

Olesha describes a clash between the envious and the envied man which is devoid of all tragedy because the 'hero' was already consumed with envy and aware of his own impotence in the face of the new society, before meeting the commissar. His envy, analysed in the novel, of the latter's way of life brings about no change in his total character. At the end of the story he is just where he began—in the gutter.

What is notable, however, is this: Even the hate-ridden, unrealistically ambitious ne'er-do-well Kavalerov cannot stand the thought that the commissar might see his letter as an expression of envy, and treat it with contempt. He is ashamed to be recognized as an envious man, for he knows how ineffectual his furious letter would then be. Hence he is glad when he thinks he has got his letter back, although, as it turns out, he in fact has the wrong letter in his pocket.

A writer in Russia ten years after the revolution, admittedly filled with resentment against those who are successful, regards it as a matter of course that envy, if recognized, is something to be ashamed of, and that the envier knows himself to be ineffectual. This is essentially no different from what human beings have felt everywhere and at all times.

Since the end of the Second World War, however, a new 'ethic' has, astonishingly, come into being, according to which the envious man is altogether acceptable. Progressively fewer individuals and groups are ashamed of their envy, but instead make out that its existence in their temperaments axiomatically proves the existence of 'social injustice,' which must be eliminated for their benefit. Suddenly it has become possible to say, without loss of public credibility and trust, 'I envy you. Give me what you've got.' This public self-justification of envy is something entirely new. In this sense it is possible to speak of the age of envy.

'Things don't like me'

Some of the passages in Olesha's novel are very illuminating for the phenomenology of envy. Kavalerov feels that he is not loved by the things of the world. He always relates the malice of objects to himself, and envies those with whom things co-operate. 'Things don't like me. Furniture tries to trip me up. . . . Soup, given to me, never cools. . . .' And, by contrast, 'things love' the commissar.[30]

From other characters in fiction, as also in clinical literature, it is evident that a man tormented by envy feels persecuted by his material surroundings. And as can be demonstrated from primitive man, such as the Dobu Islander or the Navaho Indian, what immediately rouses his envy is that whereas the other man seems to be favoured by his material environment, the envious man can only see himself as cheated by it.

Gradually Kavalerov becomes aware of the nature of his feelings towards the commissar, whom he often calls sausage-maker or grocer: 'What is it, then? Do I respect him? Fear him? No. I am just as good as he is. I am no bystander. I'll prove it.'[31] It is only much later, in the second half of the book, when Olesha himself is the narrator, that he shows Ivan before an examining magistrate and says: 'Are you interested in his dominant emotion, or in his name? . . . Nikolai Kavalerov, the Envious.'[32]

A little further on there is a conversation between Ivan and Kavalerov, who, they both recognize, bear a resemblance to one another. Ivan says to Kavalerov:

'My friend, envy is eating us away. We envy the future. It's the envy of senility, if you wish. . . . Let's talk about envy. . . .'[33]

Ivan then relates a childhood experience: as a thirteen-year-old schoolboy, he went to a party where a girl did better than he at dancing and parlour games. 'I couldn't stand it. I caught the girl in the corridor and gave her a going over . . . scratched her charming features. . . .' Ivan's explanation for his rage is significant if we remember that the most acute form of envy is provoked by someone who is almost our equal: 'I was always used to admiration, to an enthusiastic following. In class, I too was top man, a pace-setter.'

He was sent home from the party: 'That is how I came to know envy. The terrible heartburn of envy. It is appalling to envy! Envy catches you by the throat, squeezes your eyes from their sockets.'[34]

[30] Op. cit., p. 2.

[31] Op. cit., p. 9.

[32] Op. cit., p. 74.

[33] Op. cit., pp. 77 f.

[34] Op. cit., pp. 78 f.

Olesha portrays one of the early and better-known manifestations of envy in Kavalerov's letter to the commissar:

'You gave me a bed. From the height of your well-being you lowered a cloud-bed. . . . You are my benefactor. . . . Just think: a famous man made me his close companion. . . . I want to convey my feelings to you. Strictly speaking, it's all one feeling: hatred.'[35]

But why? Kavalerov answers this a few lines further on:

'Why must I acknowledge his superiority?'

When Olesha's *Envy* appeared in 1927, Soviet critics were at first unanimous in their praise. According to *Pravda*, Olesha was the leading author among those who stood closest to the group known as the 'Russian Association of Proletarian Writers.' The novel was also enthusiastically acclaimed by some Russian émigrés abroad.[36] Improbable as it may seem to the present-day reader, Soviet critics did not then see the irony and satire inherent in the portrait of the commissar. Only by degrees was the extent of Olesha's commitment to individualism realized; then the criticism began.

L. P. Hartley's utopian novel Facial Justice

During the post-war years and up to the end of the fifties, perhaps nowhere else was the subject of 'envy and equality' so much discussed as in England. Periodicals such as *The Spectator* and *Time and Tide* repeatedly published comments, articles and readers' letters on the subject of envy which sought legitimation under cover of various economic and educational measures, taxation, etc., usually in the guise of a demand for equality.[37] The debate was originally stimulated by the

[35] Op. cit., p. 38.

[36] G. Struve, *Soviet Russian Literature, 1917–50*, Norman, 1951, pp. 98, 219.

[37] 'Next to looking downwards and inwards they [the previous writers in this series] seem to like looking sideways at their neighbours—an activity which is all the more difficult to explain since its most usual effect seems to produce rage and ill-will. The simple pleasures and modest economies of the Retired School-master with his £800 a year, seemed to act on many readers like a red rag to a bull. A "wry smile" from a clergyman was about the most charitable reaction to this article. . . .

'I can't help feeling the willingness to put up with a plain swindle is one of the most alarming phenomena in post-war Britain. But to regard the relative success and comfort of more fortunate people as a cause for fury and annoyance in itself, and to regard their high standards of culture and education as an insult, is quite another

Labour Government's levelling, egalitarian measures between 1945 and 1951, and subsequently by its demands when in opposition, as well as by the excuses made by the Conservatives, who were afraid to lay a finger on the institutions created in the name of equality. It was almost inevitable that someone should write a satirical novel along the lines of George Orwell's *Nineteen Eighty-four,* having as its central theme the political exploitation of equality and envy. Such a novel appeared in 1960 from the pen of the well-known English writer L. P. Hartley (born 1895). It was called *Facial Justice.*

None of the literary works discussed by me and concerned with this subject attack it so frankly as does Hartley in this little book. The title is actually followed by the epigraph: 'The spirit that dwelleth in us lusteth to envy. St James . . . '

The action of this short utopian novel takes place soon after the Third World War. It is a satire in the Swiftian tradition on the drive towards uniformity such as the author must frequently have observed in England during the fifties. During that decade, the left wing of the Labour Party demanded, more unequivocally perhaps than any other party, a society of absolute equals. But first let us take a look at Franziska Becker's review of the novel in the *Neue Zürcher Zeitung:*

> An invisible dictator, whose voice is audible always and everywhere giving directions, treats his subjects, whom he addresses as 'patients and criminals,' as a strict but just teacher would treat badly behaved louts. He is concerned mainly with uniformity and the elimination of envy. Pretty women are seen as a disruptive element. Thus it is virtually the moral duty of anyone born with an 'Alpha' face to undergo an operation in order to acquire a 'Beta' face. Jael's vanity leads her, though with a bad conscience, to evade that duty; this is the first of other individualistic actions—eventually she loses her face after all. After this she rebels out of hatred of the

---

matter. That is just envy.' (W. Taplin, 'Making Ends Meet,' *The Spectator,* August 3, 1951, pp. 151 f.)

A leading article by Charles Curran, titled 'The Politics of Envy,' in *The Spectator,* December 6, 1957, p. 780, castigates a trend that 'will pretty certainly turn this country into an impoverished co-operative ant-hill, with no room for differential abilities to flourish.' Hartley's novel merely extrapolates the trend to its logical conclusion.

dictator, who by pushing people's egalitarian tendencies to such an extreme has unleashed their destructive drives. It ends with 'le roi est mort, vive le roi.' The book is a satire. But careful reading is needed to discover what the author is talking about and just what it is that he is attacking.

From the very start, there is never any doubt as to what *Facial Justice* is about. This new state of the future is founded upon self-abasement and equality. All citizens are criminals: none can be said to be worse than his neighbour. Everyone is dressed in sack-cloth, and 'Envy is the sole cause of personal distress and social friction.'

The novel opens with the words: 'In the not very distant future, after the Third World War, Justice had made great strides. Legal Justice, Economic Justice, Social Justice, and many other forms of justice, of which we do not even know the names, had been attained; but there still remained spheres of human relationship and activity in which Justice did not reign.'

The Equalization (Faces) Centre

On the very first page of the novel we encounter two girls on their way to the 'Equalization (Faces) Centre.' They do not notice each other until they are going into the building. Jael, the heroine of the novel, is crying. She recognizes her friend Judith, a nice-enough-looking girl, but not particularly attractive. Judith finds herself looking at a pretty girl. She is the first to collect her wits: 'I didn't expect to see you here . . . ,' and then, after looking at the pretty one again, 'I might have guessed.' Jael says: 'But you, Judith?' Jael cannot finish the hurtful sentence with 'you're not ugly enough to qualify for beautification in this country.' Nevertheless Judith replies: 'You mean I'm not so ugly? I was Gamma minus, you know, at my last Board. . . . So I've qualified for a rise. Any Gamma is, of course, below Gamma plus.'

It turns out that though Judith is not allowed to choose the model she wanted, her boy-friend still prefers the new face. Jael's problem is the reverse. She is aware of her beauty and has an Alpha face. Years before, she had scarred her own face so as to avoid debeautification on political grounds. But to no purpose.

Envy and equality in Utopia

The behaviour towards one another of all members of this society living under an omnipresent dictator (similar to Orwell's 'Big Brother' in *Nineteen Eighty-Four*), who must always be referred to as our 'darling dictator,' is determined by two values, one positive, equality, the 'good E,' and one negative, envy, the 'bad E.' Wherever these two terms are mentioned, speaker and listener must at the time or immediately afterwards perform a ritual: the word 'equality' necessitates a graceful curtsey, the word 'envy' a contemptuous spit. Understandably, people try to avoid these terms and therefore speak either in circumlocutions or in abbreviations.

Envy, the bad E, is in any case the most taboo and abominated word in the language. *But*—and this is particularly perspicacious of Hartley— the contempt is not for the envy or its subject; rather, the whole weight of official disapproval in this society falls upon those who have somehow been able to make themselves enviable to others; the highest value is envy-avoidance. In his satire, Hartley draws the logical conclusion from those tendencies of this century, especially prevalent since the Second World War, and stressed by me in this work—namely, the strange endeavour to legitimize the envious man and his envy, raising them to absolutes, so that anyone capable of arousing envy is regarded as an antisocial or criminal element to be treated accordingly.

Contrary to all earlier societies that have evolved naturally, contrary, indeed, to all human societies that may be expected to last, what we are shown in the novel is not the envious man rendered innocuous by social controls, who must hang his head in shame, but the man who is envied. Official consideration of the envious man has so inverted all values that only complete de-individualization of every person in the name of equality can find favour in the eyes of the Inspectors (who themselves, of course, are subject to somewhat different laws than apply to ordinary citizens).

To govern such a society is no simple matter. Thus some motor vehicles still survive from the time before the Third World War, and there are citizens, objects of the full weight of official disapproval, whose hearts still lust after such reactionary, individualistic and enviable things as the pleasure of going for a drive. Needless to say, no one is allowed to drive a car alone, but there are regular state-organized communal bus rides in the neighbourhood designed to keep eccentrics moderately contented. Although to go on such a trip is to court suspicion, and not only the fare but a fine has to be paid, the outings become more and more popular and the throng ever greater. This greatly displeases the dictator. He doesn't quite dare to put an immediate stop to state excursions, but he admonishes the people, pointing out that the joys of driving are non-conformist, envy-provoking and betray a wrong attitude; he then announces that one bus in six is to have a state-organized accident: no one will know which vehicle it is going to be, but there will always be dead and injured. Against all expectation, this new kind of sumptuary law fails to have the desired effect.

Sometime later, therefore, the dictator increases the obligatory accident rate. To his horror, this only increases the number of his subjects who wish to go on excursions.

Jael is the heroine of the novel. From the start, her non-conformity consists in her refusal to see why people who are better-looking or cleverer should de-individualize themselves because of other people's envy. On one of the bus trips she infringes a social taboo (no one is allowed to raise his eyes) by getting her fellow excursionists to join in a round-dance, in front of a ruined tower, in the course of which they all happily raise their eyes. On the return journey their vehicle suffers the pre-arranged accident. While she is in hospital, and before recovering consciousness, she is operated on and given the normal Beta face. She is not aware of the punishment until her discharge. The congratulations and compliments of other Betas only serve to enrage her. Through the agency of the dictator's personal physician, whom she blackmails, she is able to publish articles in which the demand for equality is taken to absurd extremes. Among other targets for envy proposed to the citizens, she includes a heart-shaped birth-mark which one of them is supposed to have on his side, below the heart. (Jael knows that the dictator, whom she mistakenly believes to be a man, has such a mark.) Incited by her, men start demanding to see each other's chests. By degrees the community is reduced to anarchy. The dictator (finally disclosed as an old woman, the key to the statutory envy of the female face) wearily abdicates and, as she dies, makes over her power to Jael.

A careful reading of *Facial Justice* reveals a catalogue of all those human qualities that have to be dealt with by the social engineers of a policy in which everything has been so levelled out that the only remaining cause of uneasiness is physical or intellectual discrepancy between individual citizens. Jael, with her Alpha face, is officially informed that all the complaints received about her at the Ministry for Face Equality originated from members of her own sex. 'One woman complained she had lost several nights' sleep just thinking about my eyelashes. She felt they were digging into her, she said.'[38]

Unfortunately, there were also snobs among Beta face wearers; those born with Beta faces considered themselves better than people who had acquired everyman's face by cosmetic surgery. Jael's brother, a model bureaucrat of the régime (he is, as Hartley hints, also motivated to some extent by sibling jealousy, although both were orphans), condemns Jael's refusal to have her Alpha face removed. When she declares that it is, after all, 'her own face,' he snorts:

'You have a right to nothing that is liable to cause Envy in the heart of a fellow-delinquent,'[39] to which Jael retorts that a pretty face might also be regarded as a source of pleasure to others. Her brother replies that, on the contrary, she should think of the envy of those who are angered by the fact that it is her face—and not theirs—that pleases the beholder, etc.

Even when the dictator has proclaimed compulsory accidents for pleasure buses, so that people crowd to go on them, those who have not booked their tickets complain that it is unfair and not in accordance with the principle of equality if everyone cannot enjoy the new risk.

There are only two kinds of person in this utopia: those naturally engendered by parents, and babies raised by the state. But couples who have children are not held in high esteem because it gives them a suspect sense of identity.[40] It is also forbidden to use the word 'my,' which ought really to be 'in my care.'[41] The gradual extirpation of Alpha faces is not enough, however. Below the pleasantly average Beta faces are the somewhat less agreeable Gamma faces. Thus a new protest movement arises, the League of Facial Disarmament, with the object of abolishing the Beta face, which the state has allowed to remain too good-looking. In a significant and pungent satire on actual reformers, Hartley makes the

[38] L. P. Hartley, *Facial Justice*, London, 1960, p. 13; New York, 1961.
[39] Op. cit., pp. 43 f.
[40] Op. cit., p. 78.
[41] Op. cit., p. 86.

discontented Betas turn against the Beta face, on the grounds that it isn't fair that there should still be Gammas whose presence causes Betas to suffer from a sense of guilt. Everyone should look exactly alike. There must be no more facially underprivileged.[42]

In her articles intended to bring about the downfall of the system, Jael demands that health should also be equalized: no one must feel too well.[43] And, of course, she soon demands control of language, since no one ought to write better, or use more cultivated prose, than anyone else. In future, only the simplest words should be allowed.[44] The campaign in the Third Reich against the use of foreign words in German, which was compulsory in secondary education, might be seen as anticipating this aspect of utopia.

In our discussion of some of the books of Herman Melville, and especially his story *Billy Budd,* we have already encountered the blind spot of American literary criticism in relation to any work that has envy as its central problem. Exactly the same blind spot is to be found in Peter Bien's monograph on L. P. Hartley. Bien, a young American, spent a year in England for the purpose of this study, and during that time he had discussions with the author and corresponded with him. Bien's account appeared in 1963. Nearly fifteen pages of a book less than three hundred pages long are devoted to the novel *Facial Justice.* Now, Bien performs the feat of commenting on and interpreting it without once using the word 'envy' or 'envious,' or giving the reader any idea that this is perhaps the one novel in the whole of literature to investigate and criticize explicitly, page by page, without circumlocution, the role of envy and the problems of a society that seeks to obviate it. Bien confines himself to mentioning 'fairness' once or twice, in the name of which people are de-individualized by the state. But nowhere does the reader learn with what psychological understanding and in what detail Hartley examines and repeatedly illustrates the function of envy in making an absolute of the value 'fair.' In my view, with which L. P. Hartley agrees, Bien's peculiar balancing-feat is best explained by the fact that the moral of this story is an acutely uncomfortable one for the typical American

[42] Op. cit., pp. 170 f.
[43] Op. cit., p. 201.
[44] Op. cit., p. 207.

progressive liberal of today, whose social philosophy agrees in many respects with that of the novel's egalitarian dictator. Hence Bien, having chosen L. P. Hartley as his subject, and unable to beat a retreat, could do no better when faced with the subject of the last novel than ignore the novelist's true and obvious intention and select peripheral aspects of the story for his interpretation.

Now, in Hartley's novel cosmetic surgery performed on women's faces, for the socially desirable purpose of avoiding envy among less pretty women, is simply the most obvious means of de-individualization (the satirist's whole onslaught being against utopian egalitarians who believe they have achieved an envy-free society as soon as they have put all citizens on an equal financial and educational footing). Peter Bien, however, manages to see this as a critical attack on the medical profession: Hartley, he declares, wishes to 'warn us of the not-at-all preposterous role the medical profession is already playing as an instrument to abridge our liberties!'[45] It is, of course, notorious that doctors and the art of medicine can be misused by dictators and wielders of power, just as other sciences and technology can be misused. And the doctor who 'Beta-fies' Jael's face, and who is, besides, the dictator's medical attendant, is not shown by Hartley in a very attractive light. The hospital staff in the novel are probably much like all others in average, overworked hospitals throughout the world. But it is difficult to understand how a literary scholar could manage to suppress the work's actual social criticism, which concerns the mania for equality in face of potential envy, and to set in its place an attack on the medical profession.

For Bien has occasion more than once to speak of Hartley's political philosophy, which, in a number of novels and essays, invariably involved the defence of the individual against the claims of the collective. Bien quotes, for instance, an autobiographical note of Hartley's which clearly reveals what impelled this particular author to demonstrate in one of his later works that a dictatorship or totalitarian régime could make the duty of non-provocation of envy in others the chief means of social control. Hartley tells of his life-long aversion to all forms of state coercion. When he was up at Oxford, from 1915 to 1919, Herbert Spencer, Mill and all other champions of individualism had already been proscribed. The

---

[45] P. Bien, *L. P. Hartley,* London, 1963; University Park (Pa.), 1963, p. 221.

writers to be admired were now Hobbes, Locke, Rousseau and others, because they all glorified some form of association (generally the state at the cost of the individual). In Hartley's own words: 'As I thought that all our troubles came from the State, I was infuriated by this—and the idea of the State having a sort of entity of its own, to which we must sacrifice ourselves, drove me nearly frantic. . . . '[46]

Chaucer and Milton

Poets have repeatedly stressed three basic facts in connection with envy, and these must be decisive in its sociological study: (1) Envy is a phenomenon of social proximity. Its worst form is directed, not against the prince enthroned at an infinite height, but against one's fellow worker. (2) The envious man is ubiquitous. There is no form of human existence that precludes envy. (3) Envy is an affect of long duration, nourished by the imagination, and generally involving physical, and hence physiological, changes.

In Chaucer's works, envy is mentioned more than eighty times, mostly in the *Canterbury Tales*. 'The Parson's Tale' concerns the Seven Deadly Sins. Having discussed pride, Chaucer goes on to 'the foule sinne of Envye,' which, like St. Augustine, he defines as sorrow at another's prosperity and joy in his harm. If a man rails against the favour bestowed by God upon his neighbour, he is guilty of the sin of envy; and in so far as the Holy Ghost is kindly, and envy originates in evil, envy is the worst of sins.

But Chaucer also sees envy as the worst of sins because nearly all the rest oppose only one virtue, whereas envy turns against all the virtues and against everything that is good. It denies, as we would now say, every value in the scale or table of values. Because the envious man takes exception to his neighbour's every virtue and advantage, the sin of envy is distinct from all others. Every other kind of sin is in itself pleasurable, to some degree productive of satisfaction, but envy produces only anguish and sorrow. Chaucer holds envy to be a sin against nature because it consists in the first place of distress over other people's goodness and prosperity, and prosperity is naturally a matter of joy. In the second place envy consists of joy in the ills and suffering that befall

---

[46] Op. cit., pp. 276 f.

others. This envy is like the devil, who always rejoices in human suffering.

Envy, according to Chaucer, breeds malice. If attempts to annoy one's neighbour fail, there are plenty of ways of doing him harm, such as burning down his house or poisoning or stabbing his cattle.

In Milton's *Paradise Lost*, the function of envy is clearly evident in the story of man's creation:

> *Who first seduced them to that foul revolt?*
> *Th'infernal serpent! He it was, whose guile,*
> *Stirred up with envy and revenge, deceived*
> *The mother of mankind. . . .*
> *Satan—so call him now, his former name*
> *Is heard no more in heav'n—he of the first*
> *If not the first Archangel, great in power,*
> *In favour and pre-eminence, yet fraught*
> *With envy against the Son of God, that day*
> *Honoured by his great Father, and proclaimed*
> *Messiah King anointed, could not bear*
> *Thro' pride that sight, and thought himself impaired.*

Now Satan speaks:

> *. . . Revenge, at first thought sweet,*
> *Bitter ere long, back on itself recoils:*
> *Let it; I reck not, so it light well aimed,*
> *Since higher I fall short, on him who next*
> *Provokes my envy, this new favourite*
> *Of heav'n, this man of clay, son of despite,*
> *Whom us the more to spite, his Maker raised*
> *From dust: spite then with spite is best repaid.*

Adam says to Eve:

> *. . . for thou know'st*
> *What hath been warned us, what malicious foe,*
> *Envying our happiness, and of his own*
> *Despairing, seeks to work our woe and shame*
> *By sly assault; and somewhere nigh at hand*

Watches, no doubt, with greedy hope to find
His wish and best advantage, us asunder,
Hopeless to circumvent us joined, where each
To other speedy aid might lend at need:
Whether his first design be to withdraw
Our fealty from God, or to disturb
Conjugal love, than which perhaps no bliss
Enjoyed by us excites his envy more . . .

Envious intrigue among literati

It is in no way due to certain peculiarities of our own time that the majority of the so-called intelligentsia, especially men of letters, have adopted towards their own society a somewhat malicious attitude of defiance. This goes back even further than the eighteenth century. The tendency of many writers to become the spokesmen of social resentment, to appeal, that is, for envy directed against all those who have in any way succeeded by conventional means, must rather be understood in terms of the psychological situation of genius, above all, of unrecognized genius.

We find an example of this in the section of Edgar Zilsel's book on the origin of the concept of genius devoted to L. B. Alberti. As a young man in the late sixteenth century, Alberti enviously compares, in his writing *On the Advantages and Disadvantages of the Sciences,* his lot as a man of letters with professions that are economically more rewarding, and adopts an attitude not often found until the eighteenth century. Alberti begins by listing all the hardships that await devotees of the sciences, such as all-night study, lack of time for pleasure and so on, and goes on to ask why so many men of learning are forced to live in wretched circumstances. He even provides figures, according to which only three out of three hundred literati can ever achieve any success, while knaves have no difficulty in reaching the summit. He maintains that only three kinds of brain-worker grow rich—lawyers, judges and doctors.[47]

Zilsel points out the tendency in other writers around the middle of the sixteenth century to paint a gloomy picture of the brain-worker's life.

[47] E. Zilsel, *Die Entstehung des Geniebegriffes, Ein Beitrag zur Ideengeschichte der Antike und des Frühkapitalismus,* Tübingen, 1926, p. 198.

According to Vasari, the *Ingegni* had to produce their precious results in poverty and without hope of reward. The blame lay with those who might have helped, but who took no interest in men of letters.[48]

Poets in the age of humanism and the early Renaissance must have suffered quite exceptionally from the envy of those around them. For this there was a very concrete, sociological reason which is put forward by Zilsel in his exemplary history of the concepts of genius, in the section dealing with envious intrigue. Unlike later times, including the present, the

> struggle for existence of Renaissance writers was not the struggle of the individual against a vast flood of books. . . . He did not have to defend himself against a compact mass of competitors personally unknown to him . . . the struggle for existence of Renaissance writers was confined to a very real game of intrigue between relatively few competitors, all very well known to each other, and found expression in a web of envy, petty jealousy, bickering, slander and polemic, in the growth of perpetually changing cliques . . . when everyone was fighting everyone else. This game of envious intrigue was frankly admitted by Renaissance writers, generally without metaphysical interpretation.[49]

This kind of unembarrassed and straightforward discussion of envy—so unlike the convention of the twentieth century—is shown by Zilsel in the greatest detail in his section on Petrarch, who devotes a whole chapter of his consolatory essay *De remediis* to envy, calling it a pestilence against which no man of parts is proof. But Zilsel also finds remarks in Boccaccio, Alberti, Verini, and Giovio which show that these men took for granted that they would be persecuted by the envious. Again and again intrigue, malicious actions and discontent are depicted as being the obvious machinations of the envious man.

Thus Verini was long uncertain whether to include living celebrities in his poem in praise of Florence. 'If he included them, he was afraid of seeming a flatterer, if he left them out, of seeming filled with envy, "the reciprocal Erinyes of men of learning." '[50]

[48] Op. cit., 200.

[49] Op. cit., pp. 194 f.

[50] Op. cit., p. 196.

Envy is also seen as the inevitable accompaniment of fame other than literary. For instance, Zilsel tells us that about the middle of the fifteenth century, Aeneas Sylvius Piccolomini mentions as perfectly natural the fact that the condottiere Picinino should forthwith begin to envy his celebrated *confrère* Sforza. Zilsel also recalls the role of envious intrigue as encountered in Cellini's autobiography or Bramante's intrigues against Michelangelo. This Zilsel sees as in part a consequence of the institution of patronage. It seems perfectly clear that competitors dependent on capriciously distributed and limited patronage are subject to particularly intense envy. For they do indeed experience the prototype of a closed economy, as understood by socialism in the nineteenth and twentieth centuries, where envy was invoked as a principle of distribution. Socialists were unable to believe in the possibility of a steadily rising national income that would eliminate poverty, and therefore laid emphasis on redistribution: increasing taxation of the prosperous would put money into the pockets of the poor—a method which, had it been logically applied, would have made impossible the improvement that has taken place during the last hundred years in the standard of living. But within a group dependent on a few patrons, the most gifted man who attracts the patron's favour, and hence his commissions, does in fact deprive all the less gifted artists and writers of real assets. Their envy is objective and rationally justified. With the rise of institutionalized patronage in the twentieth century, specifically, the foundations in the United States and more recently in some European countries, envy would appear once again to have been provoked among similarly situated groups of potential beneficiaries.

11

Envy as the Subject
of Philosophy

UNTIL ABOUT THIRTY YEARS AGO philosophers quite often dealt with the problem of envy as one of the inescapable questions of existence. They sought to define its terms and to establish its phenomenology. This chapter does not aim at a complete account of the problem of envy in the history of Western philosophy, but rather is concerned with demonstrating the regularity with which this subject has been considered.

Aristotle

In his *Rhetoric,* Aristotle perceives plainly the degree to which envy is felt only towards those who are themselves our equals, our peers. What is decisive is that we do not ourselves really wish to have what we envy, nor do we hope to acquire it in the course of our envy, but would like to see it destroyed so far as the other person is concerned. The more nearly we are equal to the man with whom we compare ourselves, the greater is our envy. Equality may be that of birth, of kinship, of age, of situation, of social distinction or of material possessions. A sense of envy results, in effect, when what we lack, by comparison with the other, is small. Aristotle quotes Hesiod: Potter against potter. We envy those whose possessions or achievements are a reflection on our own. They are our neighbours and equals. It is they, above all, who make plain the nature of our failure. Aristotle goes on to discuss emulation, a feeling often mistaken for envy.[1]

[1] Aristotle, *Rhetoric,* Book II, 10, from: Ross, W. D. (ed.), *The Works of Aristotle,* Vol. XI, Oxford, 1924, p. 1387b.

Francis Bacon

Bacon's ninth essay, which is also one of the longest of the fifty-eight, is entitled *Of Envy*. In some of the other essays, too, he stresses the role of envy in human activity, against which he warns us, advising us how best to guard against it, as in the essays on ambition, bodily deformity and seditions and troubles, for example.

As many of Bacon's biographers and commentators on his *Essays* have pointed out, there is no doubt that he himself suffered the effects of other people's envy and observed it among his fellow courtiers. His discussion of the problem of envy, which he saw as one of the most ineluctable and fundamental factors of social life, contains rules of great importance concerning envy and its avoidance, while with unerring sociological vision he lays bare the essentials.

Bacon begins by discussing the evil eye, which may stem from envy and can be synonymous with it, and draws attention to the relationship between envy and witchcraft. It is improbable that Bacon believed that envy was based on witchcraft, as nearly all primitive peoples do; he simply recalled this primal motive for sorcery.[2] Whether this is meant to be ironic or serious is irrelevant. Since the envious act contains an element of witchcraft, the only way envy can be averted is by the method used in a case of sorcery or an evil spell. Thus, he says,

> the wiser sort of great persons bring in ever upon the stage of life somebody upon whom to derive the envy that would come upon themselves; some-times upon ministers and servants; sometimes upon colleagues and associates; and the like; and for that turn there are never wanting some persons of violent and undertaking natures, who, so they may have power and business, will take it at any cost.[3]

Tactics to counter envy

While the tactics recommended by Bacon for countering envy are always applicable, they have seldom been as clearly discerned as here. His

---

[2] F. Bacon, *The Essays of Counsels, Civil and Moral,* ed. S. H. Reynolds, Oxford, 1890, p. 56.

[3] Op. cit., p. 60.

conviction that the only way to assuage envy is by propitiation or providing a substitute is illuminating. Yet Bacon suggests one other form of envy-avoidance, which is deliberate self-harm or abasement: '. . . whereas wise men will rather do sacrifice to envy, in suffering themselves sometimes of purpose to be crossed and overborne in things that do not much concern them.'[4]

Nevertheless, Bacon goes on to suggest that the man who carries his greatness in a plain and open manner will attract less envy than one who does so craftily and hypocritically. The man who seeks, but clumsily, to conceal his greatness—his luck, reputation, etc.—or to belittle it, seems to be saying what he does not himself truly believe, that fate is to blame for treating him better than he deserves. Such a man gives the impression of being conscious of his unworthiness and lack of desert, thus truly arousing the envy of others.[5] Elsewhere Bacon suggests that what especially inflames the envious man's animosity is the observation that his envy has rendered its object unsure of himself, so that he seeks to conciliate the destructive feelings by half-hearted gestures. Why is this?

An indirect answer is found in Bacon's phrase for the clumsy avoidance of envy, 'to disavow fortune,' which gives the appearance of casting doubt upon good fortune itself. It might be further added that if those who ought to benefit thereby—those, that is, who are favoured by fortune—reproach fortune, for the benefit of the envious, with unjustified partiality, they shatter the convention implicit in the concept of fortune or luck which is acknowledged by both the well placed and the less well placed in society, so that envy is given free rein.

From the start, Bacon distinguishes between two kinds of envy, public and private. Public envy is not merely envy that is openly admitted, but more exactly it is envy for the benefit of the public weal. This concept is similar to E. Raiga's 'indignation-envy.' Bacon could not have guessed that two centuries later a few social philosophers would succeed in so camouflaging or repressing private envy as almost always to present it in the guise of advocacy of the common weal. What since the nineteenth century has been called 'democratic envy' is most often, though by no means necessarily always, the presumed aggregate of the electors' private envy.

[4] Op. cit., p. 60.
[5] Op. cit., p. 60.

Public envy manifested in the public interest is a form of which no one need be ashamed, and by contrast with private or secret envy, as Bacon quite rightly recognized, there is something to be said in its favour.

> For public envy is as an ostracism [presumably the source of Bacon's insight], that eclipseth men when they grow too great. And therefore it [the fear of envy] is a bridle also to great ones, to keep them within bounds.
>
> This envy, being in the Latin word *invidia,* goeth in the modern languages by the name of *discontentment*; of which we shall speak in handling sedition.

Bacon is probably wrong in believing that *invidia,* literally 'a hostile look,' is concerned only with envy expressed in public opinion and not with the private person's spiteful envy. At any rate the current words in Spanish that derive from *invidia* all have the meaning of private envy. And by equating public envy with discontentment, Bacon circumscribes it. As is observable in a modern democracy, this form of envy, which keeps a check on politicians who have grown over-powerful, is also manifested in times of prosperity and by people who are far from having any cause for complaint.

Bacon devotes most space, however, to private or personal envy, which is a constituent of the 'public' form of envy and which probably plays a greater role in all societies. First he presents us with a typology of the envied and the envying man. The man devoid of virtue, who lacks all hope of ever attaining virtue, enviously causes the downfall of his more worthy fellows.[6]

His next observation is more interesting sociologically: 'Men of noble birth are noted to be envious towards new men when they rise. For the distance is altered, and it is like a deceit of the eye, that when others come on they think themselves go back.'[7]

Here Bacon is describing what might be called the envy of kings, which operates from the top downwards. One might call it the envy of aloofness, and it is a form that will be encountered repeatedly. This, perhaps, is absolute envy, because the man at the top truly has nothing to lose should others, through their own attainments, begin emulating his luxury and his wealth.

[6] Op. cit., p. 56.

[7] Op. cit., p. 57.

A mortgage with the world bank of fortune?

Bacon observes that those who are particularly envy-ridden are often the
deformed, the lame and eunuchs—in his own words, persons who
cannot possibly mend their case and hence attempt to impair another's.
Yet he mentions heroic exceptions who by their selfless deeds have
ennobled their very defects. But those whom Bacon regards as peculiarly
liable to envy are persons who have endured temporary setbacks, cata-
strophes or deprivations: 'For they are men . . . who think other men's
harms a redemption of their own sufferings.'[8] An instance that exactly
fits this case is the one given by the ethnologist Karsten concerning
South American Indians (see p. 54).

This is extremely revealing. It is easy enough to understand that
someone imprisoned in a vale of tears should look enviously upon those
who are more fortunate. But why does Bacon lay so much stress on
people who are *recovering* from a calamity? After the First World War
there were, for instance, certain people who came back unscathed and,
on the grounds of the privation they (and more especially others) had
suffered, set themselves up as the strictest of moral arbiters at a time
when privations were virtually a thing of the past. It might be supposed
that a person who has emerged in good fettle from a bad spell would
gratefully and gladly demonstrate his goodwill towards those whom fate
has favoured. Perhaps, in fact, Bacon discovered a motive of decisive
importance. For it might be that one who has escaped calamity, uncertain as to why fate has spared him, and filled with guilt towards those of
his companions who were not spared, will take out a retrospective
mortgage with 'fortune's tribunal,' the world bank of fortune, not only
by doing penance himself but by insisting that others should do so too.
One might interpret in the light of this hypothesis some of the ill-tem-
pered, exigent, pseudo-ascetic character of many Central European,
English and American writers since the Second World War.

In his catalogue of men especially prone to envy, Bacon mentions
those in close proximity: '. . . near kinsfolks, and fellows in office, and
those that have been bred together, are more apt to envy their equals
when they are raised. For it doth upbraid unto them their own fortunes,
and pointeth at them and cometh oftener into their remembrance, and

---

[8] Op. cit., pp. 57 f.

incurreth likewise more into the note of others.'[9] Bacon also gave some thought to those who are not as a rule so readily envied.

Among these are persons whose advancement takes place when they have already achieved eminence. They appear to have earned their luck, and no one, Bacon believes, envies a man the settlement of his debt. What is of significance for the sociology of envy is that 'envy is ever joined with the comparing of a man's self; and where there is no comparison, no envy; and therefore kings are not envied but by kings.'[10]

Bacon is also aware of the subjective time-element in envy, which is a function of the awareness of time in one who observes another's good fortune: '. . . unworthy persons are most envied at their first coming in [to an exalted position], and afterwards overcome it better; whereas contrariwise, persons of worth and merit are most envied when their fortune continueth long. For by that time, though their virtue be the same, yet it hath not the same lustre; for fresh men grow up that darken it.'[11]

In this, as in the ensuing instances, Bacon chiefly has in mind the life at court where people may gain or lose the monarch's favour for a variety of reasons. Thus he thinks that those of low degree, partly because their reputation is already such that little can be added to it: 'and envy is as the sunbeams, that beat hotter upon a bank or steep rising ground, than upon a flat. And for the same reason those that are advanced by degrees are less envied than those that are advanced suddenly and *per saltum* [at a bound].'[12]

The only antidote to envy named by Bacon is pity. Hence those who have earned their honours by great travail, perils and cares are less exposed to envy. They are sometimes pitied. 'Pity ever healeth envy.' It is therefore wise and prudent in politicians, having attained greatness, to lament continually their toilsome existence. Not because they themselves find it so, but in order to take the sting out of envy. Yet caution should be observed; the toil must stem only from those duties that

[9] Op. cit., p. 58.
[10] Op. cit., pp. 58 ff.
[11] Op. cit., p. 59.
[12] Op. cit., p. 59.

devolve upon them. Self-imposed, superfluous cares might rather intensify envy.[13]

Adam Smith

In his *Wealth of Nations,* after considering envy, malice and resentment, Adam Smith leaves no room for doubt that only the containment of this motive by a society founded upon law and order will permit inequality of property, and hence economic growth. Men can, indeed, co-exist with a fair measure of public safety even without any authority to shield them from injustice arising out of these passions. But not in a society with great disparity of property.

> Wherever there is great property, there is great inequality. For one very rich man, there must be at least five hundred poor. The affluence of the few supposes the indigence of the many, who are often both driven by want, and prompted by envy, to invade his possessions. It is only under the shelter of the civil magistrate that the owner of that valuable property, which is acquired by the labour of many years, or perhaps of many successive generations, can sleep a single night in security. He is at all times surrounded by unknown enemies, whom, though he never provoked, he can never appease, and from whose injustice he can be protected only by the powerful arm of the civil magistrate continually held up to chastise it. The acquisition of valuable and extensive property, therefore, necessarily requires the establishment of civil government. Where there is no property, or at least none that exceeds the value of two or three days' labour, civil government is not so necessary.[14]

Adam Smith is quite definitely wrong, however, in believing that there could exist any property so small that the owner would be safe against envious aggression.

Immanuel Kant

In his late work, *The Metaphysic of Morals* (1797), Kant discusses envy, which he regards as belonging to the 'abhorrent family of ingratitude and

---

[13] Op. cit., p. 59.
[14] A. Smith, *The Wealth of Nations.* Modern Library edition, p. 670.

Schadenfreude.' These he calls 'The vice of human hate that is the complete opposite of human love.' It is a hate that is not 'open and violent, but secret and disguised, so that baseness is added to neglect of one's duty to one's neighbour, and thus one's duty to oneself also suffers.'

Kant gives full expression to the philosophical doctrine and ethic of values, according to which envy is the very antithesis of virtue, the denial of humanity. His is one of the most complete definitions of envy:

> Envy (*livor*) is a tendency to perceive with displeasure the good of others, although it in no way detracts from one's own, and which, when it leads to action (in order to diminish that good) is called qualified envy, but otherwise only ill-will (*invidentia*); it is however only an indirect, malevolent frame of mind, namely a disinclination to see our own good overshadowed by the good of others, because we take its measure not from its intrinsic worth, but by comparison with the good of others and then go on to symbolize that evaluation.[15]

In more primitive societies, as we have seen, for instance, among the Pacific Dobuans or the North American Navaho, it is held that another person's good is factually the cause of a man's own ill. A certain degree of rationality and maturity, or at least complete freedom from a magical view of things, is required before the envious man can fully realize that the man he envies does not possess something which, but for the possessor's existence, he, the envious man, might otherwise have.

Kant goes on to discuss an expression that neutralizes envy. It is so current today, particularly in America and England, that one may assume that it serves to repress the knowledge of envy's true nature and function in human relations. Kant writes: 'It is no doubt for this reason that the harmony and happiness of a marriage, family, &c., is sometimes described as *enviable,* as if it were permissible in certain cases to envy a person.' It is a turn of speech often used today, as it was used apparently in Kant's time, to give expression to genuine envy but in a socially acceptable form—sometimes, even, to warn the envied man against one's own envy or that of others. This may, indeed, represent a social control whereby influence is gained over another person's style of life, or over the pleasure he takes in life. The following sentence of Kant's

[15] I. Kant, *Metaphysik der Sitten* (The Metaphysics of Morals) in *Sämtliche Werke,* ed. K. Vorländer, Vol. 3, 4th ed., Leipzig, 1922, p. 316.

introduces three further fundamental insights into envy which are valid
for any society:

'The impulse for envy is thus inherent in the nature of man, and only
its manifestation makes of it an abominable vice, a passion not only
distressing and tormenting to the subject, but intent on the destruction of
the happiness of others, and one that is opposed to man's duty towards
himself as towards other people.'[16]

It is therefore natural for man to feel envious impulses. He will always
compare himself with others, generally with those who are socially not
too remote, but the vice that threatens personal relations, and hence
society as a whole, becomes manifest only when the envious man
proceeds to act, or fails to act, appropriately (by deliberate failure to
warn or help), to the detriment of another, or at the very least gives
enough play to his envy to cause himself harm.

Because envy is a purely destructive passion, quite unproductive of
any positive value either for the individual or for society, Kant declares it
to be an infringement of duty, both of the envious man towards himself
and of the envier towards the envied man. Kant could scarcely have
guessed that out of the roots of the French Revolution, of which he
himself was so attentive a witness, there would within a hundred years
arise for all mankind a new version of his categorical imperative, whose
wording would be: 'Envy others so fiercely that the appeasement of your
envy (impossible though that be) will become the foundation of all
lawgiving.' Or more precisely: 'Envy others in such a way that your
envious demands become the yardstick of all lawgiving.' (Only one word
has been changed in Kant's phrasing—the word 'envy' has been substituted for the word 'act.')

The psychology of ingratitude

With an insight into psychological correlations that is scarcely available
to us now, Kant presents his psychology of *ingratitude*. The word 'envy'
does not appear in this particular section, but Kant counts ingratitude
among the 'horrid family of envy.' Almost a hundred years later
Nietzsche gave a very similar interpretation of ingratitude, but our own
age, obsessed by the desire to 'do good' to the most distant nations and

---

[16] Op. cit., pp. 316 f.

peoples, is unwilling to admit that the recipients of its welfare, for reasons that are obvious, deeply envy and hate the givers and, in extreme cases, live only in the hope of the latter's destruction. Kant then goes on:

'Ingratitude towards a benefactor which, if taken to the point of hatred of that benefactor, is qualified ingratitude, but otherwise is termed thoughtlessness, though it is generally held to be a very dreadful vice; yet it is so notorious in man that to make an enemy as a result of benefactions rendered is not regarded as improbable.'

How can this discovery have been lost from sight so completely that, since 1950, the West has supposed that foreign policy could be superseded by development aid to the 'Third World'? One mentions this simply in order to show that we cannot afford to ignore the problems of envy.

What is significant in Kant's description is the remark that 'indeed, in the public view it is a vice greatly abhorred.' No one admits publicly, and hence public opinion does not admit, that ingratitude is the norm. It is astounding that countless benefactors allow themselves to be persuaded over and over that ingratitude with the resultant hatred is a rare and special case. It could be that by ignoring ingratitude many benefactors are able to repress in themselves a consciousness of their *own* envy of someone else. If a person were to admit that the recipients of his welfare were in fact envious of him, he would be forced to recognize that his own ambivalent feelings towards benefactors might be something as contemptible as envy and hatred. Since most people are both recipient and benefactor they retain a memory of earlier benefactions, which may cause the benefactor to harbour ambivalent feelings throughout his life.

How, then, does Kant explain the constant recurrence of ingratitude?

The reason that such a vice is possible lies in the misunderstanding of a man's duty towards himself, in that he imagines, because the benefactions of others subject him to an obligation, that he does not need them; nor will he ask for them, but bear the burdens of life alone, rather than put them upon others and thus become indebted to them: for he fears that by doing so he will sink to the level of client in relation to his patron, and this is repugnant to true self-esteem.

Thus, according to Kant, uninhibited gratitude is possible only towards those (ancestors, parents) whose benefactions cannot but precede our own. But our gratitude towards our 'contemporaries is but meagre—indeed, in order to conceal the inequality that lies between us and them it may well become the very opposite'—namely, hatred and animosity.

To Kant ingratitude is a reprehensible vice not only because its example may cause men to desist from benefactions and hence diminish the amount of mutual human aid (which no social system can dispense with entirely), but also because 'it is as though love were turned upside down and a mere lack of love further debased into an urge to hate the person who loves us.'[17]

Kant believes, however, and experience has repeatedly proved him right, that a display of ingratitude will not necessarily bring about a decrease in benefactions, because the benefactor 'may well be convinced that the very disdain of any such reward as gratitude only adds to the inner moral worth of his benefaction.'

However, I would add, benefaction in the face of hostile ingratitude only serves to intensify the passion and the principle of ingratitude, the giver having proved himself so much bigger, better and more un-assailable than he previously appeared. Most of the observations made between 1955 and 1965 in areas receiving aid from the major industrial countries provide what is tantamount to experimental proof of Kant's maxims. This large-scale example of international benefaction is pecu-liarly clear because in the age of the Cold War only sovereign govern-ments as opposed to private recipients could afford to show immediate and ostentatious ingratitude, an ingratitude almost proportionate to the benefits received.

Before Kant's discussion of the family of envy, and hence of ingrati-tude, he also examined the duty of gratitude, and in doing so he indirectly touched on some of the problems of envy.

That gratitude is a moral obligation essential for a peaceful society is deduced by Kant from the ineluctable fact, arising from our existence in a time-continuum, that 'no requital of a benefaction received can ever absolve us of the debt.'[18]

The recipient can never catch up with the giver because the latter, from

---

[17] Op. cit., p. 317.
[18] Op. cit., p. 312.

the viewpoint of merit, has the advantage of having been first in the field of benevolence. (Significantly, some primitive peoples have succeeded in evolving a practice and ethic of giving that eliminates the problem of priority in giving.) Kant considers that gratitude is not a mere opportunist maxim to secure a further benefit, but that the respect due to a person on account of his benefaction to us is a direct requirement of the moral law, in other words, a duty. But he goes even further:

'But gratitude must be seen as a *sacred* duty, as one, that is, whose infringement . . . may destroy the very principle of the moral desire to do good. For that moral object is sacred in respect of which an obligation can never be fully redeemed by an equivalent act.'

If Kant sets so high a value on gratitude, because it is not humanly possible ever fully to requite the benefactor, it is surely because he sensed the social discord, the chronic envy and resentment, that must arise in a society where envy, and hence ingratitude, came to be sanctioned as the accepted response. The moral obligation of gratitude thus indirectly inhibits envious feelings of aggression. Without such an inhibition—exerted upon the individual by the cultural ethos, by the axioms of decency and by religion—there would be a danger that unconsidered benefactions in a society might have altogether unexpected consequences.

Kant also shows the frame of mind in which the duty of gratitude should be performed and the manner of its performance:

The lowest degree is to render *equal* services to the benefactor, should he be able to receive them (if still living), and if not, to extend them to others; not to regard a benefaction received as a burden of which one would be glad to be relieved (because the recipient stands one step below his patron, so that his pride is wounded); but to accept the occasion of it as a moral blessing, i.e., as a given opportunity to pledge this virtue of human love [gratitude] which represents both the sincerity of the benevolent mentality and the tenderness of benevolence (attention to the finest nuance of this in the concept of duty), thus cultivating human love.[19]

Most of us know people who find it almost impossible to accept help, a kindness, a present or a benefaction. Psychiatry has described extreme

[19] Op. cit., pp. 312 f.

forms of such pathological modesty. What is in fact involved is not the
virtue of modesty, but the idea of even the smallest obligation (i.e., the
duty of gratitude) being so intolerable to some people that they would
rather make themselves ridiculous, or hurt others' feelings, than accept
anything from anyone. Are such people afraid of their own envy, or of the
vice of ingratitude? Do they realize that they are simply incapable of
gracefully accepting a natural benefaction without suffering from a
corrosive sense of inferiority towards the benefactor, a feeling that will
develop into hatred and ostentatious ingratitude?

Schopenhauer on envy

In Schopenhauer we find an analysis of human wickedness which concludes with an inquiry into envy. This philosopher believes that everybody has within him something that is morally altogether bad and that
even the noblest character will at times display a surprising streak of evil.

Schopenhauer recalls that, of all animals, man alone torments his own
kind for entertainment. 'For truly in the heart of each one of us there is a
wild beast that only awaits the opportunity to rant and roar, to hurt
others, and, should they seek to bar its way, to destroy: it is here that all
lust for war and fighting originates.' This leads Schopenhauer on to an
analysis of envy: 'The worst trait in human nature, however, is *Schadenfreude,* for it is closely related to cruelty . . . generally . . . appearing
where compassion should find a place. . . . In another sense, envy is
opposed to compassion, since it stems from an opposite cause.'[20]

In his chapter 'On Judgment, Criticism, Applause and Fame,' Schopenhauer describes in detail the manifestations of envy. If the acerbity of
his language betrays his disappointment and bitterness regarding contemporary philosophical criticism, some of his observations still remain
valid and significant for the sociological study of literature.

Envy he describes as 'the soul of the alliance of mediocrity which
everywhere foregathers instinctively and flourishes silently, being directed against individual excellence of whatever kind. For the latter is
unwelcome in every individual sphere of action. . . .'[21]

[20] A. Schopenhauer, *Sämtliche Werke,* ed. A. Hübscher, Leipzig, 1939, Vol. 6,
pp. 223–39.
[21] Op. cit., p. 491.

Schopenhauer believes, for example, that it was the envy of German musicians that had caused them for a whole generation to refuse obstinately to recognize the merit of Rossini.[22]

Even more remarkable, however, is what Schopenhauer has to say about modes of behaviour to avoid arousing envy: '. . . the virtue of modesty was only discovered as a protection against envy,' and he quotes Goethe's saying: 'Only scoundrels are modest.'[23]

Envy, Schopenhauer believes has two favourite methods—to praise what is bad or, alternatively, to remain silent about what is good: '. . . for every one who gives praise to another, whether in his own field or in a related one, in principle deprives himself of it: he can praise only at the expense of his own reputation.'[24]

Among his remarks, Schopenhauer includes a quotation from an article in the London *Times* of October 9, 1858, a passage which gives 'the most unadorned and strongest expression' to the fact that envy 'is irreconcilable in regard to personal advantages.'[25]

> There is no vice, of which a man can be guilty, no meanness, no shabbiness, no unkindness, which excites so much indignation among his contemporaries, friends and neighbours, as his success. This is the one unpardonable crime, which reason cannot defend, nor humility mitigate. 'When heaven with such parts has blest him, Have I not reason to detest him?' is a genuine and natural expression of the vulgar human mind. The man who writes as we cannot write, who speaks as we cannot speak, labours as we cannot labour, thrives as we cannot thrive, has accumulated on his own person all the offences of which man can be guilty. Down with him! Why cumbereth he the ground?

Sören Kierkegaard

Kierkegaard's deep concern with envy is exceptional. His biographers seek the reason for this not only in his personal destiny, but also in the Danish environment which was especially prone to envy. At one point Kierkegaard writes:

[22] Op. cit., pp. 491–2.
[23] Op. cit., p. 492.
[24] Op. cit., pp. 493–4.
[25] Op. cit., p. 230.

'Anyone who wishes to understand the nature of offence should make a study of human envy, a study I am offering as a luxury item and which I believe I have done thoroughly.'[26]

Kierkegaard's discussion of envy is found throughout his work. By contrast with many authors of the mid-twentieth century, he uses the ascribed motive of envy in many passages as a self-evident explanation for certain human modes of behaviour, and especially to explain sudden reversals of feeling. Kierkegaard frequently speaks of the envy of the gods or of the deity, of the envy of ostracism and the argument of the potsherd which prevails above all better ones. He regards envy and stupidity as the two great forces in society, prevalent above all in the small town where the 'repellent lust of envy' is one of the favourite pastimes.

Like Nietzsche a few decades later, Kierkegaard constantly points out the envy-motive concealed in apparently harmless and generally current turns of speech:

> Great men are defeated by the trivial things ordinary men take in their stride. . . . How strange it is. Is it not odd, really something for the psychologist to ponder, the way in which it could justly be said that life envies the distinguished man, mockingly intimating to him that he is a man like any other, like the least of men, that the human element demands its rights.[27]

And elsewhere we read:

> Envy is concealed admiration. An admirer who senses that devotion cannot make him happy will choose to become envious of that which he admires. He will speak a different language, and in this language he will now declare that that which he really admires is a thing of no consequence, something foolish, illusory, perverse and highflown. Admiration is happy self-abandon, envy, unhappy self-assertion.[28]

[26] S. Kierkegaard, *Sygdommen til Doden* (The Sickness unto Death) in *Samlede Vaerker,* ed. H. O. Lange, Copenhagen, 1920–30, Vol. XI, pp. 197 f.

[27] Ibid., *Fire opbyggelige Taler* (Four Edifying Discourses), Vol. V, p. 141.

[28] See note 26.

According to Kierkegaard, mistrust also belongs to the same genus as envy, as do *Schadenfreude* and baseness. He writes:

> And there is envy; it is quick to abandon a man, and yet it does not abandon him as it were by letting him go, no, it hastens to assist his fall. And this being once assured, envy will hasten to his dark corner whence he will summon his even more hideous cousin, malicious glee, that they may rejoice together—at their own cost.[29]

Kierkegaard sees, too, envy's role in drawing unenvious people into class conflict. Who does not envy with us is against us! His aversion to envy as a legitimate weapon in social reform naturally causes him to be reproached with conservatism. Yet he correctly recognizes the difficult position, doubtless acute in any society, of the man who either cannot or will not envy:

> And should one of the humble folk, whose heart was innocent of such secret envy of the power, honour and distinction of the powerful, the honoured and the distinguished, and who refuses to succumb to corruption from without—should he, without craven obsequiousness, and fearing no man, modestly, but with sincere delight, give due honour to those above him; and should he sometimes be happier and more joyous even perhaps than they, then he too will discover the twofold danger that threatens him. By his own kind he will, perchance, be rejected as a traitor, despised as a servile spirit; by those who are favoured he may be misunderstood and perhaps reviled as a presumptuous man.[30]

Kierkegaard's writings provide not only a running commentary on envy in human existence, but in some places a step towards a philosophy of envy which is one of the most profound treatments of the subject. Kierkegaard depicts his era: It is a revolutionary but passionless and reflective age performing the dialectical feat of 'allowing everything to remain intact, but craftily robbing it of its meaning. Instead of culminating in rebellion it enervates the inner reality of things in a reflexive

---

[29] Ibid., *Kjerlighedens Gjerninger* (The Works of Love), Vol. IX, p. 245.
[30] Op. cit., p. 245.

tension which allows everything to remain intact and yet has changed the whole of life into an ambiguity.'[31]

Thus there is no intention to do away with royal power, to tear down what is excellent, to abolish Christian terminology, but

> secretly they desire the knowledge that nothing decisive is meant by it. And they want to be unrepentant, for they have indeed destroyed nothing. They would no more like to have a great king than a hero of liberty, or someone with religious authority—no, what they want is to let what exists continue to exist in all innocence, while knowing in a more or less reflective knowledge that it does not exist.[32]

The age of levelling

From here, Kierkegaard proceeds to the principle of envy. In the same way that enthusiasm is the unifying principle in an impassioned age, so

> in a passionless and strongly reflective age *envy is the negative unifying principle*. Yet this should not be immediately understood in the ethical sense as a reproach, no, the idea of reflection, if one may speak thus, is envy, and envy is therefore a twofold quality, being the selfishness of the individual and then again that of others against him.[33]

Thus to Kierkegaard envy is primarily, as one might say, a social-psychological factor, condemning the individual to a false self-image:

> Selfish envy in the form of the wish demands too much of the individual himself, and thus becomes an obstacle to him. It pampers him as would the predilection of a yielding mother, for envy of himself prevents the individual from surrendering himself. The envy of others in which the individual participates against others is envious in the negative critical sense.[34]

The reflective envy then becomes changed into ethical envy, like enclosed air which always develops its own poison, and this is then detestable envy.

[31] Ibid., *En literair Anmeldelse to Tidsaldre* (The Present Age), Vol. VIII, p. 73.

[32] Op. cit., p. 76.

[33] Op. cit.—'against him' refers to the individual.

[34] Op. cit., p. 77.

Kierkegaard here gives a detailed analysis of the incipient age of levelling. According to a Kierkegaard expert, this was instigated by abuse in the humorous paper *The Corsair*, which had highly disagreeable consequences for him.[35] First Kierkegaard sees a playful outlet for envy in the so-called age of enthusiasm; there can, as it were, be envy with character, as when, for instance, ostracism in Greece could also bring honour to the man who was banished. And when one of the voters told Aristides that he was voting for his banishment because his reputation as the only just man was intolerable to him, this was far from being a slur on Aristides' honour. But it is an altogether different thing if envy becomes clandestine and featureless, and by concealment implies its non-existence, yet endeavours in a multitude of ways to organize society for envy's benefit:

'The envy which establishes itself is the process of levelling and while a passionate age spurs on, lifts and casts down, raises and lowers, a reflective passionless age does the opposite, it strangles and inhibits and levels. Levelling is a silent mathematical abstract activity, that avoids all sensation.'[36]

Kierkegaard at once highlights what is sociologically characteristic by his remark that rebellion, but never levelling, may be led by one individual:

'. . . for then he would become the ruler, and would have eluded levelling. The single individual in his own small circle may help towards the levelling, but this is an abstract power, and levelling is the victory of abstraction over individuals. Levelling in modern times is the equivalent in a reflective age of fate in antiquity.'[37]

A few pages further on there is an observation that is very pertinent: 'In order that levelling can really take place, a phantom must first be brought into being, its spirit a monstrous abstraction, an all-embracing something that is Nothing, a mirage—that phantom is the Public. . . .'[38]

In seeing the public, a vast nonentity, as the true instigator of the levelling process, Kierkegaard anticipates Heidegger's concept of

[35] A note by the translator, Emmanuel Hirsch, in the German edition, *Gesammelte Werke*, Düsseldorf, 1952, Vol. XVII, p. 158.

[36] Op. cit., p. 79.

[37] Op. cit., p. 79.

[38] Op. cit., p. 84.

'Them.' Hence the censorious catch-phrase 'One just doesn't do such things' usually implies a warning that to do them in fact is to display an individualism that might attract the envy of the less independent.

In his *Christian Discourses* of 1848, only a few years after his discovery of the approaching age of levelling, of which he saw the first signs a generation before Nietzsche, there is a strange application of the envy concept whereby the blame appears to be shifted to the envied man or what is enviable. He writes: 'All earthly and worldly property is, strictly speaking, selfish, envious; its possession, envious or envied, is bound either way to impoverish others. What I have, no one else can have; the more I have, the less can anyone else have.'[39]

Even entirely lawful possession or acquisition, and even a man's readiness to share his earthly goods with others, could not obviate the fact that possession is of itself envious. This does not apply, however, to possessions of the mind. Because their very concept involves communication, possession of them is without envy and is beneficial. There are, however, other, more imperfect intellectual possessions, such as insight, knowledge, ability, talent, which are not in themselves communication. By possessing these a man may provoke the envy of others, and hence be a selfish person. 'Thus the clever man becomes ever more clever, yet in the envious sense, in such a way that he seeks to derive advantage from the very fact that others become increasingly simple by comparison with the growth of his cleverness. . . .'[40]

It may at first seem strange that Kierkegaard should here designate the owner of a possession or of a skill, against which others can measure their relative inferiority, as the envious man. But if we reflect—and the view is also that of this book—that envy's inevitable presence in this world is due to the fact that one person owns something, of whatever nature, which makes another feel the want of it, this use of the word is comprehensible.

Friedrich Nietzsche

Like Schopenhauer and Kierkegaard, Nietzsche also recognized the function of envy in human society. The force of his observations must be

[39] Ibid., *Kristlige Taler* (Christian Discourses, 1848), Vol. X, pp. 120 f.
[40] Op. cit., p. 124.

attributed to countless experiences of being envied. His entire opus, from first to last, contains references to the problem of envy, but they are most abundant in his middle period, of which the central work is *Human, All Too Human*. As a classical philologist he was familiar with the Greek idea of the envy of the gods. He had, however, a tendency to idealize this and, like Kierkegaard, to underestimate the full import of envious manifestations in Athenian democracy. This realization came only much later, with the Dane, Svend Ranulf.

The concepts of envy and resentment are frequently to be met with in Nietzsche; there is no periphrasis and they are invariably understood in the sense of those authors we have already discussed. Nietzsche does not confuse the concepts jealousy and envy as unfortunately so many of his predecessors and successors have repeatedly done. In his anthropology, Nietzsche proceeds from ever latent envy, one of man's deepest tendencies, which is aroused as soon as he finds himself in society. Yet Nietzsche hardly perceived the inevitability of envy, even in cases where the difference between the individuals under comparison is infinitesimal. No doubt Nietzsche focused too much on considerable and startling differences between the great and the small, the high and the low, to notice how little the intensity of envy depends on the objective margin between the envious man and his object.

Nietzsche, the philosopher, postulates a man who has finally succeeded in overcoming the envy within him. To Nietzsche, the French Revolution and all subsequent revolutions, the idea of equality and certain conceptions of social justice were all equally abhorrent, as they had been to Goethe, on whom he here draws for support. Yet here and there we find in Nietzsche thoughts which suggest the view that the social dynamic of these motives and ideas is indispensable, that the roots of social control lie in the desire for equality and justice, or in other words the envious impulse, and that without them human society as we know it is barely conceivable. Notable, too, is the clarity with which he perceives the need for every group ('herd') to provide a safety valve for the envy of its members so as to divert it from destroying the group. In one of his aphorisms, he declares that this function has been taken over by the priest. With uncanny insight he foresaw the manner in which the envious and resentful would succeed, during the twentieth century, in making people feel that happiness was a disgrace. He literally anticipates the problem with which Paul Tournier has to struggle.

Envy among the Greeks

In December 1872, Nietzsche discusses in *Greek Philosophy and Other Essays* what he describes as Homer's contest. He suggests that nothing so much distinguishes the Greek world of antiquity from our own as its recognition of the agonistic element, the fight and joy in victory. This serves to explain the difference in tone between individual ethical concepts, for example those of Eris and of envy. The whole of Greek antiquity shows a view of resentment and envy entirely different from our own, hence the predicates resentment and envy were not only applicable to the nature of the wicked Eris, but also to the other goddess, good Eris. Nietzsche writes:

> The Greek is *envious* and conceives of this quality not as a blemish, but as the effect of a beneficent deity. What a gulf of ethical judgment between us and him! Because he is envious he also feels, with every superfluity of honour, riches, splendour and fortune, the envious eye of a god resting on himself, and he fears this envy: in this case the latter reminds him of the transitoriness of every human lot: he dreads his very happiness and, sacrificing the best of it, he bows before the divine envy.[41]

Nietzsche next supposes that this conception did not lead to estrangement between the Greek and his gods, but rather only to his renouncing all competition with them, so that he was impelled into jealous competition with every other living being, and even with the dead whose fame alone could excite consuming envy in the living. Nietzsche's interpretation of the institution of ostracism is almost the same as the argument used in America in the twentieth century to justify anti-trust laws; an institution, that is, which, by banning or silencing the greatest, safely restores competition among a number of the less great.

'The original sense of this peculiar institution however is not that of a safety-valve but that of a stimulant. The all-excelling individual was to be removed in order that the contest of forces might reawaken. . . .'[42]

The basic assumptions of these aphorisms in *Human, All Too Human* devoted to envy might be summed up as follows: Envy and jealousy, 'the

---

[41] Friedrich Nietzsche, *Collected Works*, London, 1910, Vol. II, pp. 55–6.

[42] Op. cit., Vol. 7, p. 57.

private parts of the human psyche,'[43] adopt the strangest disguises. Whereas ordinary envy clucks as soon as the envied hen lays an egg, and so is mitigated, there is another and deeper form of envy: '. . . envy that in such a case becomes dead silent, desiring that every mouth shall be sealed and always more and more angry because the desire is not gratified. Silent envy grows in silence.'[44]

Schadenfreude

There is a brilliant analysis of *Schadenfreude,* which, according to Nietzsche, came into existence only after man had learnt to see other men as belonging to his own kind, in other words, since the founding of society:

> Malicious joy arises when a man consciously finds himself in evil plight and feels anxiety of remorse or pain. The misfortune that overtakes B. makes him equal to A., and A. is reconciled and no longer envious. If A. is prosperous, he still hoards up in his memory B.'s misfortune as a capital, so as to throw it in the scale as a counter-weight when he himself suffers adversity. In this case too he feels 'malicious joy' (*Schadenfreude*). The sentiment of equality thus applies its standards to the domain of luck and chance. Malicious joy is the commonest expression of victory and restoration of equality, even in a higher state of civilization.[45]

Nietzsche believed that 'where equality is really recognized and permanently established, we see the rise of that propensity that is generally considered immoral and would scarcely be conceivable in a state of nature—envy.'[46]

This sentence is at once right and wrong. Nietzsche is right in believing, like de Tocqueville fifty years earlier, that a society thoroughly imbued with the idea of equality will become increasingly envious as this principle becomes institutionalized. Contrary to what its champions since the French Revolution have maintained, equality is, in fact, the

[43] Op. cit., Vol. 2, p. 22.

[44] Op. cit., Vol. 2, p. 37.

[45] Op. cit., Vol. 7, p. 207.

[46] Op. cit., Vol. 7, p. 209.

expression of envy and is very far from being the one and only way of curing it. But Nietzsche is wrong in assuming that there had been a primitive state of nature where men had not been envious of each other. However, he brings out clearly the connection between envy, the idea of equality and the conception of social justice:

> The envious man is susceptible to every sign of individual superiority to the common herd, and wishes to depress everyone once more to the level—or raise himself to the superior place. Hence arise two different modes of action, which Hesiod designated good and bad Eris. In the same way, in a condition of equality, there arises indignation if A. is prosperous above and B. unfortunate beneath their deserts and equality. These latter, however, are emotions of nobler natures. They feel the want of justice and equity in things that are independent of the arbitrary choice of men—or, in other words, they desire the equality recognized by man to be recognized as well by Nature and chance. They are angry that men of equal merits should not have equal fortune.[47]

In a relatively short aphorism in *Dawn of Day* Nietzsche points out the connection between envy and nihilism. Under the heading 'The world destroyers' he writes:

'When some men fail to accomplish what they desire to do they exclaim angrily, "May the whole world perish!" This repulsive emotion is the pinnacle of envy, whose implication is "If I cannot have *something,* no one is to have *anything,* no one is to *be* anything!" '[48]

Because magnanimous behaviour is more enraging to a man's enemies than is unconcealed envy, this being a 'plaintive variety of modesty,' Nietzsche suggests that envy is sometimes used as a cloak by those who are themselves not at all envious.[49]

Resentment

In his *Genealogy of Morals,* Nietzsche describes resentment.

> All men of resentment are these physiologically distorted and worm-riddled persons, a whole quivering kingdom of burrowing revenge, inde-

---

[47] Op. cit., Vol. 7, p. 209.

[48] Op. cit., Vol. 9, p. 266.

[49] Op. cit., Vol. 7, p. 172.

fatigable and insatiable in its outbursts against the happy, and equally so in disguises for revenge, in pretexts for revenge: when will they really reach their final, fondest, most sublime triumph of revenge? At that time, doubtless, when they succeed in pushing their own misery, indeed all misery there is, into the *consciousness* of the happy; so that the latter begin one day to be ashamed of their happiness, and perchance say to themselves when they meet, 'It is a shame to be happy! *There is too much misery!* '[50]

There can be no doubt that Nietzsche here forecasts one of the most momentous developments of the twentieth century, which alone made possible effusions such as Paul Tournier's on the subject of true and false guilt-feelings. Or again one need only recall the innumerable masochistic writings in which Westerners indulge in shame and self-indictment because of the inequality between them and the so-called developing countries. Nietzsche sees this development as the biggest and most fateful of misunderstandings. The world in which the happy and successful begin to doubt their right to happiness, he regards as a world turned upside down. Nietzsche follows this by writing about what he calls the tremendous historic mission of the ascetic priest in a society. The priest acts as a deflector of resentment by telling the sufferer searching for a cause, an instigator or, to be exact, a guilty instigator, of his suffering, that certainly there is a guilty person, but that person is the sufferer himself.[51] Nietzsche believes that even if this were objectively false, it would still deflect resentment from action dangerous to society. A Marxist would here reproach Nietzsche with accepting religion solely as an opiate for the people in order to avoid class war; but seen against the background of this book, Nietzsche's view, devoid of religious sentiment, may have been realistic in that fundamentally no society can be effective or even attain a tolerable social climate, if it does not possess that kind of belief that will bring the underprivileged man to see, if not himself, then the effect of blind chance as a cause of his condition. We have already seen the dead ends in which primitive peoples stagnate as a result of conceiving that every misfortune or loss of asset experienced by the individual is deliberately engineered by a fellow tribesman.

Nietzsche examines resentment in many forms, and also its physiological manifestations, as a reactive and enduring mode of behaviour.

[50] Op. cit., Vol. 13, p. 160.
[51] Op. cit., Vol. 13, p. 162.

Resentment overcomes those people who are denied the proper positive reaction and who can find indemnity only in imaginary revenge. Such resentment is slave morality, and the slave rebellion in morality begins when resentment itself becomes creative and produces values.[52]

But significantly Nietzsche opposes attempts to seek the origin of justice, in his sense of the term, in the area of resentment. Some of his contemporaries, whom he calls 'anarchists and anti-Semites,' themselves filled with resentment, made an attempt to sanctify, in the name of justice, their own thirst for revenge, as though justice, in the last analysis, were only the sense of injury carried to a further stage.

He writes: 'And that to which I alone call attention is the circumstance that it is the spirit of revenge from which develops this new nuance of scientific equity (for the benefit of hate, envy, mistrust, jealousy, suspicion, rancour, revenge).' As opposed to this, Nietzsche maintains that a man is inspired by true justice when, and only when, even under the onslaught of personal injury, contumely, aspersion, the just man's deep and tolerant objectivity, his clear and lofty vision, remain unclouded. And even the man who attacks is closer to justice than is the man who reacts resentfully.[53]

Zarathustra mocks the detractors and snivellers to whose envy his happiness is intolerable: 'How *could* they endure my happiness, if I did not put around it accidents, and winter-privations, and bearskin caps, and enmantling snowflakes!'[54]

Here we have the same thought as that already encountered in Francis Bacon, that because of the envious it is often necessary to simulate misfortune.

Max Scheler

Scheler presented a detailed analysis of the problem of envy in a study published between 1912 and 1914, *Das Ressentiment im Aufbau der Moralen* (Resentment in the Structuring of Ethics). He devotes about a hundred pages to a phenomenology of the envious man, whom, follow-

[52] Op. cit., Vol. 13, pp. 101 f.
[53] Op. cit., Vol. 13, p. 85.
[54] Op. cit., Vol. 11, p. 54.

ing Nietzsche, he sees as the resentful man. Like Nietzsche before him, he stresses the subjective time factor necessary to the development of the sense of impotence: there is, of course, the expression 'impotent anger.' Resentment arises when a man is forced by others or by circumstances to remain in a situation which he dislikes and feels to be incommensurate with his self-evaluation. Here Scheler anticipates by several decades the frustration theory of aggression, so dear especially to American social psychologists.

Scheler's approach was necessarily limited because he worked exclusively on the hypothesis of so-called resentment types to which, by definition, woman belongs since she is always subordinate to man. Scheler does not recognize envy's universal role in human existence, and more important still, he knows nothing of the conclusively significant body of data on envy among primitive peoples. He touches on envious crime, an example being the murderer who, in the early days of motoring, satisfied his hatred of motor-car drivers by fastening a wire between two trees across a main road outside Berlin, thus neatly decapitating a passing motorist. Scheler examines in detail the role of envy and resentment in political parties and in the demand for equality. Since he published his work before the First World War, it is not surprising that he felt able to make some very tart comments on the envy inherent in democracy.

Resentment and revenge

Scheler begins by explaining that the French word *ressentiment* is untranslatable, and further that Nietzsche had made of it a technical term. As such it must be retained. He believed the elements of the usual meaning of the word in French to be significant: '*Ressentiment* implies living through, and reliving, over and over, a certain emotional response reaction towards another, whereby that emotion undergoes progressive deepening and introversion into the very core of the personality, with a simultaneous distancing from the individual's sphere of expression and action.'[55] The term further comprises the meaning that the quality of this emotion tends towards hostility. Scheler then quotes at length from

---

[55] Max Scheler, *Gesammelte Werke,* Bern, 1955, Vol. 3, p. 36.

Nietzsche's *Genealogy of Morality,* stressing, as the work does, that resentment is a form of self-poisoning which culminates in the vindictive impulse. What is involved is a group of emotions and affects, to which hatred, ill-will, envy, jealousy and spite also belong. Scheler then distinguishes between a counter-attack, a defensive gesture, such as a physical blow in immediate response to an insult, and the act of revenge which presupposes a certain lapse of time during which the reactive impulse is inhibited or controlled: a postponement, that is, of the counter-reaction till later on, in the sense of 'Next time I'll show you!' But when, under the influence of this inhibition, a person is able to predict that next time, too, he will be the under-dog, resentment begins.[56]

The stressing of the time factor is important. Scheler writes:

> Impulse and emotion, as it were, progress from vindictive feelings through rancour, envy and jealousy, to spite, approximating to genuine resentment. Revenge and envy represent types of hostile negation usually directed towards some definite object. They require definite causes for their manifestation, and their progress is determined by definite objects, so that, with the cessation of the cause, the emotion also disappears.[57]

Scheler implies here that my envy will disappear when the envied property becomes my own. This is probably an over-optimistic view. He regards begrudging as a more dangerous feeling than mere envy because it seeks out those value factors in things and people from which it can derive painfully angry satisfaction. To the begrudging man, systematic destruction is, as it were, the structure of the individual concrete experience in social life. He neither sees nor experiences anything that does not correspond with his emotional situation. In the case of spite, the detractive impulse is even deeper and more internalized, while at the same time always ready to pounce, betraying itself in some uncontrolled gesture, a way of smiling, etc. Now Scheler continues:

> None of these, however, amounts to resentment, but all are stages in the development of its points of departure. Vindictive feeling, envy, begrudging spite, *Schadenfreude* and ill-will become components of resentment only in

[56] Op. cit., p. 39.
[57] Op. cit., pp. 39 f.

the absence either of its moral subjugation (as, for example, *genuine* forgiveness in the case of revenge), or of action . . . e.g., a shaken fist; and where that absence is due to the fact that such behaviour is inhibited by a pronounced awareness of *impotence*. [58]

Resentment types

Scheler distinguished various resentment types—those, for instance, which can be understood from the historical situation and others again from socio-biological differences, such as the generation gap which, he says, is usually fraught with the danger of resentment. Further, he cites the mother-in-law, especially the husband's mother, who appears in the folk literature of every nation, as a wicked, malignant figure. Scheler does not regard the active criminal as a true resentment type, only the one who commits certain kinds of crime, here characterized as malicious, coming within this category. One such is the murderer of motorists mentioned earlier. Scheler detected less cause for resentment in the industrial proletariat of his time, in so far as it was not infected by the resentment of certain leader types, than among the progressively declining craftsmen, the lower middle classes and the lower civil service. Within the framework of this study, however, Scheler does not examine more closely, from the viewpoint of class sociology, the causes of these kinds of resentment.

He believes that the structuring of ethics is affected by resentment only in so far as this brings about the collapse of an immemorial scale of values. True, he does not think that genuine or true moral value-judgements are ever based on resentment, but only false ones arising from fallacious values. This, the ethical relativist and sceptic, Nietzsche, failed to distinguish properly, although he had himself spoken of the distortion of the scale of values by resentment. The resentful man's whole perceptual mechanism is concentrated, Scheler believes, on abstracting from, and perceiving in, reality only that which is able to feed his malice and begrudging: 'Hence the resentful man is drawn as if under a spell towards manifestations such as *joie de vivre,* glamour, power, happiness, riches, strength.[59] Scheler stresses repeatedly the distorting

[58] Op. cit., p. 41.
[59] Op. cit., p. 65.

influence of resentment on the very structure and process of the perceptual act, a factor we have already shown as being applicable to envy
generally.

At one point Scheler remarks:

> Impotent envy is also the most terrible kind of envy. Hence the form of
> envy which gives rise to the greatest amount of resentment is that directed
> against the individual and *essential being* of an unknown person: *existential
> envy*. For this envy, as it were, is forever muttering: 'I could forgive you
> anything, except *that* you are, and *what* you are; except that I am not what
> you are; that "I," in fact am not "you." ' This 'envy,' from the start, denies
> the other person his very existence, which as such is most strongly experi-
> enced as 'oppression' of, as 'a reproach' to the person of the subject.[60]

Nicolai Hartmann

In his comprehensive *Ethics,* and under Scheler's stimulus, Nicolai
Hartmann discusses envy a number of times. He recognizes the function
of envy in the social revolutionary and eudaemonistic theories and
movements since the end of the eighteenth century. In contrast to the
individual eudaemonism of antiquity, the modern era has produced, in
connection with a reassessment of the problems of social living, this
form of 'social eudaemonism,' which he terms a truly practical ideal of
life on an 'altruistic' basis: 'No longer does the happiness of the individual person constitute its comfort, but the welfare of all.' Bentham called
it, more concisely, 'the greatest happiness of the greatest number.'[61]

But if the happiness, which really means the comfort, of the greatest
number becomes the standard, a strange perversion arises, as Hartmann
shows: so many and so varied are the things that may be regarded as
useful for the widest possible dissemination of comfort, that the final
goal is lost from sight in questions of distribution, and ends up as
utilitarianism. Unfortunately, this switching of concepts is not only
theoretically confusing, it also leads to distortion in the social sphere
itself, where, according to Hartmann, it gives rise to a move towards
negativism or absence of content: 'Social eudaemonism . . . is rather a

[60] Op. cit., p. 45.

[61] Nicolai Hartmann, *Ethics,* London and New York, 1950, 2nd ed., Vol. 1, p. 137.

cramping and impoverishment of the sense of value; and in its extreme form it is, as regards values, pure nihilism.'[62]

A few pages further on, Hartmann stresses the function of envy in this remarkable ethic for modern times. He speaks of the danger of false values, particularly in social existence:

> The oppressed man, the labourer, he who is exploited—or he who so regards himself—lives unavoidably under the belief that the man of means is the happier. He imagines that the rich have everything which he himself yearns for in vain. In the other conditions of life he sees only the hedonistic value. That there are in reality other values which are hidden—education, taste, knowledge—and that these are dearly paid for in effort, he does not see. He is not acquainted with the difficulty of mental work and the burden of great responsibilities.[63]

Social eudaemonism

In his critique of social eudaemonism, Hartmann points out the irresponsibility of 'short-sighted social leaders' who abuse this falsification of values, that is, envy of those supposedly more happy, in order to 'hold up before the crowd a general happiness near at hand, and to incite them thereby to action. Such a vision, when it succeeds, is the means of setting the sluggish masses in motion.'[64]

He has envy in mind when he goes on to say that this misrepresentation 'appeals to the lower instincts in man, to the crudest sense of values, and liberates passions which afterwards cannot be checked. But the tragedy is that even this arousing of passion rests upon an illusion.'

Hartmann's concluding critique, evidently having in view the times during which his *Ethics* was written, points out the inevitable corruption of eudaemonistic social movements because their only momentum was derived from envy:

> If an ordinary man is under such an illusion, it is quite natural. If a demagogue makes use of the illusion as a means to his own ends, the means

[62] Op. cit., pp. 138–9.
[63] Op. cit., pp. 144–5.
[64] Op. cit., p. 145.

becomes a two-edged sword in his hand; but it is valuable—as seen from his point of view. If, however, the philosopher allows himself to be misled into justifying and sanctioning the illusion, this is due either to un-scrupulousness on his part or to the deepest moral ignorance. Nevertheless, the social theories of modern times have trod this fateful course ever since their first appearance: and it must be regarded as the misfortune of the social movement up to our own day, that this kind of sanction has been set upon it and handed down to us. . . . Here as in so many other departments of our moral life, the principal work still remains to be done.[65]

Hartmann breaks off at this point. What he doubtless had in mind was a social philosophy capable of showing how certain altruistic tasks can be done without exploiting envy. This is, perhaps, an impossible task, because the feeling of envy is much more constitutive of our inter-indi-vidual evaluations than he ever realized.

Eugène Raiga

The only writer up to now to have written a monograph on envy is Eugène Raiga. The twenty-four chapters of his book L'Envie comprise some 250 pages devoted to the group of phenomena that go to make up envy in the narrower sense. It appeared in 1932. Raiga had already published, fairly regularly since 1900, books mainly in the field of public law, and also of the economics of war, diplomacy and public administration.

Raiga cites Spinoza, according to whom human passions and their attributes are among the natural processes that are susceptible of exam-ination. He opens with a quotation from Tartuffe, to the effect that envious men die, but envy does not. Raiga sees jealousy as the mother of envy and points out how often the one is mistaken for the other. But he regards envy as more comprehensive than jealousy. Both are of great importance in social life and are the most active and powerful motives in our behaviour. If it were possible to record an individual's jealousy and envy in the same way as the electrical impulses in his brain, it would be comparatively simple to explain his other affects and his behaviour.

Raiga then examines envy in an altogether conventional series of

[65] Op. cit., pp. 145–6.

chapters. First, he seeks its origins, shows how it is linked with jealousy, discusses the phenomenon of 'envious indignation,' and considers envy and admiration. Two chapters are devoted to various forms of general and sexual jealousy. There follows the geography of envy: in the family, among friends, in the small town, and again in circles in the big city, such as those of lawyers, doctors and surgeons, officials, the military, poets and writers, painters and sculptors, thence to the role of envy in art criticism (already incisively described by Schopenhauer), envy in the world of scholarship and between victorious generals.

Three chapters are concerned with envy in democracy, particularly the envy of the masses and its function in socialist aspirations. Finally he investigates envy in religious life and on the international plane. The concluding chapter examines the social function of envy.

Like others, Raiga sees the distinction between jealousy and envy in the fact that jealousy postulates genuine expropriation of an asset hitherto possessed. He demonstrates the difference between envy and admiration with the example of antagonists in a competition, and disinterested strangers watching a tournament: the latter are able to admire the antagonists without envy. Raiga agrees with many other writers in regarding envy as a vice, a negative and destructive characteristic. It gives rise to only *one* virtue, that of modesty. Although Raiga can see no extenuating factor in envy or its subject, although all that the typically envious man achieves by his envy is that he never becomes or obtains that which he envies, yet the modesty evoked by his fear of envy, which is so obligatory in social life, is of social importance: even though such modesty is often simulated and insincere, it still makes co-existence possible. It gives those whose situation is lower, socially, the illusion that they have not been forced into that position. Essentially Raiga's treatment of envy resembles our own. He demonstrates its ubiquity and inevitability, and the part it plays in twentieth-century politics, and he indicates the reactions to that ubiquity which help to make social existence possible. Raiga seems not to have been aware of Max Scheler's great study of resentment, nor does he mention Nietzsche. The literature to which he refers consists for the most part of a few late nineteenth-century French psychologists and historians. Théodule Ribot is very often quoted, as are some French moralists, among them Diderot, La Bruyère and La Rochefoucauld, whose views he discusses. Schopenhauer is cited once, and there are a few references to Henri Bergson's study of laughter, to Spinoza and Aristotle; J. Bourdeau, Pierre Janet, G. Tarde and Renan are mentioned a number of times.

What I miss most in Raiga is ethnographic data and the discoveries made by social anthropology concerning the phenomenon of envy among primitive peoples. However, it is in this field, particularly, that much research and writing have been done since the time his book appeared. Once he mentions envy in animals, such as the dog; but ethology, the study of behaviour, which has meanwhile made such great strides, plays no part in his investigation. Psychoanalysis exerted equally little influence on his work.

By a remarkable coincidence, only a year after Raiga brought out his book in Paris, the Danish sociologist Svend Ranulf began to publish quite independently his big, two-volume study of the envy of the gods and criminal justice in Athens, a far more scientific work than Raiga's essay.

Raiga also comments on the failure to discriminate between envy and jealousy, which we have already repeatedly encountered in English and German literature and everyday speech.

These terms, as Raiga stresses, are often seen as interchangeable, even by important writers of undoubted sensibility.[66] He gives several examples from French literature, though La Rochefoucauld, to whom the point was important, makes a very clear distinction: he sees jealousy as an attitude that is often justified and reasonable, because it keeps watch over something that we have, yet fear to lose; whereas envy is a madness to which the prosperity of others is intolerable.[67]

Envy-indignation

Rivarol, another French moralist, had already pointed out the remarkable fact that the mental faculty of comparison, which in the intellect is a source of justice, is a source of envy in the heart. Raiga elaborated this idea.[68] Envy invariably arises out of the comparison of two situations.

[66] E. Raiga, *L'Envie,* Paris, 1932, p. 13.

[67] Op. cit., pp. 14 f.

[68] Op. cit., p. 8.

By definition, the very possibility of comparison must involve the diagnosis of inferiority in one of the parties. As we shall repeatedly see, this is not at all dependent upon either the absolute level of the persons under comparison or the absolute distance between them. Comparison is potential envy, in so far as no compensatory views and feelings effectively intervene. Envy and indignation are regarded by Raiga as identical psychological processes, but there are two kinds of envy— common and vulgar envy, which is reprehensible, and hence generally concealed, and envy-indignation, which may be excused or even justified[69] (Francis Bacon's 'public envy'). Both kinds of envy, Raiga says, have the same origin. The distinction between them depends on people's impartiality and their sense of what is just and fair.

Raiga indicates that his concept 'envy-indignation' resembles the concept of nemesis described by Aristotle in the *Nicomachean Ethics*— general indignation, a feeling between envy and malignance. (Nemesis, the Greek goddess, was responsible for good measure, and was regarded as the enemy of too much happiness, this embodying what the Greeks considered to be the envy of the gods.) Raiga writes: 'The noble action demanded by morality is that one should rejoice with others in their happiness, *gaudere felicitate aliena,* a virtue, indeed, which fine natures put into practice, but envy is there, ubiquitous upon this earth, and everything that contributes to the pride and joy of others causes it to suffer.'[70]

Behind destructive and impotent envy Raiga recognizes that natural impulse or drive without which much of what we call civilization would never have come into being. The problem of the envy-ridden man is, indeed, to know whether his indignation is legitimate. We shall be confronted more than once in this book with the problem of the true and false legitimization of envy.[71]

Envy is a subdued frame of mind, and is mostly camouflaged. One of its favourite weapons is irony. Raiga recalls Bergson's study of laughter of which the original function was to denigrate and to intimidate. The strategy of envy has always included the glorification of modesty and the

[69] Op. cit., p. 11.

[70] Op. cit., p. 24.

[71] Op. cit., p. 25.

censure of pride, which is called a sin. It may be presumed that those who feel pride are fewer than those who ascribe it to others and begrudge it them.

Within the nuclear family, that is, between husband and wife, parents and children, envy, Raiga feels, should not be found. Among themselves they are equal, and the good of each one contributes to the good of the whole small group. As experience shows, however, the social structure of the family is in many cases unable to obviate tormenting and destructive feelings of envy among its members. (Here Raiga is not speaking of jealousy, to which the family is particularly prone.) Thus he postulates a possible cause for jealousy between husband and wife which has since been substantiated—in American experience, for instance. Because a number of professions and careers have been thrown open to both sexes, it can happen that one member of a couple becomes the other's competitor, earns more, gets better reviews or, if each has a different profession, enjoys more agreeable conditions of work.[72]

In his chapter on envy between friends, Raiga gives various examples, mostly from fiction, to prove the thesis that even among close friends it is better for each, by an excess of modesty, to beg constant forgiveness for his superiority.[73] Bacon, however, had early recognized the inefficacy of this tactic.

Raiga compares the proneness to envy of the inhabitants of small provincial towns to those of Paris, finding that the mutual envy so characteristic of the village community or the small town appears equally in the metropolis, but in individual circles such as the professions, neighbourhoods, between inmates of the same house, etc. In the capital city envy exists in a number of 'enclaves,' which Raiga describes in a separate chapter.[74]

Envy in France

Towards the end of the book, Raiga turns to envy in democracy. He contributes nothing to the various discoveries made by individual nineteenth-century writers, such as Jacob Burckhardt and Nietzsche. Some

[72] Op. cit., pp. 65 ff.
[73] Op. cit., p. 83.
[74] Op. cit., p. 99.

of Raiga's observations cast light on political life in Paris, making comprehensible much of what occurred in France after 1945. By nature the Frenchman is a passionate leveller, an anarchist. Raiga mentions the institution of ostracism in Athens and is faintly disapproving of Montesquieu, for viewing it as a very minor evil. The fear of the truly great, prevalent among French lower-middle-class people and the newly rich, has, it seems, given rise to the belief that the principles are all that count while individuals count for nothing. Raiga is very critical of electioneering in the twentieth century, but assumes that there are, from time to time, candidates with a sincere concern for the public weal. The hierarchy of the various ministries to be shared out by the prime minister among his followers was responsible for irreconcilable envy, particularly among politicians' wives.

Raiga is concerned about the systematic fomentation of envy and greed in the masses, but he also has hard things to say about the naïve stupidity of those who ostentatiously dissipate their inherited wealth with a complete disregard for the envy of the lower classes. He recognizes envy as a phenomenon of social proximity; a grocer will hardly ever compare himself with a millionaire. But Raiga's age—the age of socialist egalitarianism—is one in which ever wider circles harbour at least the illusion that everyone is comparable with everyone else.

Raiga then returns to the distinction already made between simple, vulgar envy and envy-indignation or legitimate envy. He admits the possibility that oppressed, underprivileged classes, when a genuine injustice is involved, may be provoked to action by envy. But, he asks, who can and may decide when envy is legitimate? And what politician, when he incites the masses to envy, asks himself whether his object is power and its concomitant privileges, or whether his aim is to eliminate the injustice suffered by others?

Raiga has a low opinion of the utopian promises and ideas of socialists who use envy as a tool with which to build a society of people liberated from envy. He is scathing about the methods of a socialism vested in envy, and employing the hatred and vindictiveness of the envious to destroy a social system while having nothing to put in its place. Yet it is precisely the constancy of envy, a factor that can always be relied on, that explains the great success of socialist movements.[75] A social revolution,

---

[75] Op. cit., pp. 233 ff.

Raiga maintains, does nothing to alter man's general lot. It creates a new privileged class, different occupants for the club armchairs, but as a rule it produces more envious people than it has succeeded in placating. Contrary to its illusion, the Marxist revolution would not change human nature. Ambition, pride, vanity, jealousy and envy are unalterable active elements in human behaviour.[76] A generation has elapsed since Raiga's little book, during which experience has increasingly taught us how right his diagnosis was.

Briefly he discusses envy between nations. These, like individuals, are capable of mutual envy and hatred. Since Raiga's book, history has furnished countless new examples of this. His prediction that the setting up of socialist governments and societies would not prevent envy between nations has, at any rate since 1945, been amply proved. Satellites of the Eastern bloc envy or are mutually envious of what they receive from the U.S.S.R. or the U.S.A., and socialist developing countries regard one another aggressively and with a jealous eye to see who is managing to get more development aid than the rest.

Raiga concludes by defining his own view of envy and its concomitant manifestations by means of a quotation from Spinoza, to the effect that there are no such things as vices, but only natural phenomena arising out of human nature. Raiga does not consider envy and jealousy to be innate, but as arising from social interplay or, as we should now say, in the course of the 'socialization process.' They are attributes of human co-existence, and since the envious must always be reckoned with, quite distinct modes of behaviour result. Raiga clearly regards some of the actions or behaviour designed to avert envy as socially highly desirable. Generally speaking, he seems to have given very little thought to the possible and perhaps extreme extent of the negative influence of this envy-avoidance compulsion, so inhibiting to cultural and individual development. What he patently lacks here is familiarity with the data of comparative ethnology.

Raiga's general definition of the envious man agrees with that of Scheler:

> All the forms of envious manifestation considered in these chapters may
> be summed up in a few words: They are nothing other than the reaction of

[76] Op. cit., p. 236.

vanquished to victor, the weak to the strong, the attitude of the less talented to those with superior talent, of the poor to the rich, the humiliated to the arrogant. What is involved are disparate reactions of varying degrees of violence, which erupt or die down according to the situation, and which are dependent on temperament and character.[77]

And because we are constantly on the defensive towards the envious, the whole of social life is correspondingly affected. According to Raiga, this is the social function of envy.

Envious political parties

Finally he reverts to the problem of socialists and of social revolutionary movements. These reject the allegation that they pander to envy, and proclaim the justice of their cause. Raiga reiterates that what members of such a party indubitably feel is envy, for they look upon themselves as the dispossessed, excluded from fortune's bounty. The feeling of sorrow and anger induced by the sight of the abundance of good things enjoyed by others, which is expressed in the cry 'Why they and not we?' deserves one name, and one only, and that is envy.[78]

Yet the sheer volume of this cry, Raiga admits, calls for reflection and close comparison. The problem of merit requires consideration. Now Raiga believes that as the virtue of modesty arises from the reaction to vulgar envy, so the reaction to envy-indignation might give rise to a necessary examination of the right to privilege. Hence, his essay concludes, it might, in fact, be possible to see the universality of envy as contributing to the relative concord of society.[79]

It is Raiga's virtue to have described the manifestations of envy in a large variety of social groups. He shows how little this problem has changed since antiquity; he warns against undue optimism regarding the possibility of eliminating envy from existence by this or that reform. For it is a basic fact of our lives and we must resign ourselves to reckoning with it, and in some measure protecting ourselves against it, by carefully calculated modesty. However, Raiga over-estimates precisely this possi-

[77] Op. cit., p. 263.

[78] Op. cit., p. 263.

[79] Op. cit., p. 264.

bility of self-protection against the envious man by means of deliberate envy-avoidance. Francis Bacon had already remarked upon the extent to which the envious man is enraged by any attempt to deprive him of the stimulus.

Raiga was a highly educated Parisian of the thirties, well versed in modern literature and the classics and familiar with French political intrigues of his day. The urbanity and courtesy of his culture may have concealed from him certain extreme forms of envious manifestation. Envious crime, for instance, is mentioned only casually. If, like his contemporary José Ortega y Gasset, he warns against the revolt of the envious masses and sees a society determined by envy hurtling towards its doom, the basic tenor of his work is confident—somehow man will succeed in dealing with envy. Raiga remains untouched by the metaphysical horror induced by envy in Herman Melville, which haunted him when he was writing *Billy Budd*.

He is far removed from the penetrating, flexible and brilliantly perceptive analysis to which Max Scheler subjected the phenomenon of resentment, and consequently that of envy. Nor can Raiga's essay be compared with Svend Ranulf's imposing study, which, while taking account of Scheler's work, methodically exploited with rare and scrupulous exactitude a comprehensive and homogeneous body of data. We have considered Raiga's book in some detail, however, because it is the only one we know that has envy as such for its subject and deals with jealousy only as a peripheral phenomenon. Strange to say, resentment as a special phenomenon hardly comes within Raiga's field of vision. Thus *L'Envie* is an example of the kinds of observation and discovery made about forty years ago, when it occurred to a clever French writer to devote a monograph to envy.

12

Politics and the
Appeasement of Envy

I T IS ESSENTIAL to a democratic system that different parties should alternate in office. Thus, from time to time one party will be more successful than the other in attacking, criticizing and casting suspicion on its rivals. Even in the unlikely event of elections being fought with precise and logical arguments on a purely intellectual plane, it is unlikely, to judge by the petty jealousy and often irrational squabbling that go on between scholars and scientists, that the level and tone of democratic debate would improve as a consequence. The aim will always be the factious annihilation of the opposition's viewpoint; and however vulnerable it may be to rational attack it will always be more profitably assailed by an appeal to basic emotions.

The affinity between envy and democracy is castigated in H. L. Mencken's essay 'A Blind Spot':

> No doubt my distaste for democracy as a political theory is . . . due to an inner lack—to a defect that is a good deal less in the theory than in myself. In this case it is very probably my incapacity for envy. . . . In the face of another man's good fortune I am as inert as a curb broker before Johann Sebastian Bach. It gives me neither pleasure nor distress. The fact, for example, that John D. Rockefeller had more money than I have is as uninteresting to me as the fact that he believed in total immersion and wore detachable cuffs. And the fact that some half-anonymous ass . . . has been . . . appointed a professor at Harvard, or married to a rich wife, or even to a beautiful and amiable one: this fact is as meaningless to me as the latest piece of bogus news from eastern Europe.
>
> The reason for all this does not lie in any native nobility or acquired

233

virtue. Far from it, indeed. It lies in the accidental circumstance that the business I pursue . . . seldom brings me into very active competition with other men. I have, of course, rivals, but they do not rival me directly and exactly, as one delicatessen dealer or clergyman or lawyer or politician rivals another. It is only rarely that their success costs me anything, and even then the fact is usually concealed. . . .

Puritanism is represented as a lofty sort of obedience to God's law. Democracy is depicted as brotherhood, even as altruism. All such notions are in error. There is only one honest impulse at the bottom of Puritanism, and that is the impulse to punish the man with a superior capacity for happiness—to bring him down to the miserable level of 'good' men, i.e., of stupid, cowardly and chronically unhappy men. And there is only one sound argument for democracy, and that is the argument that it is a crime for any man to hold himself out as better than other men, and, above all, a most heinous offence for him to prove it. . . .[1]

It would be a miracle if the democratic political process were ever to renounce the use of the envy-motive.[2] Its usefulness derives, if for no other reason, from the fact that all that is needed, in principle, is to promise the envious the destruction or the confiscation of assets enjoyed by the others; beyond that there is no need to promise anything more constructive.[3] The negativism of envy permits even the weakest of candidates to sound reasonably plausible, since anybody, once in office, can confiscate or destroy. To enlarge the country's capital assets, to create employment etc. requires a more precise programme. Candidates will naturally try to make some positive proposals, but it is often all too apparent that envy looms large in their calculations. The more precarious the state of a nation's economy at election time, the stronger the temptations for politicians to make 'redistribution' their main plank, even when they know how little margin is left for redistributive measures and, worse still, how likely they are to retard economic growth.

[1] *The Vintage Mencken,* ed. Alistair Cooke, New York, 1956, pp. 75–7.

[2] In his *Geistliche Gedanken eines Nationalökonomen* (Dresden, 1895, p. 57) the political economist Wilhelm Roscher wrote: '. . . Whereas most other sins at least begin by being pleasurable, the feeling of envy is miserable from the outset. Yet envy, in these democratic days, is particularly prevalent. How many of those moods which we supposed to be a sense of justice are infected at their very base by envious impulses.'

The appeal of envy in politics

The role of envy becomes patent when, for instance, the legislator shrinks from passing overdue measures, in themselves sensible and of undoubted economic benefit to the community, through fear of the latent envy or indignation of those to whom the measures might at first be relatively detrimental. Housing policy in various countries shows many examples of this. The factor of envy is also prominent in the case of fiscal measures of a vindictive and confiscatory nature, such as progressive income tax, death duties and other related forms of taxation. As we shall see, welfare economists are coming more and more to face the question of envy and to discuss it explicitly.

In the name of an unattainable equality the legislator uses fiscal means of disproportionate severity to tax the few who, for whatever reasons— even for avowedly legitimate reasons—are economically greatly more successful or better endowed than the majority. Sociological research has shown the extent to which this demand for levelling originates with certain groups of intellectuals, the average voter feeling hardly any definite envy towards those with really high incomes,[4] for the objects of our envy are generally those who are almost our equals.

Nor are we fully aware, as a rule, of the extent to which politicians exploit a latent guilty conscience among people or groups that are economically above average. In other words, certain economic or fiscal policies are put into effect less from evidence of any real, socially dangerous feelings of envy among the poorer classes than by playing on an irrational sense of guilt. People feel they must do something because they are so well off; but whether any effective results will accrue to the supposed beneficiaries is a question rarely asked. In this context it would be worth investigating the mania for making wild promises during parliamentary elections, which I believe is not only based on calculated vote-catching but is often a ritual device to relieve many politicians' consciences.

[3] This was particularly clear, for example, in the Labour Party's nationalization programme after 1945. See W. W. Haynes, *Nationalization in Practice. The British Coal Industry,* Cambridge, Mass., 1954, especially pp. 69, 115, 159, 163, 177, 184, 385.

[4] See, for instance, R. E. Lane, 'The Fear of Equality,' in *American Political Science Quarterly,* Vol. 53, 1959, pp. 35–51.

Things are more complicated in the case of legislation on behalf of groups which still enjoy a certain residual sympathy from the past, although their living conditions no longer call for compassion. These may be groups who at one time quite consciously played up their envy so as to make political capital out of the feelings of self-conscious guilt aroused in others. In many countries this is particularly noticeable among the farmers and the trade unions. Originally the farmers and industrial workers may have felt a justifiable combination of indignation and envy. Yet it has now become institutionalized into a political taboo, an example of the kind of political situation which we believe can only be properly understood by an analysis of the psychological motivation which lies behind it. In this instance the guilt we feel when we want to throw away a stale loaf of bread is no doubt linked in origin with the feeling that inhibits us from voting against an economically irrational measure that favours the farmers.

Both right-wing and left-wing writers have discussed the political implications of envy, with a certain degree of plausibility on both sides. Colm Brogan, for instance, wrote twenty years ago:

> Egalitarianism has its noble side, even political egalitarianism, but it is very easily perverted to envy, and socialist propaganda has lost no opportunity of so perverting it. It is a frightening thought that many people are willing to accept grave hardship so long as they are convinced that privileged people are equally afflicted. The scandalous lethargy of house-building did not anger the homeless one tenth as much as the thought that wealthy people might be able to secure a room in a hotel. Ruthless drive in the building programme would have got them a home, and the closing of all hotels would not, but they have been more angered by the open hotels than by unfinished houses.[5]

Statements such as Colm Brogan's have sometimes been answered by egalitarian authors who have not, however, said how they propose to prove the absence of envy in their programmes. The American social critic Max Lerner once defended politics by envy as follows:

> It is a theory that has become the basis of most of the attacks upon socialist and populist movements. They are born, we are told, of spite and

[5] Colm Brogan, *Our New Masters*, London, 1948, p. 207.

envy and hate. They are the product of an underlying population that, out of its anger at being denied the amenities of civilization, is willing to destroy the structure of civilization itself. No doubt some such envy, some such desire to increase one's stature, enters into all bids for power. . . . But to think of the common man as motivated wholly by this envy . . . is a sign of the arid imagination of the elite.[6]

The British socialist C. A. R. Crosland defends himself thus against allegations of envy:

It is sometimes said that one is doing something disgraceful, and merely pandering to the selfish clamour of the mob, by taking account of social envy and resentment. This is not so. . . . It is no more disgraceful to take them into account than many other facts that the politician must attend to—such as the greed of the richer classes, who claim they must have higher monetary rewards and reduced taxation as an incentive to greater effort, patriotism being evidently not enough. . . . The Socialist seeks a distribution of rewards, status, and privileges egalitarian enough to minimize social resentments, to secure justice between individuals, and to equalize opportunities; and he seeks to weaken the existing deepseated class stratification, with its concomitant feelings of envy and inferiority, and its barriers to uninhibited mingling between the classes.[7]

There is no intrinsic, scientific objection to a social movement, a political party or a sect basing its tenets on the motive of envy, or using it as an inducement to its followers and to gain new adherents. The envy latent in man is no less socially legitimate in this capacity than is, say, love, the urge for freedom, national pride, homesickness, nostalgia or any other emotion that can be used to inspire collective political action. As long ago as the last century the British writer W. H. Mallock emphasized that even though envy may be shown to be the motive behind radical, socialist and other movements, this is no argument against them.[8] There could be situations in which the only possible

[6] Max Lerner, *It Is Later Than You Think,* New York, 1938, pp. 249 ff.

[7] C. A. R. Crosland, *The Future of Socialism,* London, 1956, pp. 203 ff.

[8] W. H. Mallock, *Social Equality, Labour and the Popular Welfare,* London, 1894. R. Kirk in *The Conservative Mind,* 1953, points out this insight on the part of Mallock. German authors such as von Treitschke, writing at the same time, oversimplified their antisocialist polemic by merely stating, with much indignation, the existence of the motive of envy.

common denominator for members of a political movement would be their latent envy. One might organize an underground movement based on envy in opposition to a tyrant, an idea developed by L. P. Hartley in his utopian novel *Facial Justice*.

Moreover, mere demonstration of the fact that the provocation of envious feelings has played a part in activating an opposition group does not of itself prove that the powers which it opposes stand for a just order. But—and this is important—neither does the mere possibility of organizing an envy-ridden opposition prove that it is speaking up for greater justice. Envy can demonstrably be aroused and exacerbated by such trivial irritants and often quite imaginary inequalities that its power to weld people into groups for social action bears no relation to the quality of the viewpoint which it is invoked to promote.

A scientific critique of the manipulation of envy is, however, in order as soon as utopian ideas of an envy-free society are introduced into the arguments. If the envious are urged to take direct action, with the promise that after the overthrow of the existing order there will be a just society of equals, it almost invariably happens that power accrues to the very people whose origins and views make them least able to effect the promised economic reform or redistribution. In the name of envy the new measures are inevitably extended to ever wider areas of life and to groups of people who are relatively better placed, so that politics and economics are invaded by progressive chaos and paralysis. Clear instances of this can be seen in various emergent nations since the early fifties; another classic case of this kind is that of Cuba since 1959.

Many of the so-called developing countries suffer from the following process: as we have already seen in the chapter on the effects of envy among primitive peoples and in simple village communities, one of the decisive factors in underdevelopment or non-development is the 'envy-barrier,' or institutionalized envy among the population. The significance of this factor has recently been acknowledged by a number of cultural anthropologists. The so-called developed countries have accomplished the breakthrough to a state of constantly rising prosperity and technical mastery of the environment because fear of mutual envy could be kept in check through certain religious, social and demographic factors.

Now when, as is quite patently the case, many of the politicians in developing countries make use of all their powers of rhetoric and persuasion for the crudest exacerbation of their people's envy of the rich industrial countries (even to the point of branding the latter as the cause of their own countries' poverty), these people's sense of envy—to which their cultures already make them over-prone—is intensified. Thus the feelings and states of mind which inhibit development are not lessened but confined and given political sanction by the countries' leaders.

I would even support the view that those Western journalists and scholars whose economic theories have nourished and encouraged the envy of the developing countries have thereby involuntarily burdened their protégés with yet another psychological factor inhibiting development—and one which is the most difficult of all to discard.

An even more fundamental critique of the use of envy as a chosen tool of political action can be made if we analyse the promises which leaders make to their envious followers. A social scientist should not have much difficulty in assessing the degree of feasibility of such promises, which range from the realistic to the totally impracticable. Little objection can be raised if an opposition leader uses the extravagance of a ruling politician's private life as a catalyst for dissatisfaction that will ultimately serve to strengthen a resistance group or parliamentary opposition, so long as his followers are not promised that the tyrant's downfall will materially and lastingly improve their economic lot. After all, however great one man's private possessions may be, their redistribution is unlikely to bring about any economic improvement for the population at large.

Hence there are some cases in which envy assumes only a transitory function and is not necessarily institutionalized. Sometimes employees concerned for a firm's prosperity can bring about the dismissal of an incompetent manager by tactically exploiting his penchant for what is essentially irrelevant extravagance or morally undesirable excesses. Situations of this kind recur frequently in present-day American business reports. A case in point is the downfall of a prominent television executive in America a few years ago. This tactic is most likely to succeed if the manager is answerable to a governing board, some of whose members still have puritan tendencies and recollections of a spartan childhood. The fate of the dismissed man, however, is due not least to the envious feelings aroused in others by his success, feelings which they make out to be indignation at his frivolously self-indulgent antics.

Envy as a trap for dictators

But the envy-motive can also be employed within the framework of a dictatorial system, for when there is a struggle for power at the top, the situation resembles that in a diminutive parliament or an electoral constituency where a political popularity contest is under way. Thus those men in the Kremlin who overthrew Nikita Khrushchev at the end of 1964 patently used envy as a lever, playing up, for instance, his nepotism, his vanity and his travels abroad. Even the absolute monarch or tyrant, as shown by Leo Strauss's study, was seen by Greek thinkers as a ruler under perpetual threat from envy, and not only the envy of the gods.[9]

We ought, perhaps, sometimes to look at things in the perspective of human frailty, and not always assume a *raison d'état* when seeking the reasons behind the travels of a head of state. Nearly everyone who has attained eminence likes to travel, especially now that it has become so comfortable. Lack of freedom to travel, especially when money is no object, can be very galling. One has only to recall the relative un-freedom of a monarch, a prince consort or even a president or prime minister in the free world, who will rarely travel for pleasure beyond his own frontiers because every journey will be interpreted in terms of high politics. How much greater, then, is the lack of freedom imposed on the Soviet Union's chief of state. Every time he goes abroad his danger from sabotage at home increases. In a totalitarian system the leader's desire to go on a shopping spree in Geneva, Vienna, Paris or New York is disproportionately greater, and if one of them succeeds in fulfilling that desire he is sure to excite his colleagues' envy. The latter are far less likely than Western diplomats or journalists to credit him with the official reason for his trip abroad. It is more than probable that one of the factors contributing to the resentment which brought about Khrushchev's fall was his aptitude for organizing entertaining travel abroad for himself and his family.

The basic error of socialism

The aversion of the radical left-wing writer to any consideration of the problem of envy is comprehensible. This is a sphere that must be made

[9] Leo Strauss, *On Tyranny. An Interpretation of Xenophon's Hiero,* New York, 1948, pp. 67 ff.

taboo, and he must do all in his power to repress cognition of envy in his contemporaries. Otherwise he might lose the support of serious-minded people, who, while sharing his views for sentimental reasons, and even following him in his demands for a policy and a political ethic dependent upon common envy's being regarded as an absolute, yet are aware how little esteemed envy is and how little it is capable of legitimizing itself openly in most Western societies even today.

Or, to put it more concisely: in so far as it is a matter of exploiting latent feelings of envy against the outsider, whether among the voters, among supporters or even in entire populations (Hitler calculated on the German envy of the 'colonial powers') with the object of securing the support of the envious to attain political power, it is both rational and politically expedient to speculate on the ubiquity of envy as a human attribute. In this, socialist movements have adapted a method which became available to them during a certain phase in the growth of industrialization. Envy, as such, is politically neutral. It can be equally mobilized against a socialist government that has been in power since living memory as against a conservative or liberal one. The decisive difference, however, is this: the non-socialist politician will always direct the voter's envy or indignation against certain excesses, the extravagant spending, the way of life, the nepotism, etc., of individual politicians, but he will not pretend, either to himself or to his followers, that as soon as he is in power his aim will be a society in which everyone will ultimately be more or less equal, and that there will be no more envy.

It is only this, the utopian part of the socialist programme, that is dishonest. The pragmatic exploitation of envious feelings merely in order to bring about the fall of a government is no more directly connected with socialism than with any other political colouring. What is really deplorable in socialist ideology is the endeavour to concoct a complete economy, a programme of sanctions, out of an ostensible obligation to create a society devoid of envy. Here Marxist socialism has set itself a task that is by definition insoluble. In so far as socialism starts out from the concept of the necessary disadvantage imposed on every person by every other person whose fate is not identical, thus re-activating those very conceptions of primitive peoples which inhibit development, it is far less able to approximate to a society relatively free from envy than are the very societies whose dissolution is its avowed aim.

More than half a century ago, Scheler recognized the degree to which resentment and envy are essential to certain political parties which, as power groups, would be swept out of politics were the problems upon which their criticism rests to be eliminated.

> The more a lasting social pressure is felt to be pre-ordained, the less is it able or liable to release forces to effect any practical change in those conditions; and the more it finds expression in criticism devoid of positive goals. The characteristic of this special form of 'criticism,' which might be denoted 'resentful criticism,' is that no redress of the circumstances regarded as undesirable will afford any satisfaction—as it will in the case of all constructive criticism—but, on the contrary, will arouse dissatisfaction, since it puts an end to the increasingly intense pleasure derived from destructive criticism and censure. An axiom that applies to more than one of our present political parties [this was written in 1912] is that nothing would annoy them or their representatives so much as to *realize* part of their political demands, or so turn to gall their high sense of 'fundamental opposition' as an invitation to some of their number to participate actively in affairs of state. The peculiarity of 'resentful criticism' is that it does not seriously 'want' what it professes to want; not satisfied with criticizing any redress of a wrong, it uses this as a pretext for general recrimination.[10]

A golden crown of thorns: The 1896 United States presidential election, from the viewpoint of envy

If a politician, and more especially a candidate seeking election to high office, wishes to make use of the impulse of envy among those electors who may support him, he will find it particularly expedient to devise a plank in his platform that can ostensibly solve a host of problems by one simple legislative act. If this also happens to involve a complex matter upon which not even experts are agreed, nearly every advantage lies with the assailant. His opposite number, confronted by a sea of angry, resentful and despairing faces and having to state on what grounds he considers this law to be undesirable, impractical or premature, is in an exceedingly awkward position. Given certain historical conditions, however, he may still win.

The United States presidential election of 1896 illustrates this very well. It is one of the few instances when an election turned almost

[10] M. Scheler, 'Das Ressentiment im Aufbau der Moralen,' *Gesammelte Werke*, Vol. 3, p. 44.

exclusively upon one well-defined issue which, at least according to one of the parties, could have been resolved by a single piece of legislation which would make everyone literally equal: this was the question of bimetallism, or the double currency standard. This is an alternative currency system whereby gold and silver coin, whose ratio to each other is fixed by law, is made legal tender for all amounts no matter how great. It can be readily understood that the two most important precious metals should serve as targets in a policy based on envy, but the spectacle presented by the champions of silver claiming the support of the envious masses and declaiming against the followers of gold ('gold bugs') is instructive. Apart from its implications of egalitarianism—silver is just as good as gold; the man with silver money is equal to the man with gold money—the political exploitation of bimetallism in America at the end of the nineteenth century is proof that no striking or absolute contrast or differences are required in order to mobilize envy. Even a technical and specialized economic question and the rating of a precious metal can be turned by demagogues into the fuel for a bitterly contested electoral campaign based on class differences and the contrast between rich and poor. We will now examine some samples of electoral oratory in the 1896 American presidential election.

At thirty-six, William Jennings Bryan was Democratic candidate for the presidency. His electoral promise was the reintroduction of bi-metallism, which had been in force from the beginning of dollar currency (1792) until 1873. His Republican opponent, William McKinley, neither regarded himself as a financial expert nor considered the currency question to be of great moment. What follows is representative of statements supporting Bryan's nomination: 'Bryan represents the people—the poor people. The fight now is of the rich against the poor. . . . Everybody, except the representatives of Wall Street, corporations and syndicates will vote for him.' Thus spake a leader of the American Federation of Labor. A speaker from the Decorators' Union declared that Bryan's nomination would mean the first really democratic convention in twenty-five years, because it had driven an immense wedge 'through both parties . . . placing in direct opposition the masses on the one hand and the classes on the other.'[11]

---

[11] C. M. Stevens, *Bryan and Sewall and the Great Issue of 1896,* New York, 1896, p. 95.

During the Republican Convention a section of delegates did in fact defect on the question of silver, ranging themselves behind Bryan. These so-called Silver Republicans adopted the oratory of the debtor class:

'We support such candidates because they represent the great principle of bimetallism, which we believe to be the cause of humanity and civilization.'[12] 'Believing as we do that the return to the monetary system . . . of 1792–1873 affords the only ground of hope for the betterment of the distressed condition of all classes except those who live by the increment that money loaned gives to those who loan it. . . .'[13]

Bryan, incidentally one of the best speakers of his time, who succeeded in persuading his hosts to pay him fees and travelling expenses for nearly all his electioneering speeches, led his audiences to pin their hopes almost exclusively on the reintroduction of bimetallism: 'You must admit that the solution of this currency question is of primary importance. If it is solved there will be nothing else to do.'

Bryan managed to formulate the currency question in a way that appealed perfectly to the pseudo-socialist (populist) views of his fellow countrymen.[14] His most famous utterance, with which he dismissed his opponent, was: 'You shall not press down upon the brow of labor this crown of thorns. You shall not crucify mankind upon a cross of gold.'[15]

Gold—the bogeyman

Within a very short time Bryan had succeeded in giving such an undemocratic, wicked, indecent connotation to the very word 'gold' that his opponents sought to avoid its use. An Eastern Republican paper commented: 'Now that Major McKinley has once said the word "gold" he feels like the boy who, after long deliberation, finally ducked his head under water. . . . He will keep doing it over and over again just to show that he wasn't afraid.'[16]

[12] Op. cit., p. 268.

[13] Op. cit., p. 271.

[14] Op. cit., p. 132.

[15] H. W. Morgan, *William McKinley and His America,* Syracuse, N.Y., 1963, p. 221.

[16] Op. cit., p. 237.

In order to understand why the silver question was so hotly disputed in the United States of 1896, we must take a brief retrospective look at the currency question. Until approximately the middle of the last century, silver was the chief currency. England, however, had already introduced the gold standard in 1816, and the champions of bimetallism in America were only too ready to play up nationalist, anti-British sentiment. Since the discovery of America silver production had usually been thirty or forty times that of gold. The United States had become the principal silver producer. When, with the founding of the Union, Americans had to institute a mint and their own currency, they decided on double-standard currency. That is to say, by Federal law, gold and silver were established as legal and unrestricted currency, at a fixed ratio of 15 or 16 to 1. Anyone possessing gold or silver could take it to the mint and have it coined as legal tender. The system obtained from 1792 to 1873. During that time, the only point of dispute was the fixed ratio between the two metals.

But in 1873 there occurred the 'crime of 1873,' as it soon came to be called. The United States went over to the gold standard, which allotted a restricted role to silver coin. The decision had been brought about by the 1867 Paris Currency Conference, where the majority of the twenty nations taking part declared in favour of the gold standard. By 1874 not only the United States, but Germany, Norway, Sweden, Japan and Holland had also gone over to it. Increased gold output and the discovery of considerable gold deposits about the middle of the century had made the move seem even more expedient.

Now the United States, after the Civil War, was already in a state of monetary transition. Different kinds of bank notes and currency were in circulation whose value was uncertain and varied according to locality. Only eight years after the end of the Civil War, the United States, the world's biggest silver producer, suddenly went over to the gold standard. The white metal thus lost its status. To the layman it was a very disturbing event and one which could easily be made to look like the cause of the already perilous economic position of the farmers. The producers of silver naturally did everything they could to strengthen that impression. To the debt-ridden farmers and small businessmen it seemed as though the suspension of double-standard currency was compelling them to meet existing commitments with money that was steadily becoming dearer, whereas a silver dollar linked to gold would enable them, while the prices of their products fell, to pay their debts with 'cheaper' money. In 1878 and in 1890, therefore, some compromise currency laws were enacted which, however, only created a highly complicated and confused situation, without relieving the economic plight of the affected groups. But when, in 1893, President Cleveland demanded the repeal of the Silver Purchase clause of an Act passed only in 1890, Bryan opposed him with a fire-eating speech in Congress. This did not prevent the repeal of the law, which in any case had failed to have the desired economic effects, but silver producers distributed a million copies of the speech. Bryan saw where the opportunity would lie for presidential candidates three years later.

In 1892 Bryan was re-elected to Congress, this time as spokesman for the silver-mine owners, whose interests, luckily for this gifted if demagogic politician, corresponded at least in appearance with those of the poor. In 1894, however, Bryan did not try a third time for the House of Representatives, but ran for the Senate instead. He was not elected. His friends in the silver trade set him up as editor of the Omaha *World-Herald,* a post that enabled him to set about preparing the way for his nomination as Democratic presidential candidate in 1896. Only very few observers would have guessed, even in the early months of 1896, that Bryan would be nominated and that bimetallism would become the exclusive issue around which the election would be fought.

Even when Bryan had fought his way up through the convention, McKinley, already nominated Republican candidate, believed that within a few weeks the silver controversy would have blown over. He would have much preferred a debate on protective tariffs. The Republicans suddenly realized, however, that in Bryan they had to combat a politically highly potent combination of the silver controversy and Populist aspirations and resentment.

The Populist Party, in the last thirty years of the nineteenth century, was an American social revolutionary protest movement for which a justly discontented rural population was responsible, for it had never really recovered from the depression of 1873. These farmers saw, and more especially heard, a great deal of the prosperity of other population groups. The symbol 'gold' was enough to direct this bitter and egalitarian-minded resentment into political channels.

Ostracism—democracy and envy in ancient Greece

To Svend Ranulf, the Danish sociologist and philologist, we owe the most thorough investigations of the social history of envy in ancient Athens. A central theme of his study is ostracism, a practice introduced into Athens in the period following the battle of Marathon. This was a measure which enabled the people—at least six thousand citizens—to send any unpopular person into exile for ten years. From a legal standpoint ostracism, so called from the potsherd used to record each vote (*ostrakon* = a shell or potsherd), is a monstrous proceeding: it is a punishment that is preceded neither by a crime nor by the formal passing of sentence. Ranulf, however, regards this procedure as being completely in accord with the Athenian mentality of the first half of the fifth century B.C.:

> For the edification of men, the gods, impelled by caprice or envy, bring down disaster and sufferings not only upon offenders and their race, but also upon perfectly innocent people. Men themselves as well as gods punish offenders. It may, then, perhaps seem quite natural that men should also, like the gods, occasionally vent their envy or their caprices on the innocent, and that they should introduce Ostracism as an established official form in which pious envy and arbitrariness could manifest themselves.[17]

Ranulf compares this with the practices of the democratic citizens of present-day republics and considers that this kind of ingratitude nourished on envy and felt towards outstanding statesmen and generals is no longer prevalent in the twentieth century. He cites examples of victorious generals who are later called to fill the highest civil offices of state. We can now supplement his list with the name of Eisenhower, although this should immediately be balanced by recalling the fate of Winston Churchill, whose electoral defeat in 1945 was interpreted by many people as a reaction based on resentment, as fear of the wartime premier who had acquired too much power. De Gaulle suffered a similar fate in 1946. In a way, too, the application of the American anti-trust laws resembles the principle of Athenian ostracism. The anti-trust actions

[17] Svend Ranulf, *The Jealousy of the Gods and Criminal Law at Athens. A Contribution to the Sociology of Moral Indignation,* Vol. 1, London and Copenhagen, 1933, p. 133.

brought by the U.S. Attorney-General's office against certain firms—which are carefully selected as targets on psychological grounds—are, it is generally admitted, scarcely ever able to show purely economic grounds for the choice of a particular firm. The decisive question is usually as follows: Which firm do its commercial rivals and the general public regard with such animosity that it becomes politically worthwhile to pay the enormous legal costs of an anti-trust action? (Many anti-trust cases, including those dismissed by the judge as unjustified, cost both the Attorney-General's office and the accused millions of dollars.)[18]

Further evidence for my thesis of the repression of the envy-motive is Ranulf's observation that the 'envy-theory' as an explanation of ostracism is out of favour with present-day scholars. In his work *La Solidarité de la famille dans le droit criminel en Grèce,* [19] Professor Glotz explains the introduction of ostracism as due to an increase in humanitarian feelings among the Athenians, and not to any lack of respect for the rights of the individual. In other fields, too, besides the historical study of ostracism, there are enough examples in this century of what Ranulf regards as a laudable reluctance to link certain social institutions and individual and group behaviour in a causal relationship with the motive of envy. This inhibition is doubtless explicable by psychological factors in the individual personalities of the scholars in question as well as by a general climate of intellectual opinion which favours such repression. Instead of the clearcut motive of envy, people nowadays prefer to adduce humanitarian sentiments to justify collectivist (i.e., usually egalitarian) incursions into the private affairs of individuals or minorities which stand out from the general norm as noticeably unequal.

This modern substitution of the concept of humanitarianism for envy as a motivation should not, however, be confused with Glotz's use of it. Glotz throws doubt on the envy-theory of ostracism by suggesting that the ten years' exile may well have been a substitute for much more severe punishment, and that therefore ostracism was a humane reform of the penal system. Ranulf's answer to this is that most of the victims of ostracism were innocent of any cause for legal action or judicial penalty.

[18] See Henry A. Wells, *Monopoly and Social Control,* Washington, 1952, especially pp. 102–5, 108, 109, 150 for passages where this specialist in anti-trust legislation shows particularly clear evidence of the envy-motive.

[19] Paris, 1904.

We believe with Ranulf that these considerations in no way invalidate his basic theory of envy as the motive of ostracism. Plutarch had good grounds for describing ostracism as 'a humane way of assuaging envy.'

Ranulf would hesitate to call ostracism an institution for the appeasement of envy simply because Greek authors of the time, such as Pindar, when referring to ostracism, complained that noble deeds could expect only spite and envy in return; nor would Ranulf be satisfied with Herodotus' statement when he remarked on the monstrous envy of the Athenians. For Ranulf the decisive evidence is rather the correlation between the institution of ostracism and all the other manifestations of the envy of the Athenians and their gods. His hypothesis is supported, above all, by the attitudes of three Greek writers—Aeschylus, Sophocles and Herodotus—whose works most fully express the prevailing ethos of the time when ostracism was at its height. For an Athenian it was unthinkable that a man could be happy and prosperous in every way throughout his life. It was the duty of the gods to prevent this. Often enough, though, the citizens themselves seemed to be zealously engaged in spoiling or frustrating any such good fortune as might arouse their resentment.

Now Herodotus does not say that Aristides was banished by ostracism because his fellow citizens were envious of him, but he immediately follows his factual description of the banishment with the remark that Aristides was the best and most honourable man in Athens. The envy-motive, according to Ranulf, emerges more clearly in an anecdote related by Plutarch. It tells of a farmer, who did not know Aristides by sight, writing his name on the sherd. Aristides asked him what that statesman's crime might be, that he should be banished, to which the farmer replied: 'I do not know him, but it annoys me to hear him cried up everywhere for his righteousness.'[20]

A significant reason for the failure of so many social scientists to acknowledge the reality of envy as a motive could be the influence of such theoreticians as Emile Durkheim and Edward A. Ross, who postulate as reality a social entity that lies above or outside its individual members, i.e., the idea of 'society,' and who maintain that all restraint exercised over individuals or groups within that society are the outcome

[20] Ranulf, op. cit., p. 136.

of a wise, benevolent 'general will' (the influence of Rousseau is plain).
How, given such a premise, can such an all-embracing body, the society
or the community, be envious? Envious of whom? Of itself or of its
offspring? The question obviously lends itself to a *reductio ad ab-
surdum*. Only by pointing out how it is that individuals succeed, by
disguising their personal envy under a cloak of social concern, in raising
it into an apparently supra-personal demand, or how generalized envy
can be whipped up to pathological level by certain demagogues—i.e.,
can be exacerbated to the point of ostracism—only then does the
inconsistency between Ranulf's theory of ostracism and modern social
theory disappear.

The nature of this inconsistency emerges very clearly in Ranulf's
dispute with Professor Gernet. Gernet begins by describing ostracism in
a way that accords with Ranulf's:

'He who interferes with democracy, who disturbs the conditions of
equality, who elevates his pride above the group, draws down upon
himself the effects of a collective "jealousy." '[21]

Much to the regret of Ranulf, Gernet finds the use of the word
'jealousy' (presumably used erroneously in this case to mean 'envy')
questionable:

> To understand the expression 'jealousy of the people' in a grossly demo-
> cratic sense would be to commit that error of interpretation which consists
> in ascribing perfectly conscious and reasoned motives to an institution of
> which they would always fail to explain the peculiarities. In such a domain
> nothing is easier than to oppose psychology to psychology. There is jealousy
> in Ostracism—granted, but there is also fear. . . . There is fear of oligarchy
> and tyranny. . . . Behind this common-sense teleology it is necessary
> to seek, in the institution itself, the profound idea to which it gives
> expression.[22]

Ranulf is right in saying that a methodological reservation of this kind
is characteristic of a pupil of Durkheim. And even though a sociologist
should never be satisfied with a purely psychological explanation of the

---

[21] Ranulf, op. cit., p. 137, ref. Louis Gernet, *Recherches sur le développement de la
pensée juridique et morale en Grèce,* Paris, 1917, pp. 402 ff.

[22] Ranulf, op. cit., pp. 137 f., ref. Gernet, op. cit., p. 404.

phenomena under observation, he should nevertheless pursue the search for the specific psychological situation which has led to the consolidation of a socio-psychological motivational syndrome.

Ranulf now develops his reasoning thus:

> Jealousy [here Ranulf uses Gernet's expression, although he himself prefers what we regard as the more correct term, 'envy'], the nature of which can be studied in Aeschylus and Herodotus, and the supposed prevalence of which among the Athenian people is conjectured here to be the root of Ostracism, is probably precisely of the kind which Professor Gernet calls 'grossly democratic.' The theory built upon this supposition does not, however, imply any conscious teleology. It does not imply that the Athenians first deliberately made it their object to gratify their jealousy, and then introduced Ostracism as a means to this end. Its import is that an underlying jealousy instinctively availed itself of the means at hand. This might have happened in exactly the same way, even if the Athenians had never known, or admitted, that they were jealous. Professor Gernet's methodical principle of seeking the explanation for a social institution in the institution itself is correct as far as it goes, and it is the principle applied in the present investigation. But 'the institution itself' may be subject to my interpretations, and if the probability of one of the possible interpretations can be confirmed also independently of the analysis of the particular institution, it should evidently for that reason be preferred to the others. When there are additional reasons for supposing that 'grossly democratic' envy was a prominent characteristic of the Athenian people, this is a decisive argument in favour of the envy theory as compared with other possible explanations of Ostracism. The fact that Greek authors speak so much of envy as they do is, indeed, in itself no proof either of the prevalence of this quality or of its connection with Ostracism, but neither is it a proof of the contrary.[23]

Today politicians and reformers attribute far more envy to the average voter than empirical studies have found. As a consequence W. G. Runciman demanded recently 'uninhibited reference group choice' in regard to all inequalities. Actually such choice is what envious men rarely exercise, thus making possible complex and productive societies based on the division of labour. Runciman, however, to maximize social

[23] Ranulf, op. cit., pp. 138 f.

justice, does not want a miner to compare himself with a fitter, a farm labourer with a boilermaker. Both men, he writes, 'have equal reason to compare themselves with clerks or businessmen or Members of Parliament.'[24] Indeed, 'the poorest pensioner is entitled to a sense of relative deprivation based on the inequality between himself and the richest man.' Runciman believes that 'the poorest appear to be entitled to a greater magnitude of relative deprivation than the evidence shows them to feel.' For instance, surveys in Britain have shown people to care much less for steeply progressive income taxes than present tax laws assume.[25]

Runciman, finding less envy than expected, argues that his model of a socially just society would not require people to be more disposed to envy.[26] This I doubt. It is an ominous sign that egalitarians now wish people to develop a keener sense of envious mortification than they normally have lest they cease to care for reforms. As we have shown from the start, concepts such as relative deprivation, though useful in some types of empirical research, have helped to repress the facts regarding envy. Our book tries to show what life would ultimately be like in a society of 'uninhibited reference group choice.'

[24] W. G. Runciman, *Relative Deprivation and Social Justice,* London and Berkeley, 1966, pp. 270 ff.

[25] Op. cit., pp. 90 ff.

[26] Op. cit., p. 280.

13

In Praise of Poverty: from Sumptuary Laws to Contempt for the Affluent Society

FOR MORE THAN TEN YEARS social criticism in Western industrial societies has been focused on their material achievements. Something simply *has* to be wrong *because* the times are so good. The suspicion that this criticism is neither profound nor well founded, but is due rather to an absence of other legitimate targets, is confirmed when we recall that in modern times social criticism has never yet commended a society for obliging its members to lead a poor and wretched existence. Praise of an inadequate economy never emanates from the critics of a particular social system, but from the holders of power, the very people who should be held responsible for the austerity of the people's life. And they will invariably make out that their austere economy is only transitional. There were clear and early indications of this 'new' social criticism in the United States between 1950 and 1955. At first this was confined to occasional veiled but scathing remarks in journals such as the *Nation,* the *New Republic* and the *Saturday Review of Literature,* gradually spreading to periodicals such as the *Atlantic Monthly* and *Harper's Magazine.* So much was this tendency in evidence that as early as 1956 I was able accurately to forecast the very thesis with which John Kenneth Galbraith was to astonish the world in 1958.[1]

---

[1] J. K. Galbraith, *The Affluent Society,* Boston, 1958. See also my forecast of the 'new' criticism in the study 'Das Problem des Neides in der Massendemokratie,' in *Masse und Demokratie,* ed. A. Hunold, Zurich-Erlenbach, 1956, pp. 254 ff.

Truth and welfare

Is there any valid reason why being miserable should bring one closer to the truth? The parables of the Bible may be largely responsible for this peculiar assumption—yet what is meant by truth has long since ceased to be religious or theological truth (where the above may indeed apply), but scientific, verifiable, pragmatic truth, and why this should be revealed to the man with an empty stomach and dressed in sackcloth, rather than to one who is well dressed and well fed, is not immediately apparent.

If such were the case then man, from the Stone Age onwards, would have been in possession of progressively less truth about himself and his social relationships, since his condition has steadily improved. Perhaps, then, one should be neither too badly nor too well off if one is to comprehend one's social existence? This argument gives rise to the insuperable difficulty as to who shall decide what is too much, and what too little. This is much harder than determining extremes, for it is easier to agree upon the lowest permissible point to which human existence may descend than it is to reach the correct mean.

This peculiar inverse coupling of socially relevant truth (or authenticity) with the welfare of the majority—a main proposition in Western social criticism since the early fifties—probably represents nothing but a revival of a much older ideological suspicion of purely Marxist origin. Between 1848 and 1948 the bourgeois, free-enterprise frame of mind was believed in principle to be incapable of perceiving truth. It was a 'false consciousness,' an ideology whose content was determined by the interests of a nonproletarian class. Only the proletarian, the worker, or at least his mouth-piece, the intellectual, who shunned the middle or upper class from which he often stemmed, was possessed of genuine social truth. In the Western industrial countries since 1950, however, this theory no longer makes much impression. The general style of behaviour and the standard of living of skilled factory workers, white-collar workers and farmers are quite similar. Indeed the relative level of real incomes in many instances has become paradoxical: the factory worker may have a larger income than the white-collar worker. What could the intellectual bent on criticism then do in Europe or the United States after 1950 but extend his ideological suspicion? The bourgeois mentality is no longer held to be *per se* blind to the workers' plight, but *all* inhabitants of the affluent society are held to suffer almost equally from loss of truth, from a false consciousness *because* they are having it so good.

Goethe's 'crime'

Mistrust and indignation felt towards anyone able to afford the good life derive, however, from emotional complexes that go back a great deal further than Marxism. Two years after Goethe's death, his English admirer Carlyle sought to draw the attention of Emerson, the great American writer, to Goethe's work. In a letter dated November 20, 1834, Emerson replied to Carlyle:

> With him I am becoming better acquainted, but mine must be a qualified admiration. It is a singular piece of good nature in you to apotheosize him. I cannot but regard it as his misfortune with conspicuous bad influence on his genius,—that velvet life he led. What incongruity for genius whose fit ornaments & reliefs are poverty & hatred, to repose fifty years in chairs of state . . . the Puritan in me accepts no apology for bad morals in such as *he* . . . to write luxuriously is not the same thing as to live so, but a new & worse offence. It implies an intellectual defect. . . . [2]

Few will contest that many people, if not the majority, are diverted from serious thinking by all those good things which their prosperity enables them to attain. But we know only too well that the man who owns no more than one threadbare suit, the man who is hungry or confined perforce to monotonous food, devotes ever more thought to daydreams or plans connected with the most elementary necessities of existence.

In England, of recent years, we have also heard poverty praised in pseudo-puritan social criticism. Arnold Toynbee and his son Philip (though left-wing himself) remarked upon this new fashion in social criticism which they both repudiated.

Philip Toynbee: 'But I think there's a certain weakness in the position of people like myself who have complained a great deal in the past about

---

[2] *The Correspondence of Emerson and Carlyle,* edited by Joseph Slater, New York and London, 1964, pp. 107 f.

unemployment and poverty and so on, but who, when the Conservative Government does, for whatever motives, raise the standard of living a great deal, turn sour and high-minded about it. I think one's got to admit that it's a good thing that people should have more money. . . .' To which Arnold Toynbee assented: 'It's rather hypocritical and offensive to advocate spiritual progress without considering the material basis for it.'[3]

We know a good deal about what is called work-inhibition. This very common attitude takes the form of aversion to starting something and causes us to busy ourselves with innumerable matters rather than the work we ought to do. We are never at a loss for a reason why what is inessential should be so much more vital than what is essential. Whatever their job or position, men will always find distractions enabling them to evade serious intellectual work. Ascetic sumptuary legislation (or, because this fails to work, constant and sometimes highly lucrative denigration of the affluent society) in no way alters that fact.

True, every single thing that has ever been at the disposal of man is also susceptible to frivolous abuse. Both in work and in play there are sensible and less sensible activities, and sometimes activities that are just plain silly. Curiously enough, it is being suggested more or less explicitly today that it is the business of governing authorities to reduce the private individual's prosperity, or rather the means that allow him to pursue his chosen way of life, to a level that will prevent him from being objectionable: that will keep him, in fact, from doing anything that might annoy the particular observer.

Social agnosticism

A survey of recent social criticism inevitably leads to the question of whether, in the eyes of these doubters and critics, there has ever been a time when men could discover the truth about their own society. Obviously not. Primitive man can exist only because he has interposed a zone of superstition between himself and both the social and the physical environment. At higher stages of social development, the intervening layer consists of religion and metaphysics. And when these fade away,

[3] A. and P. Toynbee, *Comparing Notes: A Dialogue Across a Generation,* London, 1963, p. 52.

there are political ideologies which are themselves allegedly superseded by the euphoria of manipulated conspicuous consumption in the affluent society. At what previous stage, therefore, did man ever have a 'correct' relationship to his society? And what, indeed, is 'correct,' apart from what the critic of a society happens to think fit?

For the moment we can allow such *social agnosticism*. There will probably never be a true or—from the point of view of an epistemological purist—a correct relationship between members of a society and the social system as such (leaving aside the question of culture and society, as also that of the supra-individual forces that uphold and actuate the system). But is that a misfortune? Can it be turned into an accusation against the form of a given society as such? Can a social system somehow be held responsible for so misleading its members that they can never learn the truth about the nature of their society?

What for most people really counts is simply this: Always and in virtually every society or simple tribal culture, however unscientific, irrational and far removed from reality the average belief and social self-interpretation of these people, there has always been sufficient correlation between what was believed or habitually done, and what was in fact possible in any given social, political, economic and geographical environment, so that somehow, despite all the waste and inefficiency, social existence was possible. Today we know much better than in 1930, 1900 or 1800 what an unheard-of quantity of specious nonsense a social and economic system can swallow without disintegrating.

Is this really so surprising? After all, it has long been realized in natural science that, so far as our knowledge and mastery of the world are concerned, control and prediction depend on only an approximate correspondence between human intellect and matter. In many cases scientists long did not know, and in others they still do not, how or why something 'works': why a medicine cures, or a chemical compound is stable, etc.

May not the case of social existence be similar? As a rule members of a society will understand what is right, at least to the extent of being able to devise tolerable forms of social existence. Claims may vary considerably in this respect, but it would seem to me doubtful whether the people who have prospered most *qua* collectives are those who have subscribed to the most current 'scientific' theory about their social life.

High incomes 'socially just' in the socialist society of scarcity,
'unjust' in the affluent society of 'capitalism'

For several years now, both in America and in European countries,
certain young people have adopted a strange attitude of defiance. A short
conversation is enough to detect in them a persistent, smouldering
feeling: their own society, or Western society in general, does not suit
them. They feel ill at ease because it is comfortable; and this is because
not everyone is equally well or badly off, and because others are too well
off. There are some, in fact, who are very badly off but seldom, as it
happens, the person I have been talking to. His father may even be rich,
and this only makes matters worse. It is the *Weltschmerz* of the egalitarian temperament caught up in a reality which takes some account of their
problem, but not enough. Often they may be too well off to be able to
take themselves as an example, asking me rather to compare the lot of
certain unfortunate people with the luxury of some highly paid individual. But seldom, if ever, are the Kennedys mentioned, or trade union
leaders, successful authors, film stars, or the instant celebrities of show
business. Exception is frequently taken to the incomes of famous doctors, business executives and industrialists. When challenged to name
any society in this world which would suit them and assuage their
conscience, they will invariably reply: 'There isn't one, but things might
be better in Red China, in the Soviet Union or in Cuba than they are in
the United States or West Germany.'

When I have then cited economic facts from the Soviet Union, these
have generally been accepted unprotestingly as true; the fact, for instance, that in Russia in 1960 the differential between maximum and
minimum incomes was something like 40:1, whereas this ratio in Western countries such as West Germany, Switzerland, the United States and
England was more like 10:1, and further that the maximum income tax
in Russia, however high the salary, was 13 per cent.[4]

---

[4] On income structure in the Soviet Union see A. Inkeles, *Social Change in Soviet
Russia,* Cambridge (Mass.), 1968. Also Rudolf Becker, 'Lohnsystem und Lohn-
politik,' *Osteuropa-Handbuch. Sowgetunion. Das Wirtschaftssystem,* ed. Werner
Markert, Cologne-Graz, 1965, p. 412. Recent information on the social stratification
of Soviet society in accordance with income is to be found in the volume edited by
Boris Meissner for the Deutsche Gesellschaft für Osteuropakunde, *Sowjetgesellschaft
im Wandel. Russlands Weg zur Industriegesellschaft,* Stuttgart, 1966, pp. 110 ff., 147 f.

Next, I would ask: 'Wouldn't you object to the highly paid manager, general, stage director or professor in the U.S.S.R., relative to his lowest-paid subordinate, being much better-off than his equivalent in the capitalist West? Not at all discountenanced, my informant would always reply that there was no comparison, since the men I had mentioned were doing something for the people. They were working towards the day when Russians who were less well off would be better off. Thus their incomes were excusable. These angry young people think it perfectly in order if today Planning Commissar X has an income fifty times that of a worker, since he is working on a plan which (if all goes well, and quite possibly in spite of rather than because of his plan) would make the average Russian able eventually to buy a private house, and a car. But for executives and businessmen in America, whose efforts have enabled the average wage-earner to have such things for years past, our young social critic finds even an income ratio of 5:1 'socially intolerable.' Or might it be that he is upset by the fact that they make the future possible here and now, whereas he looks to the distant morrow simply because this excuses him from making a place for himself in society as it is today?

Luxury

In what was once the winter riding school, now the 'Stadtsaal' of the former Salzburg Festspielhaus, the painted ceiling (dated 1690) bears the inscription:

> What you now tread on was a mountain, as far as the ridge extends. . . .
> Of that no memory remains save the two walls of living rock. . . .
> Everything gives way to strength. And that no mean caviller shall deem
> building extravagant by reason of its size, be it known that the mighty

---

The income figures for top officials (and their expense accounts) are kept secret, but it is known from Soviet sources that in 1959 more than two-thirds of all workers and employees earned an average monthly wage of about 60 new roubles, whereas in 1960 an academic could earn up to 1,500, an opera singer up to 2,000, a plant manager up to 1,000. Even assuming that in 1965 the average monthly wage had risen to 95 roubles, a cautious estimate of the effective income of a top official would be 4,000 roubles, the income differential between the lowest class and the Soviet élite thus probably being 1:40; fifteen years ago it was still 1:100.

blocks hewn from the rock were used in the building of churches in the year
of Our Lord 1662. Guidobald, Archbishop and Prince.

The Church's prince, then, is anxious not to be accused of extravagance. It is notable that the expression 'mean caviller' should have been
used, rather than 'envious one'; the Archbishop may not have wished to
accuse his critics of a sin in the strict sense, or perhaps one cannot envy a
prince, but merely feel indignant at his extravagance. Here again, then,
we come upon the distinction between legitimate envy based on righteous indignation and vulgar destructive envy which is always directed
towards those socially comparable with oneself.

The battle waged against luxury by the envious is age-old.[5] Sumptuary laws are found in very diverse societies, among primitive peoples,
in antiquity, in the high cultures of the Far East, in the European Middle
Ages, and they persist to this day. Sometimes a man who could afford
inequality could pay ransom for the privilege, could buy off the envy of
the community, as it were, by paying, say, a special tax if his house had
more than a certain number of windows or stoves, or his waistcoat more
than the minimum number of buttons; today in some countries his car is
taxed according to its horsepower. But quite often there was no pardon
for those accused of luxury. In the West African native kingdom of
Dahomey, the commoner who used too many leaves for the roof of his
hut, or who consumed honey he had found in the jungle, paid for this
'luxury' with the loss of a limb, if not his life.

Anyone who looks into works on sumptuary laws at different periods
of history and among different peoples soon realizes that what basically
is nearly always at work in individual societies is a regular and almost

[5] There is a recent study on this subject from an economic angle, containing information on other sources, by H. Kreikebaum and G. Rinsche, *Das Prestigemotiv in
Konsum und Investition. Demonstrative Investition und aufwendiger Verbrauch
(Beiträge zur Verhaltensforschung,* ed. G. Schmölders), Berlin, 1961. The motive of
envy-avoidance in consumer behaviour is not, however, examined exhaustively. While
the authors recognize the difficulty of defining the concepts 'luxury' and 'extravagance,' and the extent to which cultural-critical resentment is concealed within the
secondary meanings of these words, yet they specifically make no attempt 'to enter
into the historical causes and reasons underlying a more or less emotional repudiation
of extravagant consumption . . . ' (p. 112).

universal envious pressure selecting for its target, more or less at random, now this, now that sign of inequality in fellow citizens or tribesmen. Luxury *as such* has never existed, and never will exist, but only *envy* of consumer behaviour that is branded as luxury. The actual yield, for instance, produced by luxury taxes, irrespective of the state of development of the economy, is almost invariably very small and often insignificant by comparison with the yield from those taxes that are paid by all, or by the majority, without regard for contingent 'luxury.'[6]

Prohibitions on luxury

The Roman *Lex Didia* (143 B.C.) laid down for the whole of Italy that not only the givers of extravagant meals, but also their guests, should be punished. Sumptuary laws were often applied to some choice morsel that had only just appeared on the market, such as shrews or mussels. If St. Louis eschewed gorgeous robes all the time he was crusading, this may have been because of (unconscious) fear of divine envy (the less finely I dress, the more likely I am to return). In 1190 Philip Augustus and Richard Cœur de Lion tried to restrict the extravagant wearing of fur by Crusaders. In the Netherlands, Charles V forbade the wearing of clothes embroidered with gold or silver, as well as of long pointed shoes, after the Church had inveighed against these things.

But sumptuary laws were enacted not only by kings and emperors:

[6] J. M. Vincent, article on 'Sumptuary Legislation,' *Encyclopedia of the Social Sciences.* Also, John Martin Vincent, 'European Blue Laws,' *Annual Report of the American Historical Association for the Year 1897*, Washington, 1898, pp. 357–72. P. Kraemer, *Le Luxe et les lois sumptuaries au moyen age*, Paris, 1920. J. Schwarten, 'Verordnungen gegen Luxus und Kleiderpracht in Hamburg,' *Zeitschrift für Kulturgeschichte*, New Series, Vol. VI, 1899, pp. 67–102, 170–90. F. E. Baldwin, 'Sumptuary Legislation and Personal Regulation in England,' *Studies in Historical and Political Science*, 44th series, No. 1, Baltimore, 1926. W. Roscher, *Prinzipien der politischen Ökonomie*, 13th ed., 1877. F. Marbach, *Luxus und Luxussteuer*, Bern, 1948.

In the *Journal of Law and Economics*, Vol. 2, 1959, pp. 120–3, there is a sarcastic demand for the foundation of a society for sumptuary legislation—the 'Sumptuary Manifesto,' in which the intellectual and emotional origins of the 'new' economy of John K. Galbraith and others are shown up in a scathing satire.

civic authorities in Italy and Central Europe were also addicts of the sport. Independent cities such as Basel, Bern and Zurich had regulations governing funerals, baptisms, weddings, banquets and the way people dressed. Sometimes a city would prescribe the quality of cloth, or the width of ribbons, to be used in clothing.

Again there is an obvious connection between European sumptuary laws and fear of divine envy, though Christians, indeed, should not have been troubled by the latter: for fifty years the earthquakes of the early sixteenth century were to serve as an admonition, as justification for the statutory limitation on luxury. From this it may be seen to what extent sumptuary legislation is at bottom a substitute for the magical propitiation of nature and spirits among primitives. I suspect that those who scorn the affluent society are partly governed by these same archaic emotional complexes.

Certain mystical agitators incline one to suspect a connection between sumptuary legislation and an early form of fanatical religious egalitarianism. Thus Hans Böhm an der Tauber (1476) demanded that no one should have more than his neighbour, and in 1521 Eberlin von Günzburg pressed for severe legislative restrictions on consumption; doctors, too, were to practise without payment, and taxation must be progressive.

By and large, it was not until the end of the eighteenth century that the rage for legislative restriction of luxury and consumption began to die down in Europe and America, making way for the inception of an expanding and economically healthier free-market economy.

The connection between Voltaire's belief in progress and his conception of luxury is indicative of the change. Voltaire cited Colbert to prove his own view that, with skilful manipulation, luxury could enrich a state. Voltaire's theory of luxury derives no doubt from certain Englishmen, for instance, Petty, North and Mandeville, but also from men such as Pierre Bayle. A century later, the notion that the luxury of the few meant work for the many was to serve a Bavarian king as a political pretext for his extravagances. In the case of Voltaire, luxury might be defined simply as 'the rich man's expenditure.' On the other hand, and quite rightly, Voltaire expressly pointed out that the term 'luxury' was purely relative. In 1738 he wrote: 'What is luxury? This is a word which we use with as little thought as we do when we speak of there being different climates in East and West. In reality the sun neither rises nor sets. The same is true of luxury—one person may think there is none, while another may see it everywhere.[7]

The paradoxical public success, with its concomitant political repercussions, achieved since the end of the Second World War by the publications of neo-mercantilist opponents of 'luxury,' is no doubt largely explicable in terms of the resurgence of archaic emotions in modern man. (If I support retrenchment of the 'affluent society' *then* I shall have done my share in helping to avert a nuclear world war, and *then* the aircraft I'm travelling in won't crash, I won't go bankrupt, etc.) Another reason for their success might be the existence of social guilt, often of an existential character (many people ask themselves why they should be alive at all), or again, the total sterility of socialist socio-economic criticism which, viewed objectively, has long since lost from sight its initial points of departure.

To indulge in luxury is to provoke envy

I admit that there will always be people who enjoy making others envious. Things that are used towards this end are called luxuries. An anthropologist once told me about his native interpreter who, having been handsomely rewarded for his work, and in answer to the question as to what he was going to do with the money, said: 'I shall buy the biggest drum I can find and beat it in the village. Then everybody will envy me.'

It is an age-old notion, of which several examples may be found in antiquity, that the only reason for treating oneself to something is to make others envious, to show them that one is bigger and better than they are—superior, in fact. Thus the object as such, its cost and its usefulness are all quite irrelevant compared with its owner's motives, or so Adriana Tilgher (1887–1941), the Italian social critic, maintained in the late twenties, in a scathing attack on the luxury of the capitalist era:

> Luxury is noxious only when it consists in a state of mind . . . of the person who associates himself with a given group of people only in order to use them as a background against which he may pose as an animal of a superior breed. Clean shirts, for instance, in the Middle Ages and during a considerable part of our own era were real articles of luxury. But today the man pulling his clean shirt over his head of a morning does not feel himself

[7] C. Rowe, *Voltaire*, p. 164; the quotation is from the Moland edition, XXII, p. 363.

superior to others because of it. The present-day person who extracts that poisonous feeling of superiority out of a shirt is the man who puts on a silk shirt which he has bought hoping to make other people envy him. . . .[8]

This definition of the term 'luxury,' and the suspicion upon which it is based, are still encountered today. But how does the critic know who wants to make others envious, and whether he is, in fact, envied? It would seem probable that the critic is deducing these conclusions from what he has learnt by introspection.

For surely only someone who was deeply envious could take this view of luxury? How might it be possible to decide whether a man is buying an expensive car because he regards it as the best trouble-free investment for the next eight years, or whether it is because he wishes to make others envious? Even in America over the years I have met people who would avoid buying a certain make of car, although this would have been the sensible thing to do, only because they were convinced that others would see it as an attempt to make them envious. An exactly similar inhibition is found in American parents when they do not want to send their child to a private school, in spite of its evident superiority and willingness to grant a scholarship.

Unnecessary, fatuous, ostentatious and frivolous spending, in most of its forms and occasions, is just as objectionable to me as to any professional critic of luxury. But I also recognize the great difficulty of establishing absolute criteria. What seems luxury to one man will appear to another the only sensible choice on grounds of the object's quality and durability. Where one man might prefer to buy the very best piano, the other will choose to go, once in his life, on a world cruise. As soon as citizens permit an authority to enact sumptuary laws, the door is wide open to every kind of chicanery and envious restriction.

'Conspicuous consumption'

But the question of what is the real attitude towards luxury is much more complex. Generally speaking, even the most impassioned democrats and egalitarians of today are little worried by certain manifestations of luxury. Between 1961 and 1963, in the United States, for example, academic and newspaper critics of the affluent society could be observed drawing in their claws as soon as President Kennedy and his wife

[8] A. Tilgher, *Homo Faber,* Chicago, 1964, pp. 218 f.

initiated a regal style in the White House which, as was generally remarked, far outdid anything that had hitherto been customary in the American republic. All of a sudden the same kind of extravagance which, only a short time before—and on a much smaller scale—had been branded as an antisocial irritant in the local manufacturer or car dealer, was found tolerable in the man elected to a four-year term as head of state.

Envy develops among equals or those who are almost equal. Where there is only one king, one president of the United States—in other words, one member only of a particular status—he can live with relative impunity the kind of life which, even on a much smaller scale, would arouse indignation in the same society were it to be adopted by successful members of larger professional or social groups. So long as the envious journalist in England or America knows that he will never be king or president, he is much less likely to be upset by the pomp or day-to-day luxury of these personages than by any display on the part of the most eminent surgeon in his locality. With a little luck, he might himself have been a surgeon. It is not the luxury itself which offends, but the impossibility in modern society of preventing the attainment of relative luxury by people like oneself.

It is possible privately to sympathize with many critics of luxury, but this is not to imply that such criticism should form the basis of a new economic policy. For this would produce something inherently different, very probably a system where not only luxury would be inhibited.

Today certain 'coming-out' affairs, like debutantes' dances, seem as absurd to me as they did to Thorsten Veblen seventy years ago. The fact of their persistence in almost equally extravagant form testifies to the impotence of the levellers; what is perhaps even more remarkable, however, is that in 1963, for instance, this kind of coming-out party, where a father launches his daughter into society at a cost of five thousand dollars for the evening, could be shown on American television without the public's batting an eyelid.

In 1955, after *Life* magazine had run a story on the grand style of life habitual to the Anheuser-Busches, a family of rich brewers, it printed (May 23, 1955) an indignant letter from Upton Sinclair, who asked: 'Sirs: Isn't it dangerous to publish pictures of the Busch family? They have an income of millions. . . . Think of the effect on millions of families who have to get along on a couple of thousand dollars a year!'

'The effect,' of course, was envy. Sinclair correctly saw a problem inherent in our mass democracies where politicians on the one hand urge everyone to compare himself enviously with everyone else, in order to create a climate of acceptance for their legislative designs, and yet where, on the other hand, the mass media have apparently discovered an insatiable demand for pictures of the grand life led by the few. Can it be that the average man is not as prone to militant envy as politicians make him out to be? Opinion polls as well as depth interviews in various countries strongly suggest this. Nor does it seem likely that, were it otherwise, the millions of readers in more modest circumstances would devour their weekly magazines so faithfully—all of them having as staple fare the intimate details of a regal style of life. If the effect were as Sinclair suspected, all these people would be so frustrated that they would brood over their envy. Some probably do, but hardly the majority.

It is possible, and is, indeed, being attempted in some socialist developing countries today, to put a ceiling on expenditure for certain family celebrations, such as a wedding. Apart from temporarily assuaging a few envious souls, however, these decrees achieve nothing, so long as they leave private means themselves untouched. Hence the next step is to pursue a policy of taxation which leaves hardly anyone well enough off to be extravagant. If, however, this wealth is not simply destroyed but removed from the private into the public sector, there arises the further question as to whether governments are less inclined to frivolous spending harmful to the community than private individuals. It would seem unlikely.

And here we need not even go so far as to consider those projects which developing countries undertake purely for the sake of prestige; it is sufficient to recall the local expenditure on bureaucratic follies familiar to most of us.

Democratic envy, which can in fact play a constructive political role—e.g., restraint on public expenditure—is the less able to put a timely brake or control on governmental or official extravagance, the higher the level at which that extravagance is undertaken.

How luxury remains politically acceptable

In the realm of politics, quite independently of any specific culture or scale of values, but simply as the accompaniment of the crystallization of power, there inevitably arise unintended processes that restrain envy and the envious. Whether envious radicals have themselves brought into being an active political movement in order to realize their ideas of a 'just' world or, as is probably more common, a group seeking power secures the acclaim and electoral support of envious people, in the final count the envious are always the loser. Arbitrary intervention in the spheres of private life, justice and economics, demanded by envy to slake its anger, merely involves, at least after an initial phase of plunder and riot, the delegation of power to a minority of functionaries who can only carry out envy's mandate if they form themselves into a hierarchy of administrators. Often enough a political party already exists that can act as the executive arm of militant envy.

National Socialism came to power in Germany with promises directed at the envious; in this connection one has only to recall Nazi Party platforms such as the limitation of income to a thousand marks a head, the elimination of 'unearned income,' etc. The revolutionary movements in South American republics, Bolshevism in Russia, the resentful Populists in the United States, all were supported by those circles who would clearly be the first to take a malicious delight in the levelling of society. But without exception, and sometimes in the course of a few decades, the new ruling caste has become a bourgeoisie or a plutocracy. It has based its style of life on that of the former ruling caste which it superseded, or on the splendour and comfort it found among its new peers, the ruling heads of those states with which relations were established. And gradually a more lavish way of life became 'socially acceptable,' that is to say, politically tolerable. Every party or group that comes to power creates, of necessity, a new privileged class with an ideology that will again render economic inequality 'tolerable.' The new inequality, however, cannot be restricted to the close circle of top party members and bureaucrats. To protect itself against the envy of those outside, the central authority is obliged to grant 'luxury' and individual inequalities to those who are not directly concerned with government. To this, technological progress contributes. In 1920 President Woodrow Wilson predicted class warfare in America that would be sparked off by the envy of the many at the sight of the few in their motor cars. Not only is it impossible today to make this fact comprehensible to a member of the younger generation in America, but in the Soviet Union the private car is gradually coming to be recognized as something relatively attainable (although it is still far from attainable in practice, even for those who have the money).

Is there then any luxury article, any pleasure, any property regardless of size, or any form of existence which, in principle, social change, technical progress or political shift is unable to legitimize and protect against envy? We would be hard put to it to name one.

What we call culture in the narrower sense—i.e., high culture— arises only where envy has been successfully diverted away from the 'alien' character of the élite minority. Spengler has stated it bluntly:

> There is one other thing that belongs of necessity to a ripe culture. That is property, the thought of which causes delirious outbursts of envy and hatred from the vulgar-minded. Property, that is, in the original sense: old and permanent possession, inherited from fore-fathers or acquired over long years by the heavy and devoted work of the owner. . . .[9]

For spending as such, for dissipation, for *parvenu* ostentation and extravagance, Spengler shows nothing but contempt, but he makes a distinction that is often overlooked:

> This must be said again and again, and particularly in these days when 'national' revolutionaries in Germany rave like mendicant friars about universal poverty and squalor—in delightful agreement with the Marxists, who declare the possession of any sort of wealth to be criminal and immoral and war upon everything that has this superiority in things of high culture and any who surpass others in the ability to acquire, maintain, and worthily use property, and that from envy of such ability, which they themselves completely lack. *High culture is inseparably bound up with luxury and wealth.* Luxury, that matter-of-course environment of things of culture that belongs spiritually to one's personality, is a premise of all creative periods.[10]

The cult of poverty

If we consider the cult of poverty in antiquity and in the Middle Ages, the German youth movement between 1900 and 1930, and Marxist movements and their disciples, drawn from both working and middle

[9] Oswald Spengler, *Hour of Decision*, London, 1934, p. 97.

[10] Op. cit., pp. 101–2.

classes, and if we then observe how invariably an increasingly aggressive and resentful attitude on the part of those who are in fact poor, neglected and often despised is spontaneously met by a show of sympathy from some members of the envied classes, we find a most remarkable congruence.

At certain times there will appear in a society a messiah and his disciples whose provocative utterances express anew the already extant social envy. There are various reasons for this: general social change, new production and trading methods, invidious comparisóns made by itinerant workers who, moving from place to place and from culture to culture, become earlier and more acutely aware of economic differences than do sedentary workers and thus, as has often been shown, form the enthusiastic vanguard of egalitarian salvationism. The messiah and his group may threaten revolution outright or, again, they may protract the revolution in sublimated form, defer the despoliation of the rich until the Last Judgement, and establish themselves as a counter-élite by stressing the glories of poverty and the ascetic life. What these people manifest is very probably envy, resentment and direct hostility to everything above their own level. But there is usually more to it than that. For the conflux of genuinely poor disciples to the cult is almost exactly matched by a similar conflux from the upper classes: in the Middle Ages, these were members of the nobility and clergy—*pauperes Christi*—who practised voluntary poverty.

These people have their nineteenth- and twentieth-century counterparts in the children of middle- and upper-class parents, in England and the United States especially, but also on the Continent and in Asia, who, apparently against all logic of class, not only attach themselves to a proletarian revolutionary movement but also adopt the frugal way of life of their chosen environment, sharing a marked contempt for all comfort and upper-class trappings, to the extent even of neglecting personal cleanliness and health. Simone Weil (1909–43), as her biographer Jacques Cabaud has shown, exemplified this personality type in a strikingly pure and consistent manner. (There are, of course, exceptions, such as the patrician or the English aristocrat who becomes a drawing-room communist without the slightest intention of giving up his comfortable life. Generally, however, he suffers from a bad conscience and seeks a compromise by exceptional loyalty and gifts to the common cause.)

Many of these 'renegades' may be moved to take this step into ostentatious poverty by personal disappointment, or resentment against parents, relations or siblings. But invariably there is the factor of envy-avoidance and its parallel, the bad 'social' conscience, the nagging sense of guilt.

Perhaps some of them believe that their own poverty will 'exonerate' their caste or class, thus saving it from punishment or destruction. But often this wish or hope applies only to the individual himself. And in a great many cases it is no more than a primarily emotional, unreflecting reaction to the 'evil eye,' to the envy, assumed or experienced, of the pariah, the disinherited, the victim of discrimination.

It might also be a case of a member of the upper classes overburdened by his social duties. One tires of behaving at all times as the well-brought-up son of the nobility, of a cleric, or as the daughter of rich parents. But ordinary, private escape into the 'simple life' is not dramatic enough, and could even lead to secret envy of those members of one's own class and family who continue to enjoy their comforts and luxury. There is an obvious way out of this dilemma, out of these ambivalent feelings: the glorification of voluntary poverty in company with the genuine (or ostensibly genuine) poor and oppressed, whose utopia or planned social revolution promises that ultimately no one will be able to afford a pleasant life. A life, although one was born to it, one did not have the courage to accept from fate—because fate, in a secular world, is thought blind. And if blind, why did it favour me and not the other? Norman Cohn's excellent work, *The Pursuit of the Millennium*, on revolutionary messianism in the Middle Ages and its persistence in modern totalitarian movements, substantiates our interpretation in a great many particulars with evidence from historical data.

The crucial factor in the feeling of envy, as we showed at the outset, is always apparent in the fact that the envious man does not so much want to have what is possessed by others as yearn for a state of affairs in which no one would enjoy the coveted object or style of life. But since envy is an altogether relative emotion, in no way dependent on the actual degree of existing inequalities, it can also happen that people leading a comfortable life will attach themselves to an envious revolutionary group of those born poor, when they wish to attack, or harm, or at the least put to shame those more highly placed than themselves.

For the lesser nobility will always find something to envy in the middle nobility, as will the latter in the higher nobility, or the prosperous parson in the bishop. The dynamic of envy, which may be provoked and inflamed by the smallest of inequalities, thus explains how it comes about that pariah movements, those of proletarian revolutionaries, are continually being swollen by recruits from the ranks of those with a standard of living higher than that of the disinherited. Moreover, it is quite conceivable that a society having no luxury-addicted upper class, or virtually none, might also exhibit this phenomenon. Generally speaking, there will usually be enough inequality within a group of people, all of whom are favoured by fortune, to cause those so predisposed to reject their own milieu in favour of a proletarian party.

It is, of course, often genuine idealism that causes people of the upper classes to go over to a pariah movement; their only desire is to do good, for they can no longer bear the sight of other people's misery. We might assume that these people feel no envy whatever of their prosperous social equals. Even though this be the case, our hypothesis is still true, in that persons of this kind think they cannot render successful aid to their protégés, even if only psychological aid, as long as there are also well-to-do families, the very sight of which gives rise to the torment of envy in the worker relieved of his poverty. Precisely this must have been in the minds of Sidney and Beatrice Webb when they wrote:

> It is not too much to say that, in Britain or the United States of today, the very existence, in any neighbourhood, of a non-producing rich family, even if it is what it calls well conducted, is by its evil example a blight on the whole district, lowering the standards, corrupting the morality and to that extent counteracting the work of the churches and the schools.[11]

In other words, even when a revolutionary or progressive reformer of good family, although perhaps envious of no one, asks for nothing more than extremely heavy taxation, he finds himself compelled by his consideration of actual, or very often merely ostensible, envy in his protégés or underdog comrades to advocate and implement a policy rooted in envy.

[11] S. and B. Webb, *The Decay of Capitalist Civilization,* London and New York, 1923, p. 31.

The recognition of these interrelationships emphatically does not mean that social reforms and compassionate deeds, for instance, furthered by the unbearable spectacle of other people's misery, are questionable as such. It is both a pragmatic policy and in keeping with the intention of most ethical teaching, secular and religious, that a society, i.e., its active members, should seek to alleviate glaring social ills. Sensible social and welfare measures, which may involve structural intervention, should not, however, be confused with structural aggression, where the satisfaction of unappeasable envy is the principle of action. Such measures are apt to have the opposite effect. They, and they alone, are self-destructive utopianism. Some of the original Levellers insisted on a more realistic, less envious assessment of their aims than their modern counterparts are liable to profess in their manifestos. A group of Levellers in Cromwell's time wrote: 'We profess therefore that we never had it in our thoughts to level men's estates, it being the utmost of our aim that the Commonwealth be reduced to such a passe that every man may with as much security as may be enjoy his propriety.'[12]

Chiliastic movements

In his discussion of the cult of voluntary poverty, which often flourished more especially among the rich and well-to-do, the sociologist W. E. Mühlmann is in agreement with Herbert Grundmann, the historian, who sees the growing prosperity of the High Middle Ages, the rise of a money economy, the increase in urban populations and incipient large-scale crafts as leading to religious movements among men of all social classes seriously desiring to lead a simple, austere Christian life. Neither Mühlmann nor Grundmann seeks to explain the cult of poverty—even in the case of the nobility—as the result of direct social changes in the lives of those deciding to adopt a different way of life. Mühlmann says:

> Meanwhile it must be asked what is actually taking place when the way of life of the 'poor,' that, indeed, of *usus taxendi,* as the occupation of a despised class, is deliberately adopted and practised. It is not the social

[12] 'A manifestation' by Lilburn, Walwyn, Prince and Overton, in *The Leveller Tracts 1647–1653,* ed. by William Haller and Godfrey Davies, New York, 1944, p. 279.

pyramid that is turned upside down, but the cultural structure. No longer do 'pariahs invert values to suit themselves'; the inversion has lost its class connotation, since it is practised by men of all classes.[13]

Yet Mühlmann goes no further towards answering his own question. What is doubtless involved, as may have been shown in this book, is a human frame of mind and a change of temperament that are by no means confined to the Middle Ages and the problems of that time. One of man's deepest desires, giving rise to what is almost a reflexive or compulsive style of behaviour and action, is the avoidance of envy. He yearns for a social situation in which he need never suspect that his fellow man (not himself) is consumed with envy of others—of him, but not necessarily of him alone. That, and that alone, would be a truly *safe* society, a social environment without potential aggressors. In as far as man evidently senses more correctly than modern theoreticians of 'frustration' that no degree of general improvement can render man permanently and completely non-aggressive, sensitive people are willing voluntarily to adopt as inconspicuous a style of life as is possible in the hope of evading aggressive envy. The nobleman or prosperous businessman, often of upper-class origins, attaches himself, as representative of his whole class—or of all envy-provoking people in the upper classes—to a chiliastic movement where, firstly, there shall be no envy among its members, and where, secondly, all *those* values giving cause for envy are denied and despised—a movement, indeed, which actually promises a new world totally devoid of all possibility of envy.

It is significant that European socialists of the nineteenth and twentieth centuries in their search for precursors picked on just those chiliastic revolutionaries, like the Cathari and the Bogomils, who themselves were enthusiasts under the domination of resentment yet never succeeded in creating any larger independent, functioning society. They were heretics who were generally claimed by the stake before they had been compelled to come to grips with a society's practical and economic problems.

Arno Borst draws attention to the discovery of the Cathari by the socialists:

[13] W. E. Mühlmann, *Chiliasmus und Nativismus*, Berlin, 1961, p. 348.

The oppressed of all periods are the heroes of those who understand freedom in terms of economics. When, in 1895, the Marxist Karl Kautsky was looking for the precursors of modern socialism, he lit on the Cathari, though he had no clear idea of what they were. Later on, in 1906, his fellow Marxist, Milorad Popovich, construed the struggle of the Bogomils, of which he had solid historical knowledge, as a class struggle. The following year, the Italian socialist and modernist, Gioacchino Volpe, portrayed the Italian heretics as representatives of the lowest classes; and in 1911–14 his pupils, Luigi Zanoni and Antonino de Stefano, took the socialist thesis to its extreme by dubbing Catharism a revolutionary movement, under the imperfect disguise of religion.[14]

The ubiquity of envy in human relations, the consideration of it even when objectively it is perhaps not especially acute in others, is one of the fundamental constituent factors of social reality. Because envy, the envy of others, is always by nature an unassuageable, negative, unproductive feeling, most successful cultures throughout history have devised inhibitions on envy.

Thus neo-Marxists today explain not only religion but all proverbs critical of envy as designed by the élite to keep the underprivileged in permanent subjection. Whether this was ever so, or whether less fortunate people coined proverbs as a sort of balm to render life tolerable, is impossible to decide now. Nor does it really matter. Whatever is thought of the comforts and humaneness of modern life compared with the past, this present civilization of ours rests on a minimum of envy-containment, which should not be considered expendable now that still more complex problems devolve upon man. Whoever attacks and undermines the 'achieving society' by dramatizing the differences between its successful members and their opposites should think twice. So long as envy and envy-avoidance are in balance, and so long as on the whole only such envy finds expression and recognition as is legitimate and functional within the framework of a given culture and its technology, neither the society's efficiency and adaptability nor the scope of its more ingenious members is restricted. Both individuals and families are to some extent protected against the pathologically envious man. The official morality of the group keeps him within bounds, and threatens with exile or other

[14] Arno Borst, *Die Katharer,* Stuttgart, 1953, p. 44.

sanctions anyone who seeks, from private envy, to harm his fellow tribesman (by means of denunciation, the evil eye, black magic, etc.).

If, however, the dividing line between private envy and justifiable envy is no longer well defined in any society, individual actions and social movements may occur with consequences that are unfortunate for the whole society. For as soon as an avowedly envious man is able to become a judge, a legislator or a leader of an important political party, social effects arise which justify man's original mistrust of envy. Envy deliberately used as a chosen instrument in political strategy or tactics is something quite different from envy that operates largely in the unconscious and upon which depend countless minor social controls and inhibitions essential to a predictable, tolerable social life.

It is, of course, true that envy can express itself as much in the desire for the preservation of inequality as in the desire to achieve equality. The jealously guarded privileges of the established can be as harmful to the welfare of others as the envy of the underdog. The notorious practices of certain unions, especially in the United States and Britain, which discriminate against ethnic minorities and against men without a family link with the trade, and which also harm the public by depriving it of adequate services, is a clear case of this type of envy. It is also to be found in the professions and their associations. Yet there can be an essential distinction. The highly paid expert, the skilled worker, etc., who protest when others with lesser skills approach their pay scales, are reacting with jealousy, not with true envy. They defend their territory as animals instinctively do when an intruder trespasses. It is therefore extremely unlikely that in any foreseeable future man will cease to react indignantly to any such act of trespass. We simply have to take this form of behaviour into account. It is also a form of psychological self-assurance: 'I deserve consideration because I have worked hard for years to get where I am; I will not tolerate people leapfrogging up into the same income bracket merely because their unions have more members.' If at the same time he insists on a 'closed shop,' such attitudes can cause labour to ossify into an occupational caste system, which is harmful to any modern industrial society. The effect on society of such jealousy and covetousness is positively to discourage enterprise, innovation and expansion. However, as soon as the skilled man is willing to admit any qualified person to his well-paid group, and merely resents the fact that others, without his qualifications and responsibilities, obtain similar rewards through group pressures based on envy, his protest is another matter entirely. Even though he is protesting on his own behalf, he is also insisting on the superior growth-potential of a socio-economic system that allows significant differences in reward for different services. By contrast, anyone who advocates a society which allows no significant differentials of reward (and many socialist parties at least in theory still retain this as a goal) is evidently prepared to see the economy collapse rather than reconcile himself to the inevitable fact that any society will always contain some potentially envious members.

In our modern societies it is still possible in cases of pathological greed and avarice to speak of acquisitiveness as a social sin. But as a general concept it no longer makes sense. The man who works overtime to afford something that he or his family covet deprives no one else of anything. It is absurd to censure such a man as if he were an absolute monarch extracting the last precious coins from his subjects in an economy with a static supply of gold or silver. As soon as there is real economic growth, and the technology to produce any item in as many copies as there is a demand for it, covetousness and acquisitiveness, as terms of social criticism, lack any real meaning.

14

The Sense of Justice and
the Idea of Equality

A NUMBER OF AUTHORS have drawn attention to the fact that those feelings and attitudes that are so vitally important to a political order—namely, the sense of equity, of justice and injustice—are inherent in man because of his capacity to envy. Envy is aroused if, in one locality, the political power allows a merchant privileges which are not conceded in another, if one man is subject to arbitrary taxation while the other remains untaxed. Something approaching equality before the law arises out of the political tug-of-war between those who make the laws and those who have to live under them. Originally it was in the interests of the authorities to leave some room for differential treatment, which could be financially profitable; moreover, arbitrary control, permitting the unequal distribution of favour, tends to an increase in power.

But gradually the legislators themselves came to be affected by the laws, and so their interest in equality before the law became more personal. Yet even in democracies there are, for a number of reasons, exceptions to this rule. Farmers, trade unions, oil-well drillers and professional groups often enjoy a special status in relation to certain laws. In general, however, the citizen of a modern democracy can rely on equality before the law. His claim to it is assured by the envy that all his fellow citizens feel towards anyone who might conceivably gain by inequitable treatment being meted out to him, even if this gain were only the pleasure felt by the powerful man in the power that enables him to be unjust.

This reasonably predictable equality before most laws and public ordinances thus creates for the individual a clear field of activity in which he is secure. In political terms envy thus has a positive and constructive function as watchdog.

But the situation is changed if the same citizens who keep jealous watch on the equality before the law, and from which they constantly benefit, now approach the state with the demand that it infringe the principle of equality before the law for those few citizens whom the state has enabled to become economically (or perhaps only educationally) unequal. Many of the advocates of equality, it would now seem, are in no way anxious to secure genuine and lasting equality of opportunity. The increasing revulsion of fanatical egalitarians in Britain towards the 1944 Education Act, once hailed as progressive and which promised real equality of opportunity in education, proves to what extent the apostle of equality disdains the consequences of his original demands.

A few years ago the Zurich professor of constitutional law, Werner Kägi, basing himself on Fritz Fleiner's *Bundesstaatsrecht,* clearly brought out the dangers of the shift from legal equality to envy. The word 'equality,' he believed, had been too long taboo, and criticism of egalitarianism ought not to be restricted to fiscal legislation. The attainment of 'uniformity' was often equated with progress. But 'Far and away beyond anything that justice demands by way of equal treatment for equals, what is unequal is often rendered uniform by democratic legislation. And that which is idealized in the form of a demand for equality more often than not turns out to be merely the expression of that egalitarian endeavour, with its mistrust of all autonomy, its resentment of any exceptional position. . . .' There follows a quotation from Fleiner's *Bundes-staatsrecht*:

' "If equality before the law is essential to democracy, it can also be a stumbling block. For it promotes that fanaticism and envy which seeks to treat men in all fields of life as equals, and repudiates as undemocratic the differences arising from higher education, upbringing, intelligence, tradition etc." '[1]

George Caspar Homans, an American sociologist, was in command of a small warship in the Pacific during the Second World War. Later he tried to put this experience to good use in social science. One mistake he

[1] W. Kägi, 'Falsche und wahre Gleichheit im Staat der Gegenwart,' *Universitas,* 1953, pp. 735 ff.

made in handling his men demonstrates the uselessness of sacrificing, for the sake of general harmony, the supposedly provocative well-being of one group in deference to the supposed envy in another. During a period of lull, the following situation occurred on board: the watch on deck was sweating in the sun, chipping off rust and painting, while the men from the engine room, who were not on watch at the time, lay about on deck sun-bathing and reading. When an officer pointed out to Homans the possible resentment of the deck watch, he ordered the engine-room crew to spend their leisure time elsewhere. Immediately, however, these men let the captain know that they felt they were being victimized. Homans writes: 'As on so many other occasions, I should have done much better if I had done nothing. . . .'[2]

Up to a point, this discovery can be generalized. Few arbitrary actions, especially those of a legislative nature, are so thankless, and few are so fraught with undesirable consequences, as an attempt to balance the scales of fate in order to assuage envy.

The sense of injustice

Why does the sense of justice, or rather the sense of injustice, demand unconditional equality? The question is asked by the professor of law Edmond N. Cahn in his book on the sense of injustice, a term he significantly uses in the title rather than 'the sense of justice.' No doubt the latter is much more difficult to attain and to put into practice than the former. According to Cahn, the existence of a general and widespread sense of injustice is not solely due to the fact that equal treatment of all who belong to a recognized class of people (of one kind for children, another for grown-ups, etc.) is a prerequisite for any sort of legal order. It is true that justice requires such uniformity, but this still does not account for our great sensitivity to injustice. (It might even be said that only man's innate sense of injustice enables him to set up legal systems.) Cahn is of the opinion that people would be unlikely to feel indignation and rage simply because a decision happened to infringe the theoretical demand for the right to equal treatment, and that what is involved must

---

[2] G. C. Homans, *Sentiments and Activities,* New York, 1962, p. 54.

be something very deep-seated in human nature, for otherwise how could it be that even the humblest and least educated people hate injustice with a burning hatred? What are the roots of this demand for equality? Cahn describes the sense of injustice as a general phenomenon denoting

> that sympathetic reaction of outrage, horror, shock, resentment, and anger, those affections of the viscera and abnormal secretions of the adrenals that prepare the human animal to resist attack. Nature has thus equipped every man to regard injustice to another as aggression against himself. Through a mysterious and magical empathy or imaginative interchange, each projects himself into the shoes of the other, not in pity or compassion merely, but in the vigor of self-defense. Injustice is transmuted into assault.[3]

A little further on Cahn says:

> The sense of injustice now appears as an indissociable blend of reason and empathy. . . . Is the sense of injustice right? Certainly not if rightness means conformity to some absolute and inflexible standard. . . . The sense of injustice is right in so far as its claims are recognized in action. Its logical justification must be found in its efficacy.[4]

Most primitive peoples, incidentally, have a marked sense of, or feeling for, equity and reciprocity, but this should not be mistaken for an idea of equality. Among the African Azande anyone who has given assistance to a relative keeps an exact mental account of everything he has done, and expects the other to do likewise, and to behave accordingly. In primitive society, there is definitely not a general cook-pot, as it were, from which everyone can help himself to what he wants as the Western, social romantic invariably imagines. For one thing, these people are much too realistic to rely on Marx's formula: *From each according to his abilities, to each according to his needs.*[5]

The sense of absolute reciprocity is also found among the simplest primitive peoples in regard to strangers. Karsten reports of the Jivaro in Ecuador and Peru that whenever a bearer failed through sickness to

[3] E. N. Cahn, *The Sense of Injustice*, New York, 1949, p. 24.

[4] Op. cit., pp. 26 f.

[5] E. E. Evans-Pritchard, 'Zande Blood-Brotherhood,' *Africa,* Vol. 6, 1933, p. 387.

accompany an expedition, he invariably returned unasked the length of cloth that he had been given as advance payment. Curiously enough, this worked better among completely primitive tribes than among those that had come under the influence of missionaries.[6]

For two hundred years, egalitarian dogmatists and social philosophers have largely failed to see how little the individual is concerned with being *equal* to someone else. For very often his sense of justice is outraged by the very fact that he is denied the measure of inequality which he considers to be right and proper. It is the same passion, whether it assails the factory hand or the opera star.

American industrial sociologists have observed again and again that what matters to the worker is not so much the amount of his wage as the recognition of the difference between him and other workers. Complaints arise mostly when the wage scale fails to express what the worker feels to be the difference in the importance, difficulty, etc. of his particular task.[7] In 1959 Risë Stevens refused to appear as guest singer at the San Francisco opera house, although she had been granted the top fee she had demanded, because her other requirement, that no other star should be as highly paid, had been rejected.[8]

But the lengths to which a society permeated with egalitarian ideology can go are demonstrated by the following paradox: In 1965 workers engaged in constructing the highest parts of a new bridge in Austria were paid danger-money. Thereupon those working lower down went on strike until they were given compensation for loss of danger-money. The motivational situation was similar to that in a complaint being made at about the same time to the West German Federal Constitutional Court at Karlsruhe. A man liable for military service demanded in the name of equality that those who, for legitimate reasons, were exempt from military service should pay a special tax of an amount comparable with the disadvantage suffered by conscripts.

---

[6] R. Karsten, *The Head-Hunters of Western Amazonas. The Life and Culture of the Jivaro Indians of Eastern Ecuador and Peru (Societas Scientiarun Fennica: Commentationes Humanorum Litterarum*, Vol. VII, No. 1), Helsinki, 1935, p. 251.

[7] F. J. Roethlisberger and W. J. Dickson, *Management and the Worker,* Cambridge (Mass.), 1940, pp. 575 f.

[8] 'Risë Stevens Protests,' the *New York Times,* July 29, 1959.

Resentment and the demand for equality

The connection between the two is formulated by Scheler in the following unequivocal terms:

> Modern egalitarian doctrine generally—whether it takes the form of a statement of fact, a moral demand, or both of these things—is, however, clearly the product of *resentment*. It is surely obvious that, without exception, the apparently innocuous demand for equality—of whatever kind, whether sexual, social, political, religious or material—in fact conceals only the desire for the *demotion*, in accordance with a selected scale of values, of those having more assets, and those who are in some way *higher up*, to the level of those lower down. In any struggle for power, however great or petty, no one feels that the scales are weighted in his favour. Only the one who fears he *will lose*, demands it as a *universal principle*. The demand for equality is always a speculation on a falling market. For it is a law according to which people can only be equal in respect of those characteristics having the *least value*. 'Equality' as a purely rational idea can never stimulate desire, will or emotion. But resentment, in whose eyes the higher values never find favour, conceals its nature in the demand for 'equality'! In reality it wants nothing less than the destruction of all those who embody those higher values which arouse its anger.[9]

Scheler emphasizes that justice as such does not demand equality, but only 'like behaviour in *equivalent* circumstances.' Here he quotes Walter Rathenau, who once said: 'The idea of justice is based upon envy,' and observes that this remark is valid only of the *falsification*, arising from resentment, of the idea of justice, and not of its true content.[10]

The confusion of justice and equality, so common today, was elucidated in at least one of its aspects in 1954 by the sociologist Richard T. LaPiere when he pointed out the intentional differences between 'equality,' 'equity' and 'justice.'

> Equity is not to be confused with equality, which is a legal concept. Men may in relatively rare instances be 'equal before the law,' and small children often insist upon strict equality in the division of pie, cake, and other tangibles. But on the whole, equality is seldom desired, infrequently

[9] M. Scheler, 'Das Ressentiment im Aufbau der Moralen,' *Gesammelte Werke*, Vol. 3, p. 121.

[10] Op. cit., pp. 121 f., footnote.

demanded, and almost never found in the social relationships of human beings. Equity, on the other hand, is everywhere and always insisted upon. And equity is frequently, if not invariably, achieved. 'Justness,' as the term will be here used, refers to the achievement of maintenance of equity, which is always relative rather than absolute, and not to that which is simply legal.

LaPiere believes that, in the long run, most legislative acts, legal decisions, etc. tend to a state of equity, although at any given moment there may be no relation between the sense of equity and the law.[11]

Now and again, although not nearly often enough, ecclesiastical pronouncements reveal the understanding that demands for equality and social justice can easily turn into envious demands. Thus, about fifteen years ago, a group of American Protestant churches declared: 'Pronounced contrasts between rich and poor in our society tend to destroy comradeship, to undermine equality of opportunity and to threaten the political institutions of a society conscious of its responsibility.'

These elastic expressions do not admit of an exact interpretation. The following sentence, however, was significant:

'Those who take advantage of such inequalities are all too liable to self-deceit if they try to justify their privileges, just as others may deceive themselves in refusing to recognize as envy their own feelings towards those who earn more or have better luck.'

To solve this dilemma, the resolution calls for undefined measures against any inequality held to be inimical to 'the broad concept of justice and the well-being of society.' But there is no suggestion as to how such conceptions can be formed into a 'just' financial and social policy.[12]

Freedom and equality

G. Simmel had earlier remarked on the necessary instability of the relationship between freedom and equality:

Where general freedom reigns, so does the same measure of equality: for the former merely postulates the non-existence of authority. . . . Equality, however, which thus appears as . . . the first consequence of freedom, is in

[11] R. T. LaPiere, *A Theory of Social Control,* New York, 1954, pp. 199 f.

[12] Resolution taken by the General Board of the National Council of the Churches of Christ in the U.S.A., September 15, 1954.

reality only a point of transition. . . . Characteristically, no one is satisfied with his position in relation to his fellow beings, but everyone wishes to achieve a position that is in some way an improvement. When the needy majority experiences the desire for a higher standard of living, the most immediate expression of this will be a demand for equality in wealth and status with the upper ten thousand.[13]

In Simmel's view, however, envy and resentment are always the product of relative social propinquity: 'The resentment of the proletarian is virtually never aimed at the highest classes, but at the bourgeois . . . whom he sees immediately above him: representing those rungs on fortune's ladder that are the first he will have to climb, and upon which his consciousness and his desire for advancement are therefore temporarily focused.'[14]

But to advance by one social rung is seldom enough; the thirst for social advancement is by definition insatiable: 'Wherever an attempt has been made to establish equality, the individual effort to outdo others from this new basis has asserted itself in every imaginable way.'

Simmel demonstrates the naïveté of the belief that to be equal necessarily means to be permanently free from authority. Freedom invariably overrides equality to establish some new superiority. Simmel illustrates this with an anecdote that rings true. In the year of the 1848 revolution, a woman coal-heaver remarked to a richly dressed lady: 'Yes, madam, everything's going to be equal now; I shall go in silks and you'll carry coal.' As Simmel stresses, people not only want the new freedom, they want to make use of it also.[15]

Good and bad luck, chance and opportunity

It is significant that concepts such as luck, chance, opportunity, 'hitting the jackpot'—what we generally regard as someone's being un-deservingly favoured by circumstances beyond his or our control—are *not* found in all cultures. Indeed, in many languages there is no way of expressing such ideas.

[13] G. Simmel, *Soziologie, Untersuchungen über die Formen der Vergesellschaftung*, 2nd ed., Munich and Liepzig, 1922, p. 164.

[14] Op. cit., p. 165.

[15] Op. cit., p. 165.

Yet where one of these concepts exists in a society, it plays a crucial part in controlling the problem of envy. Man can come to terms with the evident inequality of the individual human lot, without succumbing to envy that is destructive of both himself and others, only if he can put the responsibility on some impersonal power—blind chance or fortune, which neither he himself nor the man favoured is able to monopolize. 'Today it's the other man who is lucky—tomorrow it may be I.' We derive the same consolation from the expression 'to have bad luck.' Thus what is involved is no providential God, whose favours can be won by special zeal in worship or a pure way of life, for this would most surely induce that bitter, consuming envy of the 'holier-than-thou' fanatic, so amply corroborated by history—as in the witch trials, for instance.

Oddly enough, there is also a half-way stage: while a culture may have a concept of disparate fortunes, of inequitably distributed opportunity, members of that culture may not quite dare to count on their luck. For they continue to be afraid that there may be other powers or gods, projections of their fellow men, who will vent their anger upon those very mortals on whom the arbitrary goddess of fortune has smiled. This was the stage reached by the ancient Greeks.

In English there are two words, 'happiness' and 'luck,' for the one German word, *Glück*. But whereas the balanced and fulfilled mental state which is happiness depends in the final analysis on the individual himself, to have good or bad luck is something quite independent of effort, prediction or human intervention. It is perfectly possible to envy the other his serenity and happiness, because it is obvious how much this depends on his work and the way he behaves, but by definition it is virtually impossible to envy him for being just lucky. Thus the English language, by using these expressions, takes some of the potential envy out of human relations.

A sportsman, a schoolboy or a businessman who has scored an unusually brilliant success, thus becoming a possible object of envy, will simply shrug his shoulders and say: 'I suppose I was just lucky.' In this way, though usually unconsciously, he seeks to disarm possible envy. The English word 'luck,' indeed, derives from Middle High German *gelücke*, which in the above sense of the term is defined as follows: an aimless, unpredictable and uncontrollable power which shapes events either favourably or unfavourably for the individual, the group or the cause. Or again: a chance combination of factors, having consequences that are favourable or unfavourable to a person.

The word 'happiness,' on the other hand, originally meant something much like luck, that is, a condition due to 'haphazard' occurrences or happenings. Gradually, however, happiness began to acquire the quite different meaning of well-being giving rise to contentment, which, by its nature, could be enjoyed simultaneously by everyone. Jeremy Bentham in his formula 'the greatest happiness of the greatest number' could only have used it in this sense. For it would be a nonsensical demand, were the term 'good luck' substituted for 'happiness,' since an individual person can have 'luck' only if its distribution throughout the rest of the world is both unequal and sparse. It is, of course, possible for any number of people in a society to be happy, since this depends largely on themselves. But they can never all 'hit the jackpot' at once, all be favoured by fate. This would be impossible from a space-time point of view. Yet modern social philosophers have turned this confusion of terms into a dangerous principle, through their belief that the equality of opportunity they are always talking about would lead to equality of happiness. Exactly the reverse is true.

Contentment

The individual can come to terms emotionally with his personal lot or that of his children because in every real, as opposed to utopian, society he is fundamentally aware, or at least able to persuade himself and other people, that the reason he has failed to achieve something others have achieved in outwardly similar circumstances is that there is no such thing as equality in luck. No society can offer its citizens a lottery system to cover all situations in life and all goals. It is interesting, by the way, that even in those societies where envy reigns unchecked in fiscal legislation, as in England, betting is regarded as 'politically tolerable' whereby anyone, for a few pence, stands the extremely remote chance of winning thousands of pounds tax-free.

The absence in the German language of the two terms 'luck' and 'happiness,' for which the single word 'Glück' has to be used, gives rise to considerable difficulties, as Nicolai Hartmann's study of the term in his Ethics of Moral Phenomena Value shows.

'It is in the very nature of "happiness" to tease man and to mock him as long as he lives, to lure him on, to mislead him and leave him standing with empty hands.' Up to this point, what is really meant is 'having good luck.' Hartmann continues: 'Happiness does not depend solely upon the attainable goods of life to which it seems to be attached. It depends at the same time, or rather primarily, upon an inner predisposition, a sensitiveness of the individual himself, his capacity for happiness. It is . . . smallest where it is passionately yearned for, and striven after.'[16] But what is meant here is happiness and not good luck.

This enables us to pursue the thought to its conclusion. To begin with—perhaps before some egalitarian started to think up plans for improving the world—luck meant something unpredictable and fleeting, which one person might have rather than another, or at least not both at once. Contentment is rather nearer to the word 'happiness' but postulates that there should be no striving or yearning for luck. Towards the end of the nineteenth century, contentment became unfashionable, and to preach it was regarded as reactionary. Everyone had to be happy, and that happiness must be fully secured and guaranteed by the state. But what they failed to understand was that, in a welfare state where everyone is given everything he needs and has to contribute only what is within his means, there neither could nor should be such a thing as good or bad luck. Yet happiness—that is, contentment—can no longer exist in such as society, for it is conditional on recognizing that not everyone can enjoy good luck at the same time.

Equality of opportunity

The absolute equality of opportunity that prevails in a game of chance, which, as all the players know from the start, can be won only by a very few, has nothing to do with the greatest happiness of the greatest number. It is true that a few envious souls may be temporarily annoyed at someone else winning the luck draw, but the fact that windfalls of this kind are tax-free in Europe (not in the United States) shows that the winner of the jackpot is very little envied. This is because of the real equality of opportunity and the absolute fortuitousness of the method of

[16] N. Hartmann, *Ethics*, I, pp. 149–50.

selecting the winner. A wife will not nag her husband for not having bought the right lottery ticket. She might reproach him for selecting the wrong football team, but even here there is so great a number of permutations and uncontrollable factors that no one could seriously suffer from an inferiority complex as a result of repeated failure.

A totally different situation arises as soon as politicians and reformers start talking about equality of opportunity, and that in a field of achievement where personal qualities such as talent, character, appearance, manner of speech and many others are involved. This applies even when the state offers equal technical and financial chances to all at some stage early in life. For if not only were there equal opportunities throughout an individual's life, but people were also as alike as egalitarians assume them to be, society would be like a race in which all the runners ran equally fast, so that they all arrived at the same moment at a narrow goal through which only one at a time could pass.

In an achievement-oriented society there cannot be equality of opportunity, there can at most be adequate opportunities for different kinds of people: person and opportunity must be complementary, but the result of such a system is a society stratified along socio-economic lines in which classes or status groups, professions and prestige are clearly discernible. This will provide occasion for envy, but it is more honest and more healthy socially, in the long run, to acknowledge this fact than to behave as though equality of opportunity were really feasible.

Egalitarians, those professional engineers of political envy-avoidance, now find themselves, as a result of their misunderstanding of the term 'equality of opportunity,' on the horns of an educational dilemma from which they will not succeed in extricating themselves as long as we continue to live in a society dependent on the principle of division of labour.

There are two ways in which egalitarians propose to attain the goal of a society with a sense of equality:

1. The American way, which has been in force for years, consists in a principle, from which there are of course local deviations, of educating children of both sexes, of all classes and parentage, of all degrees of talent—from the educationally subnormal to the genius—between the ages of six and eighteen, side by side in classes and schools whose composition depends neither on where the parents live nor on the pupil's

intelligence, but on pure chance alone. The unforeseen but inevitable result of this system is merely the postponement of the struggle for status, for since all cats look the same in the dark, the individual's education up to the age of eighteen signifies little. But after he has left high school his parents begin the desperate struggle to get him at all costs into a college having the maximum prestige. Since, however, 50 per cent of all Americans are sent to some sort of college, thanks to the down-grading of high schools in the name of equality, the deterioration of the already low standards of these educational establishments is accelerated, so that today 75 per cent of all those graduating, at about the age of twenty-two, from such colleges feel as unqualified professionally as did, thirty years ago, the graduates from high school. This has recently given rise in America to yet another surge toward the so-called 'graduate schools'—those establishments, that is, at real university or technical college level, for which virtually *all* students are given scholarships, regardless of their parents' means; yet there are more free places in graduate schools today than there are applicants who meet the conditions of entry. Hence the universities send out talent scouts to find recruits. Finally, after enormous public and private expenditure, a population has been produced in which those who have been at school up to their twenty-eighth year look down on those who had to leave school at eighteen. Both groups, however, having had far too much purely voca-tional instruction, suffer equally from classroom tedium, from staleness, and thus are often spoiled, at different levels, for the very careers which would have suited them. The boy kept in school by every possible means until he is seventeen or eighteen years old cannot face the prospect of technical training because he feels he has already had enough of teach-ers; the young man who has hung around graduate school until he is twenty-six or twenty-eight to acquire his doctorate or M.A. in the (correct) belief that his college diploma was no longer of much signifi-cance is not really content to be a trainee in a bank or a business firm.

2. Again in the name of equality, over the past twenty years Britain has evolved a system that seeks to afford equality of opportunity, indepen-dent of family and income, but it differs from the American system in that, at the age of eleven, children may be divided between three types of school whose requirements vary, as consequently, does their quality. This process depends upon a stiff, general examination.

The Labour Government has now declared itself opposed to this system, which already has been either partially abolished or watered down, and this, among other things, because it has become apparent that the utopian ideas of 1944 are not the way to the egalitarian heaven.

Inequality of opportunity as an alibi

In 1954 a study was published in Britain (based, among other things, on a questionnaire sent to ten thousand adults) on the subject of social mobility, edited by D. V. Glass. In this book developments were already apparent which were to be carried through to their conclusion a few years later by a young sociologist, Michael Young, in his penetrating book *The Rise of the Meritocracy*. [17] The reactions it aroused can be seen from a review of Glass's work in the leftist weekly, the then *New Statesman and Nation*. The reviewer asked: '. . . within a couple of generations there may be "perfect mobility," except for the few attending fee-paying schools—if there are any left. But what will happen then? What will equal opportunity really mean?'[18] For, as D. V. Glass pointed out, the threefold system of grammar, technical and modern secondary schools did little to equalize and share out opportunities of mobility:

> On the contrary, the more efficient the selection procedure, the more evident those disadvantages are likely to become. Outside of the public schools, it will be the grammar schools which will furnish the new *élite*, an *élite* apparently much less assailable because it is selected for 'measured intelligence.' The selection process will tend to reinforce the prestige of occupations already high in social status and to divide the population into streams which many may come to regard—indeed, already regard—as distinct as sheep and goats.

What comes next is Glass's key sentence:

> Not to have been to a grammar school will be a more serious dis-qualification than in the past, when social inequality in the educational

---

[17] D. V. Glass (ed.), *Social Mobility in Britain*, London, 1954. M. Young, *The Rise of the Meritocracy. An Essay on Education and Equality*, London, 1958.

[18] A. Curle, writing in *The New Statesman and Nation*, August 14, 1954.

system was known to exist. And the feeling of resentment may be more rather than less acute just because the individual concerned realizes that there is some validity in the selection process which has kept him out of grammar school. In this respect, apparent justice may be more difficult to bear than injustice.[19]

At this point the reviewer takes fright. He regrets that in 1944, when the Education Act was passed with the approval of all parties, there was no sociological research to forecast possible developments. He looks back nostalgically to the good old days when primitive man, regardless of personal ability, invariably had his clearly defined place in society. (A highly contestable hypothesis.) And the perplexity of the mid-twentieth-century egalitarian who has confused the stagnant equality of primitive society with progress is seldom so patently revealed as in these words of the reviewer:

> He has emotional security, but no freedom. For us, however, the picture is reversed. We have struggled out of the close-knit and restrictive pattern of primitive life and have released our creative faculties from the embrace of taboo. But by the same token that we have gained mobility we have lost security. What is the purpose of life, what are we here for, how do we fit in, what is right and what is wrong? We no longer know.[20]

The reviewer speaks of an enormously dangerous transitional stage, but then goes on, like all egalitarians, to pin his hopes on still more education, to lead us into an age of mutual understanding and sympathy. This affords scant consolation and is hardly original.

Equality of opportunity comes to grief because individuals do not all have the same ability to make use of their opportunities with equal or comparable success. And this is a more bitter experience than one for which one can blame others rather than one's self.

To the disappointment of egalitarians, and hence to that of Labour Party intellectuals in particular, the percentage of working-class children in grammar schools remained low by comparison with the numerical ratio of the working class to the whole population, even when there

[19] D. V. Glass, op. cit., pp. 25 f.
[20] A. Curle, op. cit., p. 26.

was equality of opportunity. This has been attributed to the discrepancy in educational opportunity during the socialization process in the home. This, however, represents only one factor. For various studies have shown that even those working-class children in Britain and on the Continent whose examination results entitled them to attend a better type of school often failed to take advantage of the opportunity. Upon investigation, it was shown that many times it was fear of envy in less-gifted contemporaries, or of envy in those adults in the child's environment who themselves had never gone to grammar school, which was barring his way to a school offering greater possibilities of social mobility.[21]

For in a community or group of people there is no method of social control so loathsomely insidious as that which ensures that no one shall break away from the lower group in order to advance and to 'improve' himself. This observation has been made again and again not only in the case of British schoolchildren, but also in that of a number of minority groups in the United States. The inhibition upon progress by social envy within the group that is discriminated against is frequently more marked—and also more verifiable—than the exclusive tendency of the higher group, into which entry would be possible for individuals.

'Social justice'—private patients but no private schools

In a book on the British middle class, written after the Second World War, during the time of the Labour Government, the two authors consider the motivational complex of 'social justice,' of levelling down to achieve greater 'equality,' and, without any circumlocution, they call the real motive 'envy.' While some of the socialist government's measures had brought about evident and appreciable equality, there could be little agreement, at least during the early postwar years, as to whether there had been any real redistribution of income as compared with before the war.

This greater equality can be looked on in various ways—as an insurance against revolution, for example. It has been achieved, as has often been

[21] See, e.g., B. M. Young and P. Willmott, *Family and Kinship in East London*, London, 1957, pp. 146 ff.

pointed out, without revolution, but none the less in deference to class pressure. This is held to be one of the greatest achievements of British institutions, at least on the assumption that a halt will be called at some point. But it is a question whether, if the 'poor' covet the standard of life of the wealthier, they will ever be satisfied short of complete equality, or what may, in material terms, pass for it. In many countries, and in Britain, the manual worker may earn more than the clerk; why not more than the brain-worker? Envy does not depend upon any particular scale of magnitudes, but simply on difference. It is possible to envy a man because he earns £10 a year more than oneself; it is indeed possible to envy him for many things other than income.[22]

It is possible, for instance—and this especially in Britain—to envy a man's diction, his way of speech, partly derived from the particular school he went to, which also affords him social contacts that can help him along in his life and career. Hence it was completely logical for left-wing intellectuals in the fifties to attack the more exclusive private schools. In 1953 Barbara Wootton thus took exception to the fact that while the middle and upper classes made use of the National Health Service—which in itself was desirable, since their demands increased its efficiency—they took much less advantage of free education. From this she went on to make a radical claim:

> In the health service, therefore, we can afford to disregard the fringe of legitimate private enterprise. . . . But in education things are different. There we have to face the fact that we may never see real equality, until private enterprise schools are virtually prohibited. Not even the broadest education ladder will meet the case, if express lifts are available for a privileged minority.[23]

Wootton, and many others who hold the same view, ascribe far too great an influence to school. Even if everybody had to go to the same kind of mediocre school—because all the young in a nation could never go to schools of 'equal distinction'—there would always be those who, as

[22] R. Lewis and A. Maude, *The English Middle Classes,* New York, 1950, 1st ed. London, 1949, pp. 260 f.

[23] Barbara Wootton, 'The Labour Party and Social Services,' *Political Quarterly,* Vol. 24, 1953, p. 67.

a result of home stimuli, and their own personal motivation, would acquire, in spite of the school, an education, intellectual and linguistic discipline, good taste, etc. which would distinguish them from the rest, so that they would once more have unequal opportunities. Thus it would become necessary to forbid inequalities in the home environments— something that has been attempted only in the kibbutzim of Israel.

Housing envy

The elementary sense of property, the instinct to demarcate a sphere of possession, is found in fishes, birds and various mammals, in the form of a territorial instinct. It is now believed that this represents a fundamental biological urge. A certain living area must be kept free of rivals of the same species, or parasites, so that there is sufficient food for the animal in its immediate environment. And just as some animals over-react in defence of their territory, so a grasping man will go too far in relation to other human beings. But this does not alter the existential fact that there will always be envy and aggression so long as it is not possible for anyone to seize anyone else's physical territory at will. So long as A necessarily occupies a place in the universe—whether this be a cave, a small field, a fishing ground or a well-paid job—there will always be B, C and D, to name only a few, who would like to be just where A is. The theories put forward by socialists and the like for the solution of this problem amount to this: An authority, i.e., the state, the bureaucrat, allocates to A, B, C, etc. their respective places—such as an apartment—in order to prevent B from being envious of C and A. As we have long since discovered, such a procedure does not help at all. Rather, it increases envy. Not only will there be the envy felt by A, B, C and D of the bureaucrat or the X Committee responsible for the allocation, and which hence occupies an enviable position of power, but the fact remains that even an executive body of truly angelic equity, which genuinely sought to practise absolute social justice, would be unable so to arrange things that A, B, C and D would not envy each other their respective physical locations in the world of space and time. Anyone wanting to get an idea of this kind of envy need only turn to the Austrian daily press—in the summer of 1964, for instance—in which envious feelings were stirred up in the crudest manner against privileged tenants of new municipal houses in socialist-run municipalities.

As far as the elimination of envy is concerned, it is irrelevant whether a person rents a pleasant house on the free market because he is better off than the other man, or whether it is allocated to him because he belongs to the right political group. In the latter case he appears in a rather worse light, because impotence in the face of a political authority is experienced as much more oppressive than is impotence in the face of another man's money. For it is, after all, possible to win the football pools, but you cannot win the ruling party's favour overnight. In addition, political parties often have no interest whatever in providing equal welfare for all. They do not want to see a dilution of the power derived from their authority to allocate a limited number of houses, offices, etc.

A jocular suggestion in an American paper on the problem of equality was that, for social living to be completely just, all the tenants of a building should, as a matter of course, 'move house' at least once a year, those on the top floor moving down to the ground floor, those on the first floor moving up to the fifth, and so on, until, after a few years, everyone would have experienced all the advantages and disadvantages of the building.

Bogus equality and conspicuous consumption

According to Scheler, envy only leads to resentment, which is all the greater 'where the values or possessions involved are, by their nature, *unprocurable,* and when these also lie within that sphere where comparison between ourselves and others is possible.'[24]

In 1954 the same conclusion was reached by David M. Potter, the American historian, on the basis of developments in his own country. He used the term 'invidious proximity.' Hatred, envy and resentment appear increasingly in the United States, and, paradoxically enough, in proportion to the degree in which the individual classes are able to observe each other at times of leisure—for instance, at sports, or while travelling (everyone has a car, and almost everyone could have a motor-boat); or, again, in proportion to the degree in which every household gadget, every article of clothing and every status symbol is within everyone's reach—at least on the instalment plan—because it is here, within the framework of a democratic and broadly egalitarian sphere of

[24] M. Scheler, op. cit., p. 45.

comparison, that the remaining class barriers in America make themselves fully felt.

For in America the worker's son can drive the same car, wear the same clothes, take his friends to the same restaurant, and—in contrast with an Englishman—speak the same English as the son of the doctor or the banker, but he would stand very little chance of being accepted as a son-in-law by either of them. It is no less painful when everything is attainable and equal within the sphere of comparison and the barrier is not an occupational one, but is due to the colour of one's skin, or to the land of origin of one's parents or grandparents.[25]

Legitimate and illegitimate envy

The all-pervasiveness of envy in human existence must be apparent from what has been said so far. Nearly all those who have written about it have not only been right in what they have said, but have recognized a truth more universal than they could, from their own particular vantage points, have suspected. Envy is ineluctable, implacable and irreconcilable, is irritated by the slightest differences, is independent of the degree of inequality, appears in its worst form in social proximity or among near relatives, provides the dynamic for every social revolution, yet cannot of itself produce any kind of coherent revolutionary programme.

They have all been right, from antiquity up to the present day. There is only one group of authors who really deserve to lose their reputation and who, moreover, should be regarded as having been empirically refuted: those who have used envy for the stuff of their social and economic philosophy, and who dream of reorganizing social life in terms of a society devoid of envy—free from either the need to envy or the possibility of being envious.[26]

In so far as to be human means to be envious, because without this attribute no sort of social organization would be possible, there cannot be a society whose functioning is dependent on the disappearance of envy. A society, however, which raises the average envious man to the position of a censor or legislator is incapable of functioning for long, and

[25] David M. Potter, *People of Plenty: Economic Abundance and the American Character,* Chicago, 1954, pp. 102 f.

[26] R. E. Lane, 'The Fear of Equality,' *American Political Science Quarterly,* Vol. 53, 1959, pp. 35–51, describes these modern egalitarians.

is in any case very extravagant of resources. A society's civilizing power of achievement is dependent on that society's skill in domesticating and canalizing envy. It is not to be promoted by inflaming envy with a vain—although politically highly profitable, even if short-lived—gesture of appeasement in the name of absolute equality, under the erroneous impression that this will bring about the envy-free society of the pure in heart.

One of the most disquieting problems today is that out of indolence so many people either pretend to be or believe themselves unable to distinguish between legitimate indignation-envy (in Raiga's sense of the term) and ordinary, vulgar envy. If one considers the way in which governments and other bodies have reacted during the past twenty years to envious acts of aggression, one might think that it is enough to show resentment and envy in order to justify any kind of action or demand. Envy is used as an instrument of legitimization, and it is no longer incumbent on the envious person, group or movement to prove that its envy is righteous indignation at real injustice.

The dividing line between vulgar envy and justifiable indignation-envy, so vital for an ordered social and national life, has been blurred by an increasingly fervent egalitarianism, the misunderstanding and exaggeration of the idea of equality. Further, a dimension of time was lost. 'Justice' must be attained this very minute: its postponement until tomorrow or the next day is now considered inconceivable.

If, however, in a relaxing social situation, everyone believes himself to be on an equal footing with everyone else and if, furthermore, the idea that a higher status or standard of living must be acquired by work, and earned, falls into disuse, if, that is, the idea of equality becomes identified with complete immediacy, it will no longer be possible to distinguish between the two forms of envy. Thus every privilege, every superiority of rank, every difference in property and prosperity and every authority, no matter how legitimately elected, is basically open to attack from the street whenever people, their faces distorted with envy and hatred, gather to protest against it.

Socialism and envy

If a study of envy must, to a certain degree, concern itself with socialism, this should not be misunderstood as an attempt to associate a

somewhat questionable aspect of human existence with a social movement in order to inculpate the latter. The connection is unavoidable for
several reasons.

The various forms of socialism have always recruited a large proportion, if not the majority, of their important supporters and theoreticians
from among those people who were deeply troubled by the problem of
envy in society. These were mostly people in good, if not excellent,
circumstances, who suffered from the idea that they gave cause for envy.
Their concern was directed equally towards those who were envied like
themselves and towards those who were envious. How acute this problem was to many socialists and communists is amply illustrated by their
writings, especially their diaries, correspondence and autobiographies.

The impulse given to socialism by this viewpoint is primarily towards
a form of society in which there will be neither envied nor envious.
Unfortunately, few socialists were properly aware either of the origin of
envy or of its extent, and they failed, furthermore, to appreciate that
many of the remedies they proposed and applied would only serve to
intensify envy.

How little the intellectual bent on achieving an egalitarian society
really knows about the means of achieving that end is shown by an entry
in Beatrice Webb's diary. Her husband, Sidney, had admitted to her that
he would have preferred to see the Labour Party defeated in the latest
elections, mainly because the party had no plan whatsoever for dealing
with the unemployment problem. The proposed curtailment of unemployment benefit would, he believed, bring about the ruin of the
party. Following these notes on the actual political situation, Beatrice
Webb reflects on socialism's crucial question, the realization of a society
of equals, of which she concedes the difficulties:

> What I am beginning to doubt is the 'inevitability of gradualness,' or
> even the practicability of gradualness, in the transition from a capitalist to
> an equalitarian civilization. Anyway, no leader, in our country, has thought
> out how to make the transition, without upsetting the apple-cart. Sidney
> says, 'it will make itself,' without an acknowledged plan accepted by one
> party in the state, and denounced by the other. We shall slip into the
> equalitarian state as we did into political democracy—by each party,
> whether nominally Socialist or anti-Socialist, taking steps in the direction
> of curtailing the tribute or rent and interest and increasing the amount and

security of reward of labour. But this cannot be done without transferring the control of the savings of the country; and I don't see how that is to be done gradually or without a terrific struggle on clearly thought-out lines. And no one is doing the thinking. So we drift on into some sort of disaster as we did into the great war. Sidney says, 'All I know is that I don't know how to do it!'[27]

The reproach of envy has been levelled at the socialist by Wilhelm Roscher and Joseph Schumpeter, by Jacob Burckhardt and Nietzsche, by Max Scheler, Oswald Spengler and Justice Oliver Wendell Holmes.[28] But he, usually so ready of tongue and so well versed in dialectics, has rarely tried to defend himself against the accusation, and has, indeed, carefully avoided controversy on the subject. Harold J. Laski, perhaps the most active and rhetorically gifted of socialism's publicists in the twentieth century, had his attention drawn a number of times and with marked emphasis, by his revered correspondent Oliver Wendell Holmes, to the envy inherent in socialist theory. Laski never replied to this.[29]

The Failure of Socialism, by C. A. R. Crosland, Oxford economist and Labour Member of Parliament, first published in 1956, presents one of the rare cases in which a socialist discusses explicitly why his party invariably chooses for leverage the envy of the lower classes, even when these have long been comparatively prosperous. However, a paperback edition reissued in 1964 no longer contains the complete discussion of the 1956 edition. Crosland attributes the envy of Labour's financially

---

[27] B. Webb, *Diaries 1924–1932,* ed. Margaret Cole, London, 1956, pp. 264 f.

[28] See, e.g., Wilhelm Roscher, *Geistliche Gedanken eines Nationalökonomen,* Dresden, 1895, p. 57.

[29] *The Correspondence of Mr. Justice Holmes and Harold J. Laski: Holmes-Laski Letters, 1916–1935,* ed. M. De Wolfe Howe, 2 vols., Cambridge (Mass.), 1953. From Holmes to Laski (May 12, 1927, p. 942): 'I have no respect for the passion for equality, which seems to me merely idealizing envy—I don't disparage envy, but I don't accept it as legitimately my master. If I am to consider contributions they vary infinitely—all that any man contributes is giving a direction to force. The architect does it on a larger scale than the bricklayer who only sees that a brick is laid level. I know no *a priori* reason why he should not have a greater reward. . . . I think the robbery of labor by capital is a humbug. The real competitors are different kinds of labor. . . . Some kind of despotism is at the bottom of the seeking for change. . . .' Holmes wrote again in the same sense on August 23, 1928 (p. 1089), October 11, 1928 (p. 1101), August 9, 1939 (p. 1272).

emancipated protégés to the residual inequality between the highly educated products of schools for the élite and those with only average education.

In socialist economists such as Abba P. Lerner, we find the envy-motive used indirectly, appearing now as a social virtue. Thus, a progressively rising income tax is proposed on the grounds that, for the psychological good of the collective, the appeasement of envy in the normal wage-earner—on witnessing the penalties of the highly paid—was quantitatively more important and beneficial than the discomfiture of the few, despoiled by the state for the benefit of the envious.[30] This thesis overlooks the fact that there are countless, and often far more painful, occasions for envy than those few really large incomes or inheritances which can be mulcted; it also overlooks the fact that by raising envy to the status of virtue in the interests of the state one only intensifies the suffering of those with a truly envious disposition be-cause politicians feel compelled continually to reveal new 'inequalities' in the society.

As these envious people look around them, they become aware of innumerable other inequalities to which they react with envy and which they would therefore like to see eliminated. It becomes increasingly difficult to persuade them that they, and they alone, must endeavour to solve their problem of envy, that no one is duty-bound to provide them with a society in which there would be no occasion for envy—quite aside from the fact that such a society would be impossible.

[30] A. P. Lerner, *The Economics of Control,* New York, 1944. Here we find the claim that the most effective means to improve the situation of the needy individual, B, is simply to diminish A's prosperity, and not (which is usually impossible anyway) to transfer his property to B. On p. 36, for example, Lerner points out that—according to his own theory—the satisfaction of B is conditional not only on his own income, but also on that of A. If something is taken away from A in order to supplement what B has, a great advance towards the welfare state had been made.

Supposing A were then to take umbrage and put in less time at work, a progressive income tax could, Lerner suggests, simply be extended to that part of A's income which he would have earned had he taken less time off (p. 237).

'... those cases where an increase in the consumption of products by one person *diminishes* the satisfaction of another, are quite another story. These cases exist wherever 'invidious' expenditure occurs. . . . In fine, assuming that the satisfaction of one person does not depend on the consumption of any other involves the complete obscuration of all problems of prestige, jealousy [sic!] etc. . . . ' (pp. 65 f.).

How to diagnose justifiable envy?

From the viewpoint of an empirical social science, whether this be psychology, sociology, economics or political science, it is not possible to establish reliable norms for the diagnosis of justifiable envy, as compared with envy that is merely destructive. Envy is so universal and deeply ingrained in man that it can never be guarded from misuse by politicians and revolutionaries.

Certain recognized theories, as well as observations from quite disparate cultures, geographic regions and historic periods, do, however, permit a few scientific conclusions concerning the envy problem in social reform, and in the pre-revolutionary phase. It is, for instance, an ascertained fact that it is very difficult, once the appetite for social change has been stimulated by means of envy, to lull, tranquillize, deflect or even satisfy it, with any measure of certainty. Envy that has been stimulated beyond its normal bounds in a group, class or people is an autonomous force which feeds on its own flames, a dynamic which cannot be arrested. Again, there is something ominous about the fact that those who, on their own admission, intend to use envy as leverage, when asked to what extent and in what spheres of life they propose to establish the envious man as a norm, never give an unequivocal answer, indeed, are unable to do so. For once they base their political strategy upon envy, they unleash an independent dynamic of elementary emotions and appetites which is constantly nourished by feelings of self-pity, and which no longer permits its instigators to set and maintain a limit.

We are still on the ground of scientific evidence in pointing out how unsuited is activated envy in a collective or a gathering to the promotion of standards for a new social order that might ensure an enduring and effective social life. Whatever we may understand by the terms 'objectivity,' 'impartiality,' etc. (and it is not without reason that Justice is shown blindfolded), there can be no doubt that active envy is an emotion which, even at the physiological level of perception, makes even relative objectivity impossible. The man who discriminates out of cold contempt or snobbish revulsion is more capable of objective judgement than the man who hates or envies. It is significant in this connection that a working-class defendant will often feel uncomfortable when confronted by a jury made up of members of his own class.

Apart from a few early chiliastic social-revolutionary sects, no movements save Marxism and some schools of socialism have so far attempted to base their new society on the virtue of envy. It is significant that its theorists and publicists have omitted to show how the new society will cope with the problem of envy, after the first great levelling has taken place. All experiments so far, both in communist countries and in the small-scale socialism of certain utopian colonies or of the Israeli kibbutzim, have proved rather that such communities can function only if they allow increasingly important deviations from the egalitarian ideal, or else cynically relegate the ideal of equality to oblivion as in the Soviet Union, where socio-economic differentiation within the population is several times greater than in any capitalist industrial country.

As we have seen, societies up to now have developed various methods of keeping envy within bounds: positive law, religions that preach renunciation or the hope of compensation in another world, theories of an innately superior élite, conceptions of a capricious fate. These contents of culture enabling the individual to come to terms with an environment full of unequals, are not by any means, as socialists maintain, just an opiate used by the ruling class to protect itself against the social-revolutionary envy of the disinherited. Though it may apply in certain cases, this wish alone would not suffice to enable the élite to maintain social control over the lower classes; envy-inhibiting conceptions of this kind actually form a constitutive role in every society, for they make possible a minimum of essential solidarity, of mutual goodwill, in spite of evident inequalities. There are several examples in history of the literally 'socially impossible' situation that arises when a powerful minority of the so-called underprivileged decides that it no longer owes its own society allegiance in any sphere, so long as there is any member of that group who has not been given absolute equality, in every sphere of life, with all others in that society. While this utopian attitude of defiance has been known to exist, it can, by its very nature, only lead to a war of all against all, or almost all, unless something happens to check it. For when an existing inequality in any society has become a purportedly moral pretext for defiance of the law and repudiation of every allegiance, so that, as in a blood feud, private measures are held to be justified, it can only be expected that ever more classes and individuals will arise who will discover—even though only a principle, not genuine need, is involved—inequalities relating to themselves which must be extirpated before those classes and individuals will again conform to the norms of the society.

The envious man as informer

A tolerable and reasonable society will, rather, be that in which as few people as possible are preoccupied with their feelings of envy and resentment, and in which those few must keep such feelings to themselves, because open envy would fail to earn them sympathy, either among their fellow men or before the law. It will be a society which, on principle, ignores the informer whose envy is plain for all to see, even if this means that from time to time a tax-dodger slips through the net.

Here, however, it is essential to discuss certain special cases, in order to meet objections and obviate misunderstandings.

1. As Svend Ranulf has shown, effective criminal justice is based on ubiquitous and latent mutual envy, so that crimes are denounced even when the denouncer is totally unconnected with either deed or victim, and has himself suffered no damage. However, it is one thing to offer a reward for the arrest and conviction of a bank robber or murderer, and even perhaps to use evidence given by an envious accomplice (which is known to have happened, as when a man failed to get his share of the newspaper headlines after a joint crime), and quite another thing if the state appeals, in effect, to all envious people, with the offer of a reward, to denounce anyone who breaks some law, in itself so niggling and absurd that it would be inoperative without the help of informers. Murder and serious sexual crimes are not normal events in social life. Not only are they rare, but they do not, as a rule, need to be combated with the help of the institutionalized informer. It is dubious enough when the police systematically incite less successful (i.e., older) prostitutes to inform against more successful ones, in order to solve a problem which they were at a loss to solve in any other way. It is even more dubious when, as in the United States, the Internal Revenue Office (not the local city or state tax office) unblushingly and regularly emits an appeal to all envious people to denounce any tax-dodger, and then rewards them for doing so. After all, however much one may wish to destroy or embarrass a man, one cannot simply accuse him of murder; there are just not enough unexplained murders. But if the state has recourse to the envious

to smell out suspected wrongdoing in the course of something that is regularly done by virtually all its citizens—filing an income-tax return—if, that is, practically the whole population is presented as a potential victim to the envious man, this can only mean that envy is of exaggerated importance to the government. The envious man knows that, by denouncing his colleague or neighbour, he can involve him in time-consuming, nerve-racking difficulties, and furthermore that the authorities will be more inclined to believe the envious informer than the victim asserting his innocence.

It can hardly be supposed that the best and most just form of society is that in which achievement of justice is based upon a maximum of activated mutual envy, though it must also be doubted whether there could be any effective social controls among people totally incapable of envy.

2. A society that denies the envious its respect is not necessarily unjust. Neither the legislature nor the judiciary should allow themselves to be influenced by the point of view of ostensible envy, but should be blind—the very thing which the envious never can be.

The 'de-envified' society

Nearly all utopias in which ultimate and universal peace and contentment reign, as well as all markedly 'practical' progressive programmes for a harmonious humanity, assume that it is somehow possible to 'de-envify' human beings. If only all were well housed and fed, in good health and educated to at least minor university level, all conflict, prejudice and crime attributable to envy-motives would disappear.[31]

This belief derives partly from the mistake of considering only what provokes envy, and regarding the envious man as a normal person who would, presumably, cease to envy once the envied object had disappeared. An attempt, therefore, is made to remove envy's targets, or to raise all the envious to a level where there is nothing left for them to envy. But since envy is usually able to create its own targets, and is in no way dependent on the degree of inequality, such a solution is vain.

[31] In the years preceding the French Revolution, a number of authors broadcast Rousseau's equalizing ideas, under pretext of the need to create a society devoid of envy. Cf. the account by the Russian V. P. Volgin, *Die Gesellschafts-theorien der Französischen Aufklärung*, Berlin, 1965, pp. 322 ff.

More decisively, however, to hope for a society devoid of envy is to overlook the fact that, without the capacity for envy, no sort of society could exist. In order to be able to fit into his social environment, the individual has to be trained, by early social experiences, which of necessity involve the torment, the capacity, the temptation, of envying somebody something. It is true that his success as a member of a community will depend on how well he is able to control and sublimate this drive, without which, however, he would never be able to grow up.

We are thus confronted by an antinomy, an irreconcilable contradiction: envy is an extremely anti-social and destructive emotional state, but it is, at the same time, the most completely socially oriented. And without universal consideration of at least a potential or imaginary envy in others, there could not be the automatic social controls upon which all association is based. We need envy for our social existence, though no society that hopes to endure can afford to raise it to a value principle or to an institution.

Now, the twentieth century has gone further towards the liberation of the envious man, and towards raising envy to an abstract social principle, than any previous society since the primitive level, because it has taken seriously several ideologies of which envy is the source and upon which it feeds in precisely the degree to which those ideologies raise false hopes of an ultimate envy-free society. And in the twentieth century, too, for the first time, certain societies have grown rich enough to nourish the illusion that they can afford the luxury of buying the goodwill of the envious at ever steeper prices.

Empathy in the rebel

According to Scheler, vindictive feelings presuppose a certain empathy between the man who is wronged and the perpetrator of the wrong. Thus the tremendous explosion of resentment that occurred in the French Revolution against the nobility, and everything to do with its way of life, would have been

> utterly inconceivable had not more than four-fifths of the nominal membership of the nobility itself been permeated by the bourgeoisie who, in purchasing noble estates, also became possessed of the owners' names and titles, while at the same time noble blood was adulterated by money

marriages. Only the new feeling of being equals of the ruling class could have caused such intensity of resentment among the insurgents.[32]

Scheler further develops this insight of a pent-up sense of impotence and a new feeling of real equality into a theory of revolutionary thirst for revenge and resentment. He maintains that

> the greater the *difference* between the legal status, whether political-constitutional or established by custom and public standing of social groups on the one hand and their *factual* power situation on the other, the greater the build-up of this emotional dynamite. And this depends, not on the existence of either one of the two factors, but on the difference between them. In a democracy that was not only political but also social and tending towards equality of possession, social resentment, at any rate, would be small. But it would also be—and indeed, was—small in, for example, a social caste order such as existed in India, or in a rigidly structured class order. Therefore, the greatest amount of resentment must exist in a society where, as in our own [Germany in 1919], almost equal political and other rights, together with openly recognized, formal, social equality, go hand in hand with enormous differences in factual power, factual possession and factual education: where everyone has the 'right' to compare himself with everyone else, yet 'factually cannot so compare himself.' Here—quite apart from any individual character and experience—the actual *structure of society* cannot fail to ensure a tremendous build-up of resentment within the society.[33]

We should not, however, attempt to find in Scheler's theory the recipe for a society truly free of envy and resentment. For, as this study has already and repeatedly shown, only the smallest, the most minimal, of factual differences are required to give rise to increasingly intensive feelings of envy and hatred. Scheler is, indeed, aware of this when he points out how the vindictive man goes out in search of imaginary injury. In this respect Alexis de Tocqueville was wholly right in predicting of America that the equality laid down in the original political blueprint, the concept of equality, would prove to be increasingly incapable of fulfilment, increasingly less satisfying and less equitable, the closer American society drew to equality in all spheres of life.

[32] M. Scheler, *Gessammelte Werke,* Vol. 3, p. 42.

[33] Ibid., p. 43.

The society in which all are totally and mutually comparable cannot, by definition, ever be a society devoid of envy and resentment.[34]

What preserves modern democracies from anarchic resentment is not, indeed, the degree of *de jure* or *de facto* equality achieved, but the continued existence of institutions, of inherited patterns of experience, of literary and religious ethical ideals, which permit a sufficient number of citizens to remain aware of the limitations set upon mutual comparison, and hence ensure social peace. It is only because a sufficient number of our contemporaries are still able to concern themselves with, and are trying to understand, their own personal fate, without at once projecting it on to a 'collective fate,' orientated either in terms of class or some other group, that we have fewer pre-revolutionary dynamisms in society than might have been expected to arise from the concept of equality.

[34] Alexis de Tocqueville, *Democracy in America,* Vol. 1, New York, 1949. The extent to which factual attainment and rhetorical confirmation of 'equality' simply make men sensitive to new 'inequalities' is demonstrated by the American social historian David M. Potter, in *People of Plenty,* Chicago, 1954.

15

The Guilt of Being
Unequal

T HE GUILT-TINGED FEAR of being thought unequal is very deeply
ingrained in the human psyche. It is found among primitive peoples
and existed long before the appearance of Christianity. Yet it is striking
that so many Christians, more particularly those of the twentieth century, who feel this existential sense of guilt believe it to be a special
Christian quality. In so doing they overlook the New Testament's remarkable religious, psychological and historical achievement in freeing believers from precisely this primitive, pre-religious, irrational sense of
guilt, this universal fear of one's neighbour's envy and of the envy of the
gods and spirits. For that alone made the modern world emotionally and
socially possible. The essence of this idea is already to be found in Max
Weber's theory of the role of the Protestant, and more especially the
Calvinist, ethic in the development of capitalism.

Under a portentous misconception as to what had really happened
when, in the West and for the first time in human history, envy had been
successfully mastered, socialist thinkers in the nineteenth century again
began to popularize concepts on the nature of inequality and, indeed, to
make them morally binding. This corresponded exactly to the concepts
of primitives. Since then, however, literary left-wing sentimentalists
and their ideas of values have taken things to a point where even people
who in no way consider themselves socialists, Marxists or ordinary
progressives, among them sincere Christians genuinely concerned with
ethical imperatives, no longer know how to deal with primitive emotional complexes, nor are they able to comprehend the irrationality of
those complexes. Hence they grope desperately and endlessly for 'social'
solutions, which in fact solve nothing.

Paul Tournier

The French-Swiss doctor and depth-psychologist Paul Tournier, who endeavours to combine psychoanalysis and Protestantism in his work, has produced an uncommonly illuminating book on genuine and false feelings of guilt (1959). His honesty makes it possible to trace associations which in most writers remain concealed. I have therefore chosen this book for analysis rather than a number of others. In the first half we find autobiographical material concerning the many situations today in which feelings of guilt, often regarded as irrational, determine what a man does and what he fails to do. Anyone who supposes that we have over-estimated the extent and depth of feelings of guilt, or the part they play, should study Tournier.

Although this psychotherapist is unsparing in his revelations of different kinds of guilt feelings, both in himself and in his family, he shies away from the problem of envy. But his book is almost exclusively concerned with what happens psychologically when we are afraid of being envied. Intrinsically, Tournier knows this, and once he explicitly formulates it. The term 'envy,' however, does not appear in the index, and in all 340 pages is found on only one page. However desirous he is of uncovering social taboos, pharisaism and sublimated guilt feelings, he is noticeably reluctant to push ahead when his observations bring him to the threshold of envy. To give an example:

'Everyone has his own rhythm, and people have different rhythms from one another. In an office, the great speed of one typist will constantly arouse in her slower fellow-workers a sense of guilt which will paralyse them still further in their work.'

Why does he not say 'feeling of envy,' which is certainly more primary? The sense of guilt comes later, particularly in typists who discover that their speed may never come up to standard. Tournier continues:

'Yet it is a simple fact of nature which should be seen objectively. There is no special merit in the speed of the rapid typist any more than there is culpability in the slowness of her colleagues.'[1]

Of course not! But that is never the way envy reacts. Tournier comments:

---

[1] P. Tournier, *Guilt and Grace,* London and New York, 1962, p. 14.

'Moreover, if she is at all sensitive, the rapid typist will come to feel guilty for being the involuntary cause of umbrage among others and will do many little services for them to win their forgiveness.'

No doubt the girl who is superior is not really aware of anything like 'envy-avoidance' and 'envy-assuagement,' feeling instead a vague sense of guilt. This is not due to the facts as they stand, but to the taboo with which we surround the phenomenon of envy. On the other hand, her conciliatory gesture in rendering small services will always bring about the opposite of what was intended—even greater resentment, that is, because she has again demonstrated her superiority. Furthermore the envious person is made really angry by such an attempt to conciliate him. In many offices, as also in schools, in America particularly, those who are quicker or more talented soon lower their own performance to the average level of the group so as to avoid envy.

Tournier is aware of the self-imposed limitation resulting from un-easiness or fear of envy in the less able or less willing, but again he only speaks of the sense of guilt of the superior worker, and not of the less capable one's envy:

It is the fear of other people's judgement that prevents us from being ourselves, from showing ourselves as we really are, from showing our tastes, our desires, our convictions, from developing ourselves and from expanding freely according to our own nature. It is the fear of other people's judgement [why not 'envy'?] that makes us sterile, and prevents our bearing all the fruits that we are called to bear.[2]

Tournier rightly calls this attitude 'false guilt feeling.' I prefer the term 'envy-avoidance behaviour.' Only much later in his study, when he can no longer shut his eyes to it, does he use the word 'envy' three times on one page: the manifestation of envy *in others* arouses *in us* unnecessary, destructive feelings of guilt. He writes:

A certain sense of guilt is a corollary of any privilege even when the privilege is deserved. An employee of quality feels it towards his fellows when an appreciative chief entrusts him with the highest responsibilities. A girl who is asked to sing in church at Christmas has this feeling towards a

[2] Op. cit., p. 17.

friend who would have dearly liked to be invited instead. *Any envy or jealousy of other people* arouses some guilty conscience in us.[3]

It is precisely this envy and its social consequences with which I am concerned. Tournier is aware of these consequences when further on he writes:

> But in all fields, even those of culture and art, other people's judgement exercises a paralysing effect. Fear of criticism kills spontaneity; it prevents men from expressing themselves freely, as they are. Much courage is needed to paint a picture, to write a book, to erect a building designed along new architectural lines, or to formulate an independent opinion or an original idea. Any new concept, any creation falls foul of a host of critics. Those who criticize the most are *the ones who create nothing.* But they form a powerful wall which we all fear to run into more than we admit. . . .[4]

Tournier does not mention, however, that his observation is true of every kind of innovation and that this 'powerful wall' applies to every social situation or, for example, that it represents one of the main causes for the absence of even elementary progress in any so-called under-developed societies. A few lines further on he says: 'On reflection, we can realize how this fear of being criticized impoverishes mankind. It is a source of all the conformism which levels men and locks them away in impersonal modes of behaviour.'[5]

This is precisely where he should have written 'fear of envy,' but that term is not used. The envious man certainly does very often disguise his hostility, his damaging intention, giving it the form of apparently well-intentioned advice, of criticism or of mocking or insidious judgement, but that in no way alters the basic factor of envy.[6] Why does he use, instead, the colourless, exculpatory word 'criticism'?

[3] Op. cit., p. 37 (my italics).

[4] Op. cit., p. 98 (my italics).

[5] Op. cit., p. 99.

[6] Strangely enough, in one of his earlier books Paul Tournier studied the concepts 'envy' and 'jealousy,' using the words a number of times. (*De la solitude à la communauté*, Neuchâtel, 1948.) Thus, in the chapter on 'just demands' he appears to be fully aware of the part played by envy. This, he believes, is nothing new, but in the present day it has been more than usually provoked by egalitarian demands, and by

Here we must go back a few chapters. On page 37, in a book of more than 200 pages, he uses the word 'envy' three times. One mention has already been quoted; here are the second and third:

'So what separates people is not only the differences in their positions, nor merely the envy which the differences arouse in the less privileged, but also the fact that they awaken amongst those who are envied a guilty conscience which spoils their pleasure.'[7]

What eludes Tournier is the impossibility of a society, whether large or small, rich or poor, in which there are no envious people. Because the central figure of his study is the man ridden with genuine or false guilt, and not the envious man, and because he takes the latter for granted (the observer who is responsible for the sense of guilt in those who are superior, happier, etc.) and does not go into the question of the ethics and the psychology of envy, the solution to the sense of guilt about which he feels so uneasy remains hidden from him. Only when one has the courage to recognize the actually or ostensibly envious man for what he is, and to ignore him (realizing that he is insatiable and that nothing will escape him), can one rid oneself of false guilt. Why does Tournier not see this? He himself provides a clue on page 36, one page before the passage where for the first and last time in the book the word 'envy' escapes him.

The 'socially permissible' holiday

Tournier, a well-established doctor and writer in French Switzerland, recounts an event in his own family. After mentioning various often irrational feelings of guilt associated with the spending of money, he continues with the following 'interesting experience':

'My wife and I were talking about taking the children for a cruise along the Dalmatian coast and on to Greece. Was such an expense legitimate, more particularly was it willed by God?' (Is this an echo of the archaic, pagan fear of the envy of the gods which so oppressed the Greeks? Very possibly, since elsewhere Tournier admits that funda-

---

certain people (who, for example, will ask: 'How can you accept such humiliating work?') with stock phrases such as 'that is socially unjust,' etc.

[7] Tournier, ibid., p. 37.

mentally the Christian God never begrudges joy and fullness of life to his earthly creatures.) 'Such a thing can be argued interminably in one's own mind, with a host of plausible arguments, but without altogether silencing an inner doubt.'[8]

Tournier was afraid of the potential envy, imagined or real, of his colleagues, and no doubt associated this unease with a vague idea of luxury and social justice. Significantly he adds:

'It seemed to us also, in our own meditations, that if we submitted the question to a friend from the same social milieu, this check would not be of much value.'

But why not? Because, as can be shown again and again, envy arises mainly within the same class, the same professional group, or among equals. Tournier is unable to ask those whose envy he fears. As we learn from other admissions in his book, he is not in the least averse to, or ashamed of, asking his friends much more embarrassing questions. But he cannot ask how much 'luxury' he and his family ought to indulge in on a holiday. His solution is revealing:

'At the time I had close links with a group of workers in a near-by factory. One evening I went to the house of one of them with all my household accounts, all my bank statements and my tax declarations [!]. With his encouragement, we went for our cruise.'

Thus, our highly educated, successful, hard-working Genevan doctor goes to a working man for 'social permission' for his expensive holiday. Only when he has the assurance that the voice of the people—the circle, that is, for whose sake he was prepared to practise 'socially just' frugality and retrenchment—will grant him without envy the experience of an especially delightful cruise, does he feel safe from the envy of his colleagues, the very people who are able to afford a similar trip—an envy the awareness of which he had sought to repress by interposing this complex of social justice, of sacrifice for the benefit of the less well-to-do. It is an insight that eludes him. In a situation so painfully absurd that few people would ever divulge it, all he mentions is insuperable, irrational feelings of guilt and inhibitions.[9]

On page 146, Tournier interprets the story of Cain and Abel. Not once

[8] Op. cit., p. 36.
[9] Op. cit., p. 36.

does he mention envy or jealousy. Cain's 'wickedness,' his 'anger' even, are mentioned, but never the simple word 'envy.' And again, towards the end of the book, when the author writes of the good son's annoyance at the happy reunion of the prodigal son with his father, and later of the parable of the labourers in the vineyard, the motive of rebellion in either case is not called envy.[10]

The modern 'solution': the envied man is wholly to blame

Why the general avoidance of the word 'envy'? Alexander Rüstow once criticized my use of the term. His argument betrays something of the process of repression which I would seek to trace. Having dealt exhaustively, for a modern writer, with the idea of envy in his principal work, in connection with a discussion of the problem 'Égalité,' and having referred to an earlier work of my own, Rüstow raises the objection that I had overlooked what was most essential: 'For, indeed, it is not the envious man who is responsible for envy, but the enviable one. He has unconsciously (or even consciously) provoked envy, and his indignation on that score is feudal or plutocratic self-righteousness.'

However, Rüstow immediately adds:

> Yet none of these considerations can make envy appear in any way good, fine or desirable. It is, in every instance, an ignoble and, humanly speaking, an ugly disposition, having a disruptive effect on the envious man himself. It is not for nothing that we speak of someone being 'consumed with envy.' But here we are concerned only with the question of social causality and guilt, and with the fact that envy as a social manifestation is not a primary but a secondary mode of behaviour.[11]

That is essentially incorrect. Rüstow is wrong in believing that in a 'just' world envy could be curbed, and would manifest itself only in the form of individual pathology. He was unaware of the observational material which I have presented, and failed to realize that no society whatever can 'justly' be made equal to an extent that would eliminate

[10] Op. cit., pp. 147 f.

[11] A. Rüstow, *Ortsbestimmung der Gegenwart. Eine universalgeschichtliche Kulturkritik*, Vol. 3: *Herrschaft oder Freiheit?* Erlenbach-Zurich, 1957. Section 6, 'Égalité.'

envy. Man seeks irritants to inflame his envy. If some of these are taken from him, he falls back on whatever difference between himself and others lies nearest to hand.

Tournier, although several times indicating that he knows it is envy as such whose existence brings about the sense of guilt, is unable to look at it squarely, because to do so would mean accusing his fellow men of sin. He wrestles with the problem presented by the universality of the sense of guilt which defies all therapy and all religion. He even asks how it can persist when men have been completely exculpated or redeemed by divine or other acts of grace. But he never penetrates to the heart of the matter, that is, the fear of envy in one's fellow men. For it is owing to this fear that the feeling of guilt persists within us, even when we should really be convinced that, from a secular or religious point of view, we ourselves are innocent and our inequality is justified. We suspect that theological liberation from the sense of guilt renders us even more hateful and enviable in the eyes of others. For they say: 'First he enjoyed the sin, and now it's forgiven him. Naturally I resent it!' And this it is—fear of the envious evil eye—which keeps alive in man the sense of guilt. However much Tournier strives after this insight, and close to it though he may sometimes come, it remains beyond his reach because it necessitates a diagnosis of the average man which, in its severity, appears to him un-Christian.

Irredeemable guilt

Towards the end of his book, in a chapter entitled 'Everything Must Be Paid For,' Tournier touches on a basic trait notable in the human psyche. Not only the atheist and the Christian in the culture of the West, but also the Hindu, for instance, forever washing himself in the Ganges, and the penitents in various religions—all these are tormented by a feeling that there always remains some kind of guilt that must be expiated. Few experiences are so difficult for human beings to digest as the acceptance of a religious or secular act of grace.

Tournier associates this observation with the conception that 'man defiles and degrades everything he touches.' Man cannot conceive that evil will ever finally disappear for it must somehow conform to the principle of the indestructibility of matter and energy. Tournier then recalls the significant fact that according to Mosaic law there had to be two scapegoats, between which lots were cast: one was offered up to God, the other was driven out into the wilderness, laden with the sins of the people.[12]

Further on, Tournier describes people who, driven by an implacable sense of guilt, sometimes impose upon themselves quite absurd penances in a vain endeavour to rid themselves of that guilt which, seen rationally, has long been expiated before God and man.

He sees the problem as a psychological rather than a religious one, though it affects Protestants more than Catholics.[13]

> At the heart of all churches there are moralistically minded men who wish to impose upon others conditions for salvation. . . . It is a psychological matter because it concerns a tendency inherent in the human mind, the mechanism, in fact, for covering up guilt . . . which makes a show of one's merits, virtues and abstinences for self-justification, and eagerly presents them to others as the conditions for grace.[14]

Tournier's observation is important in that it suggests the assumption that social controls—especially those with ascetic undertones which many declare to be universally binding—might primarily have originated in uncontrolled feelings of guilt, however much they may seem to be motives inspired by envy. Our inability, puzzling to Tournier, really to shake off a sense of guilt although we have been forgiven might, however, have some connection with assumed or known envy of ourselves by others who begrudge us the state of innocence.

In promising the same degree of grace to all without exception, irrespective of previous deserts, it would seem to me that the New Testament preaches an unenvying mental attitude. On occasion it almost seems to throw out a challenge to the 'sense of justice,' which is unmasked as envy, as in the parables of the prodigal son (Luke 15:25–32) and the labourers in the vineyard (Matt. 20:1–16). Tournier rightly refers to them here.[15]

[12] Op. cit., pp. 177 f.
[13] Op. cit., p. 196.
[14] Op. cit., p. 195.
[15] Op. cit., p. 195.

The depth and primitive nature of the human fear of envy in others is seen not least in the inability of even the Christian doctrine of salvation to furnish its own believers with a clear conscience, or bring them to accept without guilt what appears to be divine injustice. The problem here is not the believer, cruelly smitten by fate, arraigning his God, but the man favoured by good luck, like the sole survivor of a catastrophe, who can never stop asking himself the guilty question: 'Why was I saved? Weren't many of those who died better than myself?' Only by studying the whole personality in all its aspects would it be possible to distinguish, in each case, between genuine and less genuine feelings of guilt.[16]

Tournier struggles to produce a phenomenological and terminological definition of the true feeling of guilt.[17] According to Freud, the sense of guilt is simply the consequence of social compulsion. The child is scolded by its parents or some other person in authority, and fear of losing their love gives rise to the feeling of guilt. Like many others, Tournier accepts this mechanism, but he asks whether Freud's interpretation of the sense of guilt as the reaction to the conscious infringement of a taboo, or as a mode of reaction engendered by upbringing and society, satisfactorily explains all feelings of guilt, or only those in which the social control is opposed to the individual's instinctual drives.

'A feeling of "functional guilt" is one which results from social suggestion, fear of taboos or of losing the love of others. A feeling of "value guilt" is the genuine consciousness of having betrayed an authentic standard; it is a free judgement of the self by the self.'[18]

Charles Odier has even tabulated the differential diagnosis of the two kinds of guilt feelings.

While inclined to describe the functional sense of guilt, normal in the child, but representing in the adult neurotic and infantile regression, as a false sense of guilt, Tournier recalls that we sometimes feel guilty in the true sense for mistakes we have made, because we were conditioned for this reaction. Is it therefore admissible to speak of a false sense of guilt?

---

[16] Op. cit., p. 196.

[17] Op. cit., p. 64.

[18] Op. cit., p. 64.

Tournier further shows that basically all human behaviour, 'however genuine it may be from a moral point of view, can be considered as "functional," that is, may be studied objectively with a concern for the mechanism of its origin.'[19]

The theories about guilt feelings of other psychoanalytic schools bring to light some other aspects of the problem. Adler sees it as the result of the non-acceptance of our inferiority, and Jung as deriving from our refusal to accept ourselves in our totality.

In the Jungian interpretation Tournier sees the conception of a genuine sense of guilt in no way suggested by the social environment. For support he looks to Martin Buber, who asks of psychotherapy that it should recognize, alongside the unfounded neurotic sense of guilt, the existence of a genuine and authentic one. This Buber considers as always present when injury is done to an inter-human relationship.[20] Tournier sees reality as a component of each of these definitions of terms, which he regards as different aspects of one complex phenomenon.

Repeatedly he states how much he has been, and continues to be, tormented by guilt feelings of an indeterminate kind, no man being free of such feelings. According to him, psychoanalysis, which seeks to free us from guilt feelings, only brings about a shift in them; there is no way of being completely just, and elsewhere he says: 'Guilt is no invention of the Bible or the Church. It is present universally in the human soul. Modern psychology confirms this Christian dogma without any reservations.[21]

Social justice

Nowhere in Tournier is there any express statement about the origin of this omnipresent sense of guilt that has beset man since long before the time of the higher religions. Yet an answer to this question lies in some of Tournier's own admissions and experiences—in situations, that is, in which he quite unmistakably feels under threat from other people's envy. An obstacle to the clarification of this problem is Tournier's occasional

[19] Op. cit., p. 64.
[20] Op. cit., p. 65.
[21] Op. cit., p. 135.

uncritical use of the term 'social justice,' which conceals from him that any inequality, however insignificant and unavoidable, can be an occasion for envy and its counterpart, the sense of social guilt.

> All of us in fact are usually so reserved . . . with so little inclination to talk freely about our financial problems, even to close friends, and especially to those who appear to be less privileged than ourselves. Important trade union officers will conceal from the workers the affluence they have achieved serving the workers' cause. It is just this lack of frankness which is the source of a sense of guilt. Then the whole of society becomes organized in an attempt to exorcise this guilt which is inexorably bound up with the privileges of freedom.

Up to this point, Tournier's description of envy-avoidance behaviour conforms with reality. But so great is his own sense of guilt about his prosperous circumstances that he continues:

> Wages are fixed by collective agreements; advancement becomes automatic with seniority. I am certainly not criticizing progress which reduces in any way the terrible guilt of wretchedness, there is also a guilt of ownership. . . . But all the social legislation . . . which is still so cruelly insufficient, appears as an inadequate veil thrown over the guilty conscience of the privileged.[22]

Tournier fails to see that envy and guilt feelings are intensified by the very fact that the utopia of an egalitarian society seems virtually to have been realized and that, in the process, existential inequalities have been emphasized. Basically Tournier realizes this, for instance when he writes:

'By a curious paradox, the employee who fully deserves his advancement and who has not asked for it is more troubled before his fellows than another, without scruples, who has deliberately set out to achieve it, by more or less doubtful means.'[23]

What is the paradox? This is hinted at in Tournier's next remarks: 'I feel uneasy at being in good health when there are so many people sick;

[22] Op. cit., p. 36.
[23] Op. cit., p. 36.

happy when there are so many people unhappy; at having money when so
many are short of it. I feel a certain discomfort too at having an
interesting vocation when so many people sigh beneath the burden of a
job they hate. . . .'[24]

In his search for the roots of the sense of guilt, however, Tournier
himself reveals what is involved: he sees himself surrounded by innumerable, potentially envious people who make him feel uneasy—in just
the same way as the primitive man suspects that every bush conceals the
magic or the spirit of an envious relative, so long as he himself remains
healthy, happy and successful.

The masochism of the Westerner

Tournier reports a conversation with a friend and colleague who told him
that his feelings of guilt were morbid and exaggerated, and that he was
suffering from 'a distorted sense of responsibility.' While recognizing
that he was not responsible for the whole world, he found that his
conversation with his friend did him little good.

'At that, I was laden with fresh guilt.' True, he is aware of human
pharisaism, which worries about Indians' dying of hunger and fails to see
the distress close at hand. But his own torment only grows on receipt of a
letter from another friend, who writes: 'I have just discovered that,
according to statistics, a large proportion of mankind is under-nour-
ished; the good things of the earth are badly distributed. As a consequence I am uneasy when I eat and when I sleep in a bed; and I don't
dare to seek amusement on Sundays and holidays.'

Tournier is unable to decide between the advice of his psychiatrist
friend and the other friend's complaint—which is worse? To repress the
sense of guilt or, as I would put it, fear of the rest of the world's envy, or to
determine the limits of one's own responsibility?

> Of course, my friend the psychiatrist will be able to say that this man,
> too, like me, is rather ill. But there is another illness as well, a universal
> illness, a vast 'repression of conscience.' If there is so much suffering in the
> world, is it not because so many good people, who are very moral, even
> scrupulous in their immediate responsibilities, reassure themselves too

[24] Op. cit., pp. 37 f.

easily by telling themselves that those distant sufferings on such a grand scale are outside their radius of action? . . . In this way flagrant injustices subsist through a sort of universal complicity.[25]

Let us analyse this: The duty to do a good deed, or to avoid a harmful action, exists in fact only if I can be causally responsible for something. Neither could there be guilt nor could I have a true sense of guilt that it would be wrong to exclude from my conscience unless I withdrew from that responsibility. Sometimes I can extend my responsibility to forebears and successors.

A person may feel obliged within reason to expiate and redeem the guilt of his forebears or successors: the *heir* is answerable for the debts of his forebears.

Yet the guilt, conscience, responsibility, so much discussed today, and of which Tournier's book and personality give testimony, have little in common with actual concepts of this kind.

Ethics—sensibility or sense?

A man may have a feeling of guilt if he has failed to do something which could be extremely dangerous to himself but which might have saved someone else's life. He can picture the accusing eyes, both of the dead man and of his dependents. If his failure to act becomes known, moreover, he also feels shame. This, however, is very different from the insincere, pretentious cosmic sense of responsibility professed, or so they think, by those who feel unhappy and guilty because somewhere on this globe there are people living in cultures and environments incapable of any kind of comparison with the Western way of life. What we see here is a wrongly understood concept of contemporaneity. Ought I to feel guilty about Indians and Chinese who starved to death a century ago, at a time when my own immediate forebears were not starving to death? For these are no more outside my effective field of action than are the Indians and Chinese who, technically speaking, are my contemporaries, yet do not co-exist with me in an economy where my activities could in any way help them. Were I to be convinced (which would be difficult) that these anonymous people were, more than anyone else, truly in need of my help

[25] Op. cit., p. 37.

and my money—in so far as these were reasonably available—I could voluntarily convey my person and my money to them. Whether I should be appreciated when I got there is problematical; but all those who are unable to escape from their ordinary lives should not have guilty feelings about what they, as scapegoats for cultural history, imagine they have failed to do in a distant, primitive land.

Anyone who harbours, or propagates, such guilty feelings must be suffering from a false perspective, explicable less in terms of ethics and theology than in terms of social psychology and depth psychology. It is possible to understand, respect and even sympathize with people who, out of a feeling of insufficiency or ineffectuality, or because they feel impelled to undergo some exceptional form of penance or expiation, go into voluntary exile in a place far removed from what we call civilization, where they devote their services to the people of the country. But it is not at all the same thing if, instead of undertaking such an 'Albert Schweitzer mission' oneself, one preaches it from one's desk in London, Paris, Washington or Zurich as a duty universally incumbent on all other Westerners, so that anybody who cannot himself be an Albert Schweitzer or a Peace Corps worker is ridden with guilt, and depreciates existentially whatever he is able to achieve within his life and his own field of activities.

'Love for the distant' as an alibi for lack of relation

The stereotyped *love for those who are distant,* today a favourite practice, may in some cases be a substitute for failure to love one's neighbour, as a certain amount of personal testimony goes to show. A number of leading figures have, on occasion, explained their abstract social idealism and their struggle for 'social justice' and radical reform movements as a result of their inability to establish uncomplicated, natural and relaxed contact with their neighbour. This poverty or lack of contact—a legitimate problem in psychotherapy—probably leads to 'distant' and generalized human love in many intellectuals.

C. P. Snow, whose characters are mostly drawn from his acute observation of real life in Britain, has depicted in several novels some of these social idealists, all of whom are distinguished by one characteristic: in normal social relations they are impossible, ungrateful, arrogant, insensitive and incapable of sensing or imagining the feelings and thoughts of others—often of the very person who is seeking to help them.[26] Incidentally, C. P. Snow, a man of many parts whom the Labour Government of 1964 entrusted with a high function, can hardly be accused of prejudice against left-wing intellectuals.

Nietzsche's Zarathustra decried love of one's neighbour and recommended 'distant love.'[27] In this case 'distant' means the superman of the future. It may be asked whether the modern prophets of distant love are aware that, with their abstract love for the man of the future (largely the so-called developing countries), they have made a social about-turn cognate with the later Nietzsche. And at that period, Nietzsche was depicting a man who had, in the material sense, broken off contact with his neighbour. Immediately preceding this event, he writes: 'Yea, my friend, the bad conscience art thou of thy neighbours; for they are unworthy of thee. Therefore they hate thee, and would fain suck thy blood. . . . Thy neighbours will always be venomous insects; whatever is great in thee,—that very thing must make them more venomous . . .[28] (read 'more envious').

Perhaps some who seek to establish overseas philanthropy as an institution know at bottom how much the patron and philanthropist is generally hated when his protégés are at close quarters. Can it be that distant love is an endeavour to escape from the practice of neighbourly philanthropy?

Emotional need for reassurance

Max Weber insists on the universal need for the legitimization of luck by a social structure and an official ideology. He has elaborated a most valuable concept—the emotional need for reassurance as to the legitimacy of personal luck:

> All other circumstances being equal, classes that are socially and economically positively privileged are hardly aware of the need for redemption. Rather do they entrust religion in the first place with the role of 'legiti-

[26] C. P. Snow, *The Affair,* New York, 1960.

[27] Friedrich Nietzsche, *Zarathustra,* London, 1910, p. 61.

[28] Op. cit., p. 62.

mizing' their own conduct of life and position in life. This very universal phenomenon has its roots in more or less general inner constellations. It is a matter of common experience that a man who is lucky, in confrontation with one who is less so, will not be content with the circumstance of his luck, but will also wish to have the 'right' to it, in other words the consciousness of having 'earned' it, as opposed to the man who is less fortunate,—similarly the latter must somehow have 'earned' his misfortune. This emotional need for reassurance as to the legitimacy of good luck is everywhere apparent whether it be in political fortunes, differences in economic status or physical health, success in erotic competition or anything else. 'Legitimization' in this inward sense is what, if indeed anything, those who are positively privileged inwardly demand of religion. Not every positively privileged class feels this need to the same extent. To the class of warrior heroes, for instance, gods are beings who are not innocent of envy. Solomon and the ancient Judaic Wisdom Literature are, indeed, united in their recognition of the danger inherent in a high position.[29]

Could it be that today this emotional need for reassurance seeks satisfaction in a preoccupation with the developing countries because the affluent society and/or the agnostic welfare state no longer allow it to be satisfied within its own society?

A few years ago Ludwig Freund, in his most penetrating book on politics and ethics, also described this remarkable and vaguely guilty unease observable in many of our contemporaries. He seeks to explain it, however, less from the standpoint of anthropology than, specifically, from that of culture and the sociology of religion.[30]

Freund rightly discerns the origins of this despondency and guilty sense of insecurity in certain incongruous ideas which were brought into Western culture: the eschatological glorification—or at least equalization—of the powerless and unpropertied within the factual social framework of a form of society whose rigid social structures were, for a considerable time, prescribed by institutionalized religion.

The painful awareness, or at least the suspicion, of actual or possible envy in others gave rise, in some members of the upper social classes in Western societies—and this perhaps most strongly in the years 1890 to 1950—to a bad conscience, an evident sense of guilt. In his auto-

[29] Max Weber, *The Sociology of Religion,* London, 1965, pp. 22, 107.

[30] L. Freund, *Politik und Ethik. Möglichkeiten und Grenzen ihrer Synthese,* 2nd ed., Gütersloh, 1961, pp. 190 ff.

biography, *Into the Dangerous World,* the Labour M.P., Woodrow Wyatt (born 1918), has described the following traumatic experience of a sudden outbreak of envy in another:

> Not, of course, that at the age of ten I had any pronounced political views or emotions, although one of my most vivid experiences had occurred earlier. I think it must have been during the General Election of 1924. Some new drains were being put in through the garden near the front of the house. I grew very friendly with the young workman, and when the election came I asked him if he was going to vote Conservative. His narrow face, which I had previously known as kindly and friendly, darkened and scowled.
>
> 'What?' he said. 'Vote for people like your father who live in big houses like that while I'm digging this drain? Why the hell should I vote for him?'
>
> He was wrong in assuming that because we lived in a large house—and a school could hardly have been in a small house—that we had any money, but I took his point and ran back into the house scared and shaken.
>
> I often used to think about that conversation afterwards. It grew to represent in my mind what I imagined to be the atmosphere of the French Revolution. I can remember thinking again and again, 'There are so many more of them than there are of us.' This was quite realistic.[31]

I have no doubt that one of the most important motives for joining an egalitarian political movement is this anxious sense of guilt: 'Let us set up a society in which no one is envious.'

The vulnerability of the class system

One of the reasons why a mobile class system is criticizable is its very virtue: it is the fortuitous product of innumerable heterogeneous individual and collective processes. For this reason, no one has ever provided a social class system with a built-in justification. And just because it is comparatively easy to ascend into a higher class, or to descend from it, this social arrangement is unable to provide any conscience-relieving explanation for individual positions such as is possible in military or religious hierarchies. Even a caste system, like that of the Hindus, is far less likely to generate guilt. Apart from superficial symbols of discrimination, now prohibited by law, such as notices outside inns, the caste system has been preserved intact, hardly touched, even, by a sense of guilt. Most Indian villages have at least four main castes, and mutual

[31] W. Wyatt, *Into the Dangerous World,* New York, n.d. (1952).

avoidance is practised just as scrupulously as before. An elderly Indian who, until a year ago, had never been outside his own country, but who had been brought up a Protestant by his parents and had worked for years as a missionary in India, told me that, in spite of conversion to Christianity, people still took the caste system more or less for granted; thus, for instance, communion often had to be served separately to people of different castes.

Indeed, even towards the end of the last century there were Indians who, out of genuine resentment of the higher castes, became members of political or religious protest or separatist movements, which either ignore the caste system or tolerate both forms of behaviour in their members. And there are also individual Indians, most of them with a Western education, whose sense of guilt about their own high caste might be comparable with the bad conscience of a scion of the British landed aristocracy. But up to now it has been true of the vast majority of Indians that they have never questioned their membership of the caste into which they have been born. The system's ideology, with the force of religion behind it, does not admit a sense of guilt on the one hand or envy on the other.

According to the Hindu religion, no one individual can substitute for the other in a spiritual sense. Even though members of the same family may perform their religious rites together, they all pray individually. If one is now well born and has a good life it is probably because one has acquired merit in some previous life; hence a privileged person's present life is the consequence of an earlier virtuous one, which was the preliminary step to the improved circumstances into which he has been reborn.

Thus what we have here is a system which, from the start, leaves little scope for envious feelings between social classes. The fear of maliciously envious people *inside* their own group is, however, very great among Indians and manifests itself in the magic normally used to ward off the evil eye.[32]

---

[32] The mutual fear, and the almost entire absence of friendship in the Western sense, among inhabitants of Indian villages are described by G. Morris Carstairs in a well-documented study, *The Twice-Born* (Bloomington [Ind.], 1958), with a foreword by Margaret Mead. The reading of this book should have a sobering effect on 'development optimists.'

16

The Eminent in the
Society of Equals

OBVIOUSLY, it is the intellectual élite in any modern society which is especially prone to a naïve and vain, yet politically relevant, form of envy-avoidance behaviour. The literature, both of biography and of political science, that testifies to the notable tendency in highly educated people—leading artists and actors, or well-known scientists—to dally with communism is extensive. This permits us to postulate that a man will opt for a philosophically decked-out, long-term communist programme (in contrast to the mob, recruited as a short-term measure for initial acts of intimidation and street fighting) all the more readily, the more unequal, distinguished and exceptional is the position he already holds in society, in so far as he combines his privileged position with a sense of guilt.

This 'paralysis' of the élite as a result of fear of the symbolic emphasizing of envy in socialist mass movements has already been well documented, as, for example, by Robert Michels. Significant, too, is André Gide's autobiographical confession in which he tells how he was cured of his prejudice in favour of communism in the Soviet Union, when, on his journey there in 1936, he did not find the hoped-for equality, but discovered how extreme was the discrepancy between the comforts and pleasures enjoyed by the élite and the circumstances of the simple people.[1]

This sense of guilt in a prominent person may arise from the knowl-

---

[1] *Psychologie der antikapitalistischen Massenbewegungen, Grundriss der Sozialökonomik,* Section IX, Part I, Tübingen, 1926, pp. 304–6. A. Gide in *The God That Failed,* p. 179, ed. by R. Crossman. Cf. also Neal Wood, *Communism and British Intellectuals,* New York and London, 1959.

edge, for instance, that his parents could not afford the same education for all their children, that he himself has achieved a great deal while the rest of his family has remained stuck in the lower classes, or, again, that he has survived while a more gifted brother has died prematurely.

Strangely enough, it would never occur to this type of personality to desire a society so simple as to need neither physicists, mathematicians, nor top-flight violinists—a society, in other words, where he could become anonymous, thus shaking off the sense of guilt engendered by his prominent position. Such an idea would be impossible because of his vanity, his vested interest in being a celebrity, quite apart from the fact that he may well be too shrewd to have recourse to an idyllic, agrarian utopia. But he believes, not altogether without justification, that an extreme socialist or communist society, or something along the lines of Germany's Third Reich, would enforce social solidarity and so bring about a kind of heaven on earth for the most unskilled and least gifted of its citizens where he would not need to feel any guilt about his exceptional position.

Actually, this hope is partly justified because, for a limited time, social-revolutionary systems may in fact bring about the identification of 'manual workers' with those once euphemistically termed 'brain workers': if a highly paid physicist and a labourer find themselves sharing a bench in the park, the former is able to flatter himself that such envy as the worker may feel towards him is really a betrayal of the ideology of total solidarity proclaimed by the Führer, party praesidium, or the like. And the labourer sometimes believes this too, though, as research has shown, he will not as a rule envy the physicist or the singer—as the latter supposes—but only the foreman or, more probably, another workman who was allowed to do a few more hours' overtime.

As in a Christian world where all shared the same belief, anyone, regardless of his worldly status or position, could regard himself as connected with his neighbour and reconciled with him through the transcendent God, and, furthermore he might not even envy him because to do so would reflect on God's wisdom; so the agnostic twentieth-century intellectual seeks a new god, promising the same protection as the Christian God's against the next man's envy (often only suspected) and the same freedom from the consuming sense of guilt engendered by his personal superiority. This substitute god is progressivist ideology or, more precisely, the utopia of a perfectly egalitarian society. It may never come true, but a mere mental pose of being in its favour helps to bear the guilt of being unequal.

Since about the middle of this century a quite remarkable irresolution and weakness towards the envious have manifested themselves in a significantly greater number of people than hitherto. Very few people today care to be in a position in which they have to decide objectively whether or not an envy-provoking situation is legitimate. The mere expression of envy, whether in a political speech or caricature, or in a satirical song etc., is now enough to convince such people that an objective infringement of justice exists. It is tempting to regard this as a form of regression. Among primitive peoples, and still today among many simple agrarian communities, the envious man's evil eye is cast upon the object of his envy seemingly on a plane of personality lower than that of the unalloyed functions of the intelligence. There are many proven cases in which knowledge of the curse of the envious man has been enough to induce symptoms of disease in the person upon whom it is cast. The whole progress of civilization presupposed that a sufficient number of people should be able to liberate themselves from this fear. The process was assisted by certain religious conceptions, as also secular ones with cultural roots, such as the concept of luck.

Today, many people in the Western industrial societies seem to be as prone to the fear of envy as are members of primitive societies. Except in rural communities and in certain minority groups, it is rare to find the use of magic antidotes against the evil eye; instead, we meet with an insufficiently reasoned reaction which accepts all forms of envy as justified in the light of the idea of equality.

Probably, the contemporary envious person, in search of social approval, benefits by the insecurity and over-sensitiveness of many of his contemporaries which are in turn responsible for the general proneness to superstition. Whoever fails to identify with the envious man and his cause is, in simple terms, pressing his luck too far.

Social conscience in the egalitarian personality

Social conscience, and the guilty feeling of having become enviable, awaken in the soul of the egalitarian upon finding himself in receipt of an income high enough to raise him above not only the manual worker but also many fellow intellectuals.

The autobiographical records of two authors—Beatrice Webb and Simone de Beauvoir—both politically committed to the left, reveal the kind of intellectual and emotional structures that serve to restore the balance of the egalitarian personality.

In her diaries, Beatrice Webb recounts the heated disputes in the Labour Party before World War II when it was on the point of taking office, and its leaders were about to receive ministers' salaries. There had been a demand that the Labour Cabinet should reduce all ministerial salaries to £1,000 a year. While Mrs. Webb could understand that a salary of £5,000 would seem enormous to the ordinary Labour member, she argues with the skill of a capitalist chairman of a board of directors that, after deduction of income tax, in addition to the necessary expenditure, the Labour minister was likely to be out of pocket. She opines that a man's just reward should be calculated over his whole career, not just over a few peak years, and mentions the financial sacrifices made by many Labour leaders before they became ministers with concomitant salaries; she does not even omit the argument according to which a retiring minister may find it very difficult to resume his former career where he had terminated it on receiving his appointment.

At this juncture, Beatrice Webb is faced with the ethical situation of those members of a Labour Government already in possession of an assured income, which they continue to receive during their term of office.

First there are the trade union officials, of whom she writes somewhat contemptuously. Not only would their period in the political limelight settle them more securely than ever in their old jobs, but they would be able to save much of their salary, and after a few years in office might be 'small rentiers' for the rest of their lives. Next, Beatrice Webb applies this difficult question of conscience to the case of her husband, and similarly well-to-do intellectuals.

> Another class of persons who are unexpectedly benefited by official salaries are persons who already live on unearned income, Trevelyan, Buxton, and, to a lesser extent, ourselves, men who will not spend substantially more than they are doing as unpaid public servants. We may spend,

owing to Sidney taking office, say £500 a year on extra entertaining and secretarial expenses—but unless we deliberately give it away, the remaining £3,000 is pure gain. . . . It is true that we have spent our lives in the public service without direct remuneration, but then we could hardly, as Socialists, have justified accepting the thousand a year unearned income if we had not done so. This same is true of Buxton and Trevelyan. . . .

Ministers' salaries

In her next paragraph, Beatrice Webb reflects that, in view of the difference in personal circumstances and the fact that many leading members of the cabinet are likely to be out of pocket as a result of their term in office, it would be virtually impossible to solve the troublesome question of conscience as to whether ministerial salaries were justified. Nor is she able to resolve the ethical dilemma in respect of herself and her husband, but finds consolation in the lame hope that the term of office would be a short one:

> However, I doubt whether the amount of the Ministerial salaries will trouble us personally: no question of conscience will arise because I believe that we shall have a short run and I doubt whether the few weeks' or months' salary will cover the expenses of the coming election. There may be a few hundreds to the good; but I doubt it.

And another jab at trade union leaders: 'Politics for the Labour man who is not a Trade Union official is a losing game.'[2]

Beatrice Webb's consoling remark on the costs of re-election has provided egalitarian-minded democratic politicians with an enduring sop to their conscience; a sop which, in the United States especially, has constantly gained in importance since the middle of the century. For since practically no limits are set there on the amount one can spend in a presidential campaign or in seeking election to the Senate, it is now possible to justify, both to one's own conscience and to that of the electorate, any inherited fortune, any wealth, no matter how dubiously acquired while in public service, any salary, however high, as elected

---

[2] Entry for February 7, 1924, *Beatrice Webb's Diaries 1924–1931*, ed. Margaret Cole, London, 1956, pp. 6 ff.

representative of the people, by drawing attention to the ever-rising cost of re-election. The end justifies the means—which here signifies money.

There can be little objection to this, perhaps, in so far as politicians would condone the same 'ethics' in other professions. For underlying it is the general problem of disparate needs in a society where there is division of labour. If a socialist politician, committed, by definition, to a society of equals (or rather: of those 'made equal' by him), manages to justify his own special financial position because of the exceptional demands made by his calling and his opportunities, and because he is so indispensable to the common weal, then other professions are entitled to similar increases. The thirty-year-old, gifted, energetic manager who would like to achieve independence can rightly argue that, because of the progressive income tax during his time as an employee, he is unable to save enough to become an employer at an early age and thus to make that contribution in the sphere of industrial organization, innovation, etc., which he feels that he alone is competent to make.

The ideal of even an approximately egalitarian society is incompatible with a cultural ethos which leaves it to the individual to determine, and to proclaim aloud, the extent of his contribution to the common weal. But it is this liberty above all that socialist writers hold so dear.

Simone de Beauvoir and Sartre

Like Beatrice Webb, Simone de Beauvoir in her autobiographical writings comes to the problem of the socialist intellectual who sees himself raised, solely by his literary success, far above the world of his fellows.

In 1945, after years of privation, the writer was faced with this problem when her friend, Jean-Paul Sartre, with whom she pooled her resources, achieved world-wide success. When she realized that from then on Sartre would always have a great deal of money she was horrified, and thought it their duty to spend it on deserving causes. But how? Neither she nor Sartre felt comfortable about the idea of turning themselves into a philanthropic institution. She tried to spend as little on herself as possible, but ended up by buying an expensive suit for her lecture tour in the United States. In tears, she told Sartre: 'It's the first concession.' Her friends made fun of her. Simone de Beauvoir, however, 'persisted in imagining . . . there could be a way out of participating in social injustice.' She felt herself to be guilty, and, she tells us, it was only by degrees that she and Sartre were able to start enjoying and appreciating the pleasant things of life, such as expensive restaurants. Their uneasiness over this indirect exploitation of the masses grew ever less intense.

But Simone de Beauvoir failed to solve the problem of how much social injustice a successful socialist author may indulge in. 'All things considered, my way of deciding whether or not I should permit myself certain "concessions," and deny myself others, was entirely arbitrary. It seems to me impossible to set up any logical principle for one's behaviour in such matters.'[3]

Arthur Koestler

In an autobiographical account Arthur Koestler has recorded an experience analogous to those of Woodrow Wyatt and Simone de Beauvoir. He, like so many others, became a communist because of his indignation that other (richer) people did not experience the same sense of guilt about their inequality that tormented him whenever he spent something on himself:

> Well aware of the family crisis, and torn by pity for my father [he was an inventor whose plans were always going wrong] . . . I suffered a pang of guilt whenever they bought me books or toys. This continued later on, when every suit I bought for myself meant so much less to send home. Simultaneously, I developed a strong dislike of the obviously rich; not because they could afford to buy things (envy plays a much smaller part in social conflict than is generally assumed) but because they were able to do so without a guilty conscience. Thus I projected a personal predicament onto the structure of society at large.

Most unfortunately (so far as the readability of modern social criticism is concerned), very few of those authors to whom socialism has come to represent the solution have attained the insight of which Koestler showed himself capable.[4]

---

[3] S. de Beauvoir, *La Force des choses,* Paris, 1963, pp. 135 f.

[4] A. Koestler, in *The God That Failed,* ed. R. Crossman, New York, 1949, p. 18.

Might not the zeal with which the socialist-minded person calls for a form of society in which he assumes that everything will be socially just spring in the first place from the need to realize, at least in so far as society in the abstract is concerned, that ideal which he has found to be unattainable in his personal life—the just society, in which no one will have to feel guilty before another's envy of his own inequality?

The assertion that the envied man is responsible for envy (and hence that not only is ownership theft, but ownership is envy in the other), a favourite thesis of left-minded writers, is just as hypocritical and, taken to its logical conclusion, just as absurd as the assertion that the envious man never has just cause for indignation. There is, however, no form of human existence in which we could ever be free from the 'guilt' of arousing envy in others. Here is the root of that general, aimless sense of guilt which, during the past hundred years, has exercised so disrupting and disorienting an influence. The pangs of guilt (social conscience), and the naïve assumption that there could ever be a form of society that was either classless or otherwise non-provocative of envy, have been responsible for the adherence to leftist movements of large numbers of middle- and upper-class people, and have made it relatively easy for communist countries to recruit spies from among the prominent in Western establishments.

It is hopeless, and hence dishonest or naïve, to strive for a form of society in which virtually no one could be 'guilty' of envy or resentment, of covetousness, in respect of another. Such a society would be incapable of functioning. It would not even have the elementary institutions to maintain, or to retain, such assets of civilization as we have so far been able to acquire; it could not admit of any innovation, nor could it succeed in bringing up a new generation. Eventually it would prove as impossible to maintain disparity between minors and adults in regard to ownership and discretionary powers over educational media as it would be to maintain disparity between those of the same ages. For the utopia of the egalitarians is invalidated in the first instance by the age-determined hierarchy existing in any society. Tensions and resentments between the generations are considerable, and among primitive peoples, indeed, there are carefully prescribed ceremonies designed to canalize them. It does not need an exceptionally vivid imagination to realize the extent to which people of different ages would become obsessed by the discrepancies arising in a society in which age was the only distinguishing feature.

Be what you are

The imperative 'To thine own self be true!' is at the heart of a number of ethical systems, both Christian and non-Christian, and yet nothing is so suspect to our fellow men as this one thing—'being oneself.' The reason is not far to seek: the more truly and fully a man is himself, the more painful will it be for others to compare themselves with him, since individuals can be equal only if each one conceals his true essence.

David Riesman's other-directed person, whom he regards as typical of the modern American, exemplifies nothing other than the socially expected behaviour of a culture that has succumbed to egalitarianism.

This dictatorship of others within our self is trenchantly described by Tournier:

> . . . we feel guilty . . . at letting ourselves be paralysed by fear, fashioned by our environment . . . sterilized by conformity; at not having been ourselves. . . . Here the opposition between false guilt suggested by society and the responsibility for oneself before God is made clear. . . . A poet tells me that he does not begin writing his poems without a feeling of guilt—for he feels he is criticized for wasting his time scribbling on paper instead of earning his living.[5]

In his great book on children in the kibbutz, M. Spiro describes an almost identical case: a young man who, with every verse he writes, thinks guiltily of his dormitory mates in the egalitarian community settlement, who cannot write poetry.[6]

There is a type of person who perpetually seeks to excuse himself for ever having been born. When he has something to say that represents his own opinion, or that might be held to be his opinion, he does so with countless reservations and genuflexions. He eschews prizes, distinctions and presents, and always chooses the worst possible seat for himself. We find this type of personality described in the literature of many peoples

[5] P. Tournier, op. cit., 1962, p. 55.

[6] M. Spiro, *The Children of the Kibbutz*, Cambridge (Mass.), 1958, p. 398.

and cultures. Its most extreme manifestation is the ritual obligatory upon any Chinese on meeting an equal, to ensure that neither could possibly get the impression that the other was even remotely superior.

We are not alone in regarding this as a universal mode of human behaviour, whereby man seeks to counteract or appease envy, supposed or real. A great deal of what has gradually become established in individual societies, throughout history, as good manners or etiquette, consists basically in rules of behaviour designed to escape envy in others. One might speak of 'prestige-avoidance,' a special form of envy-avoidance. In all cultures, from the most primitive to the most highly developed, there are varying degrees of inhibition on any expression of personality that might possibly provoke envy. It is found again in psychopathology if such behaviour becomes so strained and exaggerated that a normal existence is no longer possible.

The envious guest

Through one of his patients, a twenty-two-year-old U.S. veteran of World War II, the psychiatrist Robert Seidenberg gained a startling insight into the connection of self-effacing considerateness and repressed envy. Here is his description:

> The individual who cannot receive or accept—who cannot be a guest. To make him a gift is to make him uncomfortable. He must repay you immediately in kind, and usually outdoes the giver. He can remain obligated to no one. It is with great difficulty that he can accept your dinner invitation and remain the socially-obligated 20 minutes after dinner. Superficially an ideal acquaintance to have, he nevertheless succeeds in making his host and those around him uncomfortable. Although his motto is, 'It is more blessed to give than to receive,' his self-denial and intended consideration are anchored to innately destructive impulses.

Such a person was this man. Any dinner-party was an ordeal for him. Finally he came for treatment. During the analysis

> he began to uncover aspects of jealousy and envy of the host which heretofore had masqueraded as graciousness and apparent ultra-consideration for the host and which had negated his ability to be a guest. In truth,

he discovered that his basic feeling was desire to incorporate within himself his host and all his belongings! He could not receive from his host that of which he was envious and would steal (home, security, etc.).

Seidenberg then recalls widespread customs of various peoples, especially of rather simple cultures. With them

it is extremely bad taste to admire a possession of the host. If the guest, inadvertently or unknowingly, does so, the host is immediately compelled to offer it as a gift to his guest. The origin of the custom may be postulated on the recognition by the host of the guest's envy. To allay this envy and possibly to prevent evil from becoming attached to the possession, he presents it to his guest.

Seidenberg takes the analysis one step further:

Phylogenetically, the ability to be a guest required more emotional development than that of being a host. It took far greater sublimation and civilization for the guest, than for the host, to accept and play his role without provoking anxiety in his host and in himself. So, if we can accept the Jungian concept . . . that the emotional development of the individual recapitulates phylogeny, we find the answer for certain character traits exhibited in the psychopathology of everyday life. . . .[7]

I have met several times, in Europe as well as in America, the kind of person so vividly analysed by this American psychoanalyst twenty years ago. Probably this personality type can help us to understand the worldwide rebellion of youth since 1966. As the 'envious guest,' Seidenberg's clinical case, these young people lack the maturity to be the 'guests of our affluent society.' The overprivileged youngsters, from California to West Berlin, from Stockholm to Rome, strike out in senseless acts of vandalism as a result of their vague envy of a world of affluence they did not create but enjoyed with a sense of guilt as a matter of course. For years they were urged to compare guiltily their lot with that of the underprivileged abroad and at home. Since the poor will not vanish fast enough for their intense guilt to subside, they can ease their tensions only

[7] R. Seidenberg, 'On Being a Guest,' *Psychiatric Quarterly Supplement,* Vol. 23, Part I (1949), pp. 1–6.

by symbolic acts of aggression against all that is thought dear and important to the envied elders.

One of David Riesman's cases

David Riesman's type of 'other-directed' man presents the description of a mode of behaviour closely corresponding to what we term 'envy avoidance behaviour.' In America this type of person will, however, often seek to imitate the style of life and the consumer habits of the people surrounding him or, in other words, will buy things which could attract the envy of those who are financially his inferiors. Yet Riesman lays equal stress upon the fear, in those he questioned, of distinguishing themselves in any way, of betraying different tastes or indulging in extravagance which might provoke envy in people who could harm them.

In 1952, in his comprehensive work *Faces in the Crowd*, Riesman recorded some of the *curricula vitae* and interviews on which the theory of his *Lonely Crowd* was based. In several cases the envy-avoidance motive is quite plainly apparent. Thus he describes an advanced student who suffers from profound self-doubt. Like so many Americans of his generation, he is unable to derive any pleasure from his unusual gifts. He resembles emotionally the man studied by Seidenberg. Clyde Higgins, as Riesman calls him, makes out that he believes football to be important. Riesman suspects either that his enthusiasm for the sport, like that of many students, is assumed only in order to conceal from others what he feels or, more probably, that he needs this genuine enthusiasm as a defence against his feelings of guilt and anxiety; not only does he want to appear average, he wants to feel average. Riesman goes on:

> For gifts are dangerous things. If one is born in the upper class they can be an ornament. . . . But the mobile lower-class person is apt to have an ambivalent relation to his gifts . . . if he cultivates them, it in a way becomes harder for him to cultivate other people. . . . One's gifts push one into competitive situations where one is exposed, a target. . . . By deprecating one's gifts, one seeks therefore to achieve two convergent goals; first, to avoid 'obeying them' which might lead one into novel situations and ambitious personal claims; and second, to deflect the shafts of envy. This is

largely an unconscious process even where some of it may be attributed to the fashion of understatement.[8]

Again, Riesman writes:

> The other-directed person . . . starts group life in fear of the taunt, 'So you think you're big,' and . . . occasionally struggles *against* his gifts, lest these bring him into conflict with others. . . . The ambition of the other-directed person is primarily focused on the limitations imposed by the presence of others—such as the danger of arousing their envy or offending egalitarian attitudes.[9]

Riesman is wrong, however, in describing as specially characteristic of modern industrial society the envy-avoidance behaviour which, as he so clearly demonstrates, leads to the undermining of a person's own talents. As we are able to show, these are much more deep-seated inhibitions, and they are more pronounced in rural societies, among primitive peoples and in isolated communities, such as Norwegian fishing villages, than they are in the United States. It was rather the after-pains that Riesman observed, the offshoots of an attitude which in America, as compared with Europe, is still oriented towards intellectual rather than economic differences—income or consumer behaviour.

A human community consisting only of boasters would not be able to function for long. A minimum of conventional modesty in social intercourse is as much a precondition for society as is the incest taboo. It is no coincidence that the superstitions, proverbs and religions of all peoples invariably combine to inculcate the virtue of modesty into every new member of the community as he grows up. And it was an astonishing post-Reformation development, and a special feature of Calvinism, which enabled the individual to feel unashamedly superior to others and, what is more, to show it in his works. This was the beginning of the breach in the envy-barrier. Perhaps the development took this course because Christianity had begun by placing man in a new and special relation to the world, and had provided him with a central, logical system of values. When, however, the Reformation placed this spiritual source

[8] D. Riesman, *Faces in the Crowd,* New Haven, 1952, p. 576.

[9] Op. cit., p. 530.

of power at the disposal of the individual, one consequence was greater immunity from the threat of the evil eye exerted by the less gifted and the less successful.

The virtue and value of modesty in a society may be indispensable; yet it would be a highly questionable procedure if those seeking power should intensify, by propaganda or rhetoric, the modesty of the individual citizen, which derives from the vague fear of being envied, until it becomes an attitude of neurotic envy-avoidance, thus making possible the enactment of levelling measures which, among other things, facilitate the control of the society by those in authority.

17

The Society Redeemed
from Envy—a Utopia

WHAT WOULD A SOCIETY freed from envy be like? Those models so beloved of utopians, the tribal culture and the small isolated society, cannot help us to picture the ideal since, as we have seen, such communities are more afflicted by envy than any other. Nor is the past much more informative, except for one instance, which in the present democratic world we would sooner not recall: many observers agree that in a hierarchically structured stable society, envy raises fewer problems than in a society with great social mobility.[1] Equally, genuine transcendental religiosity associated with a moral doctrine condemning envy can do a great deal to combat it. It is very doubtful, however, whether any social institution or any form of society in the past has ever known people liberated from envy.[2]

What do we mean when we speak of a society redeemed from envy? In a superficial interpretation, and one that crops up fairly often, Alexander Rüstow for instance would have us believe that it is a social reality in which nothing is left that is enviable.[3] Envy as here understood is, primarily and exclusively, a consequence of what is enviable—another's enjoyment of great estates, learning or his zest for life. The solution that offers itself is a levelling down. Men should be made equal. Quite aside

[1] D. M. Potter, *People of Plenty: Economic Abundance and the American Character,* Chicago, 1954, pp. 111 f.

[2] I have seen this claim made only once, in the account of a Russian missionary writing in the nineteenth century about tribes in the Aleutian Islands; he states that the people in question were so good-natured and happy that they did not even suffer from envy, and would take in good part personal mishaps (such as a fall into freezing water and becoming soaked through) without ill-feeling towards their more fortunate comrades. (*Human Relations Area Files,* Yale University.)

[3] A. Rüstow, *Ortsbestimmung der Gegenwart,* Vol. 3, 1957, pp. 91 f.

from the much over-estimated practical and psychological difficulties of complete levelling, this solution overlooks the important function of material inequalities. The envious man is able to endure his neighbour's superiority as regards looks, youthfulness, children, married happiness, only by envying the other's income, house, car and travels. Material factors form a socially necessary barrier against envy, protecting the person from physical attack.

Sense of justice and freedom from envy

To picture utopia as a society of envy-free individuals does not mean thinking of people who are essentially incapable of perceiving and sensing the fact of injustice. It is possible to think of grossly unjust situations by which everyone, without question, is deeply outraged.

By an envy-free society we by no means envisage a society in which people impassively accept absurdly small differences in compensation for widely disparate performances, or big differences, no less absurd, in remuneration for identical ones. For our mental exercise in constructing an envy-free society, we have to consider long-term processes, enduring structures and institutions. What sort of character, what sort of personality structure and what socio-economic situation are required in order to obviate envy and resentment?

For such a society people are needed who are totally committed to social, economic and political equality. From early childhood until death, everyone would have to be constantly aware of the cardinal rule that he must never become unequal. His whole education would be directed towards imprinting upon him, and imbuing him with, this principle. More consistently, almost, than in ancient Sparta or in Plato's Republic, children would have to be brought up from birth in community houses by nurses who themselves were frequently replaced by others. In the schools of such a society there would be no good or bad pupils and no one would fail to move up each year; nor would there be any marks. No member of the community would want for food, medical care, clothing or shelter. For the sake of equality, all meals would be taken in a communal kitchen and no one would have his own clothes but every Friday would be given a freshly laundered outfit for the following week. A toothbrush and a pair of shoes would be the only personal objects. No private property of any kind would be allowed. Work would be so allocated that no one could occupy a special position or fill an office for more than a certain time. Even the most talented, when their turn came, would have to give up everything else for the hardest manual labour. Membership in this form of society would have to be entirely voluntary. No one could be kept there against his will. There would be no wall. Other ways of life would be known and within easy reach.

In order to test our thesis, the experiment would have to have been in progress long enough for a generation to have been raised within the realm of the new society with no personal memories of other forms of social life.

The kibbutz as a laboratory for equality

Unlikely though it may seem, such a society actually exists. There are more than two hundred community settlements of varying sizes which, though the villages may differ in certain respects, accord with the ideals and customs outlined above.[4] A further requirement would be accurate studies of these settlements by different observers, among them experienced cultural anthropologists who have done research in cultures similarly inclined towards simplicity. And these, too, are at our disposal. The society in question is, of course, that of the Israeli communal settlements, or kibbutzim. A number of social scientists have rightly described the kibbutz as one of the most important laboratories for the study of human beings under special social conditions. For these represent the first 'utopian' communal foundation, literally and deliberately based upon socialist ideals and emotions, and one which, instead of disintegrating after a year or two, has continued to function for half a century.

For comparative cultural science and anthropology, the kibbutzim are considerably more valuable than the communities of primitive peoples, because the former are settlements whose founders and subsequent

[4] Between 1948 and 1958, the population of Israel more than doubled, but kibbutzim membership increased by only about 25,000. At the beginning of 1957, it comprised some 80,000 people. In 1948 there were 177 kibbutzim and in 1958 a total of 229. A report by S. S. King in the *New York Times* from which these figures are quoted is headed 'The Kibbutzim lose their Attraction.'

members originated for the most part in the West. They are modern people who, in contrast to primitive man, know very well what the world is like outside the kibbutz.

The aim of the kibbutz is to make communal life feasible in the pure and full sense of Ferdinand Tönnies' famous and influential work of 1887, *Community and Society.*

The kibbutz goes beyond most of the earlier, natural communities, in that its object is, literally, a society of absolute equals. In the first decades of its existence, from about 1910 to 1930, this endeavour sometimes bordered on the grotesque. Then, for example, not even working clothes or underwear could be individually owned, but were sent weekly to the communal laundry and then were redistributed.

From the time the kibbutzim were first planned up to the present there has never been any doubt, either in the minds of founders and members, or of their friends, proponents and supporters in the outside world, that this was the first great experiment, the practical test of socialism. They could draw on half a century of socialist literature since Karl Marx for their attempt to realize socialism in circumstances vastly more favourable than those in the Soviet Union, although in the kibbutzim, at least until recently, the socialist experiment in Russia was regarded with intense sympathy and naïve admiration.

Today, in many cases, the kibbutzim make use of modern technological methods; processes are modernized, agricultural machinery is imported. Yet there can be no doubt at all that such methods could never have been invented or developed by a people which had never emerged from the form of community represented by the kibbutzim. In other words, the purely socialist community, and more especially the kibbutzim in the singularly difficult environment that is peculiar to them, can exist and function only by making use of the products, the technology and the achievements of individualistic societies.

A form of future society?

The claim to be a superior form of society and the form, furthermore, of the future, a claim which the kibbutzim on a smaller scale share with the communist countries, is liable in the first place to arouse our scepticism when, based on the findings presented in this book, we ask ourselves whether the society of equals would ever have been able to exist at the level to which it has now become accustomed, had it not been for the achievements of societies where individualism was permitted. And here we must emphasize the fact that the Soviet Union, in contrast to the kibbutz, is very far from being an egalitarian society. Astonishingly, those who propound the ideal of the kibbutz overlook the fact that in many spheres—in education, for instance—the egalitarianism of the kibbutz is much closer to that of the United States than to any institution in the Soviet Union, where one of the system's favourite methods is unequal remuneration of achievement.

This means that the idealist of the kibbutz movement cannot cite Russian attainments as additional evidence for the efficiency of their own system, because those attainments were acquired under a system of marked inequality, as well as by the importation of models from the free world. Or again, the apologist of the Soviet Union could not very well—and is indeed unlikely to do so—point to the kibbutzim and their surface harmony as the final and stable condition towards which Soviet society is tending. In the Soviet Union there is no single trend, goal or commitment to values capable of giving rise to anything resembling the Israeli community settlements, with their jealously guarded equality.

Hence the utopian dreamer, the egalitarian, the armchair socialist of the West cannot, so long as he sticks to the facts, construct a model out of social reality in Russia or the kibbutz that would permit of any hopeful prognostication for socialism.

There exist very few communities having so few members and conditions so simple as to lack all, or almost all, semblance of political structure and all recognized regular or delegated authority. Nearly always there are tasks where division of labour in the sphere of decision-making and executive power is indispensable. Negotiations have to be conducted with neighbouring villages or tribes, or with outside merchants etc., a function which cannot be carried out by the entire collective or by all the able-bodied men as a kind of permanent people's assembly. Somebody has to work out the plan for the next hunting or fishing expedition, or the next war against neighbouring tribes, and somebody has to see that the plan is carried out.

At very simple levels of social organization it is sometimes difficult to determine whether the leadership roles are imposed on those who were unable to shirk them in time, or whether they are taken on by exceptionally aggressive, ambitious persons, or by those concerned for the welfare of the group. A number of ethnological accounts would seem to suggest that these processes often take place concurrently.[5] At any rate, they are not mutually exclusive. For in the recent history of democratic countries, we have seen candidates for the office of head of state who have managed to project the image of completely disinterested bystanders and, while publicly stressing the undesirable aspects of office, have induced their friends to canvass on their behalf.

The smaller and closer a community and the less division of labour it either needs or has, the more egalitarian will the basic disposition of its members be. Almost irrespective of the characteristic features of any culture, however, there would seem everywhere to be deep-seated resentment and mistrust of those who have to wield authority. It is only with reluctance, and because of the need for a power or an authority, that among primitive peoples a village or tribe will agree on a leader, giving him to understand, however, from the moment of his installation and by means of specially unpleasant rituals, how low is the esteem in which the wielder of authority is held; thereafter he becomes the object of their particular mistrust, lest he should fail to place the interests of the community above his own. If ethnographers' descriptions of the thanklessness of the leader's role, among primitive peoples, and the understandable tendency of many to evade it are compared with accounts of the kibbutzim, an astonishing similarity of problems is discovered.

Problem of authority in the kibbutz

American social scientists, wholly predisposed in favour of the kibbutz experiment, have shown how the development of individual kibbutzim over the course of some thirty years has arrived at an impasse. Founded decades ago in the spirit of a literally understood, abstract egalitarianism, the kibbutzim could not opt out of modernity, out of the commercialization and industrialization that has taken place since Israel became a state. The tasks of the kibbutz multiplied. Specialists, repre-

[5] C. S. Belshaw, 'In Search of Wealth,' in *American Anthropologist Memoirs,* February 1955, p. 80.

sentatives, leaders, were needed in all spheres of life and work. But the mutual envy which they had sought to banish in perpetuity by compulsory equality, had, in fact, never been eradicated. Though prepared to elect people to positions of authority, a strict watch is kept over them from the beginning, with an intense and anxious mistrust, their every visible exercise of authority being regarded as suspect. Those who are chosen both know and feel this all too plainly. And after a few years, the community finds itself in a state of crisis, because, to use the words of one writer, a 'refusal pattern' has arisen: all seek to evade nomination or acceptance whenever anyone has to be chosen for necessary office.[6]

If a polity rewards its elected higher public servants adequately or more than adequately, the electors are not compelled constantly to ask themselves whether the holder of the office assumed it in order to exploit his position to the detriment of the community. However, should the legislators be unable to see their (envious) way, out of consideration for 'healthy' (envious) popular opinion, to grant appropriate remuneration for leading officials, democratic envy shows a different face, and people ask: 'If this man was doing so well in business or in his profession, why should he want to govern? In what way does he differ from us ordinary mortals? Is he dangerously ambitious? Is he seeking government office so as to exploit it for illicit financial gain?' This attitude is revealed in the United States in the restrictions set upon, and demanded of, leading public servants in the Federal Government by Congress (but which do not apply to members of Congress themselves).

In a society economically stratified in accordance with income, however, there are a number of possible ways to compromise, of making public office sufficiently attractive financially, that is, to allow candidacy to appear reasonably expedient and legitimate without arousing too much the envy of the elected. But if a polity such as the kibbutzim, on principle and without exception, refuses payment to its members while demanding, in the spirit of Karl Marx, of each according to his ability and allotting to each a share according to his needs, as an equal among equals, the egalitarian's dilemma is harshly revealed. Anyone assuming a leading role in a kibbutz has less time for his family and for his hobby,

---

[6] I. Vallier, 'Structural Differentiation, Production Imperatives and Communal Norms. The Kibbutz in Crisis,' in *Social Forces,* Vol. 40, 1962, pp. 233–42.

and may even have to draw upon his own meagre resources in order to carry out his duties, yet not only does he fail to receive any compensation, but his mode of life is, in fact, watched more jealously than that of other members, so as to ensure that he enjoys nothing from communal resources which other people do not also get. In the course of time the number of those who are even remotely willing to take over a leading office dwindles more and more, until at last the members of the kibbutz become acutely and uncomfortably aware that, actually, it is always the same people who are in office. This then in turn arouses real resentment. Thus, envy has produced a vicious circle; the more evident it becomes in the control of leaders, the greater the friction between leaders and led. Those studying the society of the kibbutz can see no solution for this self-generated conflict.

The application to larger societies is obvious. For, after all, the kibbutz is the model of unalloyed democracy. If existing democracies reach the stage at which those who happen to hold public office are, on principle, unremittingly attacked by a malicious public—not because they are in truth guilty, but merely because they have to exercise authority—then these resentful watchdogs of democracy will bring about an increasingly narrow circle of thick-skinned men assuming such office and proving ever less sensitive to public opinion.

Motives of the founders

There is ample evidence that a community deeply involved in a common enterprise can tolerate considerable inequalities among its members, and even maintain and encourage these as an incentive. Pioneering conditions, the need to master a difficult and dangerous environment, should not have evoked and kept alive the demand for absolute equality in the kibbutzim any more than it did in other cases of land seizure and settlement. Thus, idealistic or ideological factors must have been involved alongside objective ones. As has been pointed out by people who know the kibbutz movement well, the planning of these settlements was directly influenced by prototypes as unlikely as the German youth movement.

We are thus faced with the question whether the founders and early members knew—indeed, whether the adults in the kibbutzim of today know—that their enterprise represents an attempt at a society *devoid of envy.* They deliberately chose the ideal of equality. And it is evident, at least from the more recent literature on the kibbutz, that equality is more often mentioned than the concept of social justice. This is only logical in a community where people are truly equal and are kept so. But has there ever been any awareness of the fact that in the kibbutz an attempt was being made to realize the age-old dream of a society in which no one is either envious or envied?

The question might be put differently: Could there have been any other motive for the insistence on equality? In view of what has so far been demonstrated in this book, it would seem improbable. For the only impediment to the ideal, harmonious, altruistic community is that particular complex of emotions and drives of which envy is the nucleus. The question that must now be asked is whether, in the course of half a century, the kibbutz has succeeded in producing an atmosphere free of envy, and in bringing up a new generation unspoiled by any kind of individualistic influences and experiences, which has learnt to live without resentment, without envy and, above all, without fear of being envied.

Any scientific study of the kibbutz, even though written by ardent supporters of the experiment and not by sceptics or opponents, will provide an unequivocal answer to that question. The problem of envy has neither been solved nor been eliminated. Even in a form of community which has eradicated inequality more drastically than any monastery—where rank and authority still necessarily obtain—and which is bent on ironing out the smaller differences, there is still plenty of occasion for begrudging another his achievement, his hobby, his proficiency or some essentially minor possession.

What is of far more consequence, however, is the intensification of envy-avoidance behaviour and of the social sense of guilt about imagined or real inequalities for which people feel they are to blame. This also explains the behaviour of the children of the kibbutz described by Spiro, an authority among American anthropologists on kibbutz culture: they are inhibited, introverted and perpetually tormented by anxieties.

Children of the kibbutz

If one recalls the part played by sibling jealousy in generating and establishing envy, it seems all the more remarkable that, in parents at his kibbutz, Spiro detected very few signs of any understanding of this situation. Uninhibited preference is shown for the newly born child, which is fondled and spoiled, the next oldest sibling being abruptly deposed. Spiro describes several cases in which he observed parents with their children and was immediately struck by the elder child's bitterness and mounting jealousy, to which, however, the parents paid no attention.[7]

It is not possible to ascertain whether the culture as such of the kibbutz encourages parental behaviour conducive to sibling jealousy in their children. It is conceivable, at any rate, that the institution whereby even the smallest children are brought up in homes by strangers, as in an orphanage, and away from their natural parents, is responsible for an unusually severe sense of guilt in the parents, who, at visiting times, are apt to shower tokens of love upon the youngest child exclusively, for it is in regard to the smallest that they would feel especial guilt. Ironically, it might well be some of the special features peculiar to the kibbutz which have so influenced the emotional development and character of the children as to render them especially prone to envy, and hence less suited to the form of community in which they have to live.

Anti-intellectualism and related animosities against those who practise the arts are—in fact, by definition—the result of envy. Anyone who concentrates as an individual on intellectual activity and who has the capacity and gift for it, and indeed anyone who seems capable of deeper thought, will be conspicuous in most groups. These are activities that cannot be collectivized or socialized. They belong to the sphere of the individual, who must practise them in accordance with his own judgement and taste, or as dictated by luck or the mood of the moment. Hence, in a community whose highest avowed value is communal work, and above all physical labour, the individual who devotes himself to intellectual work will always give offence.

Now, Spiro, in his books on the kibbutz—though he lived on only one for any length of time—gives numerous examples of anti-intellectualism there. Were there no background of Jewish culture and tradition, which sets high value on scholarship, reading and intellectual pursuits, things would certainly have been much more difficult for intellectually active

[7] M. Spiro, *Children of the Kibbutz,* Cambridge (Mass.), 1958, p. 65.

members of the kibbutz. But even those intellectual occupations condoned by the collective, and pursued in a man's own time, always leave
behind a faint sense of guilt. One man told Spiro that he found it
impossible to develop his poetic gift because he could not help thinking
of his comrades, capable only of manual labour, who, as children, had sat
next to him in the latrine (his own words). There is a feeling of guilt,
such as we saw in Chapter 15 in the Genevan doctor, Paul Tournier, and
some of his friends. This sense of guilt felt by the gifted, intellectually
active man who is able to do comparatively agreeable work is, however,
nothing other than the idea of the supposed envy in others of his own
special position.[8]

If we pass under review envy's ubiquitous social control of kibbutz
members, and see to what revulsion, mockery, resentment and suspicion
anyone is exposed who seems to be even slightly different, a little more
inventive, creative, gifted, wide-awake or imaginative than the others,
one thing becomes clear: the kibbutz culture, prototype of the socialist
community and 'signpost for the future of mankind,' reflects many
aspects of the society of primitive peoples. Displayed, as in a laboratory,
we see the degree of the pressure exerted by egalitarianism, the fear of
mutual envy, upon the potential inventor, creator or innovator. The ideal
of absolute equality, the eschewing of all authority and superior status,
of all economic advantage, and the concern for the survival of this system
of equality, once established, cannot admit of any individual's success in
introducing unforeseen innovations, since he would then, by definition,
no longer be an equal, even were his invention immediately and unself-
ishly placed at the disposal of the collective.

The problem is not, in fact, so much actual rejection of innovation by
the kibbutz community as the fear inculcated from childhood onwards
into the individual that he might somehow stop being equal, might show
some sign of superiority or in some way become conspicuous. Spiro,
who studied the kibbutz with very real sympathy, describes the inhibitions of children born and brought up on the kibbutz.[9] More recently,
difficulties have arisen from the conflict between the propertyless
kibbutzim and the inheritance laws of the state of Israel.[10] A further

[8] Op. cit., p. 398.

[9] Op. cit., pp. 367–71, 453.

[10] 'Erbschaftsprobleme in Israel,' in *Neue Zürcher Zeitung,* December 13, 1962.

problem is the question of paid workers from outside who are employed by many of the kibbutzim.

The sin of privacy

Privacy is recognized by different cultures in very differing degrees. Yet we must not imagine that there is a straight path leading from a primitive first stage without privacy to a high civilization in which such privacy is definitely assured.

Significantly, if a man really makes use of his right to be alone, the annoyance, envy and mistrust of his fellow citizens will be aroused, even in cultures where a private life is a permissible and long-established institution. Anyone who cuts himself off, who draws his curtains and spends any length of time outside the range of observation, is always seen as a potential heretic, a snob, a conspirator. It is hardly surprising, therefore, that the puritans of New England felt a profound mistrust of those who valued their privacy. Besides this, there must also have been prejudice, wholly undemocratic and without religious connotations, against the man with a private existence, especially on the western frontier, where, if someone put up a fence or a hedge round his house, the consequences could be serious.

To the same degree that Anglo-Saxon culture respects and values privacy, the egalitarianism of the American polity has given rise to resentment against it. Anyone who lives long enough among Americans today must notice how greatly many of them still fear to indulge in what their fellow men might consider to be undue privacy. In so far as possible they try to show that they have nothing to hide. A drive after dark through a middle-class suburb will reveal countless families behind the uncurtained windows of living-room or dining-room, as in a goldfish bowl. With few exceptions, modern Americans still fight shy of surrounding their houses with fences or hedges, at least of the kind that might give complete concealment. In some townships these are even expressly forbidden.

There is in America one profession above all in which, for egalitarian reasons, fear of seeming to take advantage of a privacy in itself natural and necessary is particularly in evidence; it is the profession which today is most intent on egalitarianism, that of college and university professors. Not one of them would deny that intellectual work, and more especially the continual spate of academic writing that is expected of him in America more than anywhere else, is best done when he can sit at his desk undisturbed, unobserved and undistracted. But one of the hallmarks of the American campus is the sight everywhere of instructors and professors sitting with their doors wide open. If, under pressure to complete a work, one of them decides with a heavy heart to keep his door shut, he does so with a strong feeling of guilt, justifying his action beforehand to his colleagues and students, and hanging an apologetic notice on the door.

Occasionally it may happen that the chairman of a department, concerned at the advantage taken of faculty members by talkative students and colleagues, recommends a policy of closed doors. But hardly anyone can make up his mind to do this, for behind his back his motives will immediately be questioned.

To appreciate the full meaning of this custom it should be known that in nearly every American college and university, and in every faculty, a professor is expected to be available in his office daily between nine and five o'clock, even if it is a day when he has no lectures or seminars. The compulsion of the open door affects a large part of the time available for intellectual work.

A cautious probing of the motives of this privacy phobia reveals it as a deep-rooted concern not to be unequal, not to be regarded as proud, secretive or unsociable, or even as exceptionally productive—a concern, in short, not to arouse envy in someone else who himself lacks the self-discipline to work and welcomes any distraction. The delicate social psychology of privacy, including the problem of closed doors in American culture, has been examined very recently by Barry Schwartz and also by Edward T. Hall.[11]

This observation of American everyday existence throws light on many other motivational complexes in American democracy and society; it must now further be considered, however, within a different framework, that of comparative culture and also of philosophy.

[11] Barry Schwartz, 'The Social Psychology of Privacy.' *The American Journal of Sociology,* Vol. 73, 1967/68, pp. 741–52. Edward T. Hall, *The Hidden Dimension,* Garden City, N.Y., 1966.

Martin Buber and the kibbutz

Let us begin with an apparent paradox: George Orwell's cruel portrait, in his *Nineteen Eighty-Four,* of collectivism taken to its logical conclusion, shows the state prohibiting the least semblance of privacy, of the desire to be alone, which it treats as a serious crime. On the other hand, in the work of a philosopher as idealistic as Martin Buber, we find passages advocating the control and elimination of privacy, though voluntarily. Twenty years ago, before the kibbutz experiment in Palestine was as much as a generation old and when it could be regarded as the nucleus of the future communal structure, Martin Buber wrote, with reference to these egalitarian communities, a sentence which, in the light of the above observations in the United States, gains in verisimilitude. According to Buber, the kibbutzim's real survival problem is neither the relationship of the individual to the idea nor his relationship to the community or the work, but interpersonal relations. Buber does not mean anything so simple here as loss of intimacy in the passing from the small to the large kibbutz:

> I mean something that has nothing whatever to do with the size of the Commune. It is not a matter of intimacy at all. . . . The question is rather one of openness. A real community need not consist of people who are perpetually together, but it must consist of people who, precisely because they are comrades, have mutual access to one another and are ready for one another. A real community is one which in every point of its being possesses, potentially at least, the whole character of community.[12]

If these propositions are compared with practice in the kibbutzim, and with their initial efforts to suppress any kind of privacy, it can be seen what Buber, understandably and with the best of intentions, means: a community of equals, where no one ought to envy anyone else, is not guaranteed by absence of possessions alone, but requires mutual possession, in purely human terms (*not* sexual as Plato, for example, supposed). Everyone must always have time for everybody else, and anyone who hoards his time, his leisure hours and his privacy excludes himself.

Thus we see how, when the ideal egalitarian condition has been

[12] M. Buber, *Paths in Utopia,* Boston, 1958, pp. 144 f.

attained, and everything that can be communally owned has long since been collectivized, there will always be something left that will be a cause for envy and hence will constitute a danger to the community; mere time-space *existence* as an individual and private person is enough to irritate. Then there is the reverse situation: in such groups there may be individuals who enjoy exceptional popularity and respect, whose advice, encouragement and company are much sought after. These people may arouse envy in those whom nobody comes to see.

Buber's demand that everyone should be constantly available is a crucial one for the utopia of the egalitarian, envyless community. It postulates a society totally devoid of authority. A characteristic of every person having authority is his selectivity, which must be accepted by anyone seeking audience. Every hierarchy, and indeed any effective division of labour, presupposes that individuals must be able to husband their time, even to the point of avarice. It is here, in particular, that the greatest difficulties in the life of the kibbutzim have arisen.

In itself, general and friendly availability is one of the most agreeable of personal traits. But it is quite patently impossible for any minister, psychotherapist, doctor, lawyer or employer to be literally always available to everybody. The socialization of the individual's time, towards which many utopias tend, is an absurdity. Yet the fact that it must remain a prerequisite so long as man continues to strive for the 'true' community, a form of existence without any private property whatever, demonstrates the vanity of that desire.

Jealousy in the group

Thus the problem of envy is most acutely apparent in the lot of a man who wants to keep himself to himself, and seeks solitude because he wants to think and, perhaps, to create something new. The individual who is capable of the desire to be alone and of enduring, or even of enjoying, solitude for a while, affronts the rest and incites the envy of the collective. Those incapable of being alone are angered by the successful escape from social control achieved by anyone who knows how to be alone. The power of the group over the individual is almost entirely dependent on man's inability, generally speaking, to live without group approval or acceptance. This thirst for 'status' in one or more primary groups represents, indeed, the main lever of social control.[13]

The solitary man thus becomes the victim of the envy of such as begrudge him the freedom from society which he asserts. In addition to this, there is consuming curiosity, envy of whatever it may be that the individual will make of his solitude: is he going to invent or think of something that will raise him above the rest? Will he be able to give the finishing touches to his poem, his book or his private work? Hence anyone who, for the achievement of self-imposed goals, asserts his right to his personal time or, more exactly, to a small portion of his limited time, for living, and excludes others from that time, affronts in a truly existential sense those other, envious people through his creation of that most elementary of possessions, the individual experience of a personal time for living; and this he cannot do to the full unless he has the courage to withdraw himself from the presence of others.

Basically, any man who prefers his own company to that of others is always an irritant. Petrarch, who refers repeatedly to other people's envy, must both have been acutely aware of it and have feared it, since he so clearly feels he has to defend his liking for solitude no less than his advice to the poet to seek it out. Petrarch defends himself against all those arguments used by others in an endeavour to invoke rage against the champion of solitude: there are admonitions against solitude even in the Bible; Aristotle is cited, with his remark about the *zoön politikon*, and Cicero, according to whom even the autarchic, self-sufficient man invariably seeks a companion.[14] Elsewhere Petrarch speaks of the immoderate attacks to which he found himself exposed from those who believed that solitude constituted a threat to the virtuous life.[15]

In recalling Petrarch's preoccupation with the envious man, we might almost be led to suppose that the ideal of solitude among early European poets itself represented in part an escape from the eyes of the envious. For the very reason that there were then comparatively few professional writers, and that these were dependent on certain social conditions, such as the patron's court, they kept a watch on each other that was closer and

[13] R. T. La Piere, *Theory of Social Control,* New York, 1954.

[14] Petrarch, *De contemptu mundi,* also *De vita solitaria.*

[15] Ibid.

more constant than is the case with writers in a modern society. Karl Vossler's study of the literature of solitude in Spain suggests that the deliberate flight from envy in others might be a direct motive for this literary genre.[16]

Freedom from envy, a task for the individual, not for society

Judging from what we have seen so far, it is inconceivable that the elimination of all evident differences—even were this practicable—would solve the problem of envy. There would remain countless suspected differences (which already play a major role today), infinitesimal inequalities, disparate performances (even when these are unpaid) and so on.

Can personalities be so altered that the individual is less likely to succumb to envy? To achieve this, we would first have to succeed in bringing up children with no experience of sibling jealousy; but that would also mean eliminating the father-mother constellation. An impartial adult would have to bring up the child. It is problematical, however, whether this would finally produce an unjealous person devoid of envy, for the time would come when he would have to be separated from his nurse and mentor, whose attention would then be transferred to another child. From whatever aspect the task is considered, the biological facts of our existence would make it seem improbable that anyone could ever grow up to be really incapable of envy.

A partial solution of the dilemma of envy can thus be envisaged only in the child and adolescent during maturation and the time of adaptation to the adult world, its culture and its ethics. Individual influential persons in the growing child's environment can effect almost as much—either for good or bad—as the whole value system of the culture concerned. Now and again we are told by writers in their autobiographies when and how they were freed from envy. Helena Morley, the pen-name of Senhora Augusto Mario Caldeira Brant, wife of a leading personality in Rio de Janeiro, published her diary (at first privately) in 1942. Of her childhood she writes:

'When I was little I used to suffer from envy a great deal but now I

---

[16] K. Vossler, *Poesie der Einsamkeit in Spanien*, Munich, 1940.

don't any more. I'm grateful to grandma for this. She got me over it. I'm the poorest girl in my set. I see the differences between my life and theirs, but I don't envy them.'[17]

Albert Camus, when he was forty-two, wrote a preface to the 1957 edition of some earlier essays (*L'Envers et l'endroit*) in which he tells how he remained free of the emotions of envy and resentment, although his earlier life in a working-class environment might have given him cause for such sentiments. He does not consider poverty to be the cause of envy, and he condemns those doctrines and movements which do serve it.

The foregoing interpretation of literature on the kibbutzim should not be understood as implying that no one in a communal settlement of that nature can be really happy or able to develop his personality. Spiro himself, returning ten years later to the kibbutz for a short visit, was surprised to find that three adults who, as adolescents, had confessed to him their disappointment at life in the kibbutz, had now grown completely accustomed to it. It is, of course, impossible to know to what extent such asseverations of loyalty to an unusual form of society should be ascribed to an attitude of defiant resignation which would never admit any doubts to a mere outsider. What must be emphasized is the voluntary factor; anyone can leave the kibbutz, though to many this would mean a substantial sacrifice, since their whole working capacity is invested there, and in return the community will care for them, if necessary, to the end of their lives.

For our thesis, there is a further question of importance concerning the kibbutz: we have discovered no indication that this culture of maximum equality is any more natural, spontaneous or self-regulating than the culture of an open society. Individual members exert continual pressure on the system towards a society that is more 'normal' by comparison with the outside world. The extreme egalitarianism of the founders has everywhere made way for concessions to the desire for differentiation, private property and an individualistic use of leisure time. Again and again there are disputes and sharp divisions between those who want to depart even further from the original ideal and others who, faithful to the tradition, seek to tighten the reins of egalitarianism.

[17] *The Diary of Helena Morley,* translated by E. Bishop, New York, 1957, p. 117.

Utopias

The kibbutzim, like all other utopian communities that have ever been effectually realized, are by their nature agricultural enterprises, even though some of them have later introduced factory-like food-processing plants and minor industries. The crucial value is the hard toil, devoted to the land, of the ploughman and the sower, before which all other activities dwindle into insignificance. There is no utopia, let alone egalitarian settlement, which has been able to make the transition, even conceptually, from the existence of the peasant to that of the many in a complex industrial society with its division of labour, while at the same time retaining collectivism. Writers such as Erich Fromm, with his *Sane Society*, cherish the dream of a reversal of our modern society to manageable communities of some five hundred souls modelled after the kibbutzim.[18]

No great effort of common sense is needed to realize that this condition alone would make it highly improbable that the completely egalitarian communal form could ever be a possible way of life for the majority of mankind.

We generally consider that as utopian which appears unrealizable within the framework of the social system in which we happen to live. The term 'utopian' is thus often abused. On the grounds of the psychological, anthropological and historical evidence applicable to the phenomenon of envy, we may justifiably consider that in regarding as purely utopian both a society devoid of envy and the elimination of the capacity and compulsion to envy, we are not simply falling victim either to myopia induced by the present structure of society or to limitations of our imagination. Hopes and ideas such as these may, indeed, undermine and bring about the downfall of existing social systems and their ideologies, but they are quite incapable of being translated into social reality. Perhaps the utopia of equality, of a society redeemed from envy, exerts so strong an attraction upon intellectuals, generation after generation, because it promises always to remain a utopia, and perpetually to

[18] H. Darin-Drabkin (*The Other Society*, London and New York, 1962) depicts in detail, and with great sympathy, the ways of life and present-day problems in the kibbutz, but he cannot avoid noting several times the conflicts between innate human individualism and the theoretically motivated demands for equality of the collective. See pp. 152–7, 215.

legitimize new demands. Nothing could be worse for the utopian intellectual than a society where there was nothing left for him to criticize.[19]

Possibly there will be future societies whose consideration for the envious man will be even more excessive. There will be others, again, in which he will get less attention and regard than in the present democracies. The official reaction to the actual or supposed presence of the envious in a society is much more variable than the basic irritability of envy, although, as has been shown, historical and cultural changes can bring with them a different view of what is enviable, and even influence the average intensity of the personal experience of envy.

[19] There are many examples of this, especially in the notes section of Günther Schiwy's *Intellektuelle und Demokratie heute,* Würzburg, 1966. Typical, too, is the complaint of an American sociologist, Melvin M. Tumin, 'Some Unapplauded Consequences of Mass-mobility,' in *Social Forces,* Vol. 15, 1957. As we know ten years later, his worry lest the welfare society might lead to the extinction of social critics was unjustified.

18

Is Ownership Theft?

SOCIALISM CONSIDERS itself as a late consummation of the evolution of morality, and further as a necessary answer to the problem of those inequalities which developed largely from modern industrial, capitalistic life. Its advocates do not know that their way of thinking has existed, and still exists, almost universally at primitive levels of social life, and that man's envy is at its most intense where all are almost equal; his calls for redistribution are loudest when there is virtually nothing to redistribute.

It was instead only when social envy had been to some degree overcome, when it had been neutralized and outlawed by clearly defined concepts, essential beliefs and legal tenets, that the way was open to an expanding economy, not least because it gave the successful a good conscience. The more the consumer-oriented economy broadened its base, diverting the individual's attention from his emotive preoccupation with castes and classes to the acquisition of certain goods—which another might already have, but only as the result of more overtime and not of absolute privilege—the more the original envy-inhibitions on economic growth disappeared.

If, today, doctrines emanating from socialism—under whatever name—again become fashionable and proclaim abstract, social envy as the legitimate principle for the regulation of economic life, they will distract men from what individuals are able to achieve by disparate efforts, as also fortuitously. In this way those very emotions would be exacerbated—envious hatred, resentment and *Schadenfreude*—which are least likely to foster that successful design for living which alone would once again be able to calm these destructive emotions.

There is no need to quarrel about the definition of socialism. Any will satisfy me that denotes part of the current which might, perhaps, be called the spirit of our times. If Sartre refuses the Nobel Prize because, as he maintains, his contribution to the future socialist society would otherwise not be plausible, it is plain that the emotions expressed in this comment would be inadequate for the planning of a social order, even a 'socialist' one. But a politician, impressed perhaps by Sartre, might add his weight to the passing of an economically irrational law, in the vague hope that he would thus be taking a step towards the society apparently preferred by the philosopher to the existing one.

The same thing may happen if a Christian theologian today proclaims the end of the age of individualism, and the necessity for modern man to envisage himself increasingly as part of the collective structure. It is easy to predict that the politician who is influenced by the oratory of the atheistic existentialist and another who intends to follow the Christian theologian will in point of fact both tend towards laws and decrees having a common denominator. This can best be defined as action responsive to that which it is believed must be assuaged—the envy of the less well endowed, even though they need not be really necessitous—for whose benefit social reality (e.g., education) and economic reality (e.g., progressive taxation) must be legislatively manipulated. If, however, the theory of social behaviour put forward in this book is accepted and man's possibilities and limitations as an envious being are recognized, solutions of this nature can only arouse considerable mistrust.

At the same time, neither the existentialist nor the theologian, neither the politician nor the journalist echoing him, need be in any way guilty of recruiting the envious. While intentional and conscious use may be made occasionally of those whose envy has been aroused, such tactics are expendable. There is something else that is much more dangerous: sensitivity to the envy of others is so deep-rooted in the human psyche that most people erroneously interpret the sense of redemption and peace, which they feel when they have made concessions to envy, as confirmation, not only of their moral superiority, but also of the expediency of their action in the reality of the here and now.

There is a simple explanation for the powers of persuasion which revolutionary messianism of whatever complexion, whether the Marxist view of society or socialist economic criticism, is able to exert upon people of strikingly dissimilar backgrounds—upon the wealthy British aristocrat, for example, no less than on the unsuccessful Parisian painter. Nor is it harder to explain the ability of interventional or redistributive theses, when demolished by the reality of irrefutable economic data, to resurrect in a new guise.

It is not, as so many believe, because programmes subordinating the individual to some collective do in fact represent progress—that is, have a built-in affinity to the future—that they have developed such tenacity and persuasiveness. Their strength actually thrives upon the residual, primeval fear of the envious; they represent a throw-back to the primitive idea of causality (the other's prosperity must be to my disadvantage), and they derive from this fact their immunity to all refutation by reason and facts.

The economic policy of the least envy in the greatest number

We shall now take another look at the typical economic thinking of envy-ridden primitives. Very often to motivate their envy and the actions arising from it, such people will maintain that supplies are strictly limited even where there is actual abundance. A notoriously envy-ridden primitive society is that of the Dobu Islanders, of whom Margaret Mead writes: 'They create situations in which the objectively unlimited supply is redefined as being of fixed and limited quantity. No amount of labor can therefore increase the next year's yam crop, and no man can excel another in the number of his yams without being accused of having stolen (magically) his extra yams from someone else's garden.'[1]

Similar negative conceptions of their own economy and environment are found in other primitive peoples. It is not difficult to see how such envious fantasies can inhibit the understanding of a growing national product which is growing in absolute terms for everyone, but not for all in equal measure at the same time. Unfortunately, therefore, the actual point of departure for socialist—and for left-wing progressive—economic doctrines generally is identical with that of particularly envy-inhibited primitive peoples. What, for more than a century, has made

[1] M. Mead, *Cooperation and Competition Among Primitive Peoples,* New York, 1937, p. 466. Mead bases this upon R. Fortune, *The Sorcerers of Dobu,* 1932, pp. 100 ff. Other pages in Mead's work informative on the envy problem are 187, 189, 191, 451, 462, 465.

itself out to be a 'progressive mental attitude' is no more than regression
to a kind of childhood stage of human economic thinking. Alexander
Rüstow once made this implication clear though probably not realizing
how much it coincides with the custom among primitives:

> Equality may be demanded at the beginning (initial equality) in the name
> of justice, at the end only in the name of envy. To each his own, is the claim
> of justice; the same for each, that of envy. A specially unequivocal and
> crude form of envy is that directed against some innate or fortuitous
> advantage in respect of which there can be no question of a just claim
> (unless this were made upon nature or the Creator), as, for example, when a
> girl throws vitriol or acid into her more attractive rival's face. But there are
> other cases, less crude and not so generally censured, where envy is also
> indubitably involved. When, for instance, respected political economists
> unashamedly put forward, publicly and unequivocally, the thesis that a
> lower but equitably distributed national income would be better than a
> higher national income with a few very rich men: that all should be equally
> poor rather than all rich and a few even richer. And this, evidently, even
> when in the second case the absolute income of the relatively less well off
> would be higher than it would in the first. Yet it is improbable that the
> learned gentlemen in question are themselves motivated by envy; it is the
> envy of the lower class which they regard as a sociological datum and
> believe they have to take into account. Were such social-psychological
> defeatism to prevail, it would mean nothing less than a catastrophe. This
> fact alone is enough to demonstrate that a psychology and phenomenology
> of envy is an undertaking as important and immediate as it is difficult.[2]

[2] A. Rüstow, *Ortsbestimmung der Gegenwart,* Vol. 3: *Herrschaft oder Freiheit?,*
Erlenbach-Zurich, 1957, p. 90. Statements closely reminiscent of the conceptions of
the Dobu Islanders are found, for example, in L. F. Post, *Ethics of Democracy* (3rd ed.,
Indianapolis, 1916, p. 82); also, reports on the British socialist programme (e.g.,
'Malice or Charity?' in *The Economist,* December 18, 1954, pp. 973 f.); op. cit., July
1954, pp. 9 f. In 1956 British socialists, among them A. Lewis, published *Twentieth-
Century Socialism,* a book which was critically reviewed by C. Curran in *The Spectator,* July 6, 1956, pp. 7–8: 'The innocence of all this turns into something uglier when
you come to consider the electoral aspects of classless egalitarianism. For, in a Britain
without poverty, who wants equality? Let us suppose—it is not a very large sup-
position—that our national standard of life raises to the point where the luxuries of
1956 are available to everybody. Would it be a hardship, or an injustice, if, while
everybody had plenty, some people had more than plenty? If £3,000 a year, say, were

Welfare economics

Some readers may doubt that there is any school of thought in economics advocating an economic policy barefaced enough to have for its leading principle the least possible envy for the greatest number of human beings. In the English-speaking world this is widely known as 'welfare economics.' It was probably given most publicity during the years 1935 to 1955.

We are spared the proof that this doctrine is less concerned with the prosperity of all than with preventing, out of deference to envy, the greater prosperity of a rather smaller number, by an article that appeared in England in 1960, 'A Survey of Welfare Economics, 1939–1959.' It differs from most literature of this kind in that it expressly mentions envy. This short history of welfare economics by E. J. Mishan is based principally upon J. S. Duesenberry's *Income, Saving, and the Theory of Consumer Behavior,* a work that appeared in the United States in 1949. In this view, the subjective sense of well-being of every income group is prejudiced by the income groups above it. In order to be rid of this 'feeling of deprivation' recourse is had to the progressive income tax. Mishan then writes:

'Ideally, of course, the tax should suffice to cover all the initial and subsequent claims necessary to placate everybody in the lower-income

---

the minimum income, would it be monstrous if some people had £30,000, or £300,000.

'The egalitarians apparently think it would be monstrous. Ask them why, and they reply with that noble bromide "social justice." But this is merely a politician's periphrasis for "envy." Social justice is a semantic fraud from the same stable as People's Democracy. It means that when everybody has plenty it is right to hate people who have more. Even though the most dim-witted citizen, whose mental endowments barely enable him to mark a football coupon, enjoys a motorcar standard of life, egalitarianism will tell him to revolt at the polls because his car is a Morris, and other people have Bentleys. But why should he care?

'Does anybody in Britain except a neurotic feel grief, or anger, or burning bitterness when he reflects that the United States is a richer country than ours? . . . In the past the Socialist movement has flourished by exploiting the wrongs of the poor. They were real and crying wrongs. Now they have disappeared. In order to keep the movement alive the Left intellectuals want to use envy and jealousy as electoral substitutes for poverty and hardship. That seems to me the conclusion implicit in *Twentieth-Century Socialism.'*

groups, and the stronger is this envy of others, the heavier must be the tax.'[3]

Mishan continues that according to Duesenberry, who speaks for many like-minded people, there can be a situation of 'excessive' income in which

> any net increase of output—for instance, more of 'every' good without additional effort—will not advance the welfare of the community no matter how it is distributed. Indeed, any increase of output makes the community worse off, since, no matter how the additional goods are distributed, the additional envy generated cannot be adequately compensated for out of these extra goods.[4]

Mishan, who uses the term 'envy' three times on the same page, is, however, critical of this view. In his opinion, there might be a distribution of additional goods, made available without any additional effort, which, in spite of evident envy, would improve the position of everyone in the society. Yet if this book has successfully demonstrated that it is envy's nature to be on principle wholly intractable to quantitative manipulations, the fallibility of welfare economics is even more evident.

Yet Mishan does allow welfare economics some prospect of success in that they take account of the envious:

> Indeed, not only does an income tax correct for social envy, this envy itself is reduced in so far as it is provoked by disposable rather than gross incomes. The more sensitive [i.e., more envious] is the community in this respect, the steeper the progression of the tax necessary to correct the conventional conditions. In extreme cases only complete equality of disposable incomes solves the problem of interdependent welfares. In the nature of things, so extreme an institution is more likely to be encountered in an opulent society than in an indigent one.[5]

---

[3] E. J. Mishan, 'A Survey of Welfare Economics, 1939–1959,' *The Economic Journal* (London) Vol. LXX, June 1960, p. 247.

[4] Op. cit., pp. 247 f. Mishan refers to J. S. Duesenberry, *Income, Saving, and the Theory of Consumer Behavior,* Cambridge (Mass.), 1949.

[5] E. J. Mishan, op. cit., p. 254.

In his notes, Mishan discusses the hypothesis that 'altruistic' inter-dependence (joy at another's good fortune) might increase social wel-fare. The opposite he calls 'egoistic interdependence' (anger at another's good fortune), i.e., envy. Mishan rejects the hypothesis with the remark: 'If I am made happy by the thought of those with higher incomes, or advancing incomes, I must be saddened reflecting on those with lower incomes, or declining incomes.'

In this we see the part played by the 'bad social conscience,' which we have discussed at length, in welfare economics. Mishan believes that the effect of these two interdependencies, differing in each individual, depends on so many factors that it is difficult to decide in which situation he feels happier. The concept of *envy-assuagement,* so crucial to our theory, reappears almost word for word in the following reflection of Mishan's:

> A society is conceivable in which mutual envy is not such as to warrant any check on output. Thus we may imagine output to increase along with improvements in technology, this being permitted provided the additional product suffices to reward any additional factors involved and to placate additional envy generated. The additional envy may issue chiefly from one or a group of persons. Increased output is warranted, however, only so long as this additional envy, no matter how distributed, can be more than compensated out of the increase.[6]

What Mishan totally overlooks in this analysis is the envy sometimes observable in the lesser man of someone who stands so high in the esteem of his employers that they will pay him a seemingly exorbitant sum, though with prevailing income tax rates he may end up by having hardly more in his pocket than the man who envies him. For people are also envied their functional importance in a society, evidenced by some symbol or other. Incidentally, Mishan does not regard welfare economics as a subject for serious research, not because of logical difficulties, but because 'things on which happiness ultimately depends, friendship, faith, the perception of beauty and so on,' fall outside its range.[7] This is correct. But we must not overlook the fact that, stimulated by welfare

[6] Op. cit., p. 247.
[7] Op. cit., p. 256.

economics, a new generation of egalitarian social engineers is already proposing to level down these subjective values also. I know intellectuals who cannot tolerate the thought that in the ideal society there should be those for whom only pop music is a relaxation, while others enjoy and understand classical music. Some years ago I examined these problems in detail.[8]

In the affluent society, attacks upon mere differences in income are not very attractive either to the intellectuals who champion them or to those who might benefit from them; the more so, since these differences have already been largely levelled out. Hence for some years past the new theme on the left has been the equalization, reorganization and redistribution of education, this being seen less as a means towards earning a better livelihood than as a direct means to a full enjoyment of life at an intellectual level. Thus Erich Fromm, who seeks a 'humanist socialism' halfway between Americanism and the Soviet culture, writes: '. . . the idea of equality of income has never been a socialist demand. . . . As far as inequalities of income are concerned, it seems that they must not transcend the point where differences in income lead to differences in the experience of life.'[9]

Does social justice mean less all round?

Where a national product grows considerably faster than the population, there would be no reason for social envy as such to assume too considerable a role. Even when representatives of labour groups or farmers in political key positions succeed in obtaining more for themselves than would be accorded them without the consideration of envy, this does not mean that the economic policy is adapted to the envious man. Although now and again the taxpayer's money and other kinds of national income are channelled to certain groups, less because of their actual performance than because of their skilful manipulation of the organ-stops of envy-avoidance in the legislature, such processes are no more than partial manifestations of the envy-phenomenon, having little influence

[8] 'Individuality vs. Equality,' *Essays on Individuality,* ed. F. Morley, Philadelphia, 1958, pp. 103–24.
[9] *The Sane Society,* London, 1956, pp. 334 f.; New York, 1955.

on the total economy. So long as these cases do not predominate in the distribution of the national income, this will rather be a process analogous to that of an employee who, knowing his colleague's salary, might say to his boss: 'I want the same. After all, it is hardly in the interests of the firm's morale that I should be envious!'

A politically dangerous spiral begins at the point where economic policy is based on the assumption that the many can be well off only if the few are not better off; or if the income or the wealth of a polity is understood as a fixed quantity, so that 'social justice' can be practised only through the sacrifice of the minority, in order that the rest should 'feel better' about things.

What has been shown so far demonstrated how little envy is concerned with the nature or size of the objects or qualities by which it is aroused. Thus A. de Levchine reports of the Kazak-Kirghiz:

> It might be thought that a people so simple as the Kazak, with their small requirements, would be indifferent towards minor gains and losses amongst themselves, but the opposite is the case. I have observed terrible fights between them upon their having to share out objects of minimal value. When they rob caravans, they cut up the objects they have stolen into the most absurd and useless little bits.[10]

Almost all who have ever expressly concerned themselves with envy unanimously agree as to the envious man's capacity to fix upon every feature, however insignificant, in the other that will serve, as for the lover in Stendhal's theory of love, to crystallize his feelings of envy.

We must, however, also concern ourselves with the principal targets, those objects and qualities in human existence which most arouse envy and more especially with those aspects of our existence whose elimination or camouflage is demanded by theoreticians of the envyless society, because they are seen as the sole or principal causes of social discontent.

The logical and political-economic reasoning displayed by critics of a market-oriented society are sometimes surprising. During the elections in March 1952 Bernard de Voto, one of the most prominent highbrow

---

[10] A. de Levchine, *Description des hordes et des steppes des Kirghiz-Kazaks ou Kirghiz-kaissaks*, Paris, 1840, p. 343.

journalists in the United States, came out against those who promised to put a brake on progress towards the total welfare state. He remarked that A. does not happily work twelve hours a day so that B. can have an agreeable winter holiday in Egypt (*Harper's Magazine*). 'One' naturally envies the man who spent the winter—of 1952—in Egypt, and 'one' feels sympathy for the man who works seventy-two hours a week. In reality, then as now, most Americans who take expensive trips to a warmer place for the winter will probably spend the rest of the time voluntarily and enthusiastically doing perhaps seventy hours' work a week as doctors, executives, self-employed professional people.

Feelings such as those reiterated again and again by Bernard de Voto and hundreds of other like-minded journalists underlie much more sincere outbursts, like the one which appeared in 1964 on the occasion of the Belgian doctors' strike:

> My 'easily aroused social envy' was all too violently aroused. . . . I simply cannot understand that a journal such as yours, which after all does not stand for the interests of any association, should quite unjustifiably align itself with those who already are too powerful. How about a little justice for us as well, who have to finance the doctors' prosperity, without ever becoming as rich ourselves?[11]

Private property

Various critics, when considering private property from the point of view of social evolution, have represented the concept of personal property as being a late phenomenon in the history of mankind. Comparative animal psychology and behavioural physiology (ethology) should be able to put them right. But we also have at our disposal other observations which suggest that a condition where personal property is absent is something quite artificial and is generally required of individuals or of individual families on the basis of an abstract ideology. Of the Tanala, Ralph Linton records that their material needs are small and easily satisfied, but that private property is just as important to them as it is to any group of European farmers. Their attitude to it is the same. The harvest is the family's absolute property. Among relatives in direct line of

[11] *Die Zeit,* April 24, 1964, Letters to the Editor.

descent, property rights are carefully observed. Within measure, however, tools etc. may be used by anyone in the absence of the owner.[12] Here we might recall the communal villages described in the preceding chapter.

In the kibbutzim, property was communal—indeed, in many of the settlements to a degree that bordered on the impractical. The American anthropologist M. Spiro observed that small children, who had grown up in a completely egalitarian social environment in which their parents were allowed no private property, would first, while playing in their communal nurseries, for instance (the children are not brought up by their own parents), quite spontaneously claim things such as toys, towels, etc., as private property, although at this stage they could definitely have no such thing. They quarrelled about whose was what exactly like property-oriented children in a capitalist society. These children also showed envy. And they knew just what they meant by 'It's mine!' It was only during adolescence that the official ideology prevailed, being most marked in adults born on the kibbutz, and that they would begin, when questioned, to deny that there was any value in, or justification for, private property.[13]

The Hutterites in Canada, an extremely communal people, are in an even stronger position than the adults in a kibbutzim to educate their children for the propertyless life. Yet John W. Bennett in his most recent studies of Hutterian Brethren also found, on closer observation, a drive to acquire personal property, to have and experience it even if 'the ideology of communal property is so pervasive that queries assuming an ideology of ownership are not clearly understood.' Hutterites do have personal property, cherish it, and it is respected (e.g., things such as an electric razor or some other fancy tool). Bennett observed instances of 'a pure gift to the self, a reflection of a basic acquisitive residue in its owner's thinking . . . almost every Hutterian male known intimately [by Bennett] owned a few such unnecessary possessions.'[14]

[12] Ralph Linton, *The Tanala. A Hill Tribe of Madagascar* (Publications of the Field Museum of Natural History, Anthropological Series, Vol. 22), Chicago, 1935, pp. 127 f.

[13] M. Spiro, *The Children of the Kibbutz,* Cambridge (Mass.), 1958, pp. 373–6.

[14] John W. Bennett, *Hutterian Brethren. The Agricultural Economy and Social Organization of a Communal People,* Stanford (Calif.), 1967, pp. 171 ff.

Significant data are available on the child's idea of property in various tribes among primitive peoples, many of which recognize the small child's private property and remain true to this principle to an even greater extent than would seem fitting to parents in Western Europe or in the United States today. Among the Navaho in North America, even small children are regularly given domestic animals with the child's own property mark. However, the child is sometimes expected to contribute to the family cook-pot. Among themselves the Tlingit Indians, too, show a pronounced respect for private property.[15]

If these observations are combined with the results of research into the behaviour of various species of animal, it can only be concluded that the concept of personal property, together with the whole of its emotive substructure, is a primary, natural and deeply rooted phenomenon, which is not necessarily engendered by a particular type of society and does not necessarily wane under the aegis of another. Thus the hope that it would be possible, by abolishing private property, to educate, within the course of a few generations, a new human being free of all those characteristics and drives which the critic of the acquisitive society finds unpalatable would seem vain indeed.

The Russians are today just as acquisitive and as ingenious in getting what they want as they ever were; not that the Soviet Union ever seriously sought to abolish private property—in some spheres, such as tax progression, it is much less hostile to it than the United States. Probably a more important example is that of the kibbutz, a social environment where most private property has been effactually abolished, but one which still does not enable children to grow up in such a way that the idea never occurs to them and has, indeed, been eradicated later by the collective and its educational organs.

Thus the purely socialist society can never be a self-propagating institution. Renunciation of private property has to be exacted from, and hammered into, each generation anew. Whether, small settlements apart, this would be a very healthy and efficient form of society seems

---

[15] *American Anthropologist*, Vol. 59, 1957, p. 534. In some instances private property seems to have developed in cultivated trees (fruit trees, coffee trees etc.), prior even to the recognition of private property in land. See René F. Millon, 'Trade, Tree Cultivation, and the Development of Private Property in Land,' *American Anthropologist*, Vol. 57, 1955, pp. 698 ff.

questionable. For it would above all be a society which would produce a considerable resentment among its members with every new generation. Enough tensions are generated already, as psychoanalysis has shown, when society exerts control only over the primary sexual drives during childhood and adolescence, the time of socialization and the development of identity. But if the urge for property also represents a natural, primary and universal desire in man, then a form of society that equipped the superego with commandments prohibiting private property would be extremely distasteful to the individual.

Significantly, in his behavioural studies based on depth psychology on the personality of native members of the kibbutz, Spiro found numerous signs of ambivalent feelings towards the collective, of resentment and of bitterness.[16] It is certainly no coincidence that in many kibbutzim today, people confess to a desire for private property and privacy which would have been regarded by the founders as rank heresy. In addition, there is the fact that the kibbutz movement, which must be seen as the only large-scale 'utopian' experiment ever genuinely to have sought to abolish private property, has obviously begun to stagnate and, if only from the viewpoint of population, can hardly now be considered as the nucleus of, or model for, a new epoch.

Hired goods instead of property

In 1959, when the Soviet Union had already set its course unequivocally in the direction of private property and a consumer society, one of the younger officials, a protégé of Khrushchev's power machine, Komsomol leader Semichastny, was to declare at the 21st Party Congress that 'manifestations of egoism and individualism, as well as other remnants of the psychology and morality of private property owners, must be eradicated in the Soviet Union.' Semichastny's proposed method was as follows:

> From his earliest days we say to the child: That's your toy, that's your book, that's your bicycle. When he grows up he says: That's my car, that's my country house, that's my motor-bike. We ought increasingly to introduce

[16] M. Spiro, op. cit., pp. 367 f.

the wonderful word 'our' into the practice of socialist communal living. This is a great problem. Let us take rental shops, for example. Why should such shops not be set up everywhere, so that those who wished to do so could hire a bicycle, a car, a motor-bike, a motor-boat and other things for a short time at little cost?[17]

Now it seems probable that Semichastny was an extremely envious man. This is not only suggested by the challenge quoted above, but also by the part he played in the ostracism of Boris Pasternak in the autumn of 1958, when Pasternak was awarded the Nobel Prize. The Komsomol leader called the poet a swine and demanded that he leave the Soviet Union. This invective was too much for intellectuals even in Russia. It is not difficult to imagine what an official might feel about poetic gifts great enough to win the Nobel Prize, when this same official actually takes offence at a child's saying 'my bicycle.'

Against the background of our entire analysis, Semichastny's proposal is instructive for several reasons. The fanatical advocate of communal ownership correctly saw that the feeling for private property was ineradicably inculcated into and stamped upon the child during the process of its personality formation. He probably did not know that decades before, in some of the Israeli kibbutzim, for just such reasons, if not perhaps very successfully, an attempt had seriously been made to set up a rotation system, even for work clothes, so that no one could talk of 'his' shoes or 'his' trousers. Nor did he know that even the simplest primitive peoples, who are not yet 'corrupted by capitalism,' both recognize and encourage an unconditional and secure title to ownership, even by young children, of certain commodities. Strong evidence suggests that private property is a constitutive factor in any social existence, and the attempt to exclude it legislatively from the process of the individual's socialization cannot appear until relatively late in cultural history, when a process of political messianism has begun.

It is, indeed, a matter of some irony that the one place where Semichastny's pet method has first taken on is America, that allegedly materialistic stronghold of capitalism: increasingly, objects of daily use, brand-new motorcars, motorboats, small aircraft, motor mowers, office equipment of all kinds, clothing, pictures, etc., are regularly rented or

---

[17] *Neue Zürcher Zeitung,* foreign edition, April 11, 1959, p. 2.

leased, and that by average people who see the temporary hire of a new or well-maintained object as more economical and practical than its lasting possession.

This new attitude towards material possessions becomes possible only if the individual has unconditional faith in his economic system, knowing that he will always find in it a sufficient supply of commodities for rent or hire. This 'communal economy' arises from faith in a consumer-oriented market economy and foreshadows a new phase of the capitalist, as distinct from a socialist, system. For the individual will renounce concrete, lasting ownership in important areas of daily consumption in favour of hired objects only if he no longer has cause to fear that a political authority may introduce arbitrary restrictions on his access to those objects.

Moreover, these human modes of behaviour, characteristics and drives related to the concept of property, against which the purist criticism of property as such is directed, would not simply disappear with the elimination of private property in the narrower sense. Where the individual, within the framework of family group, clan or village community, has no private property, all the intentional and emotional manifestations which occur at the frontier dividing owner from non-owner are simply shifted to the frontier between family and outsiders or between individual villages. One often gets the impression that the pride of ownership and greed for possession in a small collective is greater and more irrational (nationalistic) than in the individual.

We find it difficult to take seriously a critique of property which opines that, once measures have been taken to abolish individual and family property, all the most crucial problems will have been solved. For the transfer of property does little to alter its meaning in terms of human existence; whether the discretionary powers are in the hands of ten, thirty or three thousand people, a man still knows that he is in a world that must draw a boundary between thine and mine, where all transactions have to be accounted for, where there is crime against property and where a group will always seek to increase its property, if necessary at another group's expense.

Nor is the matter very different if we draw a fine line between private property as such and private property as the 'means of production.' After all, many more things can serve as means of production than just steel mills or fleets of trucks. Some authors deem private ownership of the means of production unjust because it allows one person, after having done his own initial work (e.g., planning a product and its marketing), a continuous share in the proceeds from subsequent labour, done by others for wages. However, on this analogy, would a playwright not then be in the same position as an industrialist? Both have put together, by mental effort, a system of directives that must employ other men whose labour results in the enrichment of the innovators, even after they have ceased to work themselves.

A play or a musical composition, once written, can be performed all over the world simultaneously by hundreds of people. Actors and musicians will sweat just for wages night after night. In a stage hit the same group of people may have to slave in monotony, as if in the harness of an assembly line, for one or two years. They receive their wages, of course, but so do factory workers. Each night the play is performed, its author, without any additional work on his part, shares in the earnings made possible by other men's labour. Is he then a capitalist too?

Removing from an economic system every opportunity for anyone to take his cut from the result of other men's labour would require drastic changes affecting authors, composers and inventors.

19

Social Indignation

WHAT OTHERS, whether for good reasons or frivolous, actually or allegedly do with foodstuffs has often led to an impassioned critique of society. If you ask a student what, in his opinion, is the first thing with which capitalism might be reproached, he will rather surprisingly even today answer that it is the destruction of food. Often he will actually know that what was chiefly involved was coffee, which could save no one from starvation. Arthur Koestler's recollection of what contributed to his conversion to communism in 1931 is typical:

'The event that roused my indignation to a pitch never reached before, was the American policy of destroying food stocks to keep agricultural prices up during the depression years—at a time when millions of unemployed lived in misery and near starvation.'[1]

Yet the same man who, understandably enough, finds this terrible, remains strangely indifferent to, say, a strategically effective strike of relatively well-paid technicians which indirectly puts many other, uninvolved employees out of work for months, or, again, to a strike of transport workers that threatens a big American city's food supplies. When private interests cause working time to be squandered and irretrievably lost, far less indignation is aroused than by the burning of something tangible like grain, although in both cases motives and results may be the same.

In fact, the destruction of provisions for price policy or political reasons is an offence in no way peculiar to capitalism or the free-market economy. Since the Second World War such incidents seem not to have

[1] A. Koestler, *Arrow in the Blue. An Autobiography,* London and New York, 1952, pp. 240 f.

been infrequent even in socialist economic planning. In 1964, of all cocoa-exporting countries, it was fanatically socialist Ghana which alone began the destruction of the cocoa crop in order to raise world prices. And Robert E. Lane, an American political scientist wholly sympathetic to economic control, when investigating problems of socialist economic planning in Great Britain between 1945 and 1951, arrived at the sobering conclusion that it is precisely the officially regimented and controlled economy which, under egalitarian pressure, will allow goods and provisions to spoil rather than allow some consumers to have more than others. One of the examples he gives is the prohibition by the Ministry of Food, in the spring of 1950, on the production of Devonshire cream by Exmoor farmers from their surplus milk, on the grounds that it was more 'just' to allow the milk to go bad than to enable some people to enjoy cream at a time when the rest of the country could not be supplied with it.[2]

Lane has numerous other examples from different areas of life and economics, all of which demonstrate that in its endeavour to guarantee total 'justice,' thus avoiding the envy of the great unknown, the state is continually promulgating measures and inflicting prohibitions and punishments which are felt to be uneconomic and unfair by those who are not wrapped in the cotton wool of utopia.

'Give us this day our daily bread'

Further insight into these associations may be gained by an investigation of the deep-rooted inhibition against throwing away stale food, especially bread. It does not stem from avarice, though this is not necessarily excluded. The saying 'Sooner meak tha belly suffer, than help to fill t'landlord's coffer' would seem to imply envy. But this particular inhibition I consider to be related to existence as such; it might even be possible to associate it with the prehuman phase in phylogenesis like the inhibitions described by Konrad Lorenz, for example.[3]

Now grain may also be used for the production of alcohol, which is drunk for pleasure. Yet very few people will feel uncomfortable when

[2] Robert E. Lane, 'Problems of a Regulated Economy. The British Experience,' *Social Research*, Vol. 19, 1952, p. 297.

[3] K. Lorenz, *On Aggression*, London and New York, 1966, Chapter 7.

they pour away the dregs from a brandy glass as they would do if they threw away milk or bread. For this is an irrational inhibition. At this very moment, a glass of water might save the life of someone somewhere in the world, yet no one is worried by the equivalent of a hundred glasses of water going unused down the drain. We are afraid and ashamed of destroying the symbol, not the substance. Perhaps religious conceptions are also involved. ('Give us this day our daily *bread*' . . .) But again, religions have succeeded in placing a taboo, for hygienic reasons, on foodstuffs that are inherently agreeable, such as the meat of hoofed animals. Neither in the Old or the New Testament is there, to my knowledge, any rule that encourages the consumption of any kind of food when once its condition is in doubt. The cultures which gave birth to these writings were far too concerned with the danger of food poisoning for such a precept to be likely. Evidently we interpose a seemingly religious commandment in order to disguise our irrational inhibition.

The uncomfortable sense of guilt that comes over us when we have to throw away stale food—or even fresh food, if we happen to be going away for a long time—has nothing to do with any particular economic system, though a system's critics will happily exploit it if they want to confuse us morally. It is a peculiar feeling which has caused many to scratch their heads in vain.

In October 1959 the *Stuttgarter Zeitung* printed an article entitled 'Bread and Machines.' This ran: 'Prosperity, according to the implacable critics of our way of life, is not good for morality; this they set out to prove by means of all manner of horror stories . . . '—the one, for example, about the 'dry roll somebody left on a park bench.' The writer of the article counters the argument by citing the result of an opinion poll made in 1959, when people were asked: 'Is it right for a bachelor or a professional woman to throw away stale bread?' (It is significant, incidentally, that the opinion seekers only dared to put a question with a built-in excuse. Clearly, no family ought ever to throw anything away.) Of 100 adults, only 21 condoned such behaviour in bachelors, and only 14 per cent in professional women. From this the article concludes:

What we have before us is clearly an almost intact moral survival unimpaired either by industrialization or by the resulting overproduction of consumer goods of all kinds. The average consumer, on the other hand, had no moral feelings about the technical aids used in the production of the goods—the tools, that is, of prosperity. . . .[4]

I have, however, observed certain inhibitions about the junking of obsolete industrial products. But let us return to bread. What really underlies this 'intact moral survival'? Exactly five years after the publication of the article quoted, the front page of the *Frankfurter Allgemeine Zeitung* carried a leading article by Nikolas Benckiser entitled 'Bread in the Dustbin.' He, too, ponders upon what he calls a short-sighted passion, but takes the analysis one step further:

> How, as a person of sensibility, in the face of the mountains of available grain, meat, fruit and vegetables . . . could one fail to think of all the starving millions. . . . Yet these goods are left to rot, and are even systematically destroyed. And then come the inevitable indignant remarks such as: A society that tolerates want anywhere is not worthy of existence. . . .

Benckiser then proves to these agitated critics how difficult and even impossible it is, if only for reasons of transport, so to distribute a local food surplus throughout the rest of the world as to waste nothing at all. (He could also have culled many examples from what happened in the case of development aid. If it proves impossible to deal rationally with the forwarding of materials such as cement, wood and steel, not to speak of machinery, after arrival at the ports of the developing countries, what would happen to perishable foodstuffs?)

Benckiser states the moral dilemma in microcosmic terms: in the average household's dustbin remains of food may often be found which could, in theory, fill some other person's empty stomach (whether he would accept it is another question). How would this person feel on seeing food in the dustbin?

> He wouldn't like it. He would think, 'Give us this day our daily bread'; there is always something sinful about throwing away bread, which is at once a symbol and a staple. And again, one is aware that in the same city, only a few streets away . . . there are people to whom the few pennies that food would have cost before it went bad would really mean something.

[4] *Stuttgarter Zeitung,* October 17, 1959, p. 3.

Benckiser then correctly points out what latitude we now have, even in household economics; an undeniable fact of modern life, without which much else would not be possible. No one need be ashamed of the fact that we do not 'live a stunted, hand-to-mouth existence.' And he goes on to ask why those warehouses full of unsaleable industrial products constantly mentioned in the Soviet press of recent years do not arouse the same feeling of shame as does a grain surplus in the capitalist West.[5]

But Benckiser's view that our feelings on seeing bread in a dustbin emanate from a piety which modern man wishes to preserve is not sufficient explanation, and we shall attempt one that is more far-reaching. If we take into consideration certain aspects of psychoanalysis, and add to this what we know of the uncertainty for primitive peoples, even today, of finding enough to eat, and of the concentration of all their efforts on sustenance—a drive which is even stronger than the sexual drive—it might not be too far-fetched to assume in man a primeval fear of starvation.

The comparative unconcern, in part due to the climate, with which food that is no longer quite fresh is thrown away in the United States, must surely have some connection with the fact stressed by the historian David Potter that the average American, almost from the start of his history, has never experienced any real shortage of food.[6]

What passes through our minds when we hesitate before throwing away a stale loaf of bread, or when we make excuses to ourselves, or anyone who happens to be present, for doing so? We are afraid of a disapproving, even a punishing, authority. We know that the bread in its present condition is of little use to anybody, and are glad if there is a near-by pond where we can feed it to the fish or the ducks. Our sense of guilt is irrational. For we feel little or no guilt about the non-use of an entrance ticket, and none at all about a broken plate. Could it be fear of the envy of the gods that is again obtruding? It must be a pre-Christian conception, and is reminiscent of the Greeks.

The reason we dare throw away food is that we feel certain it will not be needed. But somewhere, perhaps, there is an angry god of fate who,

[5] *Frankfurter Allgemeine Zeitung,* August 13, 1964.

[6] D. Potter, *People of Plenty: Economic Abundance and the American Character,* Chicago, 1954.

begrudging us our frivolity and boldness, will think: 'Here's a man who had better go hungry for a while!' And perhaps we are suddenly beset by the thought, 'If I throw away this loaf now, might there come a day, sometime in the future, when I shall remember this, and long for a bit of stale bread?' We know how little this could be influenced by our present, reasonable decision to eat nothing but wholesome and agreeable food. And yet the uncomfortable feeling remains with us.

Individual precautions are unsocial

Anyone taking a precaution which does not in the least impair the opportunities of others must nevertheless often reckon with malicious animosity and outraged indignation or contempt, behind which lurks peculiar envy. In order to understand this, we have to go back to primitive superstitions. Among many primitive people, but also among ourselves, it is regarded as reprehensible frivolity so much as to name a disaster which might at some time befall the tribe. Thus, if someone provides against a possible catastrophe in a really original and thoroughgoing way, he will arouse the ill-will of his potential comrades in misfortune, who are partly angered by his foresight and partly fear unconsciously that his precaution will attract disaster.

Anyone who makes earlier or better provision than other people is no longer an equal in the fellowship of misfortune, and hence becomes an object of envy. I have never seen this more plainly manifested than by the following observation.

About ten years ago I took part in an innocent, casual conversation with members of a European family. The talk turned to anxiety about another war. Someone mentioned the fact that early in the fifties a European intellectual had deposited a large sum of money with friends in the United States for the express purpose of being sent food parcels after the Third World War. To my astonishment, the expression of all those present immediately changed to annoyance. In tones of the utmost indignation, and in terms more applicable to a visitor who had stolen the silver, a woman doctor began to abuse this prudent, and to her quite unknown, individual—whose only desire, if seen rationally, was that he should not have to beg.

What taboo had he infringed? It should first be said that the people concerned had had plenty to eat during and after the Second World War. Thus it cannot have been the memory of real deprivations which unleashed their fury upon a person who had taken precautions. This was due in part rather to the superstitious fear that precautions taken by a private person (as opposed to government measures, or those officially recommended, such as the storage of food supplies by families) might draw upon them a Third World War. Another factor might have been the projection of their own feelings into the hypothetical years of hunger after the Third World War, in which they compared themselves with the hypothetical recipient of regular food parcels.

Envy in fellowship in misfortune

Let us imagine two Central Europeans, both in comfortable circumstances. The first buys an Irish farm on which to spend his summers. The other deposits a large sum of money in an Australian bank, with instructions that after the Third World War he is to be sought out and provided for. We can be fairly certain that if the second tells other people, who are equally well situated financially, about his precaution, he will arouse considerably more concealed ill-will and envy than will the first. Why?

After a catastrophe, our tolerance for interhuman inequalities dwindles. The concept of fellowship in misfortune explains why this should be. For the more specifically someone is concerned with a better position in a potential future fellowship in misfortune, the more anticipatory envy will he incur. And the more his concern has to do with present, and perhaps even frivolous, luxury, the less will be the indignation among possible fellows in misfortune.

Envy, understandably enough, is the more 'existential,' and the more irrational and pitiless, the more it is extended to inequalities in the mere provision for existence: food and personal survival are elementary values. Anyone who, as compared with ourselves, arranges for himself some future advantage which we would also be able to afford, were we not too lazy, too superstitious, stingy or consumption-oriented, will, oddly enough, arouse our animosity more than a neighbour who is quite obviously eating his way into the grave. For in the case of the greedy neighbour, we can always tell ourselves with hypocritical *Schadenfreude* that we shall probably outlive him. Evidence for this is the envious rage to which American families are exposed if, in certain districts, they build themselves air-raid or tornado shelters.

Success in power politics and the superior tactics of the manipulators of envy derive from their ability to play upon the most vulnerable nerve in human social existence. Though they may not have suspected this at the start, by degrees they begin to exchange knowing and cynical smiles. Everyone, the second from bottom in the primitive tribe, as the one before last in the modern industrial concern, fears the envy of the one whom he senses to be his inferior. No human existence is really conceivable in which man was liberated from the sense of guilt which culminates in the questions: 'Why am I better off than the other man? What does he think of me, what's he going to do?' This primeval anxiety can be shown to exist throughout all cultural development. It has undoubtedly led to individual actions and to social institutions which have made life more tolerable than in earlier epochs. But it would seem improbable that man would be able totally to repress any of his primeval motives. They always return.

Now the blind reaction of alarm set up in those whom he accuses, by the agitator who manipulates the social egalitarian keyboard, proves neither the validity of the accusation nor the efficacy of the social and economic system to which the accused are to be bullied into giving their assent. And the latter no longer have confidence enough to question whether that system will be able to assuage either their own bad conscience or the torment of other, envious dispositions.

20

Envy as Tax Collector

NEITHER DEMOCRACIES nor dictatorships are averse to depending upon the supposed mutual envy in the population to produce maximum honesty in tax matters. It is true that in the United States tax returns are treated as confidential, but an article that appeared a few years ago in *Time* Magazine expressed surprise at the efficiency of the direct tax system and declared outright that this was due to the mutual envy of taxpayers, who keep a watch on each other. Something that is perhaps less well known is the morally dubious procedure of the U.S. Internal Revenue Service when, every spring, before tax returns are finally due, it makes known how much it has paid in rewards to informers. It is not rare to see in the press caricatures or photographs depicting a clearly ill-intentioned individual looking over a taxpayer's shoulder, with the caption: 'Be honest; envy is watching you!' On April 1, 1962, just in time for the April 15 deadline for making the returns, the *New York Times* Magazine, for instance, obligingly aided the Internal Revenue Service by printing a terrifying story about tax informers: 'The tax collectors—volunteer division,' and a handsomely rewarded one at that. The article remarked: 'No one is quite sure how many communications the Treasury receives each year, but educated guesses put the number at 100,000. It is hard to say what motivates these people. Revenge, *envy,* anger, patriotism, spite—all play a part, perhaps a greater part than greed.'

It is notable that a method deliberately counting on envy for the purpose of tax collection was unblushingly commended in the nineteenth century—by Jeremy Bentham, for example. Bentham suggested that the state should evolve the sort of taxation best suited to enlist envy as an inexpensive watchdog. He had in mind, for instance, the success and easy collection of a special tax on bankers:

> If antipathy to this class [the bankers], an innocent at least, not to say a very useful one[!], of His Majesty's subjects, if ill-will, and not the necessity of providing for the exigencies of the state, were the fit motive for the common father of all and his advisers to be governed by, the rigour of the tax would be a recommendation of it [and] nothing would be listened to that exhibited a tendency of softening it. . . .[1]

Today this method might be successfully applied, say, to American doctors, who have for many years been the whipping boys of envious public opinion.

The procedure of making tax returns public is found, incidentally, in Swiss communities, where it is possible to find out, without valid reason, the amount of income and assets declared by one's neighbour or competitor. But a small community near Lucerne goes one better.

In Wolhusen (and one or two neighbouring communities) a list is printed, and sold by schoolchildren from door to door, with the names, assets and incomes of all local residents. For weeks after its publication, there is ample food for malicious and envious gossip. In front of me now is the 1964 register. It starts off with A. A., factory hand, with assets of 2,000 francs and a taxable income of 3,400 francs. The same page contains the name of Direktor E. B., with assets of 270,000 francs and an income of 45,400 francs. Of two farmers of the same name, J. B., one has assets of 153,000 and an income of 9,100 francs, and the other only 3,000 and 2,000 francs respectively. The list becomes interesting where assets and income had to be 'assessed by the special commission,' in cases, that is, of individuals whose control by their fellow residents' envy might be especially welcome. Among these there is the doctor J. B., with assets of 469,000 francs and an annual income of 75,600 francs, while the dentist J. F. has no assets, but nevertheless earns 41,500 francs per annum. Another dentist makes no more than 20,000 francs, while the photographer earns 17,400 francs per annum. The cinema owner is little better off than the self-employed gardener. Printer, butcher, painter, taxi-man and tiler all earn about the same, some 12,000 francs a year.

The list costs three Swiss francs; the publisher is not named. From what I was able to learn, it is published by the Social Democratic Party,

[1] 'Proposal for a Tax on Bankers,' from Jeremy Bentham's *Economic Writings,* critical edition by W. Stark, New York, 1952, Vol. 1, p. 408.

after permission has been obtained from the town council. But here, as so often elsewhere, many are able to turn to their own account the social control supposed to be exerted by the potential envy of fellow citizens. In this town, so we are told, peasants with daughters to marry off or people who wish to obtain credit declare their assets and income to be much higher than they are in reality. They are quite prepared to pay, in consequence, taxes that are unnecessarily high.

Progressive taxation

A poll carried out in the United States, albeit twenty years ago, revealed that members of the lowest classes, when asked how much tax people in different income groups having incomes of $10,000 or over ought to pay, invariably named as 'right' or 'fair' a figure lower than the very high one at the time imposed by the government.

Nor did other investigations, which sought to test the poor man's 'sense of justice' in regard to the income tax, ever succeed in finding any empirical proof for the 'political' necessity for rates of taxation which absorbed up to 90 per cent of income. It is inconceivable to the simple mentality, however badly off a man may be and however envious of those at the top, that anyone should be so wealthy that he could be deprived of much more than 50 per cent of his income.[2]

For what is remarkable about severe progressive taxation is the claim that it is sociologically or politically expedient, based, that is, on window-dressing, in spite of the admission that the top rates are fiscally meaningless. Whose egalitarian feelings, and whose envy, are they supposed to satisfy? Surely not those of people to whom it would be unimaginable that the state should take away so large a portion of anyone's income?

In some Western democracies, mainly since the Second World War, rates of income and inheritance taxes, while failing to achieve an egalitarian paradise, have attained such a level that in some cases they amount

[2] G. Knupfer, 'Portrait of the Underdog,' *Public Opinion Quarterly*, Vol. 11, 1947, pp. 103–14. Striking data from more recent interviews of British voters, showing much less envy of high income earners than official tax policy leads one to suspect, are reported, with chagrin, by W. G. Runciman, *Relative Deprivation and Social Justice*, London, 1966.

to confiscation of property. Such measures are usually introduced by socialist governments in response to the express wishes of intellectuals (e.g., proponents such as Harold J. Laski and Sidney and Beatrice Webb), but also in the belief that they correspond to the insatiable emotional need of the electorate at large. In this way, very similar taxation rates were applied in both Great Britain and the United States, in spite of the fact that the observable envy in lower-income groups in the United States, as we now know, was hardly comparable with that in Great Britain, and even less so after 1950.

In democracies such as the United States, Western Germany and Switzerland progression of income tax has now become less harsh; this is not so in Great Britain, Austria or Sweden. In the former countries at least, it is no longer a main subject of controversy, though there, too, it represents consideration of presumed envy in the majority, and not any fiscal necessity. Had national income tax in Sweden (1960) been limited to 25 per cent, the exchequer would have lost only 2 per cent of all tax revenues. A top rate of 45 per cent—instead of the existing 65 per cent—would have entailed a loss of only 45 million kroner (out of a total revenue of 16.5 thousand million). In the United States (1962), progressive income tax over 30 per cent brought in only 6.4 per cent, over 50 per cent only 1.9 per cent and over 65 per cent a mere 0.6 per cent of the total revenue. Rates of 75 per cent to 91 per cent yielded only 0.2 per cent. Yet not even conservative governments, when they succeed a left-wing administration, are able as a rule to do much towards dismantling this steep progression. They are too afraid of the envy they suppose this would arouse in the electorate.

If proponents of extreme progression are asked for their reasons, most of them will as often as not actually admit that it is fiscally meaningless. The reason for steep tax rates is said to be the ideal of equality, which has to be pursued, if only symbolically. If this argument is demolished (by reference to the steady demand for certain luxury goods and to the similar consumer habits in the middle and upper classes which is very apparent at least in the United States), the invariable retort is that extreme progression militates against unequal distribution of *power.* For it is wrong that one citizen should have at his sole disposal the power that goes with considerable property. In this, the egalitarian naturally overlooks the fact that the moderately paid Member of Parliament, official or executive has far more power than someone who earns or inherits an exceptional sum. The 'power' of the three or four experts in a modern democracy able to suggest at what point tax progression should assume confiscatory proportions is indubitably and considerably greater by comparison than the power of a widow who has inherited a few millions from her husband.

To claim 'humanitarian motives,' when the true motive is envy and its supposed appeasement, is a favourite rhetorical device of politicians today, and has been for at least a hundred and fifty years. Twenty years ago an Australian premier, for instance, declared in Parliament:

> . . . seven years ago, about £17 million was being expended each year on social service benefits. This year, social services will cost about £88 million. I do not deny that this scheme involves a redistribution of the national wealth, and I make no apology for the fact. Our policy arises from humanitarian motives, which many other people must share, because other-wise we should not have been returned to power at the last two elections. We aim to compel those who can well afford to do so, to surrender some of their income to help those who do the hard and tedious work of the country. . . . The workers are the people who really make the wheels go round. . . .

These were the closing words of the Budget Debate on September 29, 1948, by the then Prime Minister J. B. Chifley. Fittingly, they were also the closing words, so to speak, for the Labour Party's rule in that country until today. Electorates seem far less grateful for this concern for their presumed envy than politicians always seem to think. The fact that envy as an imputed motive to most members of a society is as inherent in the preference for progressive taxation as it is untenable logically and prag-matically has been emphasized by serious scholars again and again. In 1953 two professors at the Law School of the University of Chicago, Blum and Kalven, published a slim volume under the title *The Uneasy Case for Progressive Taxation,* in which they asked what our attitude towards 'equality' would have to be

> if by a convenient miracle the wealth and output of society trebled over-night without any changes in its relative distribution among individuals. Would the issue of lessening inequality . . . appear any less urgent? . . . what is involved is envy, the dissatisfaction produced in men not by what they

lack but by what others have. . . . If this is what is primarily involved, the remedy, however impractical, would seem to be one suggested by Aristotle, that it is the desires of men and not their possessions that need to be equalized. Nor is there much basis for optimism about the impact on envy of the redistribution of material goods. Every experience seems to confirm the dismal hypothesis that envy will find other, and possibly less attractive, places in which to take root.[3]

How little punitive taxation has to do with social progress, or indeed with anything modern, representing rather a direct regression, very common in present-day politics, to the motivational state of undeveloped primitive peoples, becomes apparent from a consideration of some of the latter's customs which usually affect those who have been favoured by fate, or who are a little more prosperous. For it can then be seen that envy succeeds in becoming an institution, regardless of what is involved, whether this be a million dollars, a pound, a mark or just a dozen mussel shells.

Ethnological data towards an understanding of the motive of extreme progression

One of envy's most remarkable institutions, and one which bears a great resemblance to the 'social justice' emotional complex today, is the *muru* attack among the New Zealand Maori. Among the original New Zealanders none were either very rich or very poor. Material equality extended to the chiefs, who, while enjoying financial advantages, were also subjected to perpetual expenditure, such as obligatory hospitality, which made the accumulation of riches extremely difficult.

The Maori word *muru* literally means to plunder, more specifically, to plunder the property of those who have somehow transgressed in the eyes of the community. This might be seen as unobjectionable in a

---

[3] W. J. Blum and H. Kalven, Jr., *The Uneasy Case for Progressive Taxation,* Chicago, 1953, pp. 74 ff. C. Föhl, 'Kritik der progressiven Einkommensbesteuerung,' *Finanzarchiv,* New Series, Vol. 14, 1953, pp. 88 ff. The impossibility of determining a 'socially just' progressive tax is also demonstrated by Kurt Schmidt, *Die Steuerprogression,* Tübingen, 1960, pp. 75 f. His bibliography gives other works on this question.

society with no judicial apparatus. But a list of the 'crimes against society' which were visited with *muru* attack might give pause for reflection. A man with property worth looting by the community could be certain of *muru,* even if the real culprit was one of his most distant relatives. (The same kind of thing was observable during European witch trials.) If a Maori had an accident by which he was temporarily incapacitated, he suffered *muru*. Basically, any deviation from the daily norm, any expression of individuality, even through an accident, was sufficient occasion for the community to set upon an individual and his personal property.

The man whose wife committed adultery, the friends of a man who died, the father of a child that injured itself, the man who accidentally started a grass fire in a burial ground (even though no one had been buried there for a hundred years) are all examples—among innumerable others—of reasons on account of which an individual might lose his property, including his crops and his stores of food. But just as in America today there are people who are proud of the magnitude of their income tax, there would seem to have been Maori who regarded the *muru* attack as a distinction, as a sign of enviably high renown.[4]

The *muru* attackers sometimes converged upon the victim from a distance of a mile; it was attack with robbery by members of the tribe who, with savage howls, carried off everything that was in any way desirable, even digging up the root crops.[5]

In the early days, before the Maori had adopted much from the European immigrants, it was enough for a man to possess an axe or a spade for him to be surrounded by envious watchers on the look-out for anything that would justify *muru* and hence the 'legal' theft of the tool.[6]

In practice the institution of *muru* meant that no one could ever count on keeping any movable property, so that there could be no incentive to work for anything. No resistance was ever offered in case of a *muru* attack. This would not only have involved physical injury but, even worse, would have meant exclusion from taking part in any future *muru* attack. So it was better to submit to robbery by the community, in the

[4] E. Best, *The Maori,* 2 vols., Wellington, 1924, Vol. 1, p. 87.

[5] Ibid., Vol. 2, pp. 358–60.

[6] F. E. Manning, *Old New Zealand,* London, 1876, pp. 92 f.

hope of participating oneself in the next attack. The final result was that most movable property—a boat, for example—would circulate from one man to the next, and ultimately become public property.[7]

Could it be, perhaps, that a citizen today in an exceptionally egalitarian democracy, when submitting without protest to a very tiresome and high tax rate, secretly hopes that, like the Maori, some special government scheme might enable him in some way to dip his hand into the pocket of someone better off than himself?

The custom of *muru* attack should not be understood to mean that the Maori had no clear concept of private property. Quite the contrary. It is from them that the term 'taboo' (*tapu*) comes, a concept that was evolved for the protection of personal property. Anyone of any importance could, with his *tapu,* place a taboo on the whole of his movable property— clothing, weapons, ornaments, tools, etc.; that is to say, he could make them immune to damage or theft by others (except, of course, from *muru*). The higher a man's social rank, the stronger his *tapu.* He need lend nothing to others, and could leave his possessions unguarded for any length of time. In the case of a fishing net, for instance, the *tapu* was regarded as being so strong that only its maker could go near it.[8]

The Maori also had a sense for unequal pay for unequal performance. Thus, in the communal distribution of the catch after a fishing expedition, the share received by a man's family was in proportion to the efforts he had expended.[9]

From this it again becomes evident how wrong it is to imagine that there can be almost pure types of 'socialist' or, alternatively, 'individualist' society, or to think of any direct line of social development. In reality, any closer inspection of human groups, societies and cultures will reveal motivational structures for the attainment of completely private as well as clearly communally profitable goals. In many respects the neighbours, citizens and business people of a modern nation oriented towards private enterprise are much better adapted to really genuine communal undertakings than are members of primitive groups or of

---

[7] Op. cit., pp. 83 ff.

[8] Manning, op. cit., pp. 94 ff. Best, op. cit., p. 251.

[9] R. Firth, *Primitive Economics of the New Zealand Maori,* New York, 1929, pp. 279, 284.

most simple peasant communities, such as those in South America or southern Italy. Since one can never be quite certain that the other person will not extract from the 'public interest' a greater benefit than oneself, communally useful co-operation can never really be achieved until primitive, primeval envy has been largely suppressed.[10] Once aroused, mutual envy turns blindly and savagely upon private gain and possession but, as observation of innumerable communities has shown, also upon the very suggestion of organizing supra-individual undertakings, even if this be only the search for a better water supply for the whole village.[11]

By fomenting, often on a 'scientific basis,' and by activating and legitimizing the envy of the people, already too strong as it is, the extreme socialist programmes, especially in some of the younger developing countries, are paradoxically undermining and/or delaying those very attitudes and modes of thought without which there can never be trustful co-operation among a number of people for the attainment of supra-individual goals.[12]

---

[10] 'In any society the aim must be to keep the less successful from blocking the creative activity of the more far-seeing. This aim is reached by making envy "not respectable" either to the envying individual himself or to his neighbours. . . . The laissez-faire ideology of the 18th and 19th centuries was very effective in dealing with these problems of envy and freedom to experiment.' David McCord Wright, 'Moral, Psychological and Political Aspects of Economic Growth,' *Särtryck Ur Ekonomisk Tidskrift,* Uppsala (Almquist & Wiksells), 1954, p. 193.

[11] A. Holmberg, 'The Wells that Failed,' *Human Problems in Technological Change,* ed. E. H. Spicer, New York, 1952.

[12] E. Banfield, *The Moral Basis of a Backward Society,* Glencoe, 1958.

21

Social Revolutions

W HICH SOCIAL REVOLUTIONS and historical situations allow the
most play for envy? The possibilities are four in number:

1. Social revolution, including the pre-revolutionary and post-revolu-
tionary phases, operates upon, and is supported by, the envy-motive.

2. Within a certain group, a sect, minority or group of workers, at
least within a social class, envy can assume considerable proportions
and lead to pronounced, envy-motivated social criticism over a period of
centuries without ever effecting a revolution in the true sense. Here the
appropriate word would be 'resentment,' to which is added, according to
Max Scheler and Nietzsche, the impulse of long-felt impotence.

3. In the case of a socially critical group envy may play a demonstrably important role, although the aim is not actual revolution, but gradual
reform.

4. Envy may play a part in economic political programmes having no
enduring and important structural reforms in view. In the 'equalization
of burdens law' after the Second World War in West Germany, one of the
determining factors was consideration of social envy in the victims. It
was not a question of the alleviation of need, or of compensation paid out
of taxes to which all alike contributed according to their income (as in
other countries that had to compensate war victims), but of direct
equalization between the better-off (the inhabitant who had escaped
damage) and the victim by means of the deliberate burdening of the
former, the fellow citizen whom luck or fate had favoured. But this type
of equalization, even if it goes on for decades, reminding the individual,
or even perhaps his heirs, that once upon a time in history he was more
fortunate than other people, does not represent structural social change
as seen from the perspective of envy. Quite the contrary. The period of

'equalization of burdens' in West Germany was at the same time a phase of economic history in which there was great economic growth, permitting the building up, largely unhampered by social envy, of considerable personal fortunes by people many of whom had started from scratch in 1945, i.e., after the currency reform of June 1948. If, when the equalization of burdens was first being discussed, there were demands for a redistribution of all remaining material assets (natural equalization), the laws passed after the currency reform of June 1948 were in no way concerned with levelling. The compensation received by the beneficiaries of equalization was proportionate to what they had owned before the war. Clearly, then, a policy so radical as to have been inconceivable at an earlier date, and enacted in the name of social justice, need not, in theory, culminate in a state of equality or an ostensibly envyless society of virtual equals. (Only in Finland, by the way, in respect of the population from areas ceded to the Russians, was there anything resembling the West German equalization of burdens.)

From the viewpoint of the man low down in society, or from that of his spokesman, there can never be, on the part of the privileged or more successful, an action that would be universally valid and acceptable to society as a whole seeking to make envy illegitimate. Whoever opposes social envy opposes social advancement, reform, innovation, justice, the redistribution of property, etc. The agitator always appears more just and more reasonable than the man who defends the social balance. No doubt this is due to a particular political and emotional perspective. For, on closer consideration, it is difficult to see exactly why a person who wants to have something that he has not got (or who would, at least, like to see others deprived of it) should be less hedonistic and egoistic than those who simply want assets and values to stay where they are. The case, however, is a special one, if redistribution is a matter of survival for the less well off; if, that is, he cannot obtain by any other method, or even by reasonably postponing the satisfaction of his need, what is necessary for his existence.

Types of revolutionary situation

In his history of German political economy (1874), Wilhelm Roscher dealt more specifically with the envy-motive in revolutions. In every revolution of any significance he discovered socialist emotions and expectations. By 'socialism,' he understands collective property that goes beyond the communal sense already present in the society in question, and which therefore necessitates compulsory measures. In so far as any revolution, by definition, involves a weakening of legitimate authority, there will always be people only too ready to believe that this means anything is permissible. Roscher mentions the manifestations of socialistic feeling, for instance, in England in Wycliffe's time, or in Bohemia during the Hussite wars.[1]

Explicit doubts as to the legitimacy of private property will arise, Roscher says, only if three conditions are simultaneously fulfilled:

1. A direct confrontation of rich and poor, resulting in the envy of desperation.

2. A highly evolved division of labour, promoting the growth of mutual dependence and hence of potential points of friction, thus making it more and more difficult for the less-well-educated man to recognize the connection between performance and reward.

3. Unrealistic demands by the lower classes after the introduction of democratic institutions: the contrast, for example, between theoretical rights and the practical inability to make much use of them. Roscher sees these factors at work in the peasant wars, when the wealth of the Fuggers existed alongside organized bands of beggars.

The lower classes had fallen on bad times through the devaluation of gold and silver. Many people, at the time of the peasant wars, inveighed against the luxury indulged in by some people, and against imported goods. The more foreign trade increased, the greater was the division of labour. These made possible luxury and conspicuous consumption, so arousing the greed of the ordinary man, who further misunderstood many of the reformers' sermons on the equality of all Christians before God, taking them to mean equality in the material sense.

Anti-colonial movements

A similar situation has arisen from time to time since the Second World War in various underdeveloped areas—Asia, Africa and South

---

[1] W. Roscher, *Geschichte der Nationalökonomik in Deutschland,* Munich, 1874, pp. 80 f.

America—where the revolutionaries paradoxically directed the envy of the mob against those institutions and persons which, though they may have given rise to envy, were at the same time a prerequisite for any economic development: export-import merchants, foreign concerns or compatriots in slightly better circumstances as the result of certain services rendered, etc. The French sociologist René Maunier has already stressed the envy-motive, on the one hand in opponents of 'colonialism' and on the other in anti-colonial revolutionary movements. Maunier, as a member of the French Académie des Sciences d'Outre-mer, considered these questions in his great work on the sociology of colonies.[2]

His book relates mainly to Algeria. About thirty years after the first appearance of his work, an account in the *Neue Zürcher Zeitung* of the revolution that had since taken place in Algeria contains an observation which clearly implies the envy-motive:

> If the wealthy foreign society in Algeria collapses, this ought to give a dim feeling of satisfaction, rather than of dissatisfaction, to many classes of Mohammedans—even though it might mean a slight lowering in their standard of living [invariably the real criterion for the envy-motive!] because their former employers will leave the country and close their businesses. Yet they cannot live at a much lower level than before without actually starving. The new employer, in the shape of the state, will, however, be capable—with the help of gifts of American grain, for example—of maintaining, or perhaps here and there of improving, the miserable standard at which the great mass of Algerians would have been living in any case. But the state as new employer will not in all probability be capable of producing the same surpluses and profits out of the country as private enterprise succeeded in doing.[3]

Envy's targets prior to revolution

It is my own impression that, since the Second World War, direct social envy of the middle class has been more in evidence in England than in

[2] R. Maunier, *The Sociology of Colonies. An Introduction to the Study of Race Contact*, 2 vols. (International Library of Sociology), London, 1949. (The first French edition appeared in Paris in 1932.) The passages mentioned in the text will be found on pp. 343–7, Vol. 1, English edition.

[3] 'Algerien im zweiten Jahr seiner Revolution. Der Weg der Zerstörung,' *Neue Zürcher Zeitung*, December 14, 1963.

the United States and West Germany. It is significant that during the fifties a greater number of indignant letters were written to newspaper editors about the middle classes than about the upper classes. A member of the working class would presumably find the middle classes, to which he is closer, more irritating than the remote upper classes. Generally speaking, envious dispositions would seem to select definite targets, such as doctors, executives, bankers or bakers (during the French Revolution, these were businesses and callings concerned with the production and sale of foodstuffs). To be angry about capitalists, the middle classes, etc., a faculty of abstraction is required; people are not always altogether sure what they mean by these terms.

Envy's habit of concentrating on a definite victim regrettably leads the politician, agitator or propagandist almost invariably to seek out and to proscribe a scapegoat—money-changers, Chinese greengrocers, or today Jewish merchants in Negro areas of U.S. cities—even where his object is to direct the discontent of the population elements required for his revolutionary goals against the more prosperous in general.

The actuating images and causes of moral indignation, which in turn nurtures the bitterness leading to revolution, are largely determined by time. An action performed by a small minority seems to many almost a moral justification of the most grisly revolutionary terrorism; but as soon as it is perpetrated by the masses or, more precisely, by those emancipated by the revolution, it is at most languidly relegated to criminal statistics.

Many readers will be acquainted with Dickens's powerful description in which he shows the social tensions preceding the French Revolution in a scene where a French marquis's coach has accidentally run over a working-class child in the streets of Paris. This particular marquis stopped to throw a gold piece to the child's parents—at least somewhat better than the total absence of concern for their victims in today's hit-and-run drivers. Whatever social explosions may occur in the future, one thing is fairly certain: later historians will *not* count among the things that provoked it the arrogant heartlessness with which many motor-vehicle drivers mow down pedestrians. At a time when, in America, any tramp can tear about in a motorized vehicle, a driver who makes off after murdering someone with his car is no longer the material of which social dynamite is fashioned. Other catalysts are needed for public indignation.

Thus the egalitarian viewpoint plays a dual role in preparing a revolution: not only can any form of property or leisure activity be branded as intolerable provocation only so long as it remains in the hands of the few, but misdeeds, malefactions and crimes are socially explosive only until such time as members of all or of several classes have the means with which to commit them. Fox-hunting, which until a few years ago was regarded even in the United States as one of the last preserves of a truly aristocratic upper class, has latterly been taken up in England by horsey miners.[4]

As criminologists have realized, not only are everyday, common crimes largely determined by their culture, which defines as crimes certain forms of behaviour under certain conditions, but those misdeeds or offences against so-called healthy public opinion, exploited for propaganda by every revolution, are equally relative. We do not, by the way, mean the unabashed way in which practically all real revolutions as a matter of course immediately, or almost immediately, adopt and put into practice precisely those despotic measures and infringements of civil rights upon which their accusations against society were based. What we have in mind here are longer periods of time, and also the less obvious phenomenon that not only are revolutionary governments quick to make a virtue out of the faults of their predecessors, but that individuals today, in so far as they do not belong to a single, small class, can also indulge safely, or at minimal risk, in provocation of their fellow men, in perversion of the law and in crime to an extent which in earlier times would have sufficed to unleash a revolution. The regular blackmail of the public, of which some American trade unions are guilty, and which cannot in any sense be ascribed to their members' real needs, is an obvious example of the way in which even economic extortion gradually comes to be seen as normal.

Francis Bacon provides a profound insight, based, no doubt, upon his own observations, into the role of envy in the pre-revolutionary phase; he mentions public envy, which can also be beneficial in that it exercises control over tyrants. Bacon sees public envy as a symptom of discontent:

> It is a disease in a state like to infection. For as infection spreadeth upon that which is sound, and tainteth it; so when envy is gotten once into a state,

---

[4] L. Fellows, 'Miners Assailed for Fox Hunting. Welshmen Ride to Hounds in Sport of Aristocrats,' *New York Times,* October 6, 1963, p. 4.

it traduceth even the best actions thereof, and turneth them into an ill odour. And therefore there is little won by intermingling of plausible actions. For that doth argue but a weakness and fear of envy, which hurteth so much the more, as it is likewise usual in infections; which if you fear them, you call them upon you.

What Bacon has correctly noted in regard to envy's role in the early history of a revolution is this: once discontented elements have directed public suspicion, envy and resentment against unpopular government measures and institutions, little can be done to counter 'the evil eye' by adulterating unpopular measures with popular ones. So long as the holder of power shows fear of envy, that state of mind will spread, and will eventually tear down the last barriers that have held back insurrection.

A number of revolutions have already proved Bacon correct in his view that fear of envy by the government plays a part in unleashing revolution.

Bacon concludes his consideration of public envy with the observation that it is directed chiefly against leading officers and ministers, much less 'upon kings and estates themselves.' There must thus always be a person whose individual actions can be subject to testing and criticism. There is one sure rule, however: if envy of the minister is great, and if the cause he gives for envy is small, or if envy extends to all ministers and officers in a government, the resultant envy, though concealed, will be envy of the state itself. It might be described as total alienation between the state and the spokesmen of envy.[5]

Oswald Spengler on revolution

In his polemical *Hour of Decision,* Oswald Spengler probably devotes more attention to the role of envy in revolution than any other more recent author. The book came out in July 1933 but, as the preface explains, the whole, up to page 160, had been printed before January 30, the date the National Socialists assumed power. In these pages there is the most scathing indictment of the existing envy-motivated revolutionary who stirs up envy; and the words closely fit the men and the

[5] Francis Bacon, *The Essays of Counsels, Civil and Moral,* ed. S. H. Reynolds, Oxford, 1890, pp. 60 f.

classes representative of National Socialism in the narrower sense. Spengler must have realized this; he even writes of the hollow men who conceal their envy behind the façade of patriotism. In the preface, however, he welcomes Hitler's seizure of power of January 30 on the grounds that it will militate against those things he warns against in his writings. Perhaps Spengler, like so many other Germans during the first months of the new régime, genuinely believed that the all-embracing social and national solidarity propagated by the Third Reich would also alleviate those class conflicts that throve on envy.

There is no doubt that many people in 1933 thought of Hitler as the lesser evil, because his programme for German society appeared to assuage the class-conscious envy stirred up by the parties of the left, an envy which, during the last years of the Weimar Republic, and especially since the start of the world-wide economic crisis, had given propertied Germans real cause for fear.

In the last chapter of his *Hitler's Social Revolution* (1966), David Schoenbaum gives striking examples of that specific relief felt by many Germans at the time from their own envy as well as the envy directed against them.

It is significant that, after the seizure of power, National Socialist propaganda very quickly abandoned its class-conscious, egalitarian tone, directing the abundantly available social envy against Jews and the 'colonial powers.'

Spengler's polemic against the engineers of envy is one of un-exampled bitterness and anger. Yet basically he has little to say about envy since the French Revolution, and in particular its consuming presence in socialist democracy, that could not be found in Alexis de Tocqueville, Nietzsche, Max Scheler, Georg Simmel, Ortega y Gasset or Jacob Burckhardt. All that Spengler sees is the envy which certain types of writer unerringly and cynically stir up in unwarped, simple minds. He is no doubt correct in thinking that the artisan of earlier times, conscious of his status and fitting snugly into his own place in his town, felt no envy of the patrician house where he sometimes went on business. So long as it is not tapped by the agitator, envy, as we have seen, is usually confined to people and groups in social proximity. Envy of remote classes or groups has to be demonstrated and inculcated in the general run of people engrossed in everyday affairs.

But Spengler gives no thought to the general role of envy and its prevalence among primitive peoples where no agitator has ever been at work. He is scathingly contemptuous of those priests of all confessions who give free rein to their envy under the cloak of religion. His diagnosis of the sleight-of-hand whereby certain concepts or types of ideal have been raised to infallible gods of envy is sociologically correct: the abstract 'worker,' specifically, may and should be an egoist, but not the peasant, artisan or white-collar worker.[6] This prejudice in favour of certain sections of a population has persisted with remarkable plausibility; in fact, it has long been other groups which have been genuinely handicapped economically.

The role of the envious man in innovation

The role played in revolutions and insurrections by the envy and resentment of individuals under-endowed by nature or society is further examined by H. G. Barnett, who observed these processes as a cultural anthropologist among primitive peoples in non-Western communities.

Resentment (a term he uses almost synonymously with envy) is found in class-structured societies among those people who are dissatisfied with their subordinate position. Barnett stresses, however, that in themselves class differences or class distinctions are not productive of envy; they would not always and everywhere elicit the same reactions, but only in cases where a deliberate attempt was made to induce the victims to compare themselves with more favoured people. Individuals in specially unfavourable personal circumstances—halfbreeds, orphans, illegitimate children, outcasts, and the seventh son of a seventh son—may serve to crystallize the discontent in a larger group or class.

Again, Barnett does not regard sensitiveness or envious reaction to the fact of discrimination as a natural phenomenon. Rather, he sees discrimination as an idea which, like any other idea, will at first seem novel to some people, and he further shows that the socio-political concepts of democracy and communism tend to attain their goals by making people aware of real or imaginary discrimination.

In his fundamental work on the process of innovation, as the basis of cultural change, Barnett describes in detail the role of the envious man

[6] O. Spengler, *The Hour of Decision,* Part I, London, 1934, pp. 121–2.

in the adoption of an innovation. No society really offers complete equality of opportunity. Basically, there can only be coveted objects and values in a group because these assets are fewer than the individuals who seek to possess them. And the written or unwritten laws of every group proscribe unrestrained competition for the valued objects. Whereas most people will accept their lot, there will always be some who feel resentment. These are described by Barnett:

> Unlike the indifferent individual, they are the have-nots instead of the care-nots. They are negativistic toward their roles but enamored of those of more favored individuals. They are envious and resentful of those who enjoy the things which they cannot. They are not resigned to their fate; and by contrast with the complacent individuals whom they envy, they are markedly receptive to the suggestion of a change which will at least equalize opportunities or, perhaps even better, put them on top and their smug superiors on the bottom.[7]

The envious man generally has less to lose than the satisfied one. He can advocate risky changes. Thus, basing oneself on Barnett, one might say that in so far as no cultural tradition is able to satisfy everybody equally and simultaneously, and in so far as in every group there are always a few people whose envy is above average, every society will always contain a few potential rebels through whom an innovation will be possible. It is quite conceivable that from a long-term point of view a society might benefit from innovations initially introduced as a result of resentment among some of its members. In other words, the man whose envious defiance leads him to reject the social controls opposed to innovation, and forces him into the role of a peripheral member, may, under certain circumstances, introduce innovations that last long enough to be adopted and end up by promoting the very society and élite which he was seeking to harm. For instance, the man in question may be a discontented, disregarded member of a primitive tribe who makes a show of being the first to be inoculated or treated by a Western doctor, in order to put his own medicine man's nose out of joint. But his 'courage,' and the success of the treatment, induce other members of the tribe to

[7] H. G. Barnett, *Innovations. The Basis of Cultural Change*, New York, 1953, pp. 400 ff.

follow his example, so that by degrees scientific medical care can be introduced. Thus, in this particular case (and disregarding certain side-effects), the envious man 'who always sought to do harm' had achieved something beneficial for his group.

It is possible to conceive similar cases in which perhaps an industry, a hospital or a district stagnates economically because its leading figures adhere to tradition and, being satisfied with the existing power structure, are averse to all innovation. Only one of the less successful, less influential employers or executives, motivated largely by resentment against the others, will risk any really original innovation, since he has, in effect, very little to lose by it. Against his expectations, however, this turns out to be so successful that his example leads to a general easing of tradition and to innovation throughout the concern or the region.

Cultural contacts

A special form of revolution results from cultural contacts. Whenever a primitive, or relatively primitive, culture has come into contact with that of Europe or America, the majority of those natives who have transferred their allegiance to the representatives of the West has consisted in those people who, for one reason or another, were unable to participate fully in their own culture. Barnett mentions two Indian tribes, the Yurok and the Tsimshian, according to whose traditions social and political position was entirely dependent on inherited privilege, those born without it having very little prospect of attaining rank or renown. Now, these were the very people who would be the first to throw off tradition and to adopt the customs and faith of the white man.[8]

Before the Second World War, Barnett relates, he himself was told by members of the Yurok tribe who still adhered to tradition that they blamed the difficulties of their position explicitly on both the white man *and* on the lower-class members of the tribe, because the latter had, from the first, aped the white man's culture. In the same way, studies of caste societies have shown that the somewhat subordinate (but not the very lowest) castes are quicker to show sympathy for the alien culture.

This would seem to suggest that Christian concepts and political

[8] Op. cit., p. 404.

democracy's ideas about the equality of man should be held responsible for arousing rebellious, envious feelings in the less favoured, particularly where these concepts, within the framework of a cultural contact, are introduced into a rigidly stratified society. Barnett rightly points out, however, that the typical process of aristocratic rejection and popular acclaim of foreign innovations is a universal phenomenon, quite irrespective of the moral, political or religious principles of the newcomers. Thus, during the Second World War, when the Japanese occupied the Palau Islands, they made no attempt to implant in the very class-conscious islanders the idea of human equality which, indeed, Japanese teaching and practice both denied; Palau children were taught that they belonged to a biologically inferior race. Nor could the Japanese have any objection to the local hierarchy, based on family and age, which corresponded to their own. But, as American researchers under Barnett were to discover after the islands had been recaptured, the results of the Japanese occupation were the same as everywhere else: only families of traditionally high rank retained their original forms of cultures and their customs.[9]

Barnett cites two examples from missionary history; one is of the influence gained by Mormons among the New Zealand Maori, where the Western preachers obtained access to the primitive culture through chiefs who had been unsuccessful in the internal struggle for power. Barnett sums this up in one sentence:

'Envious men innovate to compensate for their physical, economic or other handicaps; and other envious men who are struggling under the same handicaps, find their solutions appropriate and appealing; certainly more so than do their complacent rivals.'[10]

Yet it should be asked whether Barnett's expression 'envious men'— to whom he attributes so considerable a role in innovation—does not rather mean persons who, whatever their motives, are cold and distant in regard to their own culture, their tradition and the power élite of their own group. It is true that a faint sense of envy may lead to a decision, in the sense of '*Now* we shall see!' or '*I'll* show them!' and hence may represent a creative motive in the civilizing process. But it might be

---

[9] Op. cit., p. 406.
[10] Op. cit., p. 403.

better to adhere to the exact definition of terms set out in this book: the man who is really envious, the pure type of envious man, is usually much too absorbed by hatred and self-pity to be capable of, or open to, compensatory, constructive innovation which, were it successful, would eliminate the cause for his envy. The envious man may wish to promote certain forms of innovation, such as new taxation, a revolution or restriction of the free market, which would harm, destroy, impoverish and cramp those he envies, but only very seldom, and then almost against his will, will he, as an envious man, carry out any constructive innovation.

Yet there may be a task for envy which will be meaningful in the sense of a society's quality; for if, in the absence of social controls, no tradition were possible, so that any innovation, however frivolous and slapdash, could be realized, no stable culture could arise. And again, envy of those who profit by an inefficient system can also act as an incentive to the envious, who may then actually succeed in introducing a new and better system. It depends entirely upon the nature of the revolutionaries. The American colonists were angry and felt something like indignant envy, on seeing how men in far-away England were benefiting from the tax on their own achievement. This kind of envy-indignation need not be destructive.

Envy in the French Revolution

G. Rudé has made a careful study of the motives by which the actual mob, the *menu peuple,* were impelled during the French Revolution as compared with the outraged bourgeoisie. Their discontent was, in fact, always and literally concerned with their daily bread. We can hardly call it envy if, out of hunger, someone hits out blindly, or attaches himself to a revolution he does not really understand. His revolutionary impulse would immediately die down were it possible to provide and distribute food, or sell it at economical prices. Rudé suggests, for instance, that we might very well sympathize with the Parisian workers and their readiness to help the bourgeoisie in destroying the Ancien Régime if, after reading C.-E. Labrousse's studies, we visualized the daily life of the lowest classes.

A chronic grain shortage reached its climax during the years

1787–89. In August 1788, a Parisian building worker would have had to spend 50 per cent of his income to get enough bread, and in the period from February to July 1789, more than 80 per cent. In contemporary documents on the insurrections of 1778 and the first years of the Revolution, Rudé found that a constant cause for complaint was the shortage or the high price of bread. He gives details which show how, often month by month, or week by week, certain social uprisings in Paris, and the intervals between them, coincided with the rise and fall in the price of bread.[11]

It was only gradually that unrest arising from these shortages led to a more purposive motivation, of which the term 'envy' might be used. With the help of the radical *Hébertistes,* and even more with that of the *enragés,* the Parisian *sans-culottes* evolved a programme of social demands. Their rage now turned against the grocers, whereas previously its object had been the bakers and millers. The revolutionary mob tried, for instance, to compel the grocers to sell their wares at pre-Revolution prices. Rudé sums up the results of his research in the following passage:

> The inescapable conclusion remains that the primary and most constant motive impelling revolutionary crowds during this period was the concern for the provision of cheap and plentiful food. This, more than any other factor, was the raw material out of which the popular Revolution was forged. It alone accounts for the continuity of the social ferment that was such a marked feature of the capital in these years and out of which the great political *journées* themselves developed. Even more it accounts for the occasional outbreaks of independent activity by the *menu peuple,* going beyond, or running counter to, the interests of their *bourgeois* allies. . . . Yet without the impact of political ideas, mainly derived from their *bourgeois* leaders, such movements would have remained strangely purposeless and barren of result.[12]

Unlike some other writers, Rudé also believes that the *sans-culottes* could have absorbed the more abstract theories. Only thus can the depth and extent of the Revolution be explained.

[11] G. Rudé, *The Crowd in the French Revolution,* Oxford and New York, 1959, pp. 201 f., 202 ff.

[12] Op. cit., pp. 208 f.

We are given similar insights into the primary motives of mostly South European, urban rioters in a study by E. J. Hobsbawm, who exchanged observations with G. Rudé during the course of his work.

Primitive rebels and social bandits

Hobsbawm attempts to portray from primary sources the thoughts and feelings, the targets and methods, of socially minded bandits and other primitive rebels in the nineteenth and twentieth centuries, in whom he recognizes archaic forms of social movements. He is mainly concerned with western and southern Europe, especially Italy, since the French Revolution.

On the general question of the role of envy in revolutionary processes, I consider the following to be among his most instructive observations. Both before and after the French Revolution, the *menu peuple,* the populace, the small craftsmen, manual workers and those who eked out a meagre existence as day-labourers in a major European city, particularly when this was the seat of supreme political or ecclesiastic authority, periodically resorted to rioting, in order to extort from the upper classes or from the court those privileges, commissions, cheap provisions, etc. to which they had become accustomed.[13] Basically it is in the interests of all, both upper classes and masses, that a balance should be maintained in the city. The revolts are accepted, even expected, as though they were natural phenomena. Everyone knows what must be done. The social system is not destroyed; indeed, the rebels would have no idea of what structural alterations they should demand.[14]

Even long after the French Revolution these insurrections, as the author demonstrates, lacked all egalitarian impulse.[15] More was wanted from the wealthier circles and classes, but not their demise; nor did anyone want to join them.[16] To the little man in the city, unlike the peasants, or small-holder, the attainment of equality is not really con-

---

[13] E. J. Hobsbawm, *Social Bandits and Primitive Rebels. Studies in Archaic Forms of Social Movement in the 19th and 20th Centuries,* Glencoe (Ill.), 1959, pp. 114 f.

[14] Op. cit., p. 121.

[15] Op. cit., p. 122.

[16] Op. cit., pp. 116, 118.

ceivable. What irritates or angers him—the luxury, perhaps, of the urban upper class—cannot simply be shared out. A fine carriage, a palace, expensive clothing and an entourage of servants are property that can be destroyed but not shared. Their destruction would rarely be in his own interests, since the extravagance they represent means work for him. Hence what he seeks from the upper classes is, basically, a ransom. By contrast with the primitive urban rebels, however, rural areas have known, for centuries before the French Revolution, social movements, insurrections and incipient revolutions with a markedly egalitarian character: everyone must be equal. Anyone who lives off the soil and the cattle in the field, anyone, that is, who has only a small parcel of land and one or two beasts, or anyone who works on a farm as a day-labourer, will not find it difficult to imagine a redistribution of these things. For this reason many pragmatic communists, like Stalin, have spoken contemptuously of the egalitarianism of the peasant mentality. For, after all, it would scarcely be convenient for the communist leader of an industrial society if his followers were literally to demand their visible share of the means of production. Such a solution to social claims can be provided only by private enterprise, whose shares can be distributed as desired.

When the urban populace breaks out, however, as Hobsbawm shows, it is guided, in many cases very accurately, by envy: it destroys what belongs to the rich, especially things that are of no use to it. But this momentary destructive rage does not, unless abetted by an egalitarian-minded bourgeois intellectual class, give rise to a programme from which a successful revolution might develop.

Hobsbawm discusses in detail the social banditry in Ivan Olbracht's Czech novel about the bandit Nikola Shuhaj. The bandit is helpless when confronted by the modern world, which he cannot understand and can only attack. He would like to destroy it, as Olbracht says, 'to avenge injustice, to hammer the lords, to take from them the wealth they have robbed and with fire and sword to destroy all that cannot serve the common good for joy, for vengeance, as a warning for future ages—and perhaps for fear of them.'[17]

This is not only a nihilistic outburst of anger but 'a futile attempt to eliminate all that would prevent the construction of a simple, stable,

[17] Op. cit., p. 25.

peasant community: the products of luxury, the great enemy of justice and fair dealing.'[18]

To anarchistic peasants and the bandits who emerged from their ranks it might well seem, in the chiliastic sense, that, after the destruction of the rich and their property, a simple, good life of equality could be expected.[19] The poor of the big cities could not share such ideas. For their existence depended on somebody's administering the town and keeping their economy going. For this reason Hobsbawm has been unable to discover, even within the last two hundred years, a single chiliastic city mob. The utopia of a new and perfect world was something the *menu peuple* in the city found uncommonly difficult to imagine.[20]

Envy as a decimating factor in the developing countries

The victims claimed by a revolution or a civil war are incomparably more numerous among those who are more gifted and enterprising, but the proportion will fluctuate according to the level of cultural development. When a society has achieved really widespread and evenly distributed division of labour it is easier for many of the more gifted to remain out of sight; also, in such a society not everyone who gives evidence of education and some personal success becomes automatically suspect to the revolutionary tribunal. Thus, even supposing a European country, A, whether in 1950 or today, experiences a revolution in which 10 per cent of the population is destroyed, it is very improbable that this 10 per cent will comprise 95 per cent of the intellectually more keen. But if, by comparison, a territory in Africa that has recently become 'independent' undergoes a period of pseudo-revolutionary terror directed almost exclusively against the 'better people' among the population, it is to be feared that a disproportionately large number of the more gifted and hard-working people will lose their lives. They are much easier to identify. The process is aggravated if, as in Nigeria, ethnically or religiously distinct groups have reached different levels of efficiency.

The above consideration may be thus applied: many of the so-called developing countries have, since 1945, entered a phase of permanent

[18] Op. cit., p. 26.
[19] Op. cit., p. 187.
[20] Op. cit., p. 122.

revolution. But because the most reliable and talented individuals among the population still, for the most part, live in small settlements so that each of them is very conspicuous, it follows that they will form a disproportionate number of the revolution's victims. In this way these areas have entered upon long-term development entailing a 'negative selection' of those who might eventually have been responsible for economic and educational development. According to the reports before us, the rebels first massacre those who are 'better' than themselves, which may often mean nothing more than two years' attendance at a mission school or the possession of a sewing-machine or of a bicycle. In the *New York Times* of October 4, 1964, we read:

> Medara Aka, 23 years old, was considered a Congolese 'intellectual' by virtue of a year at the University of Oregon. He had taken a teacher-training course on an American scholarship, gone back to Léopoldville to teach English in a secondary school and three weeks ago returned here to see his family. The next day the rebels took Lusaka. Mr. Aka was immediately singled out. 'You're an intellectual, aren't you?' asked the rebel leader. 'You have even been to America, our greatest enemy. You are too smart. You are an enemy of the revolution.' With that, the young man was taken to the town square and beheaded.
>
> His death is but one of thousands of examples of the rebel army's deliberate liquidation of anyone with more than a rudimentary education.
>
> With rebel units of the Stanleyville Congolese People's Republic now in control of roughly a fifth of the Congo, this liquidation has reached staggering dimensions.
>
> No one knows how many 'intellectuals' have been slain. Congolese with some degree of higher education are still few in the Congo. Under Belgian rule, the Congo's educational pyramid was broadly based but reached a peak at the secondary level. Few Congolese at the time of independence held posts higher than a clerk.
>
> Now, in the northern and eastern provinces of the Congo, where the rebels hold sway, even the clerks have been wiped out.
>
> 'Here in Moyen Province,' said a Catholic missionary in Lusaka today, 'there is hardly a Congolese alive with more than a primary education.' He added: 'This means, quite simply, that this part of the Congo has been set back thirty years.'[21]

---

[21] B. L. Garrison, 'Congo Rebels Kill "Intellectuals" as Enemies of Their Revolution,' *New York Times,* October 4, 1964, p. 4.

There is also a report about the systematic decimation, by the dictator's strong-arm police, of the relatively successful middle class in Haiti today. The massacres in Indonesia in 1966, this time of communists, with one hundred thousand victims, also involved the death of many who had in some way provoked the envy of their fellow villagers—by starting up a taxi service, for instance. According to the available reports, this Indonesian 'blood-letting' killed off not only communists but more particularly those who were 'unequal.'

Our thesis that it is the most talented in the developing countries who are exterminated is borne out by what has happened in Nigeria since 1962, where the Ibo, more intelligent and more adaptable to modern requirements, are being systematically persecuted and killed by the other tribes, who feel themselves to be inferior.

Whereas in many rebels, blood lust against the 'leading' members of the community may simply derive from primitive envy-hate, there is also the possibility that such massacres are based on the calculations of specialists trained in these 'revolutions.'

Widely different ideas and concepts, and their concomitant emotive states, will serve, either singly or together, for a polity's social and political basis. To integrate human beings there are concepts such as progress, solidarity, honour, renown, love, transcendental ideas, the concept of an historical mission, and even outward-directed hatred, or feelings of inferiority fed by envy, in regard to other groups. But there is one state that no society can live in for any length of time, accepting it as official doctrine, and that is mutual envy. It is, of course, possible to use it as a rallying-point in order to prepare for, and successfully carry through, a class revolution, but no sooner has this been achieved than the envy must be deflected onto a few scapegoats within the society which are regarded, perhaps wrongly, as expendable—or, better still, deflected onto groups and symbols of prosperity situated outside the nation.

22

A Theory of Envy in
Human Existence

THERE ARE SOME three thousand known and distinct cultures, varying from small tribes to complex civilizations. The social consequences of the emotions of envy and fear of envy are not found in anything approaching equal measure in the various cultures; neither can a straight line of development be traced leading inevitably from more envious up to less envious cultures. To keep a society going, and to ensure that essential social processes take place, only a minimum of envy in that society's members is requisite. Envy in excess of that minimum is a surplus which can, as often as not, be 'digested' by the social system, but it will certainly do more harm than good in so far as the potential development and standard of living of the society are concerned.

There can be little doubt as to the economically inhibiting effect of the envy-motive: there is an envy-barrier in the backward cultures of the so-called developing countries today, but special consideration of other people's envy is found in poor cultures as well as rich. The frequency, direction and intensity of mutual envy in a society, or the consideration taken of the envious man in the cultural ethos, bears very little relation, as is plainly demonstrable, to the actual state of inequality, the wealth of poverty of the individual. The differentiation in performances and the level at which a culture admits (or rewards) socially relevant actions resulting in an improved standard of living for the majority, are dependent on those gaps which, so important organizationally, economically, politically and technically, sometimes perhaps by chance, occur in envy's net.

When it succeeds in establishing itself (and this includes sadistic social controls or subversive secret societies) envy, or the envious man, endangers any group and any society. By definition, envy threatens every individual who can never be sure that, somewhere, an envious man is not waiting for an opportunity to avenge the fact that the other is doing better than himself. Even in the rural districts of industrial countries this fear lingers on. In Bavaria and Austria old peasants still mix 'envy herb' with fodder to protect the cattle against *Verneiden,* a term that corresponds to 'envious sorcery' among primitive peoples. In the Gmünd district of Carinthia, a beast that will not eat is said to have got 'envy.' The following spell is put on its disease: 'Turn, envy,/chafe thyself, envy,/out with thee, envy.'[1]

In their understandable and necessary concern about envy, nearly all its observers and critics have overlooked the indispensable function and universal role it alone can play in social life. And even those authors who, in about 1930, studied envy and recognized that it had a certain positive function—Svend Ranulf and Eugéne Raiga—failed to draw upon any series of observations of primitive peoples' simple societies. They regarded envy as little more than an occasionally desirable corrective for extreme luxury, irritating unsocial attitudes, etc. They hardly recognized how little the emotion of envy is dependent on the absolute extent of inequality between people, the degree of 'luxury' and so on, and that it is, indeed, wholly independent of it. Envy plays a negligible part where it is a question of restraining a prince, a head of state or a tycoon from absurd expenditure, but it plays an important part when one among almost equals has got out of step.

There are *two* contrasting social processes in which the envious man plays a considerable role: inhibiting processes, which serve tradition by thwarting innovation, and the destructive processes of revolution. The ostensible contradiction disappears as soon as it is realized that in both cases envy is the motive for the same action: the sarcasm, sabotage and menacing *Schadenfreude* towards anyone who seeks to introduce some-

---

[1] Heinrich Marzell, 'Neidkräuter,' *Bayerisches Jahrbuch für Volkskunde,* ed. J. M. Ritz, Regensburg, 1953, pp. 78 ff. Cf. also Robert Mielke, 'Neidinschriften und Neidsymbole im Niederdeutschen,' *Niederdeutsche Zeitschrift,* Vol. 10, 1932, pp. 178 ff. The 'intimate connection' between the superstition of the evil eye and envy is well attested by the vast collection of material made by S. Seligmann, *Der böse Blick und Verwandtes, Ein Beitrag zur Geschichte des Aberglaubens aller Zeiten und Völker,* Berlin, 2 vols., 1910, esp. pp. 41–3 in Vol. I and 417, 420 in Vol. II.

thing new, and the gloating, spiteful envy with which revolutionaries seek to tear down the existing order and its symbols of success.

Anyone who inveighs against innovation in the name of tradition because he is unable to tolerate the individual success of the innovator, or anyone who rages, in the name of the downfall of all tradition, against its upholders and representatives, is likely to be impelled by an identical, basic motive. Both are enraged at another's having, knowing, believing, valuing, possessing, or being able to do, something which they themselves do not have, and could not imagine having.

In cultural history, the envious constitute a double threat to the works of man: in the first case, a jealous tradition endeavours to fend off any new creation. Should the latter succeed, however, and become a powerful institution, its beneficiaries may well arouse the envy of a younger or subordinate class. Thus private enterprise was at first compelled to defend itself against and evade princely envy until, once successful, it became the target of every unprincely critic: though, indeed, aristocratic envy of later private enterprise and its owners in the nineteenth century was not infrequently the ally of the early socialists.[2]

This poses a crucial question: Should man's capacity to envy be regarded as an entirely negative impulse, capable only of inhibiting or suppressing innovation and more advanced economic and technological development? Are the opponents of envy, who succeed in domesticating it within the framework of a culture, the only institutions and forces that promote culture? Or does a positive role in cultural change and the progress of civilization devolve indirectly upon envy as such?

Power domesticated by envy

Envy is a drive and a mental attitude so inevitable, and so deeply rooted in man's biological and existential situation, that no scientific consideration of this phenomenon ought to start from the postulate that its consequences in the process of social change and the differentiation of social forms were exclusively negative. May it not rather be supposed

---

[2] There are various examples of this in *Capitalism and the Historians*, with contributions by T. S. Ashton, L. M. Hacker, W. H. Hutt and B. de Jouvenel, ed. F. A. Hayek, Chicago, 1954.

that certain social controls, dependent in part on the capacity to envy, are not only necessary to maintain the *status quo* of a society, but are also sometimes essential to the processes of development? Envy is not just a constant threat to property; it also motivates the countless unofficial watchdogs of property who, simply because they begrudge the swindler, the thief and the robber their loot, assume unasked the function of police. It was Svend Ranulf's achievement to have demonstrated this 'disinterested tendency to punishment' in the Athens of antiquity.[3]

It might almost be regarded as fortunate that envy also extends to the values held by asocial, criminal and semi-criminal elements. In the case of the notorious gangs during the thirties in the United States, the crime squad was occasionally enabled to get hold of the leaders through the jealousy of an accomplice who had himself failed to make the newspaper headlines. In other words, the pre-eminence or predominance of any one group in a society is potentially limited by the mutual envy among members of that group, or by their envy of the leader. This also applies to the absolute tyrant.

In so far as the ubiquity of envy runs counter to the unlimited monopoly of power, and hence will often lead to its dispersal, and in so far as it is only through the domestication of power that most creative innovations, and, indeed, humanity, become possible, envy cannot be regarded as a purely negative phenomenon.

Envy, however, plays a more direct part in innovation. As has been shown by Max Scheler and H. G. Barnett, it is above all the resentful man who welcomes innovation. The defiant 'Now I'll show them' attitude has productive results as well as destructive ones. A distinction must, however, be made. All who have written about it describe pure envy as an exclusively negative, destructive, value-denying and value-depreciating attitude. Only when a man realizes the futility of brooding on invidious comparisons between his own lot and that of others, when a person realizes that the torment of envy is ineluctable because it will never lack stimuli and, out of that realization, is able to turn his feeling of envy into an agonistic impulse, endeavouring to 'outdo' the others by his

[3] His principal works are: *The Jealousy of the Gods and Criminal Law at Athens. A Contribution to the Sociology of Moral Indignation*, 2 vols., London and Copenhagen, 1933, 1934.—*Moral Indignation and Middle-Class Psychology. A Sociological Study*, Copenhagen and New York, 1938.

achievements, will he attain, by intent though motivated by envy, a fundamentally new plane of value-enhancing, competitive behaviour.

Contrary to the superficial view, the way out of envy is not the way of asceticism, or ostentatious abstinence, of the monastery or of solitude. All such activities and states of mind—should they derive from envy— remain bound up with the envious intention: by the emphasis on poverty the pleasures of the rich are turned to gall; yet others are to be tormented with feelings of guilt because of their comfortable circumstances. Whether this will make the envious man happy is questionable. The only activity that liberates from envy is that which fills us with new, different impulses, feelings and thoughts which, to be of help, have to be value-asserting, dynamic and forward-looking. To many, the desire to overcome their envy may have been a genuine incentive for positive achievement, and hence have led to satisfaction in a sense of achievement.

It is true that in all cultures envy-avoidance behaviour is the norm, but in a great variety of cultures there may also be cases of individuals who deliberately aim at or achieve something in order to evoke in their critics, rivals or relatives the impotent rage of envy. In such a case, the provocation of envy in others is a means of revenge or punishment. Unlike most other actions and methods that may be used in revenge or punishment, the provocation of a tormenting sense of envy in his rival is not a negative or destructive act so far as its instigator is concerned, for he cannot as a rule cause envy in the other unless he himself achieves a particular object, proving himself the *better* rider, fisherman, hunter, fighter, lover or writer. We are here not concerned with spurious attempts, whose falsity is apparent to the envious man, and which are therefore bound to fail; a case in point is that of the proverbial American who gets into debt so as to outdo his neighbour in conspicuous consumption.

The limits of envy

The ubiquity of the envious man, who should not be mistaken for the thief, poses the following question: How is it possible that property and circumstances of life should vary to the degree that we observe them to do? Why is it that the envious have so rarely succeeded, and then only transitorily—as in a revolution or an ephemeral sect—in shaping the world according to their own standards? A comparison might be the sexual drive, whose ubiquity and intensity have never made promiscuity the norm. No society permits totally uninhibited promiscuity. In every culture there are definite rights of ownership in the sexual sphere, for no society could function unless it had foreseeable and predictable restrictive rules as regards selection of the sexual partner.

Envy-inhibitions rooted in culture may be similarly understood. Envy is a passion so exclusively oriented towards human relations, and is, indeed, so negative, that no group or society could function without first having managed to outlaw envy to some extent and—in so far as it is extant—to deflect it to values which are not crucial for the survival of the society.

The domination of envy as an institution and the tyranny of the envious as separate individuals are further restricted in every society in that it is emotionally impossible for most people to live with a picture of the world as prescribed by envy. The word 'hope' is an indication of this. The envious man is convinced that it is always other people who are lucky, 'they get all the breaks,' and he alone is unlucky. Yet it is hardly possible, even physiologically, to live for very long with this exclusive expectation of the future. More succinctly, the extremely envious man does not live long. In the course of phylogenesis there must have been fewer chances of survival, and hence of shaping behaviour patterns, for those people who were most intensely envious.

Anyone who does not succeed in concealing his envy from his fellow tribesmen is nearly always suspected of sorcery and is often eliminated. Unlike some social philosophies since the end of the eighteenth century, human societies have never recognized envy as a positive value but have only, and that precisely because the envious man was regarded as malicious, evolved specific or general envy-avoidance behaviour. The extremely envious man always belonged to a minority. It is only in Marxism, the abstract and glorified concept of the proletariat, the disinherited and exploited, that a position of implacable envy is fully legitimized. And even this is possible only because of the implied promise that, from the revolution for which it was necessary to mobilize the envy of the masses, there will arise a classless paradise of equality devoid of envy. It would be absurd to seek to proclaim envy as a permanent institution over and above that which, without official sanction, it has already assumed in every society.

The cultural ethos, those temporal and supernatural conceptions that rule everyday life, are generally supported by views which oppose the excesses of the envious. That which man, during the past millennia, has succeeded in making of himself and his environment, is in itself sufficient evidence of his intense need to envisage a world of possibilities understood in the personal sense. An existence in which I can see a number of possibilities for myself will leave little room for the principle of envy.

From the fact of continual conflict between sorcerers and their victims, to which ethnological literature overwhelmingly testifies, it is clear that, almost always and everywhere, there must be people who, even in confrontation with a world full of the dangerously envious, insist upon their personal idea of the future and upon a betterment of their environment. The first and only owner of a sewing-machine or bicycle in an African village knows what awaits him, but nevertheless still risks the 'step forward.'

The path of inequality, however, is less rugged for the man living in a community whose culture has evolved conceptions, such as varying degrees of luck, which can assuage his own conscience and disarm the envious. A doctrine, highly successful in the suppression of envy, is that of predestination taught by Calvinism.

Pressure of envy as a civilizing factor

Escape from the next man's envy can often be favourable to civilization. The importance of cultural diffusion in the development of mankind's more complex skills and attainments is well known. Inventions, innovations, the creation of new concepts and new procedures may initially be confined to a single family in one locality. New ideas and methods are more likely to be conveyed to, and reproduced by, other population groups and tribes if the innovator meets with prejudice in his own country.

Proverbial wisdom has long known that no man is a prophet in his own country. While there are, of course, examples of people's unwillingness to accept lessons and help from strangers, such unwillingness is even more apparent, as a general rule, in those to whom an innovation, which they were not the first to discover, is proposed by a neighbour or relative, a person, that is, known to them long before the discovery of the innovation.

The reason is not far to seek. If my fellow villager, schoolmate or work mate suddenly comes up with an invention, a discovery or some new process whose objective value and quality are undeniable, this will excite my envy much more than if a stranger does the same thing; for in that case I can console myself with the thought that he has previously had certain opportunities, experienced certain influences and enjoyed possibilities of learning and observation which were denied me. His superiority is neither so crushing nor so much of a reproach as that of the successful innovator from my own circle, which forces me to ask: 'Why didn't I think of it myself? What had he learned and seen that I didn't learn and see as well?'

If an innovation is to contribute to culture and civilization, there must be an opportunity for migration and an incentive for horizontal mobility. Hence, as has been pointed out, the early development of science, technology and modern economic practice in those areas where inland waterways (a good system of rivers) or a long, indented coastline permitted easy travel at a time when there was no suitable overland transport. Innovators, inventors and resourceful men would in any case have travelled far afield out of mere love of adventure and desire for gain; but it is not difficult to imagine that the incentive to leave home (in the narrower sense) was the hostility, mockery and mistrust to which the creative man is most exposed where he has been longest known.

Thus the universal factor of envious reprisal against the man who makes himself unequal by introducing an innovation (in whatever sphere) is desirable in so far as it promotes the overall development of cultural achievements and hence mastery of the environment.

Of envy's function, it may therefore generally be said that it not only makes possible social controls upon which human societies depend but also, by way of emigration, has far-reaching consequences in promoting civilization. Only at the cost, however, of the innovator's native locality. Up to a point, these consequences may be self-compensatory, so that the overall effect on a civilization—or on a certain trade—will be the same: where, for instance, an inventor is driven out of town A by the hostility of the inhabitants, and arrives in B, where he is successful, while another inventor takes the opposite course, from B to A. In such instances, even if they were multiplied indefinitely, the rate of growth of innovations in a country or a continent would be roughly the same as it would were the factor of envy entirely absent. Yet there will be certain places, more especially large cities, offering favourable conditions to the inventor who has left home in disgust: more often than not, inventive men will gather in a few places, with results favourable to the general development of skills.

Again, a situation may arise in which talent is driven out of a country by social and economic controls which are basically envy-motivated, to take refuge in a region offering considerably better means for its effective employment.

The meaning of envy in the phylogenesis of man

The following might be a plausible general theory of the meaning of envy in man's phylogenetic development. Social co-existence, and especially any co-operation, requires reasonably efficient social controls. That is to say, instructions, commands and prohibitions must be issued and respected, even if the person from whom they emanate is not physically present. This means that the unsupervised members of the group, impelled by what are often only mildly envious feelings, must keep jealous watch upon each other, lest any deviate from the appointed task: none can be certain that he will not be denounced. The chief who sends several envoys to another tribe is able to count on the loyal execution of their mission because each one of them would be inhibited by the envious anger of his companions from attempting to compromise with the opposite group for his own advantage.

This situation can probably be most easily illustrated by the incest taboo: in the father's absence, none of the sons can afford to take liberties with female members of the family, because he has to reckon with jealous denunciation by at least one of his brothers. The same kind of thing will obtain in a working group of equals: no one will let anyone else idle, since this might mean that he would himself have to make up the other's deficit of work. Thus he would be envious of any work-breaks or skimping on the part of a fellow worker, which he would therefore seek to prevent. In British coal mines, long after nationalization, it was found that work groups of about seven or eight had less absenteeism than groups, say, of seventeen men where absenteeism soared. It is not enough to say, the family-type smaller group is so cosy, so intimate that in it men enjoy working more. Rather, the difference is in fear of the envy of those who showed up for work. If a man of a group of fifteen goes fishing, he can assume that at least one other man will also be absent, thus diverting the shafts of envy from himself. As a member of a group of only seven men, the one considering taking a day off for fun must risk being the only one missing that day, thus all the ugly looks the next day will fasten on to him, and him alone. Such facts of social life, unfortunately, rarely convince management, be it private or public, which prefers to let the kind of technical equipment determine the optimal size of a work team.

It may thus be said that a being who has become largely independent of instinctive activity and biologically determined behaviour can use the opportunities afforded by his new freedom in a socially constructive way only if deviant behaviour and innovations are reduced to a minimum.

Thus the individual scope for action of a being who has outgrown instinct must once again be so restricted as to permit the proper functioning of a larger social group. No motive that we have been able to discover, however, ensures conformity more certainly than fear of arousing envy in others and the sanctions this entails. To the degree, therefore, that man has developed the capacity of mutual control out of suspected envy in the other, larger social groups with division of labour for their members have become socially possible. The exceptionally long, biologically determined period of at least ten years, during which the human character is formed within the framework of a sibling community, has meant that this social consideration of envy has become a constitutive part of the personality.

It may be imagined that those smaller groups and families, whose members *failed* to develop sufficient sensitivity towards the threat of envy in others, fell behind phylogenetically because they were unable in the long run to form themselves in the larger groups necessary for the mastery of their environment.

Hence man, as an envious being and by reason of his capacity to envy, became truly human. There are still some very simple primitive peoples in existence today, organized in groups of an extremely primitive character, which have remained at about this stage. The Siriono Indians offer, perhaps, the clearest example of a group in which, while a man's personal behaviour may be greatly influenced by the others' envy, he is not yet in a position to take the next step forward. The tribe, which A. Holmberg studied twenty-five years ago in Bolivia, consists of hordes of some twenty members. These people, out of fear of the others' envy, seldom eat except when they believe no one is looking: usually alone and at night. This mutual envy, however, has not in their case become a social system of control such as would permit communal action by the group, or by several groups together.[4]

Nor is very much achieved by the formation of enduring larger groups of, say, fifty to five hundred members. Depending on environment, they will, of course, achieve more than autonomous bands of ten to twenty, but if they are to be the nucleus or point of departure for higher cultural structures they must develop and institutionalize another capacity, restricting mutual envy's ubiquitous social control. A differentiated culture, a definite division of labour, a political structure, economic growth and diversity of trades can arise within a group only if individual innovations and disparate gains, acquisitions of wealth, etc., have again become socially possible, at least for a time. A certain amount of inequality on the grounds of unpredictable individual deviations from the group norm must be tolerated. The binding culture of the group— which by now may be termed a society—must therefore attain a state of equilibrium in which sufficient envy is unleashed on the one hand— which also means consideration of envy—to power the social controls necessary to the polity as such, while, on the other, envy of certain individual performances and achievements must be so far suppressed and outlawed as to leave sufficient room for those innovations which are essential if the growing group is to adapt to its environment.

Our second premise is therefore the following: Man, being envious, can become a genuine, culturally creative being only if the envious within the group are to a large extent disarmed by certain concepts, e.g., of a religious nature, or rationalization of the inequality of fortune (the idea of luck), or politically created reservations for those who are unequal.

[4] A. R. Holmberg, *Nomads of the Long Bow: The Siriono of Eastern Bolivia,* Smithsonian Institution. Institute of Social Anthropology Publication No. 10, Washington, 1950.

Most ethical systems and religions under whose aegis there has been cultural, economic, technical and generally civilizing development, have usually fallen in with the requirement, perhaps only through right intuition and conjecture, that envy be suppressed. There is no ethical or religious system that has sanctioned envy as such, even in one individual towards another. But while execrating crude envy, most long-developing normative systems (at least where they have not been distorted for particular political ends) have numerous prohibitions, restrictions and precepts unequivocally opposed to the provocation of envy. And these ready-made sanctions call for a sufficient number of the envious in a society to press for observance of the envy-avoiding forms of behaviour. This explains the apparent paradox whereby, on the one hand, religions keep the envious man within bounds, expressly rewarding in their allegories the one who is able to master his envy, while on the other they demand a kind of social justice tending towards the ideal of equality, which only consideration of the envious can explain.

Capitulation to the envious

Unfortunately for the general understanding of economics, some social philosophies, as also some ideas evolved within the Church since the late eighteenth century and reinforced during the past hundred years or so, have laid their whole emphasis on the satisfaction and assuagement of envy, having, indeed, virtually handed over to it the determining of social norms. This shift of emphasis is attributable, not only to some publicists and politicians who were themselves highly envious and resentful people, but also to very magnanimous, unenvious persons tormented by a sense of social guilt. It is doubtful whether the latter themselves were often aware of this combination of the sense of social guilt and the fear of primeval envy.

The great success, often running wholly counter to reason and convention, of manifestos and social-political or philosophical theories addressed to the envious and against the enviable, is explicable in terms of this phylogenetic root. The appeal could not have been made to any more elemental emotional level in man than this one.

Yet two decisive facts have been overlooked by those who have capitulated. Firstly, the efficient functioning of every larger human group depends no less on restraining envy than upon consideration of the envious man. Secondly, there is no possibility whatever of setting up an enduring human polity in such a way that it will contain neither envious people nor people with a bad social conscience.

The member of a primitive people comes to terms with the malice of his fellow tribesmen, whose envy he incorporates as a definite factor into his picture of the world. He cannot and does not need to believe in the goodness of man. To him, the other is always an envious enemy, and probably all the more so for being closely related. His own inequality, modest though it may seem to us, is no great problem to the primitive man, because the others' envy is an unavoidable fact. Though this may be a cause for fear, it would seem improbable that there could be any question, in primitive peoples, of a man's inequality and other people's envy engendering a bad conscience, in our sense, capable of social and political activations.[5]

Not so the sensitive European and American (Western man) towards the middle of the eighteenth century, who had been gradually losing his nerve in the face of envy in others. A further question might be whether social destratification since the French Revolution has been furthered by a growing fear of envy, or whether the social reshuffle, the demolition of hierarchies whose legitimacy had hitherto gone unquestioned, has increased the fear of being envied. Whatever the cause, during the past two hundred years the need to believe in the goodness of man, independent of the society that spoils him, has become ever more pressing. Yet if we are to believe in the possibility of the absolutely good, benevolent and unenvying man, we must also insist upon the utopia of egalitarianism, the idea of equality progressively understood as an historic mission: under the evil eye of our contemporary and neighbour we seek to create a comforting alibi, if only by committing ourselves, whether ideologically and politically, or merely in naïve and sentimental play-acting, to a future programme promising a society of absolute equals, or in other words a community from which envy has been eliminated because of universal

---

[5] Cf. also J. Clyde Mitchell, 'The Meaning in Misfortune for Urban Africans,' *African Systems of Thought,* International African Institute, London, 1965, pp. 192 ff. This volume contains a number of new studies of the sociology of sorcery. That the sorcerer is regarded primarily as an envious man is shown with particular clarity in *Witchcraft and Sorcery in East Africa,* ed. John Middleton and E. H. Winter, London and New York, 1963, p. 29; and in John Middleton's *Lugbara Religion,* London and New York, 1960, pp. 239 f.

equality. This is impossible, as we have seen, because the ability and need to envy is inherent in man. A society in which no one need fear any one else's envy would not have those social controls necessary to its existence as a society. How little the fact of everyone's being almost equal is able to eliminate mutual envy is surely evident from the simpler cultures. Again, from the viewpoint of developmental psychology the hope of ever attaining a society in which no one would suffer from envy proves unfounded.[6]

Pure envy as the basic concept or supreme norm of a society is just as intolerable and destructive as, for instance, the raising to an absolute of pure sexual jealousy, which would demand a condition of permanent promiscuity. If we disregard precarious experiments, it is on principle socially impossible to legitimize as a central value a mentality and an emotion which proclaim privacy and private property as invalid.

The unalloyed concept of envy and of man as an envious being, from primitive man to the modern city-dweller, is sheer irrationality. It is irreconcilable with the concept of rationality, of rational action, of purposeful ordering of the world if someone—outside of a comprehensible competitive or conflict situation—insists that another shall not have or be something if the same asset is not attainable by himself, even though it may not be worth attaining. It is remarkable that, in the course of several millennia and in various societies, man has gained sufficient control over this basic drive to be able to realize civilizational achievements through the individual process of becoming unequal.

The capacity to envy is a fact. In so far as man is a being who is able to reflect upon his existence, he will inevitably ask: 'Why am I myself and not someone else?' The next question follows naturally: 'Why is the other person's existence so different from my own?' The degree of the questioner's self-estimation will determine which ensues, envy or a sense of guilt. Both may torment the same individual, and one may reinforce the other. In so far as the person experiences himself as an individual, however indistinctly in certain societies, he can never be sure that someone else might not rather be he. There will always be some other he

---

[6] George M. Foster, 'Cultural Responses to Expressions of Envy in Tzintzuntzan,' *Southwestern Journal of Anthropology,* Vol. 21, 1965, pp. 24–35. See also, Humberto Rotondo, 'Percepción de envidia o sentimiento de ser envidiado como mecanismo de defensa,' *Revista de Sociologia,* Universidad Nacional Mayor de San Marcos, Lima, Vol. 3, No. 4, 1966, pp. 90–8.

cannot trust and towards whom he feels a sense of guilt. This is inevitable. It cannot be conjured away by social reforms. The only liberation from this useless and destructive sense of guilt comes from the realization that there is no way of eliminating what causes one to be envied. Envy's culture-inhibiting irrationality in a society is not to be overcome by fine sentiments or altruism, but almost always by a higher level of rationality, by the recognition, for instance, that more (or something different) for the few does not necessarily mean less for the others: this requires a certain capacity for calculation, a grasp of larger contexts, a longer memory; the ability, not just to compare one thing with another, but also to compare very dissimilar values in one man with those in another.

Today we can state on a better empirical basis than would have been possible fifty or a hundred years ago that the world cannot belong to the envious, any more than the causes of envy can be eradicated from society. The society devoid of all traces of class or status, and similar refuges for wits'-end thinking and uncomfortable feelings, should no longer be considered worthy of serious discussion. The sciences concerned with man must come down to earth, incorporating man in the equation as he is and not as they imagine he will be when, for obscure reasons, he has lost that motive force which alone, as we hope we have shown, has enabled him to construct larger social groups and polities characteristic of our species.

Even those who have never taken seriously utopias of classless societies and pure socialism have been seduced in the course of the last hundred years into falsely concluding that the critical role in society is the prerogative of envious dispositions whom a single concession would supposedly placate. Of course there is much social stupidity that can and must be avoided. There is no virtue in rubbing salt into a wound. But historical observation and rules deducible from basic human behaviour would seem to suggest that there is something like a hardening towards exaggerated sensitivity to envy. Francis Bacon had already realized that nothing is more calculated to exasperate the envious man and to feed his discontent than irrational action, an abdication from a superior position with the removal of his envy in view. The time has surely come when we should stop behaving as though the envious man was the main criterion for economic and social policy.

A Selected Bibliography

For complete references to all works and articles drawn upon, compare footnotes.

Bacon, Francis: *The Essays of Counsels, Civil and Moral.* Ed. by S. H. Reynolds. Oxford, 1890.

Banfield, Edward C.: *The Moral Basis of a Backward Society.* Glencoe: The Free Press, 1958.

Barnett, H. G.: *Innovations. The Basis of Cultural Change.* New York: McGraw-Hill Book Company, 1953.

Belshaw, Cyril S.: 'In Search of Wealth. A Study of the Emergence of Commercial Operations in the Melanesian Society of Southeastern Papua.' *American Anthropologist Memoir 80,* February 1955.

Bentham, Jeremy: *Bentham's Economic Writings.* Crit. Ed., by W. Stark. Vol. 1. New York: Burt Franklin, 1952.

Berelson, Bernard, and Steiner, Gary A.: *Human Behavior: An Inventory of Scientific Findings.* New York: Harcourt, Brace & World, 1964.

Berkowitz, Leonard: *Aggression: A Social Psychological Analysis.* New York: McGraw-Hill Book Company, Inc., 1962.

Best, Elsdon: *The Maori.* (Memoirs of the Polynesian Society, Vol. 5.) 2 Vols. Wellington: Tombs, 1924.

Bettelheim, Bruno: *Symbolic Wounds. Puberty Rites and the Envious Male.* Glencoe: The Free Press, 1954.

Bien, Peter: *L. P. Hartley.* Pennsylvania State University Press, 1963; London, 1963.

Bohannan, Laura: 'The Frightened Witch,' in Casagrande, Joseph B., ed.: *In the Company of Man. Twenty Portraits by Anthropologists.* New York: Harper, 1960.

Bohannan, Paul: 'Some Principles of Exchange and Investment Among the Tiv.' *American Anthropologist,* Vol. 57, 1955.

Brachfeld, Oliver: *Inferiority Feelings in the Individual and the Group.* New York: Grune & Stratton, Inc., 1951.

Brandt, Richard B.: *Hopi Ethics. A Theoretical Analysis.* Chicago: University of Chicago Press, 1954.

Buber, Martin: *Paths in Utopia.* (Beacon Press Paperback Edition.) Boston: Beacon Press, 1958.

Buss, Arnold H.: *The Psychology of Aggression.* New York: John Wiley and Sons, Inc., 1961.

429

Buss, Arnold H., et al.: 'The Measurement of Hostility in Clinical Situations.' *Journal of Abnormal and Social Psychology,* Vol. 52, 1956.

Cabaud, Jacques: *Simone Weil. A Fellowship in Love.* New York: Channel Press, 1965.

Cahn, Edmond: *The Sense of Injustice. An Anthropocentric View of Law.* New York: New York University Press, 1949.

Carstairs, G. Morris: *The Twice-Born.* Bloomington: Indiana University Press, 1958.

Clinard, Marshall B., and Wade, Andrew L.: 'Toward the Delineation of Vandalism as a Sub-Type of Juvenile Delinquency.' *The Journal of Criminal Law, Criminology, and Political Science,* Vol. 48, 1958.

Cohen, Albert K.: *Delinquent Boys. The Culture of the Gang.* Glencoe: The Free Press, 1955.

Cohen, Y. A.: 'Four Categories of Interpersonal Relationships in the Family and Community in a Jamaican Village.' *Anthropological Quarterly,* Vol. 28, 1955.

Crosland, Charles Anthony Raven: *The Future of Socialism.* London: Cape, 1956; New York: Macmillan, 1957.

Darin-Drabkin, H.: *The Other Society.* London: Gollancz, 1962; New York: Harcourt, Brace & World, 1962.

Davidson, William L.: 'Envy and Emulation,' in Hastings, James, ed.: *Encyclopedia of Religion and Ethics,* Vol. 5. New York and Edinburgh: Scribner/Clark, 1912.

Davis, Kingsley: *Human Society.* New York: Macmillan, 1948 and 1949.

Devereux, George: *Reality and Dream. Psychotherapy of a Plains Indian.* New York: International Universities Press, 1951.

Dodds, Eric R.: *The Greeks and the Irrational.* Berkeley: University of California Press, 1951.

Donaldson, Dwight M.: *Studies in Muslim Ethics.* London: S.P.C.K., 1953.

Erasmus, Charles J.: *Man Takes Control. Cultural Development and American Aid.* Minneapolis: University of Minnesota Press, 1961.

Evans-Pritchard, E. E.: 'Witchcraft (Mangu) Among the Azande.' *Sudan Notes and Records,* Vol. 12, 1929.

Evans-Pritchard, E. E.: *Witchcraft, Oracles, and Magic Among the Azande.* Oxford: Clarendon Press, 1937.

Evans-Pritchard, E. E.: 'Zande Blood-Brotherhood.' *African,* Vol. 6, 1933.

Firth, Raymond: *Primitive Economics of the New Zealand Maori.* New York: Dutton & Co., 1929.

Firth, Raymond: *Primitive Polynesian Economy.* London: Routledge & Sons, 1939.

Fortune, Ree Franklin: *Sorcerers of Dobu. The Social Anthropology of the Dobu Islanders of the Western Pacific.* New York: Dutton & Co., 1932.

Foster, George M.: 'Interpersonal Relations in Peasant Society.' [With Comments by Julian Pitt-Rivers and Oscar Lewis.] *Human Organization,* Vol. 19, Winter 1960/61.

Frankl, Viktor E.: *From Death-Camp to Existentialism. A Psychiatrist's Path to a New Therapy.* Boston: Beacon Press, 1959. New Edition: *Man's Search for Meaning. An Introduction to Logotherapy.* Boston: Beacon Press, 1962.

Fromm, Erich: *The Heart of Man: Its Genius for Good and Evil.* Ruth N. Anshen, ed. New York: Harper, 1964.

Fromm, Erich: *The Sane Society.* London: Routledge & Kegan Paul, 1956; New York: Holt, 1956.

Fyvel, T. R.: *Troublemakers. Rebellious Youth in an Affluent Society.* New York: Schocken Books, 1961 and 1962.

Galbraith, John Kenneth: *The Affluent Society.* Boston: Houghton Mifflin Company, 1958.

Gibbons, Don C.: *Changing the Lawbreaker.* Englewood Cliffs: Prentice-Hall, 1965.

Gide, André, in Crossman, Richard, ed.: *The God that Failed.* New York: Harper, 1949.

Gillin, John Philipp: *The Culture of Security in San Carlos. A Study of a Guatemalan Community of Indians and Ladinos.* New Orleans: Tulane University of Louisiana, 1951.

Glass, D. V., ed.: *Social Mobility in Britain.* London: Routledge & Kegan Paul, 1954.

Gluckman, Max: 'Lozi Land Tenure' in *Essays on Lozi Land and Royal Property.* (Rhodes-Livingstone Paper No. 10.) Livingstone (Northern Rhodesia): Rhodes-Livingstone Institute, 1943.

Glueck, Sheldon, and Eleanor: *Delinquents in the Making. Paths to Prevention.* New York: Harper & Brothers, 1952.

Granqvist, Hilma Natalia: *Child Problems Among the Arabs. Studies in a Muhammaedan Village in Palestine.* Helsingfors: Södorström, 1950.

Green, Arnold W.: *Sociology.* 4th Edition. New York and London: McGraw-Hill Company, 1964.

Greenacre, Phyllis: *Trauma, Growth, and Personality.* (International Psycho-Analytical Library No. 46.) London: Hogarth Press, 1953.

Gutheil, Emil Arthur: *The Language of the Dream.* New York: Macmillan & Co., 1939.

Hartley, L. P.: *Facial Justice.* London: Hamish Hamilton, 1960.

Haynes, W. W.: *Nationalization in Practice. The British Coal Industry.* London: Bailey Bros. & Swinfen, 1953; Cambridge (Mass.), 1954.

Hobsbawm, Eric John: *Social Bandits and Primitive Rebels. Studies in Archaic Forms of Social Movement in the 19th and 20th Centuries.* Glencoe: The Free Press, 1959.

Holmberg, Allan R.: *Nomads of the Long Bow: The Siriono of Eastern Bolivia.* (Smithsonian Institution. Institute of Social Anthropology. Publication No. 10.) Washington: U.S. Government Printing Office, 1950.

Holmberg, Allan R.: 'The Wells that Failed. An Attempt to Establish a Stable Water Supply in Viru Valley, Peru' in Spicer, Edward H., ed.: *Human Problems in Technological Change. A Casebook.* New York: Russell Sage Foundation, 1952.

Holmes, Oliver Wendell, and Laski, Harold J.: *Holmes-Laski Letters. The Correspondence of Mr. Justice Holmes and Harold J. Laski, 1916–1935.* Mark de Wolfe Howe, ed. 2 vols. Cambridge: Harvard University Press, 1953.

Homans, George Caspar: *Sentiments and Activities.* New York: The Free Press, 1962.

Hsien-chin, Hu: 'The Chinese Concept of "Face."' *American Anthropologist,* Vol. 46, 1944.

Hunter, Monica: *Reaction to Conquest: Effects of Contact with Europeans on the Pondo of South Africa.* London and New York: Oxford University Press, 1936.

Inkeles, Alex: 'Social Stratification and Mobility in the Soviet Union 1940–1950.' *American Sociological Review,* Vol. 15, 1950.

Inkeles, Alex: *Social Change in Soviet Russia.* Cambridge (Mass.), 1968.

Kardiner, Abram: *The Individual and His Society. The Psychodynamics of Primitive Social Organization.* New York: Columbia University Press, 1939.

Karsten, Sigfrid Rafael: *The Head-Hunters of Western Amazonas. The Life and Culture of the Jivaro Indians of Eastern Ecuador and Peru. (Societas Scientiarum Fennica. Commentationes Litterarum,* Vol. VII, No. 1.) Helsingfors: Finska Vetenskaps-Societeten, 1935.

Klein, Melanie: *Envy and Gratitude. A Study of Unconscious Sources.* New York: Basic Books, 1957.

Kluckhohn, Clyde: *Navaho Witchcraft. Papers of the Peabody Museum of American Archeology and Ethnology,* Vol. 22, 1944.

Kluckhohn, Clyde, and Leighton, Dorothea Cross: *The Navaho.* Cambridge: Harvard University Press, 1946.

Koestler, Arthur, in Crossman, Richard, ed.: *The God that Failed.* New York: Harper, 1949; London, 1950.

Koestler, Arthur: *Arrow in the Blue.* New York: Macmillan, 1952; London, 1952.

Krige, E. J., and J. D.: *The Realm of a Rain-Queen. A Study of the Pattern of Lovedu Society.* London and New York: Oxford University Press, 1943.

Lane, Robert E.: 'Problems of a Regulated Economy. The British Experiment,' *Social Research.* Vol. 19, 1952.

Lane, Robert E.: 'The Feat of Equality.' *The American Political Science Quarterly,* Vol. 53, 1959.

Lane, Robert E.: *Political Ideology. Why the American Common Man Believes What He Does.* New York: The Free Press, 1962.

La Piere, Richard T.: *A Theory of Social Control.* New York: McGraw-Hill Book Company, 1954.

Lerner, Abba Ptachya: *The Economics of Control. Principles of Welfare Economics.* New York: Macmillan, 1944.

Lerner, Max: *It Is Later than You Think: The Need for a Militant Democracy.* New York: Viking Press, 1938.

Lewis, Oscar: *Life in a Mexican Village.* Urbana: University of Illinois Press, 1951.

Lewis, Roy, and Maude, Angus: *The English Middle Classes.* London: Phoenix House, 1950.

Lifton, Robert Jay: *Death in Life: Survivors of Hiroshima.* New York: Random House, 1950.

Linton, Ralph: *The Tanala. A Hill Tribe of Madagascar.* (Publications of the Field Museum of Natural History, Anthropological Series, Vol. 22.) Chicago, 1935.

Lorenz, Konrad: *On Aggression.* New York: Harcourt, Brace & World, 1966; London, 1966.

Mallock, William Hurrell: *Social Equality. A Short Study in a Missing Science.* London: Bentley & Sons, 1882.

Marbach, Fritz: *Luxus and Luxussteuer.* Bern 1948.

Mead, Margaret, ed.: *Cooperation and Competition Among Primitive Peoples.* New York and London: McGraw-Hill Book Company, 1937.

Meissner, Boris, ed.: *Sowjetgesellschaft im Wandel. Rußlands Weg zur Industriegesellschaft.* Stuttgart, 1966.

Merton, Robert K., and Barber, Elinor: 'Sociological Ambivalence' in Tiryakian, Edward A., ed.: *Sociological Theory, Values, and Sociocultural Change. Essays in Honor of Pitirim A. Sorokin.* London and New York: The Free Press/Collier-Macmillan, 1963.

Middleton, John: *Lugbara Religion.* London and New York: Oxford University Press, 1960.

Middleton, John, and Winter, E. H., eds.: *Witchcraft and Sorcery in East Africa.* London: Routledge & Kegan Paul, 1963; New York: Praeger, 1963.

Milgram, Stanley: 'Nationality and Conformity.' *Scientific American,* Vol. 205, 1961. Reprinted in O'Brien, Robert William, et al., eds.: *Readings in General Sociology,* 3rd Edition. Boston: Houghton Mifflin, 1964.

Mills, C. Wright: *White Collar. The American Middle Class.* New York: Oxford University Press, 1951.

Milobenski, Ernst: *Der Neid in der griechischen Philosophie.* Wiesbaden: Otto Harrassowitz, 1964.

Mishan, E. J.: 'A Survey of Welfare Economics, 1939–1959,' *The Economic Journal,* Vol. 70, 1960.

Mitchell, J. Clyde: 'The Meaning in Misfortune for Urban Africans' in *African Systems of Thought. Studies Presented and Discussed at the Third International African Seminar in Salisbury, December 1960.* (International African Institute.) London: Oxford University Press, 1965.

Mowat, Ronald Rae: *Morbid Jealousy and Murder. A Psychiatric Study of Morbidly Jealous Murderers at Broadmoor.* London: Tavistock Publications, 1966.

Murdock, George Peter: *Social Structure.* New York: Macmillan, 1949.

Nilsson, Martinus Persson: *Geschichte der griechischen Religion.* Vol. 1, *Bis zur griechischen Weltherrschaft.* (Handbuch der Altertumswissenschaft. W. Otto, ed., 5th Sect., 2nd Part, 1st Vol.). 2nd Edition. Munich, 1955.

Olesha, Yuri: *Envy and Other Works,* New York: Anchor Books, 1967.

Paul, Benjamin D.: 'Symbolic Sibling Rivalry in a Guatemalan Indian Village.' *American Anthropologist,* Vol. 52, 1950.

Pepitone, Albert: *Attraction and Hostility. An Experimental Analysis of Interpersonal and Self-Evaluation.* New York: Prentice-Hall/Atherton Press, 1964.

Piers, Gerhart, and Singer, Milton: *Shame and Guilt. A Psychoanalytical and Cultural Study.* Springfield: Thomas, 1953.

Potter, David: *People of Plenty: Economic Abundance and American Character.* Chicago: University of Chicago Press, 1954.

Raiga, Eugène: *L'Envie.* Paris: Alcan, 1932.

Ranulf, Svend: *The Jealousy of the Gods and Criminal Law at Athens.* 2 vols. London and Copenhagen: Norgate Ltd./Levin & Munksgaard, 1933–34.

Ranulf, Svend: *Moral Indignation and Middle-Class Psychology. A Sociological Study.* Copenhagen: Levin & Munksgaard, 1938; New York: Schocken, 1964.

Reichel-Dolmatoff, Gerardo, and De Reichel, Alicia D.: *The People of Aritama. The Cultural Personality of a Colombian Mestizo Village.* Chicago: University of Chicago Press, 1961.

Richards, Audrey I.: *Land, Labour and Diet in Northern Rhodesia.* London and New York: Oxford University Press, 1939.

Riesman, David: *The Lonely Crowd. A Study of Changing American Character.* London and New Haven: Yale University Press, 1950.

Riesman, David: *Faces in the Crowd. Individual Studies in Character and Politics.* London and New Haven: Yale University Press, 1952.

Rosenthal, Celia S.: 'Social Stratification of the Jewish Community in a Small Polish Town.' *American Journal of Sociology,* Vol. 59, 1953.

Rudé, George: *The Crowd in the French Revolution.* London and New York: Oxford University Press, 1959.

Runciman, W. G.: *Relative Deprivation and Social Justice. A Study of Attitudes to Social Inequality in Twentieth-Century England.* London: Routledge & Kegan Paul, 1966; Berkeley: University of California Press, 1966.

Rüstow, Alexander: *Ortsbestimmung der Gegenwart. Eine universalgeschichtliche Kulturkritik.* Vol. 3, *Herrschaft oder Freiheit?* Erlenbach-Zurich and Stuttgart, 1957.

Scheler, Max: 'Das Ressentiment im Aufbau der Moralen.' (*Gesammelte Werke,* Vol. 3.) 4th Edition. Bern: Francke, 1955.

Scheler, Max: *Ressentiment.* (Lewis A. Coser, ed. and intro.) New York: The Free Press, 1961.

Schmidt, Kurt: *Die Steuerprogression.* (Veröffentlichungen der List-Gesellschaft e.V. Vol. 20) Basel and Tübingen, 1960.

Schoenbaum, David: *Hitler's Social Revolution. Class and Status in Nazi Germany.* Garden City, New York: Doubleday & Company, Inc., 1966.

Scott, John Paul: *Aggression.* Chicago: University of Chicago Press, 1958.

Seidenberg, Robert: 'On Being a Guest.' *Psychiatric Quarterly Supplement,* Vol. 23, Part 1, 1949.

Seligmann, Siegfried: *Der böse Blick und Verwandtes. Ein Beitrag zur Geschichte des Aberglaubens aller Zeiten und Völker.* 2 vols. Berlin, 1910.

Shils, Edward, and Young, Michael: 'The Meaning of the Coronation.' *The Sociological Review,* Vol. 1, 1953.

Shils, Edward: 'Professor Mills on the Calling of Sociology.' *The World Politics,* Vol. 13, 1961.

Simmel, George: *Soziologie. Untersuchungen über die Formen der Vergesellschaftung.* 4th Edition. Berlin, 1958.

Simpson, George: *Sociologist Abroad.* The Hague: Martinus Nijoff, 1959.

Simpson, George Eaton: 'Haiti's Social Structure.' *American Sociological Review,* Vol. 6, 1941.

Smelser, Neil J.: *Theory of Collective Behavior.* New York: The Free Press, 1963.

Spiro, Melford: *Children of the Kibbutz.* Cambridge: Harvard University Press, 1958.

Spiro, Melford: *Kibbutz: Venture in Utopia.* New York: Schocken, 1963.

Steiner, F. G.: *Malice.* Chancellor's English Prize Essay. Oxford: Basil Blackwell, 1952.

Strauss, Leo: *On Tyranny. An Interpretation of Xenophon's Hiero.* (Political Science Classics.) New York: The Free Press, 1948.

Sullivan, Harry Stack: *The Interpersonal Theory of Psychiatry,* New York: Norton, 1953.

Suttie, Jan Dishart: *The Origins of Love and Hate.* London: Paul, French, Trubner & Co., 1935.

Tanner, R. E. S.: 'The Sorcerer in Northern Sukumaland, Tanganyika.' *Southwestern Journal of Anthropology,* Vol. 12, 1956.

Tax, S.: 'Changing Consumption in Indian Guatemala.' *Economic Development and Culture Change,* Vol. 5, 1957.

Thrasher, Frederic M.: *The Gang: A Study of 1313 Gangs in Chicago.* Chicago: University of Chicago Press, 1927. New Ed. by James F. Short Jr., 1963.

Tournier, Paul: *Escape from Loneliness.* Philadelphia: Westminster Press, 1962.

Tournier, Paul: *Guilt and Grace. A Psychological Study.* New York: Harper, 1962.

Toynbee, Arnold J., and Philip: *Comparing Notes: A Dialogue Across a Generation.* London: Weidenfeld & Nicolson, 1963.

Tumin, Melvin M.: 'Some Unapplauded Consequences of Social Mobility in a Mass Society.' *Social Forces,* Vol. 15, 1957.

Vallier, Ivan: 'Structural Differentiation, Production Imperatives, and Communal Norms. The Kibbutz in Crisis.' *Social Forces,* Vol. 40, 1962.

Vincent, John Martin: Art. 'Sumptuary Legislation,' in *Encyclopedia of the Social Sciences,* Vol. XIV-XV. New York: Macmillan, 1937.

Wallis, R. Sawtell: 'The Changed Status of Twins Among the Eastern Dakota.' *Anthropological Quarterly,* Vol. 28, 1955.

Watson, James B., and Samora, Julian: 'Subordinate Leadership in a Bicultural Community. An Analysis.' *American Sociological Review,* Vol. 19, 1954.

Watson, William: *Tribal Cohesion in a Money Economy. A Study of the Mambwe People of Northern Rhodesia.* (The Rhodes-Livingstone Institute.) New York: Humanities Press, 1958.

Webb, Beatrice (Potter): *Diaries, 1912–1932.* (Margaret Cole, ed. and intro.) London and New York: Longmans, Green & Co., 1956.

Weber, Max: *Wirtschaft und Gesellschaft.* Vol. 1. Tübingen, 1922. 4th Edition, 1956.

Winter, E. H.: 'The Enemy Within. Amba Witchcraft and Sociological Theory,' in

Middleton, John and Winter, E. H., eds.: *Witchcraft and Sorcery in East Africa.* London: Routledge & Kegan Paul, 1963; New York: Praeger, 1963.

Wolf, Eric R.: 'Types of Latin American Peasantry. A Preliminary Discussion,' in *American Anthropologist,* Vol. 57, 1955.

Wood, Neal: *Communism and British Intellectuals.* New York and London: Columbia University Press, 1959.

Yerkes, Robert M.: 'The Life History and Personality of the Chimpanzee.' *American Naturalist,* Vol. 78, 1939.

Yerkes, Robert M.: 'Conjugal Contrasts Among the Chimpanzees.' *The Journal of Abnormal and Social Psychology,* Vol. 36, 1941.

Yerkes, Robert M.: *Chimpanzees. A Laboratory Colony.* New Haven and London: Yale University Press/H. Milford, Oxford University Press, 1943.

Young, Michael: *The Rise of the Meritocracy: An Essay on Education and Equality.* London: Thames & Hudson, 1958.

Index

Name Index

Aberle, David F., 87
Adler, Alfred, 318
Aeschylus, 143, 151, 249, 251
Alberti, L. B., 191–192
Alexander, Franz, 82, 91
Alpert, Hollis, 20
Aristides, 211, 249
Aristotle, 194, 226–227, 356, 390
Asch, S. E., 98, 99
Ashton, T. S., 415

Bacon, Francis, 4, 195–199, 200, 218,
    227–228, 232, 339–340, 400, 427
Baldwin, F. E., 261
Banfield, E., 393.
Barber, E., 113
Barnett, H. G., 37, 402–405, 416
Baumgarten, Eduard, 95–96
Beauvoir, Simone de, 41, 330, 332–333
Becker, Franziska, 182
Becker, Rudolf, 258
Beit, H. v., 141
Belshaw, Cyril S., 72, 346
Benckiser, Nikolas, 380–381
Benedict, Ruth, 43, 126–127
Bennett, John W., 371
Bentham, J., 222, 286, 385–386
Berelson, Bernard, 120–122
Bergson, Henri, 227
Berthoff, W., 171
Bertholet, F., 142
Best, E., 391

Bettelheim, B., 84
Bien, Peter, 188
Bleuler, Eugen, 113
Blum, W. J., 390
Bohannan, Laura, 70
Bohannan, P., 70
Böhm, Hans, 262
Borst, Arno, 273–274
Bowen, Merlin, 169
Brachfeld, Oliver, 13
Brandt, R. B., 43
Brogan, Colm, 236
Bryan, William J., 243–244
Buber, Martin, 318, 354–355
Burckhardt, Jacob, 145, 228, 299, 401
Burn, A. R., 152
Buss, A. H., 88
Butler, Joseph, 22

Cabaud, F., 269
Cahn, Edmond N., 279, 280
Camus, Albert, 358
Carlyle, 255
Carstairs, G. Morris, 326
Cellini, 193
Chaucer, 189–190
Chifley, J. B., 389
Clinard, M. B., 135
Cohen, A. K., 135
Cohen, Y. A., 60
Cromwell, Oliver, 272
Crosland, C. A. R., 237–238, 299

439

Subject Index

The text of this book is set in Times Roman, a typeface created by and for the London *Times* under the supervision of Stanley Morison and first used in the October 3, 1932, issue of the newspaper. The *Times* used its new typeface for one year before releasing it for general use. Since then the simple and direct design of Times Roman has made it a practical choice for a wide variety of books, periodicals, and ephemeral publications.

Book design by Madelaine Cooke, Bonita Springs, Florida
Typography by Typoservice Corporation, Indianapolis, Indiana
Printed and bound by Edwards Brothers, Inc.,
Ann Arbor, Michigan